PHOTOGRAPHY AND THE OPTICAL UNCONSCIOUS

PHOTOGRAPHY

—— AND THE ——

OPTICAL UNCONSCIOUS

SHAWN MICHELLE SMITH AND
SHARON SLIWINSKI, EDITORS

Duke University Press | Durham and London | 2017

© 2017 Duke University Press
All rights reserved
Cover design by Matthew Tauch;
interior design by Mindy Basinger Hill
Typeset in Arno Pro by Tseng Information Systems, Inc.

Library of Congress Cataloging-in-Publication Data
Names: Smith, Shawn Michelle, [date] editor. |
Sliwinski, Sharon, [date] editor.
Title: Photography and the optical unconscious /
Shawn Michelle Smith and Sharon Sliwinski, editors.
Description: Durham : Duke University Press, 2017. |
Includes bibliographical references and index.
Identifiers: LCCN 2016048393 (print)
LCCN 2016050623 (ebook)
ISBN 9780822363811 (hardcover : alk. paper)
ISBN 9780822369011 (pbk. : alk. paper)
ISBN 9780822372998 (ebook)
Subjects: LCSH: Photography—Psychological aspects. |
Psychoanalysis and art. | Photography, Artistic. |
Art, Modern—21st century.
Classification: LCC TR183.P484 2017 (print) |
LCC TR183 (ebook) | DDC 770.1—dc23
LC record available at https://lccn.loc.gov/2016048393

Cover art: Zoe Leonard, *100 North Nevill Street*, 2013.
Installation view, detail. Chinati Foundation, Marfa, Texas.
Photo © Fredrik Nilsen, courtesy of the artist, Galerie Gisela
Capitain, Cologne and Hauser & Wirth, New York.

Duke University Press gratefully acknowledges
the School of the Art Institute of Chicago, which provided funds
toward the publication of this book.

CONTENTS

ACKNOWLEDGMENTS

The idea for this book was hatched at a conference on "The Madness of Photography" in Savannah, Georgia, in 2011. During conversation in between panels we began to ask ourselves why the discourse of psychoanalysis, which had been so influential for film, had by and large failed to permeate the field of photography studies. The roving conversation eventually turned into more pointed questions: Why had the field so favored the Marxist aspects of Walter Benjamin's work on photography while ignoring its associations with Freud? Could Benjamin's germinative concept — the "optical unconscious" — be turned into a more potent analytic tool for exploring the psychological dimensions of the medium? The questions felt urgent enough that by the close of the conference we were committed to investigating further. The first foray consisted of a symposium that was graciously hosted by the Toronto Photography Seminar at the University of Toronto in 2013. Many of the chapters in this book were discussed and developed during this workshop and we would like to express our gratitude to the presenters and attendees — and especially the members of the Toronto Photography Seminar — for their goodwill and good thoughts on the project.

We would also like to express our appreciation to the various individuals and institutions that have granted permission to reproduce the images appearing in this book, and especially to the artists who have generously contributed their work to the project. We would like to thank the School of the Art Institute of Chicago, and especially Dean of Faculty Lisa Wainwright, as well as the Western University Ontario for supporting the production of this book. We are grateful to Ken Wissoker, Jade Brooks, and the rest of the team at Duke University Press for bringing the project to fruition with such care.

Finally, Shawn would like to thank Joe Masco for engaging and sustaining a conversation about Benjamin over the course of many years, and for the generosity of his support and enthusiasm for this book, and Sharon would like to thank Melissa Adler for teaching her how to look at the world through a different lens.

INTRODUCTION

———

SHAWN MICHELLE SMITH

AND SHARON SLIWINSKI

Photography mediates our experience of the world. Of this fact there can be little dispute. The technology has come to permeate almost every domain of contemporary life: images and cameras are a ubiquitous presence in our homes, hospitals, museums, schools, and war zones alike. An astonishing amount of human knowledge—of ourselves, of other people, and of the phenomenal world—is bound up with this medium. In public and private, individually and collectively, and in both productive and consumptive modes, photography has become one of the principal filters between the world and us.

What has gone relatively unexplored are the ways that photography mediates our experience and knowledge of the world in *unconscious* ways.[1] Perhaps not surprisingly, Sigmund Freud was one of the first to intuit this idea. He began using photographic processes as a metaphor for his concept of the unconscious mind as early as 1900; however, it was not until the 1930s when Walter Benjamin began writing about the medium that the profound implications of this connection started to become evident. In the course of his studies of the revolutionary changes in perception that the technology introduced, the German cultural theorist proposed that the camera revealed something he named the "optical unconscious." And while Benjamin has subsequently become one of photography's most important and influential thinkers, his ideas about the medium's relationship to the unconscious have remained curiously latent.[2] As the interdisciplinary interest in photography continues to expand, this book seeks to broaden and reframe the significance of photography's relationship to the unconscious, extending Benjamin's germinative concept into a more potent critical tool.

Given Freud's repeated use of the photographic metaphor in his theory of the mind, it seems astonishing that he never constructed an explicit theory of unconscious perception.[3] Benjamin recognized and took up this challenge, in part, by reversing the emphasis between the two central terms, highlighting the optical nature of the unconscious. He was interested in the way photography as a visual technology both affected and offered unprecedented access to this dynamic domain. Benjamin's writings on this topic unseat the fantasy of mastery that surrounds the desire to see and to know. His consideration of the optical unconscious attunes us to all that is not consciously controlled in the making, circulation, and viewing of photographs, the contingency involved in the production and consumption of images, as well as the unexamined motivations and effects of this technology's pervasive spread into wider and wider spheres of human and nonhuman activity.

Benjamin's concept also opens questions about the nature of unconscious communication. He recognized early on that photography was becoming a favored tool for everyday users to sort and process their lived experiences — a fact that has become ubiquitous in today's era of social media. The theorist helped pioneer the now commonplace idea that our image technologies facilitate and shape social relations. He was part of a lively conversation that was occurring in Germany in the 1920s and 1930s that tried to grasp the social and political significance of the explosion of new information technologies.[4] For his part, Benjamin was particularly interested in the way the instruments of mass communication — radio, film, and photography — served as virtual and actual prostheses for human perception. A central aspect of his work involved the attempt to rethink the embodied, cognitive processes through which we engage the world around us. One of his signal contributions to this larger conversation was the idea that photography was organized by "another nature," which is to say, he emphasized the ways this technology mediates human relations through unconscious means.

For the past thirty years, the cultural study of photography has been dominated by narratives about power and regulation and, in particular, by narratives about how photography has served as a disciplinary apparatus of the state. John Tagg and Allan Sekula have contributed exemplary work in this vein. Sekula's study of criminological and scientific systems explicitly defines photography as a technology of surveillance in the nineteenth century. During this period, police departments and other state agencies began producing archives in which bodies were transformed into images, and subsequently into types, which became the key tools of population control. Such institutional archives, as well as broader shadow archives, offer evidence of photography's repressive logic.[5]

Responding to this disciplinary model, feminist, queer, antiracist, and post-colonial scholars have subsequently demonstrated that photography also allows for slippages and resistances, forms of double mimesis, disidentification, and double consciousness that resist official, normative strategies of categorization and containment.[6] Elizabeth Edwards, for instance, has proposed that photographic archives contain myriad contradictions and disruptions; Robin Kelsey has explored the centrality of chance in the history of photography; Tina Campt has studied the ways black European subjects used photography to create community in diaspora; and Elspeth Brown and Thy Phu have proposed that affect profoundly shapes and organizes photographic meaning in ways that elude more rationalized processes.[7] In concert with these studies, this book aims to pursue the unknown, the unseen, and the uncontrolled—even as we recognize the real forms of domination and coercion that photography continues to propagate.

Photography and the Optical Unconscious uses Benjamin's concept as a pivot in order to bring questions about photography and photographic processes closer to questions about the human mind and its psychical processes. We are interested in exploring how the medium engages and shapes perception and lived experience, forms of seeing and unseeing, sovereignty and agency, and time and space. We are also interested in extending one of Benjamin's central wagers: that thinking photography through the lens of the unconscious can help us grasp the revolutionary optical dynamic that permeates the domains of history and politics.[8]

Our present era, just as in Benjamin's time, is marked by war, extreme nationalism, mass dislocation, high-speed information, and an accelerated consumption cycle driven by global capital. Our contemporary moment, like Benjamin's, is also seized by dramatic technological changes in image making and circulation. The ascension of digital technologies—and the smartphone in particular, with its convergence of visual imaging and communication technologies—means that more photographs are being taken and they are circulating more widely than ever before. According to a 2013 report, more than 250 billion photographs have been uploaded to Facebook, with another 350 million being uploaded every day. This makes the social networking service the world's largest photographic repository by far.[9] The vast majority of these images, moreover, are produced on cell phone cameras, and the sheer ubiquity of these devices has inspired new terminology such as "mobile photography" and the "fluid image."[10] The time seems right to follow Benjamin's invitation to consider the new image worlds that photography has helped bring into view, as well as the unconscious dimensions of our imaged and imagined communities.

Although it is the chief subject of this book, the optical unconscious remains elusive. This concept is not something that is directly available to sight, but it nevertheless informs and influences what comes into view. By attending to this idea, one might become newly aware of previously unnoticed details and dynamics, as well as the material, social, and psychic structures that shape perception. In several of his books, the British psychoanalyst Christopher Bollas described this disavowed dimension as the "unthought known." This refers to material that is either emotionally undigested or actively barred from consciousness.[11] As Bollas teaches us, this "unthought" material is, in fact, an integral part of knowledge. And indeed, it seems photography may be one of the principal means to circulate this unconscious material that remains vexingly obscure. Like latent memories, details of photographic information snap into focus and become visible in unpredictable moments. As Benjamin put it, they "flash up" in moments of danger and desire—and they can quickly fade from view unless seized in a moment of recognition.

The contributors to this volume offer a number of innovative ways of defining or elaborating the notion of the optical unconscious: attending to perceptions (chapter 8), developing latent images (chapter 10), discovering things hidden in plain sight (chapter 11), focusing on the disavowed (chapter 12), and perceiving the slow (chapter 15). Together they explore the realm of the unseen that photography paradoxically introduces as it probes the outer edges of the expansive terrain of the human imaginary.

As a means to frame and ground the subsequent chapters and artists' portfolios, this introduction outlines the ways in which photography functions as metaphor and paradigm in the writings of Benjamin as well as Freud. It is important to emphasize that although Benjamin was deeply influenced by Freud's writings, his sense of the optical unconscious was not coterminous with the psychoanalyst's notion of this dimension. Freud himself constantly revised his ideas about the unconscious over the course of his long career, but as he did so he frequently returned to the metaphor of photography to elaborate his views. In other words, Benjamin was not alone in imagining that photography could help us better understand the structure and force of this other agency.

A Concept in Transition

Benjamin seemed to recognize and emphasize the medium's proximity to the unconscious from the outset. His first published discussion of photography appeared in 1928, when he wrote "News about Flowers," ostensibly a short review of Karl Blossfeldt's photo book, *Originary Forms of Art*.[12] Even in this brief entrée, Benjamin seems preoccupied with the unconscious aspects of perception that the camera revealed. Marveling at Blossfeldt's enlargements of tiny pieces of plants, Benjamin declared, "A geyser of new image-worlds hisses up at points in our existence where we would least have thought them possible. . . . Only the photograph is capable of this."[13] For Benjamin, as for many of his generation, Blossfeldt's technological innovations irrevocably shattered the boundaries of human perception. The art teacher had built a camera with unprecedented magnifying capacity, which he used to photograph plants in hitherto unseen detail. He meticulously arranged tiny part objects—twig ends, tendrils, seedpods, leaf buds—on stark backgrounds, revealing elegant architectural forms seemingly hidden in the organic world. In these enlargements Benjamin discovered a world of unconscious resemblances. In Blossfeldt's photograph of horsetail, Benjamin saw ancient Greek columns; saxifrage seemed to reveal miniature cathedral windows; a bishop's crosier appeared in fern fronds; and totem poles seemed to arise out of maple shoots (figs. 1.1 and 1.2).[14] Blossfeldt's photographs revealed otherwise unseen dimensions of the visual landscape, and Benjamin would spend the better part of the next decade thinking about this "geyser of new image-worlds" that the medium exposed.

In "Little History of Photography," published three years after "News about Flowers," Benjamin boldly proclaimed, "It is another nature that speaks to the camera rather than to the eye: 'other' above all in the sense that a space informed by human consciousness gives way to a space informed by the unconscious."[15] Despite being a human invention, Benjamin seems to say, photography exposes the limits of human intentionality. The theorist was keen to explore how the technological processes of photography could reveal aspects of existence that elude our conscious grasp: "It is through photography," he insisted, "that we first discover the existence of this optical unconscious, just as we discover the instinctual unconscious through psychoanalysis."[16]

As with many of his enduring concepts, Benjamin's definition of the optical unconscious remained vexingly protean. That said, the idea seems to have been initially sparked by technological experimentation. In "Little History," Benjamin returns to his praise of Karl Blossfeldt's close-ups and adds an allusion to Eadweard Muybridge and Étienne-Jules Marey's motion studies: "Whereas it is a commonplace that, for example, we have some idea what is involved in the act of walking (if only in general terms), we have no idea at all what happens during the fraction of a second when a person actually takes a step. Photography, with its devices of slow motion and enlargement, reveals

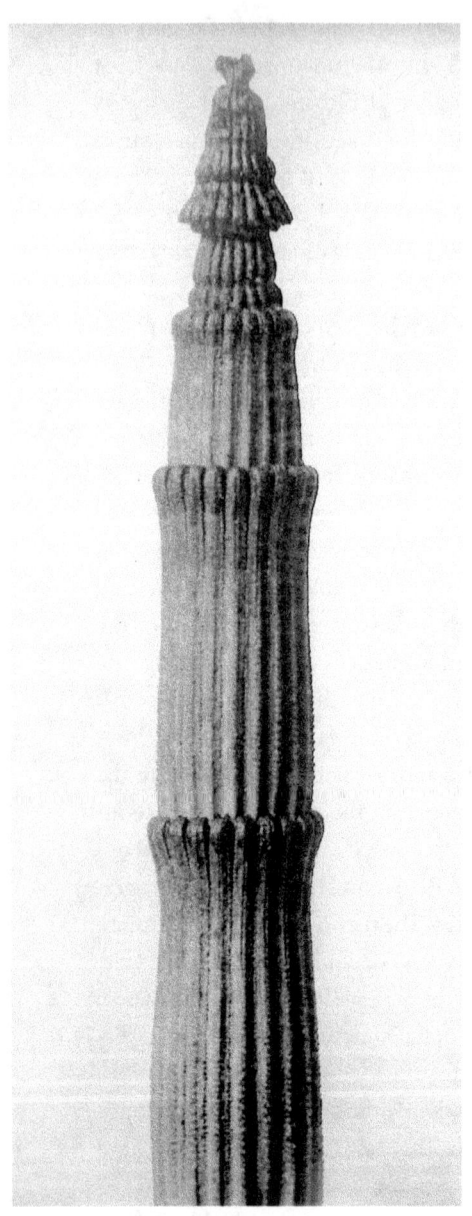

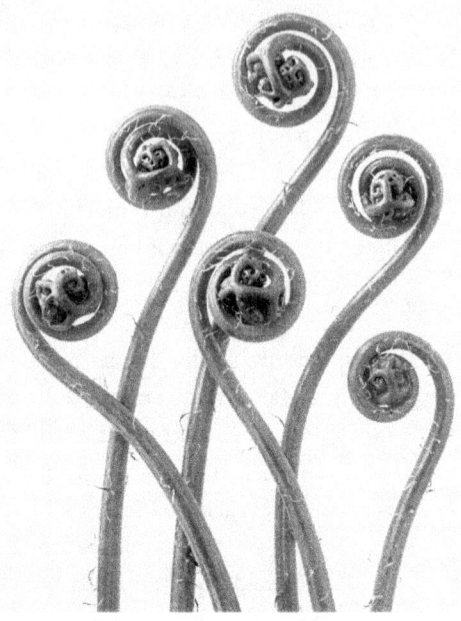

FIGURE I.1 *left* Karl Blossfeldt, *Equisetum hyemale*, 1898–1928. Gelatin silver print, 23 7/16 × 9 5/16 inches (59.5 × 23.7 cm). Thomas Walther Collection, gift of Thomas Walther, the Museum of Modern Art. Digital image copyright the Museum of Modern Art/licensed by SCALA/Art Resource, New York.

FIGURE I.2 *above* Karl Blossfeldt, *Adiantum pedatum*, American maidenhair fern, before 1928. Young rolled-up fronds enlarged eight times. Gelatin silver print, 11 5/8 × 9 5/16 inches (29.5 × 23.6 cm). Thomas Walther Collection, purchase, the Museum of Modern Art. Digital image copyright the Museum of Modern Art/licensed by SCALA/Art Resource, New York.

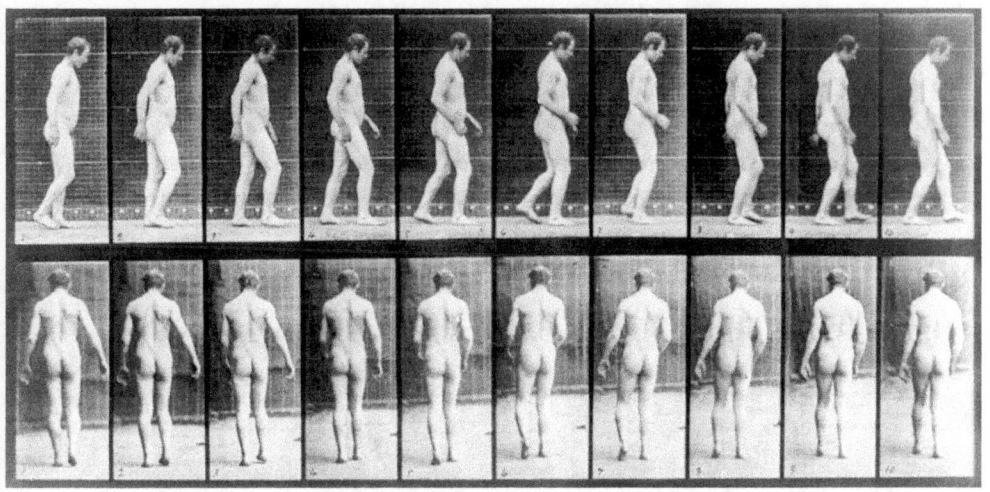

FIGURE I.3　Eadweard Muybridge, *Animal Locomotion*, Plate 443, circa 1887.
Library of Congress, Prints and Photographs Division.

the secret."[17] The camera allows us to grasp what remains otherwise imperceptible to the powers of human sight: what is either too miniscule or too rapid for the unaided human eye to see (fig. 1.3). And yet, Benjamin insists, the technology's capacity to glimpse these alternate image worlds is merely how "we *first* discover the existence of this optical unconscious."[18] In its initial iteration, Benjamin's sense of this domain corresponds to dimensions of the visible world that appear to be beyond the natural limits of human sight—microstructures that dwell "in the smallest things" and the deconstruction of space that slow motion affords—but which nevertheless seem to have a "secret" influence on human imagination.

As Miriam Hansen has pointed out, Benjamin's discussion of the optical unconscious is inextricably knitted to his equally complex notion of the aura.[19] Neither concept remained static in his work. Hansen traces three distinct definitions of the aura in Benjamin's thought, and one could produce a similar trajectory of the optical unconscious. Even within the space of his "Little History," Benjamin's sense of the term shifts from being an inherent property of a particular object (i.e., a microscopic image world hidden in maple shoots) to an agency of perception itself. In this second iteration, the optical unconscious names a particular structure of vision (which is not limited to the visible) that endows objects with the power of the gaze. Perhaps the clearest articulation of this version of the concept arrives with Benjamin's citation of the nineteenth-century photographer Karl Dauthendey recalling his early experience with daguerreotypes: "We didn't trust ourselves at first to look long at the first pictures. . . . We believed the tiny faces in the picture could see *us*."[20] Leaning on a sense of the uncanny, here the image itself carries the powers of sight.

This second definition of the optical unconscious—as a gaze that belongs to the other, as something in excess of the spectator's agency but which seems to show itself to the camera—was revived and expanded a few years later, in Benjamin's well-known essay, "The Work of Art in the Age of Its Technological Reproducibility." By the mid-1930s, Benjamin's concentration was almost entirely absorbed by his *Arcades Project* (*Das Passagenwerk*), a sprawling cultural history of the emergence of urban culture in nineteenth-century Paris. "The Work of Art" was among a trio of essays that arose as an offshoot to this massive (and ultimately unfinished) project.

In the second, 1936 version of the "Work of Art," Benjamin included an entire section that addressed what he describes as the "equilibrium between human beings and the apparatus." In this section, he develops a kind of rolling definition of the optical unconscious that gathers up and builds upon all his previous insights: slow motion and close-ups open "a vast and unsuspected field of action. . . . With the close-up, space expands; with slow motion, movement is extended . . . bringing to light entirely new structures of matter."[21] In this third iteration, the optical unconscious is spatialized, referring, among other things, to the hidden dimensions of a place—an idea he expands in his discussions of Eugene Atget's photographs of Paris. Benjamin also repeats his claim that the camera enables the discovery of the optical unconscious, just as psychoanalysis enabled the discovery of the instinctual unconscious. This statement is followed by a remarkable passage that deserves to be quoted in full:

> Moreover, these two types of unconscious [the optical and instinctual] are intimately linked. For in most cases the diverse aspects of reality captured by the film camera lie outside the *normal* spectrum of sense impressions. Many of the deformations and stereotypes, transformations and catastrophes which can assail the optical world in films afflict the actual world in psychoses, hallucinations, and dreams. Thanks to the camera, therefore, the individual perceptions of the psychotic and the dreamer can be appropriated by collective perception. The ancient truth expressed by Heraclitus, that those who are awake have a world in common while each sleeper has a world of his own, have been invalidated by film—and less by depicting the dream world itself than by creating figures of collective dream, such as the globe-encircling Mickey Mouse.[22]

In this dense passage, Benjamin's speculations begin to take an acutely politi-cal turn, although surprisingly, the pivot point is not photography's so-called indexical relationship to reality, but rather its proximity to fantasy. What mat-ters to Benjamin here is photography's ability to capture and circulate the "de-formations" and "stereotypes" that make up the psychotic's and the dreamer's perceptions. Benjamin is proposing, in other words, that "collective percep-tion" is more akin to a shared unconscious fantasy, and, moreover, that mod-ern technology can allow us to access these ways of seeing that are actively disavowed or otherwise unavailable to consciousness. He sees photography's political potential not in its ability to document material reality, but rather in its profound link to psychic structures. In this third iteration of the optical un-conscious, therefore, Benjamin begins to elaborate a theory of mass communi-cation that is centered on the notion of the unconscious rather than rationality or reason. Here photography becomes a key medium for the circulation of a culture's unconscious desires, fears, and structures of defense.

A Photographic View of History

As his varied articulations of the optical unconscious suggest, Benjamin's en-gagement with photography was more profound than the small handful of his works that directly discuss the medium might suggest. Photographic technolo-gies also informed and inspired his critical method of writing history; indeed, his complex notion of the dialectical image as well as his discussion of "time at a standstill" are both structured by his thinking about photography.

In one striking instance, Benjamin describes the dialectical image as a kind of stereoscopic image.[23] Borrowing words from Rudolf Borchardt, he explains the "pedagogic side" of his massive compendium *The Arcades Project* in this way: "'To educate the image-making medium within us, raising it to a stereo-scopic and dimensional seeing into the depths of historical shadows.'"[24] This "image-making medium within us" is yet another iteration of the optical un-conscious, here an internal mechanism of perception that animates and shapes our recognition. Benjamin sought to educate and harness this internal mecha-nism to the project of historical materialism. As Susan Buck-Morss proposes, Benjamin's collection of scraps, notes, and images of outmoded commercial forms found in the Paris arcades were meant to provide half a text—or rather half an image, to which readers would supply the other half by bringing images of their own historical moment to bear on these antiquated artifacts. Taken together, Benjamin imagined that these doubled images might crystallize, as in

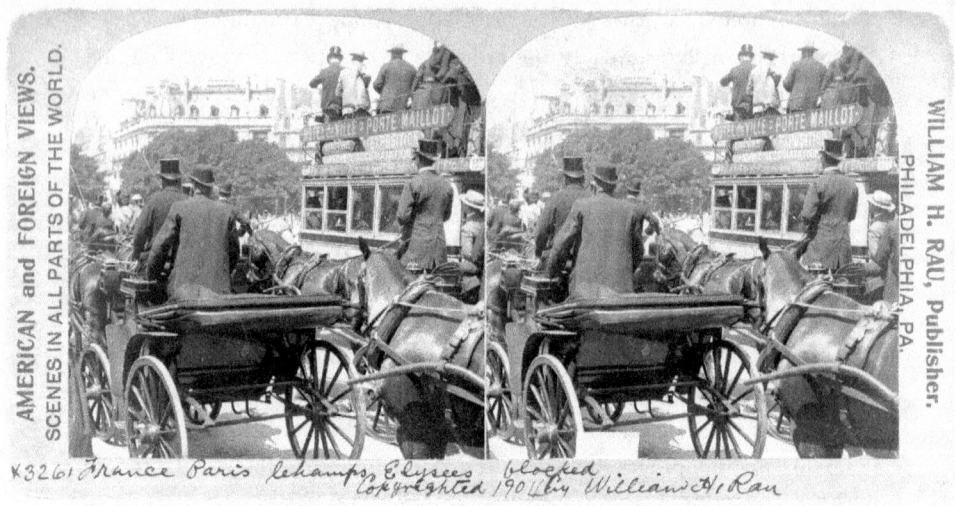

FIGURE I.4 William Herman Rau, *Champs Elysees Blocked*,
Paris, France, circa 1904. Photographic print on stereo card.
Library of Congress, Prints and Photographs Division.

the stereoscope, into a single, dialectical image — a revelatory vision that would awaken the viewer by demystifying the present, enabling one to see and understand the unchanging sameness of capitalism's purported progress. Training our unconscious perception in this way, Benjamin hoped, would awaken us from capitalism's "dream-world."[25]

It is important to emphasize that the stereoscopic image, fully realized in the age of photography, is a virtual image. This image becomes visible only through the interplay of human binocular perception with the stereoscopic device, as Jonathan Crary has elaborated.[26] The stereoscopic image does not exist in the world, but only in the mind's mechanically enhanced eye. It is made through the combination of three components: a viewing device (the stereoscope), a doubled image (the stereo card), and human binocular vision. The stereo card presents two slightly different images, side by side (fig. I.4).[27] When placed in the viewing device, and engaged by a viewer, the two photographs of the stereo card coalesce into a single image that provides an illusion of depth. When the image snaps into focus as one gazes through the device, it also snaps into relief, revealing planes that divide the newly realized space of the image. In this way, the stereoscopic image evokes, but does not reproduce actual three-dimensional perception: the planes recede in discrete rows, as if they are stage sets that might be rolled offscreen, and individual figures stand out from one another in too pronounced a manner, almost as if they are miniatures that have been pasted into a small diorama. Thus, the stereoscopic image provides an illusion of depth and dimension, but not an illusion of reality. It is an entirely imaginary scene that cannot be envisioned otherwise.

Benjamin borrowed the stereoscope's conflation and transformation of two images into a startling new view as the salient technique of his historical writing. His dialectical image, like the stereoscopic image, is not part of the phenomenal world, but an image that is activated by present readers gazing upon the past. Again, it is not something that is directly perceptible (nor reproducible), but only emerges in the imaginative interaction between reader and text. Benjamin aimed to invigorate readers, to create conceptual models that would galvanize the subject into an awakening: a fragment from the past, read in light of the present, triggers the "image-making medium within," effecting a dialectical image through which the subject might see the mirage of capitalism exposed.[28]

One finds another analogy for Benjamin's historical method in the temporal disruption of photography. In his late, aphoristic essay, "On the Concept of History," Benjamin describes the work of the historical materialist as "blast[ing] open the continuum of history," perceiving a present "in which time takes a stand and has come to a standstill"—just as it does in a photograph. In this way, Benjamin's historical thinking depends not simply on "the movement of thoughts," but on "their arrest as well."[29] More than any other medium, photography offered Benjamin a model for his thinking about the arrest of time and thought. In the photograph, historical configurations crystallize and come into focus in the "dynamite of the split second."[30]

Benjamin's thoughts on the temporality of the photograph remain startlingly innovative. The photograph not only stops time, Benjamin argues, but also works to project the future out of the past. The photograph is a forward-looking document, so to speak, anticipating a future viewer who will recognize in it a spark of contingency that cannot be contained to one temporal moment. As Benjamin puts it in his "Little History of Photography": "No matter how artful the photographer, no matter how carefully posed his subject, the beholder feels an irresistible urge to search such a picture for the tiny spark of contingency, of the here and now, with which reality has (so to speak) seared the subject, to find the inconspicuous spot where in the immediacy of that long-forgotten moment the future nests so eloquently that we, looking back, may rediscover it."[31] Benjamin was fascinated by the contingency of photography, by those moments of chance that exceed human intentionality and the narrative of history as progress, and in those "tiny sparks of contingency," he found not only the past, but also the future.[32] Similarly, Vilém Flusser has seized upon the medium's sense of futurity in his more recent ruminations on photography and history. Flusser describes photographs as "projections, that is, as images of the future." Despite our persistent understanding of photographs as "copies of scenes, that is, as images of the past," Flusser argues, they are actually visualizations that concretize images out of myriad possibilities, and in this way, they direct the future.[33]

Benjamin divined the future from the past of the photograph. Over and over, photographic technologies served as a potent analogy for his radical historical project. He produced an understanding of the present through images of the past that blazed up before him, and he championed the idea that we should seize hold of this memory "as it flashes up at a moment of danger."[34] Blasting open the mirage of time as linear and progressive, the historical materialist recognized in the dialectical image a historical reality laid bare.

The Latent Image

Although he rarely acknowledged it directly, Benjamin took many of his cues from Sigmund Freud, who repeatedly relied on the metaphor of photography in his own work. In this respect, the technology offered both thinkers a powerful means to conceptualize psychological processes. Freud also wrote of "the image-making medium within us," which he posited as a complex interplay between direct sensual perceptions and latent images (memory traces and fantasies), all of which must be "processed" before becoming conscious. One of the first uses of this metaphor appears in *The Interpretation of Dreams*, published in 1900, where Freud mobilized a variety of optical devices — including a "photographic apparatus" — to figure the workings of the mind.[35]

Where Benjamin favored the metaphor of the stereoscope, Freud initially preferred the telescope to figure his model of human perception. Both analogies hinge on a virtual image that is produced through the alignment of two or more images that are physically askew. Explaining the relationship between the inner and the external world, Freud suggests, "Everything that can be an object of our internal perception is *virtual*, like the image produced in a telescope by the passage of light-rays."[36] He stresses the fact that we must actively process the perceptions that arrive from the external world. Perceptual data is captured and filtered through our senses, and then transformed to make a virtual image. This transformation is not neutral because the information that arrives through our senses encounters unconscious interference, so to speak. For Freud, each of the psychic systems functions like "the lenses of the telescope, which cast the image."[37] Psychic operations such as repression, projection, negation, or scotomization serve as evidence of the dynamic force of the unconscious. Following Freud's own analogy, repression works like the refraction of light as it passes from one lens (or psychic system) to another, thus distorting the image perceived in the mind's eye.[38]

Nearly four decades after he first drew on visual models to describe the human psyche, Freud returned to the photographic analogy in *Moses and Monotheism*, which was published in English the same year he died, 1939. In the course of a discussion about the structural significance of early childhood experiences, Freud proposes that the relation of unconscious memories to conscious perception is like that of the negative to the photographic print: "It has long since become common knowledge that the experience of the first five years of childhood exert a decisive influence on our life. . . . The process may be compared to a photograph, which can be developed and made into a picture after a short or long interval."[39] The powerful force of early childhood experiences remains latent and inaccessible, just as a negative can remain unprocessed for a long period of time before being made into a positive print. The photographic analogy underscores the deferred temporality that dominates psychic life. Latency—by which Freud means the way past experiences are refashioned to suit the present—is key to understanding the ways in which unconscious thoughts can exert an influence in the time afterward.[40] Put differently, Freud proposes that the past can return to haunt the present, and photography offers a prime model for how this strange deferred temporality works. The medium's unique relation to time—its capacity to figure multiple temporal moments simultaneously—becomes a model for understanding the workings of the dynamic unconscious, which, Freud famously insisted, knows no time.[41]

In her evocative reading of Freud's use of photographic analogies in *Moses and Monotheism*, the French philosopher Sarah Kofman stresses the fact that latency does not require or necessitate development: "In the psychic apparatus, the passage from negative to positive is neither necessary nor dialectical. It is possible that the development will never take place."[42] Many childhood experiences remain unconscious. Further, when and if development does take place, what is remembered is actually something that went unobserved in the first instance. According to Freud, latent memories are constituted by what a child has experienced and "not understood," and indeed, "may never be re-membered."[43] He speculates that some of this structural latency has to do with human development: unconscious memories correspond to experiences that a child undergoes at a time when "his psychical apparatus [i]s not yet completely receptive."[44] These experiences nevertheless organize and direct the adult's un-conscious, including the style and structure of our perception: the way each of us "unconsciously scans" the world, observing, collecting, and scrutinizing par-ticular phenomenal objects based upon early patterns of experience.[45]

There is a direct echo here of Benjamin's optical unconscious, which, he claims, photography can help us to grasp. The camera can capture scenes that pass too quickly, too remotely, or too obscurely for the subject to consciously perceive. By enlarging details, or by slowing down or stopping time, the cam-era pictures phenomena that the viewer has encountered and unconsciously registered but not consciously processed. This sense of the optical unconscious is not about making latent memory traces visible, however, but rather demon-strating the reach and complexity of unconscious perception.

Race and the Optical Unconscious

As several of the chapters in this book attest, optical understandings of race and racialized understandings of optics are latent in the writings of Benjamin and Freud. Both thinkers wrote in the shadow of Nazi imperialism and eugen-ics, and it is perhaps not surprising that race is at play in their thoughts about the workings of the human psyche. In the wake of European colonialism and slavery in the Americas, race served as a defining feature of modern social and psychic structures. Several twentieth-century theorists—perhaps most promi-nently W. E. B. Du Bois and Frantz Fanon—offer articulations of the ways race is imbricated in self-imaging, at both the conscious and unconscious levels.

Although they are not exactly in sync, Du Bois's double consciousness and Benjamin's optical unconscious both aim to describe visual worlds that shape the psyche. The idea of a gaze that belongs to the other, a component of Benjamin's understanding of the optical unconscious, was also central to Du Bois's experience of double consciousness. For Du Bois, racial conscious-ness was a visual dynamic, an effect of an exterior gaze, and his concept names the psychic strain that African Americans experienced living in a segregated world: "It is a peculiar sensation, this double consciousness, this sense of always looking at one's self through the eyes of others."[46] He described a self-understanding alienated by a colonizing gaze that one sensed, even if one did not see it. Such an understanding of oneself through the gaze of the other was a dynamic structuring element that Du Bois strove to make visible in order to expose and resist its power.

The dynamic splitting and doubling of self and gaze also produced, for Du Bois, the revelation of "second-sight," that is, the capacity to see the material structures of segregation and colonialism as well as the visual and psychic technologies of racial domination.[47] Indeed, Du Bois deemed himself "singularly clairvoyant" about the "souls of white folk": "I see in and through them. . . . I see these souls undressed and from the back and side. I see the working of their entrails. I know their thoughts and they know that I know."[48] Du Bois perceived the lens through which he was seen, he sensed others looking, and he also looked back at them with piercing eyes.

Du Bois's insights, like those of Benjamin and Freud, were founded on long-standing visual conceptions of race produced by the convergence of scientific discourses and photographic technologies in the nineteenth century. His capacity to see the souls of white folk "undressed and from the back and side" eerily recalls (and perhaps even reverses) the gaze imposed in Joseph T. Zealy's infamous daguerreotypes of enslaved men and women commissioned by the polygenesist Louis Agassiz in 1850 (see figs. 8.10 through 8.13 in chapter 8).[49] In Zealy's daguerreotypes, enslaved men and women stand stripped before the camera, photographed from a variety of angles — ogled at from "the back and side." The images render visible the radically visceral dimension of racism, that is, the way race can be optically inscribed onto the human body. In this respect, the daguerreotypes are part of a much larger American archive, a quasi-scientific set of dividing practices that, as Ta-Nehisi Coates puts it, "all land, with great violence upon the body."[50] These images also record, as Suzanne Schneider has argued, Agassiz's racialized sexual desire, cloaked in the discourses of scientific scrutiny, hidden in taxonomic sight.[51]

Zealy's daguerreotypes are striking examples of the way modern conceptions of race were produced with the camera. Scientists devised visual typologies to define and differentiate racial groups, mapping physical characteristics they claimed to read in the body and through the photograph. In the late nineteenth century, Francis Galton, the founder of eugenics, devised a system of composite portraiture to delineate racial types, "the Jewish type" prominent among them (see fig. 4.1 in chapter 4). Working with preselected groups, Galton photographed individuals from the front and side, and overlaid exposures proportionately so that each individual's face was equally represented in the composite image.[52] Such techniques of visual compositing profoundly influenced the way race came to be seen. As Jonathan Fardy discusses in chapter 4, following Sander Gilman, Freud's racial anxieties come into view in one of his dreams via the mechanism of the composite image. Startlingly, a racialized composite image enables Freud to recognize that his unconscious is functioning photographically.

The photographic experiments of Agassiz and Galton fundamentally shaped modern understandings of race as visual, and their work helped generate vast photographic archives in the late nineteenth and early twentieth centuries. As Allan Sekula has argued, the archives of race scientists and criminologists consolidated the dominant ideology that people could be read and categorized visually, that exterior signs could reveal interior essences.[53] In the same period, photography was put into the service of colonialism; indeed the colonial archive is a particularly dense repository for this racialized gaze, as Gabrielle Moser demonstrates in chapter 10. The colonial archive also records its own uncertainties, and Moser, following Ann Stoler's work, pursues several "nonevents" in a specific colonial photographic archive, proposing that the latent details of such nonevents reveal unconscious colonial anxieties about race and power.

Writing from the colonial contexts of France, nearly five decades after Du Bois, Frantz Fanon would similarly describe his experience of a colonial gaze as a splitting, doubling, and even tripling of the self. Caught in the gaze of the other, he is forced and yet unable to heed a white child's hail: "Look, a Negro!" a child calls out at the sight of Fanon on a train in the early 1950s.[54] The encounter throws Fanon's body into view and imprisons it in the same stroke, projecting a distorted bodily image—a white fantasy of blackness—that Fanon is forced to confront but with which he cannot identify. The result of this collision is a profound psychic splitting, a crumbling of Fanon's internal sense of self: "nausea . . . an amputation, an excision, a hemorrhage."[55]

According to Fatimah Tobing Rony, Fanon's central concern is this: "What does one become when one sees that one is not fully recognized as Self by the wider society but cannot fully identify as Other?"[56] For David Marriott, the question is even more formidable: "What do you do with an unconscious which appears to hate you?"[57] In Marriott's reading of Fanon, the visual dynamics of looking that animate segregated and colonized worlds also structure the very composition of the imago/ego in Lacan's famous "mirror stage."[58] According to Marriott, "The black man is already split, preoccupied, by a racist, a conscious-unconscious, imago."[59]

Du Bois's second sight might serve as antidote to the devastating dynamics of psychic colonization described by Marriott. Second sight might parallel what Rony deems "the third eye," an appropriate form of vision for Fanon's "triple person."[60] It is the ability "to see the very process which creates the internal splitting, to witness the conditions which give rise to the double consciousness."[61] Du Bois's second sight is able to see the visual dynamics that inform and are formed by racist social structures. Although he describes this critical insight in almost mystical terms as the "gift" of "the Veil," it is also an insight he shares in *The Souls of Black Folk* as a lesson to be learned. It is a critical visual strategy not only for registering race and racism, but also for combating it — for working through the social dynamics that split and double the self.[62]

As a number of the chapters in this book demonstrate, race and the optical unconscious both come into focus photographically in the twentieth century. Mark Reinhardt draws out the visual constructions of race subtly figured in Benjamin's "Work of Art" essay to show how the optical unconscious of race in the United States breaches the limits of psychic sovereignty (chapter 8). Laura Wexler uncovers the colonial past registered in Roland Barthes's famous Winter Garden Photograph (chapter 11). Thy Phu and Sharon Sliwinski both study the material, technological, and psychic limitations of photography under racialized war and violence (chapters 13 and 14). Together these chapters, along with those of Fardy and Moser (chapters 4 and 10), demonstrate how Benjamin's thoughts about the optical unconscious, and even about modernity itself, were imbricated with colonialism and scientific racism, even if Benjamin himself did not always see it.

The Shape of the Book

Photography and the Optical Unconscious explores the revolution in human perception — and the unconscious aspects of perception in particular — that the invention of photography opened. It also investigates the wide range of image worlds that the medium has both generated and discovered. Together the essays and artists' portfolios gathered here provide a collective and sustained investigation of photography and the optical unconscious. The book aims to be both focused and broad enough to encompass the breadth of the optical unconscious as well as to suggest new modes of engagement with photographs and texts. Some of the chapters center on works by Benjamin and Freud, others on the historical periods in which they wrote, and still others on disparate archives, images, and texts ranging from the nineteenth to the twenty-first century.

As Benjamin looked to photographs to theorize the optical unconscious, and Freud turned to optical technologies to understand the psyche, it makes sense that this book would also explore the optical unconscious through photography, allowing photographs to do the work of revealing the unseen aspects of sight itself. Three artists' portfolios offer visual entry into thinking about the optical unconscious: Zoe Leonard's camera obscura installations, which are documented in photographs (chapter 5); Kelly Wood's images of homeless carts, which bring disavowed cultural subjects into view (chapter 12); and Kristan Horton's composite portraits, which open questions about unconscious perception and the formation of subjectivity (chapter 9).

These portfolios are included in an effort to allow photographs to communicate at least partly on their own terms. Benjamin's "tiny spark of contingency" is not something to be discovered in words, but rather in looking, and specifically by looking at photographs, visual documents that resist the creator's control, "no matter how artful the photographer, no matter how carefully posed his subject."[63] This book endeavors to engage the optical unconscious through images as well as words, to allow for resistance to our usual analytics and verbal modes of argumentation. Each portfolio is briefly framed by textual material that does not so much explain the body of work as provide a platform through which the images might be engaged. Leonard presents a conversation about her camerae obscurae; Wood offers an account of the motivations that inspired her photographs; and Horton has written a creative text that runs parallel to his composite portraits. None of this textual material aims to contain or restrain the meaning of the images. Rather we hope the portfolios will solicit viewers' responses, courting curiosity and surprise. The images provide a means to explore the dynamics of perception, drawing attention to the ways photographs can technologically reveal what the physical and cultural parameters of sight obscure.

———

To begin the conversation, Andrés Mario Zervigón situates Benjamin's thoughts on the optical unconscious in the wake of the rapid expansion of the illustrated press in 1920s Weimar Germany (chapter 1). By the 1930s, intellectuals in Germany both celebrated and condemned the proliferation of photographic images, lauding the expansion of perception offered by photographs while at the same time fearing the ways in which "photo-inflation" overwhelmed perception and understanding. In this atmosphere of both enthusiasm for and anxiety about the proliferation of photographic images, Benjamin theorized an optical unconscious that functioned parallel to the photograph itself, recording a plethora of details and information not consciously perceived in one's environment and encounters. As Zervigón argues, "photography itself imprinted the nearly invisible phenomena that only the unconscious was prepared to perceive at the actual unfolding of such events." Articulating a new mode of perception, Benjamin also began to postulate a new understanding of the modern photographic subject who might see beyond the surface of things to their underlying structures. The photographic subject, trained precisely by the proliferation of images, might come to see and understand photographs as "dialectical images" that revealed in a flash the capitalist structures that undergird the world of commodities and images. Catalyzed by his thoughts on the optical unconscious, Benjamin began to propose a new model of the photographic subject, one that reserved and reinvented the revolutionary power of photography in the midst of the medium's accelerated proliferation.

Taking another tack on the photographic contexts in which Benjamin theorized the optical unconscious, Shawn Michelle Smith looks to the history of photography that Benjamin drew upon in formulating his ideas (chapter 2). In her discussion of Benjamin's signal essay on the medium, "Little History of Photography," she examines the photographers and images Benjamin called upon to define the photograph's "magical" qualities, especially the work of the early Scottish practitioners David Octavius Hill and Robert Adamson, who were receiving renewed attention in Germany at the time of Benjamin's writing. In other words, she understands Benjamin's thoughts on the optical unconscious as emerging within a historiography of photography. Even as Benjamin was critical of the vast commercialization of photography in the nineteenth century, and increasingly afraid of the destructive potential of the visual culture that surrounded him in 1930s Germany, he preserved an early moment in the history of the medium as both magical and revelatory. In Hill and Adamson's work from the 1840s, Benjamin saw the potential of the new technology to capture not only a moment from the past, but also a moment of futurity that called out to later viewers, and he seized upon this temporal disruption as key to photography's revolutionary optical unconscious.

While the first two chapters explore how Benjamin's theory of photography was informed by psychoanalysis, chapter 3 reverses this trajectory. Here the French philosopher Sarah Kofman examines the role that photography played in Freud's thinking about the psyche. This short chapter was initially the middle section of a book called *Camera Obscura: Of Ideology*, which was first published in French in 1973 (in English in 1998). This was Kofman's third book, and it continued her characteristically close reading of Freud's oeuvre. Here the philosopher tracks the ways Freud explicitly and repeatedly used the metaphor of photography—and the photographic negative, in particular—in order to illustrate his theory of the unconscious. Just as the positive print originates from a negative (in the analog photography of Freud's day), there is an unseen counterpart to consciousness. Kofman's careful parsing of the metaphor puts pressure on the idea that photography is an instrument of transparency. Far from simply producing a clear-eyed copy of reality, here the photograph is something closer to phantasmagoria—a kind of illusion or dream designed to suit the needs of the ego. Kofman provides several tantalizing threads that lend support to Benjamin's protean notion of the optical unconscious as well as his particular brand of ideological critique.

Following Kofman's lead, Jonathan Fardy delves into some of the ways in which psychoanalysis was informed by photography (chapter 4). Fardy assesses the optics in Freud's theory of the unconscious, proposing that Freud's dream "R is my Uncle" is structured by "seeing photographically." Specifically, he shows how Freud understands his dream to have visually combined, in the manner of Galton's composite photography, the faces of two men: his friend and his uncle. Thus Freud's analysis and understanding of his dream, and the very mechanism of the dream itself, incorporate a "photographic vision." Fardy suggests that Freud's dream used the technique of composite photography without recognizing it as such, or in other words, that the unconscious is itself working photographically. Building from Freud's own associations to his dream, Fardy also encourages us to consider the unconscious as a racialized agency. He takes note that Freud's dream, like Galton's composites, betrays a preoccupation with "the Jewish type." Seeing photographically, then, is a form of seeing that will always be burdened by the anxieties haunting the subject's particular time and place.

In her interview with Elisabeth Lebovici, Zoe Leonard explains how her camerae obscurae explore photographic seeing without resorting to or resulting in the fixed image of a photograph (chapter 5). These images provide a way to go back to the beginning of photography, and to expand the ways in which we experience, understand, and see photography. The camerae obscurae provoke "questions about how we see, how we look, and what we take for granted about sight." For Leonard these are both psychological and political questions. Like Benjamin, she proposes that "the space of the camera obscura is related to the space of the unconscious." In the camera obscura one experiences images before they have been corrected, before they have been turned right side up by the brain, and before they have been comprehended: "The camera obscura makes the mechanics of sight visible." Together in a darkened room, viewers are asked to think about how we see and how we look. Understanding how we inhabit space and observe together, yet differently, is for Leonard a profoundly political experience.

Mary Bergstein considers the forces that shape collective looking in her chapter on the turn-of-the-twentieth-century visual culture in which Freud developed the theory and practice of psychoanalysis (chapter 6). Focusing on scopophilia, she discusses early theories of hysteria and the famous case of Anna O. alongside Johann Schwarzer's Saturn film erotica. The overlap between medical themes and popular culture is striking, especially with relation to hypnosis and hysteria. Bergstein is interested in these historical resonances without trying to make a directly causal argument. She grounds science and scientific research in its historical contexts, demonstrating how psychoanalysis shared themes, gendered assumptions, and even scenes and settings with visual erotica in 1920s Vienna. Bergstein's analysis subtly suggests that a shared optical unconscious informed the development of psychoanalytic treatment in the talking cure, as well as the scopophilia of early film erotica.

As Bergstein studies the visual culture in which Freudian psychoanalysis emerged, Mignon Nixon assesses Freudian psychoanalysis in visual culture in her essay "On the Couch" (chapter 7), first published in *October* 113 (summer 2005). Looking at film, photography by Shellburne Thurber, and archival art projects such as those of Susan Hiller, Nixon considers the analytic scene, the "frame," namely the analyst's office, and especially the couch, thereby making the practice of psychoanalysis visible. By focusing on the couch in the analytic scene, the artists Nixon discusses show the place the analysand inhabits, and also reveal the chair behind the couch, the place the analyst occupies, out of sight. In this way, these images reveal the blind spot in the analytic scene. Drawing out the parallels between the scene of psychoanalysis and Conceptual art further in her discussion of Silvia Kolbowski's audiovisual installation *an inadequate history of conceptual art*, Nixon demonstrates how the Vienna Freud Museum was established in the historical context of Conceptual art and suggests that it was even modeled on similar forms and strategies. Ultimately Nixon proposes that we see the practice of psychoanalysis and remember its history in the visual terms of Conceptual art.

Mark Reinhardt's provocative chapter explores the optical unconscious in representations ranging from the frontispiece of Hobbes's *Leviathan* to Kara Walker's installation *A Subtlety* in the former Domino Sugar Refinery in Brooklyn (chapter 8). Looking at pre- and postphotographic technologies of reproduction, as well as daguerreotypes, he reads Benjamin's optical unconscious as a subversion of sovereignty in which "side perceptions," including unauthorized views as well as nonoptical sensations, shape what is seen and understood. Decisively conjoining the optical to the unconscious in Benjamin's formulation, he examines both literal instances in which a detail in an image is not seen but may nevertheless be perceived affectively, as well as the unconscious impulses and desires that guide visual perception, especially with regard to race as a visual construct. Drawing out the visual construction of race in Benjamin's artwork essay through the figure of Mickey Mouse, Reinhardt turns to Kara Walker as the preeminent artist of the optical unconscious of race in the United States, showing how her work "invites viewers to experience the limits of psychic sovereignty." For Reinhardt, the optical unconscious not only disrupts the social contract, it also calls into question one's own fantasies of mastery, "destabilizing the contractual subject to its core." Finally he encourages us to understand "the optical unconscious as a subversion of psychic sovereignty."

Kristan Horton's *Sligo Heads* might also be said to subvert the psychic sovereignty of the subject by attending to side perceptions (chapter 9). Amalgamated images, the portraits resist the reduction of the traditional portrait and combine gestures and impressions into composites. Although we may not recognize these grotesque and haunting forms, they might represent the layered process of perception quite accurately. Our impressions build up over time, not in the discrete images we might recall, but morphing into one another. Mixing together different facets of features and personalities, Horton's portraits explore the process of perception, just as his written piece about the *Sligo Heads* traces the circuitous development of his thinking in making the work. Both the images and the essay open up the process of seeing and conceiving, refusing end points and conclusions, in an effort to communicate the fleeting and ephemeral qualities of perception.

Gabrielle Moser considers the photographic archive as the optical unconscious of British empire (chapter 10). Examining the massive Colonial Office Visual Instruction Committee's (COVIC's) archive of over 7,600 photographs made by Alfred Hugh Fisher between 1907 and 1910, she suggests that latent anxieties about the limits of imperial citizenship register through the figure of the female "coolie" in the photographic archive. Fisher's photographs were used by COVIC to create lantern slide lectures and texts for children of the colonies, instructing them in forms of imperial belonging. Focusing on photographs of female "coolies" whose liminal legal status troubled the logics of imperial citizenship, Moser models a form of archival research that follows Ann

Stoler's strategy of "developing historical negatives," finding in images of the "coolie" "alternative visions of the future," repressed meanings and uncertainties that COVIC continually sought to manage. Moser interprets the photographic archive as a repository of images in which latent meanings can be developed by the researcher in ways that are analogous to the analyst's interpretation of dream images. In her understanding, the archive becomes not simply a static repository of already developed images that cohere according to colonial ideology, but an unstable resource that, through careful analysis, might also reveal the unsettled desires and fears of colonial authority.

In another effort to expose imperial anxieties, Laura Wexler turns to Roland Barthes's famous Winter Garden Photograph to discuss what the absent image hides in plain sight (chapter 11). Scholars have long debated the existence of the Winter Garden Photograph, the impossible image that captures his mother's essence, and that Barthes, mourning her death, refuses to reproduce in *Camera Lucida*, knowing that readers would see in it only the banality of studium information. Despite his comments otherwise, Wexler discovers, through a reading of Barthes's posthumously published *Mourning Diary*, that the photograph did indeed exist, and that Barthes reproduced it for himself, and allowed a photographer to show it hanging on the wall in Barthes's study. More profoundly, Wexler suggests that Barthes may have been reticent to reproduce the photograph in *Camera Lucida* because it would tie his mother to her brother (also depicted in the image), and link them both forcibly to their father, Louis-Gustave Binger, a French colonial official in Côte d'Ivoire. Barthes's uncle, Philippe, took up his father's work, and continued the imperial project. Wexler proposes that by refusing to reproduce the photograph in *Camera Lucida*, and by keeping readers focused on his mother in his emotional writing about the image, Barthes obscures the evidence of his family's colonial past, creating a blind spot in which a troubling heritage can be hidden in plain sight.

Kelly Wood creates an archive of latent images in her Vancouver carts series (chapter 12), a collection of photographs of repurposed shopping carts used by the homeless and other economically marginalized people. The carts, found stashed on the street, not abandoned but temporarily left alone, stand in for the politics of gentrification, the problem of homelessness, and the contest over property rights, citizenship rights, and civic space. Wood's photographs of the carts also subtly consider her own role, as an artist, in the gentrification that displaces the poor and underemployed, including artists, in developing neighborhoods. Her careful exploration of such disavowed problems and people brings the collusion of cultural and economic forces into view. Conversely, the refusal of gallery owners to see these carts, in Wood's photographs and outside their own doors, highlights a general refusal to acknowledge the ways in which galleries and developers together disenfranchise the impoverished in the process of gentrification.

Thy Phu examines limited vision in another way. In her essay on revolutionary photography in Vietnam (chapter 13), Phu provides a reinterpretation of Benjamin's thoughts on photography as a revolutionary medium. Working with oral histories and archival documents, Phu offers a detailed examination of the work of several Vietnamese socialist photographers who pictured the war with the United States. This chapter works both with and against the prevailing mode of ideological critique that has dominated photography studies (in the wake of the war in Vietnam in particular), showing how Vietnamese patriots turned to the camera precisely because of its revolutionary promise. One of Phu's intriguing findings is that the idea of disability surfaced both literally and symbolically in this body of work, through both the figure of injured bodies and the flawed quality of images. The narrative is not a uniform one, however, as later efforts to retouch the visual records suggest a conceptual shift in the unconscious optics. Taken together, these competing visions illuminate the ways photography can shape a shared fantasy of the past.

In her essay on the Bang-Bang Club, a group of four white photojournalists who documented the end of apartheid in South Africa, Sharon Sliwinski also considers the material and psychological constraints of "dark times" and the effects of such deprivations on the imagination (chapter 14). She argues that sovereign strictures and structures can be registered in these photographs, indeed, that the images demonstrate the ways the imagination can be leveled by political violence. Borrowing from Benjamin's sense of photography as mobilizing collective fantasy, Sliwinski reads the Bang-Bang Club's images not as realist documentary, but as documents that unconsciously reproduced the mentality of apartheid. This is a case in which photographs do not offer a view of reality so much as reveal how imagination and vision can be stunted by the material realities of racial violence. The Bang-Bang Club's photographs show a flattened world, which in turn teaches us something about the unconscious optics of apartheid.

To close the book, Terri Kapsalis returns to the expansive perceptual capacities of photography that Benjamin hoped would predominate in the medium (chapter 15). She explores those capacities in her essay "Slow," which is an extended meditation on James Nares's 2011 film *Street*. Nares used an ultrahigh-speed camera to make *Street* six seconds at a time, producing forty minutes of real-time footage that he then converted into extremely slow motion and edited. The results are a hypnotic look at everyday life on the street transformed into an almost spiritual meditation. The slowness changes everything. In Benjamin's words, "Slow motion not only reveals familiar aspects of movements, but discloses quite unknown aspects within them."[64] Kapsalis shows how attentive the artist is to the perceptual reorientation of his work. She includes parts of an interview she conducted with Nares, and together they discuss the work in terms uncannily similar to Benjamin's gestures toward the optical unconscious. Nares tells her, "To the same extent that the high-speed camera reveals things which we cannot experience or which we cannot see with the natural eye, it also obscures and creates things that don't exist." The chapter, like this book, is about the ways in which technology can transform perception, and new perceptual capacities can alter the way we live our lives.

Notes

1. Generally speaking, the unconscious refers to those processes of the mind that occur outside of conscious awareness, but which nevertheless have an impact on human behavior. The term was coined by the eighteenth-century philosopher Friedrich Schelling and greatly developed by Sigmund Freud throughout his vast oeuvre. It should also be noted that contemporary neuroscientists have turned to the question of nonconscious states of mind, and, in some cases, have developed their own aggressively nonpsychoanalytic notion of the unconscious. See *The New Unconscious*, ed. Ran R. Hassin, James S. Uleman, and John A. Bargh (Oxford: Oxford University Press, 2005). Others have attempted to marry psychoanalytic notions of the unconscious with the new cognitive models. See Antonio R. Damasio, *The Feeling of What Happens: Body and Emotions in the Making of Consciousness* (San Diego: Harcourt, 1999) and Mark Solms, *The Feeling Brain: Selected Papers on Neuropsychoanalysis* (London: Karnac, 2015). Contemporary media theorists who explore questions about the nonconscious ways humans intersect with technology have tended to favor these theories of the cognitive neuroscience. See N. Katherine Hayles, "The Cognitive Nonconscious: Enlarging the Mind of the Humanities," *Critical Inquiry* 42 (Summer 2016): 783–808, and Wendy Hui Kyong Chun, *Updating to Remain the Same: Habitual New Media* (Cambridge, MA: MIT Press, 2016).

2. Although it has not been systematically elaborated, a number of scholars have found ways to engage the optical unconscious in compelling ways. Most prominent among them is Rosalind E. Krauss with her book of the same name, *The Optical Unconscious* (Cambridge, MA: MIT Press, 1993), although Krauss's monograph is not focused on photography per se or on Benjamin's work. Eduardo Cadava has written extensively about Benjamin's theorizations of photography, although Cadava's primary focus is on

the link between photography and conceptions of history: *Words of Light: Theses on the Photography of History* (Princeton, NJ: Princeton University Press, 1998). Film scholars such as Miriam Bratu Hansen have productively discussed Benjamin's optical unconscious in relation to time and the medium of film: *Cinema and Experience: Siegfried Kracauer, Walter Benjamin, and Theodor Adorno* (Berkeley: University of California Press, 2011). More recent books on photography, such as Christopher Pinney's *The Coming of Photography in India* (London: British Library, 2008), and Elizabeth Abel's *Signs of the Times: The Visual Politics of Jim Crow* (Berkeley: University of California Press, 2010), broach the concept as a critical tool, even if it is not their primary focus. Mary Bergstein has approached Benjamin's insight from the other direction. In her *Mirrors of Memory* (Ithaca, NY: Cornell University Press, 2010), Bergstein outlines how visual culture, and photography in particular, fed Freud's thinking about the terrain of the human psyche. Ulrich Baer's book, *Spectral Evidence: The Photography of Trauma* (Cambridge, MA: MIT Press, 2005), offers a distinct intervention into these fields by tracing the connection between the experience of trauma and the photographic image. Much of this literature builds upon the French philosopher Sarah Kofman's chapter on Freud in *Camera Obscura: Of Ideology*, trans. Will Straw (Ithaca, NY: Cornell University Press, 1999), a groundbreaking study of the ways the metaphor of the photographic apparatus came to play a central role in Freud's oeuvre (see chapter 3, this volume). Kofman was a contemporary of Jacques Lacan, whose own use of optical diagrams and metaphors to describe the workings of the unconscious has been a subject of considerable scrutiny.

3. Christopher Bollas, "What Is Theory?," in *The Christopher Bollas Reader* (London: Routledge, 2011), 229. Subsequent psychoanalytic theorists have engaged this question in compelling ways. Apart from Bollas's work, see Darien Leader, *Stealing the Mona Lisa: What Art Stops Us from Seeing* (New York: Faber, 2002).

4. Throughout the 1920s, Benjamin pursed a relationship with the Frankfurt School, which was undertaking a sustained interrogation of mass media. Benjamin formed close friendships with the architect and film theorist Siegfried Kracauer, the philosopher Theodor Adorno, the chemist Gretel Karplus (later Gretel Adorno), the poet and playwright Bertolt Brecht, and the Latvian journalist and theater director Asja Lacis. He also became involved as a fringe member of the G-group—a circle of avant-garde artists, architects, and filmmakers, who came together in Berlin in the early 1920s to launch a journal called *G* (an abbreviation of the German word *Gestaltung*, meaning formation or construction). The members of the G-group included Ludwig Mies van der Rohe, László Moholy-Nagy, El Lissitzky, Raoul Hausmann, and Hans Richter. For more on Benjamin's work and role in this scene see the "Editors' Introduction" to Benjamin's *The Work of Art in the Age of Its Technological Reproducibility and Other Writings on Media*, ed. Michael W. Jennings, Bridgid Doherty, and Thomas Y. Levin (Cambridge, MA: Belknap, 2008).

5. Allan Sekula, "The Body and the Archive," *October* 39 (winter 1986): 3–64; John Tagg, *The Burden of Representation: Essays on Photographies and Histories* (Minneapolis:

University of Minnesota Press, 1988); John Tagg, *The Disciplinary Frame: Photographic Truths and the Capture of Meaning* (Minneapolis: University of Minnesota Press, 2008).

6. Mary Ann Doane coins the term "double mimesis" in *The Desire to Desire: The Woman's Film of the 1940s* (Bloomington: Indiana University Press, 1987), 181. José Esteban Muñoz theorizes "disidentification" in *Disidentifications: Queers of Color and the Performance of Politics* (Minneapolis: University of Minnesota Press, 1999). W. E. B. Du Bois famously articulates "double consciousness" in *The Souls of Black Folk* (1903; reprint, New York: Library of America, 1990).

7. Elizabeth Edwards, *Raw Histories: Photographs, Anthropologies, Museums* (London: Bloomsbury, 2001); Robin Kelsey, *Photography and the Art of Chance* (Cambridge, MA: Harvard University Press, 2015); Tina M. Campt, *Image Matters: Archive, Photography, and the African Diaspora in Europe* (Durham, NC: Duke University Press, 2012); Elspeth Brown and Thy Phu, *Feeling Photography* (Durham, NC: Duke University Press, 2014).

8. Vanessa R. Schwartz, "Walter Benjamin for Historians," *American Historical Review* 106, no. 5 (December 2001): 1721–1743.

9. On September 16, 2013, Internet.org — the global partnership formed by Facebook, Ericsson, Qualcomm, and others — released a report, "A Focus on Efficiency," which noted that "more than 250 billion photos have been uploaded to Facebook, and more than 350 million photos are uploaded every day on average." Internet.org has subsequently deleted this report from their online archives, but it can be viewed at http:// www.slideshare.net/FiratDemirel/facebook-ericsson-rapor. Compare these numbers to the Library of Congress's Prints and Photographs collection, which contains a mere 14.4 million visual images (many of which are nonphotographic).

10. Stephen Mayes describes the transformation that digital photography has wrought in terms of the difference between the "fixed image" and the "fluid image." See his interview with Pete Brook, "Photographs Are No Longer Things, They're Experiences," *Wired*, November 11, 2012, http://www.wired.com/2012/11/stephen-mayes -vii-photography/. On the topic of photography in the digital era, see also Fred Ritchin, *After Photography* (New York: Norton, 2009).

11. See Christopher Bollas, *The Shadow of the Object: Psychoanalysis and the Unthought Known* (New York: Columbia, 1987), and *Cracking Up: The Work of Unconscious Experience* (London: Routledge, 1995).

12. Benjamin had been thinking about photography since at least 1924, when he translated Tristan Tzara's 1922 preface to Man Ray's photographic album for the June 1924 issue of *G: Zeitschrift für elementare Gestaltung* (*G: Magazine for Elementary Form.*)

13. Walter Benjamin, "News about Flowers" (1928), in *Walter Benjamin: Selected Writings, vol. 2, part 1, 1927–1930*, trans. Rodney Livingstone et al., ed. Michael W. Jennings, Howard Eiland, and Gary Smith (Cambridge, MA: Belknap, 1999), 156.

14. Benjamin, "News about Flowers," 156.

15. Walter Benjamin, "Little History of Photography" (1931), in *Walter Benjamin:*

Selected Writings, vol. 2, part 2, 1931–1934, trans. Rodney Livingstone et al., ed. Michael W. Jennings, Howard Eiland, and Gary Smith (Cambridge, MA: Belknap, 1999), 507–530, 510.

16. Benjamin, "Little History of Photography," 510–512.

17. Benjamin, "Little History of Photography," 510.

18. Benjamin, "Little History of Photography," 510–512, emphasis added.

19. Miriam Bratu Hansen, "Benjamin's Aura," *Critical Inquiry* 34 (winter 2008): 336–375.

20. Benjamin, "Little History of Photography," 512.

21. Benjamin, "The Work of Art in the Age of Its Technological Reproducibility," Second Version (1936), in *Walter Benjamin: Selected Writings, vol. 3, 1931–1938*, trans. Rodney Livingstone et al., ed. Michael W. Jennings, Howard Eiland, and Gary Smith (Cambridge, MA: Belknap, 2002), 117.

22. Benjamin, "The Work of Art," 117–118, emphasis in original.

23. Susan Buck-Morss, "The Flaneur, the Sandwichman and the Whore: The Politics of Loitering," *New German Critique* 39 (fall 1986): 99–139, 109.

24. Walter Benjamin, *The Arcades Project*, trans. Howard Eiland and Kevin McLaughlin (Cambridge, MA: Belknap, 1999), 458.

25. Buck-Morss, "The Flaneur, the Sandwichman and the Whore," 109. See also Susan Buck-Morss, *The Dialectics of Seeing: Walter Benjamin and the Arcades Project* (Cambridge, MA: MIT Press, 1989).

26. Jonathan Crary, *Techniques of the Observer: On Vision and Modernity in the Nineteenth Century* (Cambridge, MA: MIT Press, 1990), 116–136.

27. Indeed, the paired images on the stereo card are often difficult to differentiate, but a close look at their distant spaces reveals a slight shift in point of view. Stereoscopic cameras mimicked the binocularity of the human eye, so that a single camera was given two lenses in order to make two slightly different views of any given scene.

28. Eli Friedlander insists that "language is the *medium* in which the dialectical image can emerge at all," and certainly Benjamin's *Arcades Project* is a compendium of snippets of texts. However, interested as we are here in Benjamin's expansive thoughts on photography, we have been struck by the photographic allusions and direct photographic references that permeate Benjamin's discussion of history, the work of the historical materialist, and the dialectical image. It is true that these ruminations occur in language, but in a language laden with photographic references. Eli Friedlander, "The Measure of the Contingent: Walter Benjamin's Dialectical Image," *boundary* 2 35, no. 3 (2008): 1–26, 2.

29. Walter Benjamin, "On the Concept of History" (1940), in *Walter Benjamin: Selected Writings, vol. 4, 1938–1940*, trans. Edmund Jephcott et al., ed. Howard Eiland and Michael W. Jennings (Cambridge, MA: Belknap, 2003), 389–400, 396.

30. Benjamin, "The Work of Art," 117. See also Cadava, *Words of Light*, 59–63. As Vilém Flusser proposes, the photograph "has interrupted the stream of history": "Photo-

graphs are dams placed in the way of the stream of history, jamming historical happenings." Flusser, "Photography and History," in *Writings*, trans. Erik Eisel, ed. Andreas Ströhl (Minneapolis: University of Minnesota Press, 2002), 126–131, 128. Scholars have begun to understand such disruptions of linear time as queer. Elizabeth Freeman specifically proposes that many queer historiographers take their cue from Benjamin, in part, because the theorist's radical nonlinear temporality "suggests a potentially queer vision of how time wrinkles and folds as some minor feature of our own sexually impoverished present suddenly meets up with a richer past, or as the materials of a failed and forgotten project of the past find their uses now, in a future unimaginable in their time." Elizabeth Freeman, "Introduction," GLQ 13, nos. 2–3 (2007): 159–176, 163.

31. Benjamin, "Little History of Photography," 510.

32. Miriam Hansen, "Benjamin, Cinema and Experience: 'The Blue Flower in the Land of Technology,'" *New German Critique* 40 (winter 1987): 179–224, 208.

33. Vilém Flusser, "Photography and History," 129.

34. Benjamin, "On the Concept of History," 391.

35. Sigmund Freud, *The Interpretation of Dreams* (1900), in *The Standard Edition of the Complete Psychological Works of Sigmund Freud* [hereafter SE], ed. and trans. James Strachey (London: Hogarth, 1953), vol. 5, 536.

36. Freud, *The Interpretation of Dreams*, 606.

37. Freud, *The Interpretation of Dreams*, 606.

38. Freud elaborated these mechanisms of defense over the course of his oeuvre. As Martin Jay has discussed, he initially rejected the idea of scotomization as "unsuitable, for it suggests that the perception is entirely wiped out." The term nevertheless became significant to Jacques Lacan, who wrote about it as early as 1938, and later tellingly referred to Freud's failure to recognize the ego's ability to scotomize as an instance of *méconnaissance*. See Martin Jay, *Downcast Eyes: The Denigration of Vision in Twentieth-Century Thought* (Los Angeles: University of California Press, 1993), 354.

39. Sigmund Freud, *Moses and Monotheism* (1939), in SE, vol. 23, 125–126. We have modified Strachey's translation slightly using Katherine Jones's edition (New York: Alfred A. Knopf, 1939), 198–199.

40. In *Moses and Monotheism*, Freud tries to bring his theory of latency to bear on historical processes (and specifically the early period of Judaism). Here latency is used in a parallel way to *nachträglichkeit* ("deferred action" or "afterwardsness"). Both terms refer to a psychic temporality in which earlier experience, impressions, and memory traces are revised at a later date in order to fit in with fresh experiences or with a new stage of development. See Jean Laplanche and J. B. Pontalis's entry on "deferred action" in *The Language of Psychoanalysis*, trans. Donald Nicholson-Smith (New York: Norton, 1973), 111–114. Also Jean Laplanche, "Notes on Afterwardsness," in *Essays on Otherness* (New York: Routledge, 1999), 260–265.

41. It must be noted that from 1920 onward, Freud revised his theory of the psychic apparatus. The shift is marked by a change in terminology: in his 1923 article "*Das Ich*

und Das Es" (translated into English as "The Ego and the Id"), Freud borrowed Georg Groddek's term *das Es* (literally, "the It") to designate the dynamic agency of the unconscious. In his second topographical theory of the psyche, Freud proposed a second form of unconscious: he added the idea of unconscious process to his earlier sense of unconscious contents. There is not the time or space to discuss the details of his evolving definition here, but it bears pointing out that there is a parallel to Benjamin's own changing definition of the optical unconscious. Seemingly taking his cue from Freud, Benjamin realized that photography not only pictures the unseen, but that it has a dynamic mode of organization, sorting psychically valuable experiences at an unconscious level. See Freud, "The Ego and the Id" (1923), in *SE*, vol. 19, 3–68. For a more fulsome discussion of Freud's various models of the unconscious, see Bollas, "What Is Theory?," 228–237.

42. Kofman, *Camera Obscura*, 21–28, 27. Reproduced in this book as chapter 3.

43. Freud, *Moses and Monotheism*, 126.

44. Freud, *Moses and Monotheism*, 126.

45. See Anton Ehrenzweig's theory of "unconscious scanning" in *The Hidden Order of Art: A Study in the Psychology of Artistic Imagination* (Berkeley: University of California Press, 1967), 32–46. Christopher Bollas has also greatly elaborated Freud's views about unconscious perception; see *The Evocative Object World* (London: Routledge, 2009) and *The Infinite Question* (London: Routledge, 2009).

46. Du Bois, *The Souls of Black Folk*, 8. For an extended discussion of double consciousness as visual culture, see Shawn Michelle Smith, "Envisioning Race," in *Photography on the Color Line: W. E. B. Du Bois, Race, and Visual Culture* (Durham, NC: Duke University Press, 2004), 25–42.

47. Du Bois, *The Souls of Black Folk*, 8.

48. W. E. B. Du Bois, "The Souls of White Folk" (1920), in *W. E. B. Du Bois: Writings*, ed. Nathan Huggins (New York: Library of America, 1986), 923.

Du Bois draws whiteness itself into view, unsettling the cultural privilege of its invisibility. As Richard Dyer has argued, whiteness has often remained unmarked in the visual field as the position from which unseen subjects gaze at others. Richard Dyer, "White," *Screen* 29, no. 4 (1988): 44–64, and *White* (London: Routledge, 1997). Other important studies of whiteness and visual culture include: Michael Rogin, *Blackface, White Noise: Jewish Immigrants in the Hollywood Melting Pot* (Berkeley: University of California Press, 1996); Eric Lott, *Love and Theft: Blackface Minstrelsy and the American Working Class* (New York: Oxford University Press, 1993); bell hooks, "Representations of Whiteness in the Black Imagination," *Black Looks: Race and Representation* (Boston: South End Press, 1992), 165–178; Martin A. Berger, *Sight Unseen: Whiteness and American Visual Culture* (Berkeley: University of California Press, 2005).

49. For further discussions of the daguerreotypes Joseph T. Zealy made for Louis Agassiz, see Brian Wallis, "Black Bodies, White Science: Louis Agassiz's Slave Daguerreotypes," *American Art* 9, no. 2 (summer 1995): 38–61; Lisa Gail Collins, chap-

ter 2, "Historic Retrievals: Confronting Visual Evidence and the Imaging of Truth," in *The Art of History: African American Women Artists Engage the Past* (New Brunswick, NJ: Rutgers University Press, 2002), 11–36; Molly Rogers, *Delia's Tears: Race, Science, and Photography in Nineteenth-Century America* (New Haven, CT: Yale University Press, 2010).

50. Ta-Nehisi Coates, *Between the World and Me* (New York: Spiegel and Grau, 2015), 10.

51. Suzanne Schneider, "Louis Agassiz and the American School of Ethnoeroticism: Polygenesis, Pornography, and Other 'Perfidious Influences,'" in *Pictures and Progress: Early Photography and the Making of African American Identity*, ed. Maurice O. Wallace and Shawn Michelle Smith (Durham, NC: Duke University Press, 2012), 211–243.

52. Francis Galton, Appendix A: "Composite Portraiture," in *Inquiries into Human Faculty and Its Development*, 2nd ed. (London: J. M. Dent and sons, 1907), 221–241.

53. Allan Sekula, "The Body and the Archive."

54. Frantz Fanon, *Black Skin, White Masks*, trans. Charles Lam Markmann (New York: Grove, 1967), 111. Lewis Gordon, among many others, describes this encounter as a defining moment for Fanon. See Lewis R. Gordon, *What Fanon Said: A Philosophical Introduction to His Life and Thought* (New York: Fordham University Press, 2015), 48.

55. Fanon, *Black Skin, White Masks*, 112.

56. Fatimah Tobing Rony, *The Third Eye: Race, Cinema, and Ethnographic Spectacle* (Durham, NC: Duke University Press, 1996), 6. See also Kaja Silverman, *The Threshold of the Visible World* (New York: Routledge, 1996), 27.

57. David Marriott, *On Black Men* (New York: Columbia University Press, 2000), 90.

58. Jacques Lacan, "The Mirror Stage as Formative of the Function of the I as Revealed in Psychoanalytic Experience," *Écrits: A Selection* (1966), trans. Alan Sheridan (New York: Norton, 1977), 1–7.

59. Marriott, *On Black Men*, 80. See also Stuart Hall, "The Afterlife of Frantz Fanon: Why Fanon? Why Now? Why *Black Skin, White Masks*?," in *The Fact of Blackness: Frantz Fanon and Visual Representation*, ed. Alan Read (Seattle: Bay Press, 1996), 12–37, 26–27.

60. Rony, *The Third Eye*, 4; Fanon, *Black Skin, White Masks*, 112.

61. Rony, *The Third Eye*, 4.

62. Building on Du Bois's insights, scholars in performance studies have assessed the ways in which African American performance artists have seized upon the disruptive force of the black body in the visual field as a site of insurgency. See Daphne A. Brooks, *Bodies in Dissent: Spectacular Performances of Race and Freedom, 1850–1910* (Durham: Duke University Press, 2006), and Nicole R. Fleetwood, *Troubling Vision: Performance, Visuality, and Blackness* (Chicago: University of Chicago Press, 2011).

63. Benjamin, "Little History of Photography," 510.

64. Benjamin, "The Work of Art," 117.

CHAPTER ONE

——

PHOTOGRAPHY'S WEIMAR-ERA PROLIFERATION AND WALTER BENJAMIN'S OPTICAL UNCONSCIOUS

——

ANDRÉS MARIO ZERVIGÓN

In his 1931 essay "Little History of Photography," Walter Benjamin offered the following phrasing to introduce his notion of an optical unconscious:

> For it is another nature which speaks to the camera rather than to the eye: "other" above all in the sense that a space informed by human consciousness gives way to a space informed by the unconscious. Whereas it is a commonplace that, for example, we have some idea what is involved in the act of walking (if only in general terms), we have no idea at all what happens during the fraction of a second when a person actually takes a step. Photography, with its devices of slow motion and enlargement, reveals the secret. It is through photography that we first discover the existence of this optical unconscious.[1]

Students of modernism have grown closely familiar with these words, and, after his partial rephrasing, with Benjamin's description of the optical unconscious in the 1936 essay "The Work of Art in the Age of Its Technological Reproducibility." What is less recognized, however, is that these same ideas would also have struck readers of the 1931 essay as commonplace. At this moment in the late Weimar era, modernists and popular advocates of the medium regularly claimed that photography surpassed and thus aided human vision. The examples of this are legion. Erstwhile Bauhaus professor and photo enthusiast László Moholy-Nagy famously wrote in 1927 that "the modern lens is no longer tied to the narrow limits of our eye; no manual means of representation . . . is capable of arresting fragments of the world seen like this . . . [or fixing] the quintessence of a movement," as in his picture of the dancer Gret Palucca, caught midair in one of her signature springs (fig. 1.1). According to Moholy, such photographic capacities "have allowed us to see beyond the specific instance" and made available an "objective vision" compelling us "to see that which is optically true."[2] Similarly, the graphic artist Johannes Molzahn observed the surfeit of images in illustrated papers and declared that "it is the photo that continually informs us and suggests new phenomena."[3] Gallerist Karl Nierendorf compared the camera to a microscope that "reveals whole systems of life in drops of water" and to "the instruments of the observatory [that] open up the infinity of the universe."[4] Photographer Albert Renger-Patzsch contrasted the camera to older means of representation and declared that "photography works faster, and with greater precision and greater objectivity than the hand of the artist." For him as for Moholy, this notion of objectivity was implicitly linked with modern truth and a purity of vision.[5] For all these observers, the medium had begun to realize new modes of perception and analysis that could be disseminated on a mass scale. Because of photography's inherent reproducibility, new ways of seeing and understanding could be made immediately available to mass audiences. This expanded mode of perception was thereby exponentially extending the laudable project of clear-sighted enlightenment.

But there were clouds rolling toward this utopian horizon, even for Benjamin. From the mid-1920s on, misgivings about photography's expanded role emerged in the long shadow of a profusion of images. At issue was the great abundance itself—the illustrated press being the chief culprit in this spike of imagery—and how the era's pictorial surfeit transformed human consciousness. Referring in 1927 to the "weekly photographic rations" that the numerous *Illustrierten* delivered, for example, Siegfried Kracauer famously worried that "the assault of this mass of images is so powerful that it threatens to destroy the potentially existing awareness of crucial traits." Ominously, Kracauer felt that "in the hands of the ruling society, the invention of illustrated magazines is one of the most powerful means of organizing a strike against understanding."[6] His was a concern with photography's capacity for mass reproducibility, precisely the same thing that excited so many other Weimar-era commentators.

But Kracauer also worried about the potential profusion of meanings produced by any single image, and the perceptual consequences of this cascade of significations for the experience of modernity. Increasingly, other observers also awoke to the capacity of one print to speak many wildly different things. Willi Münzenberg, publisher of the radical-left *Arbeiter-Illustrierte Zeitung* (*Worker's Illustrated Magazine*, or AIZ), complained in 1931 that by employing

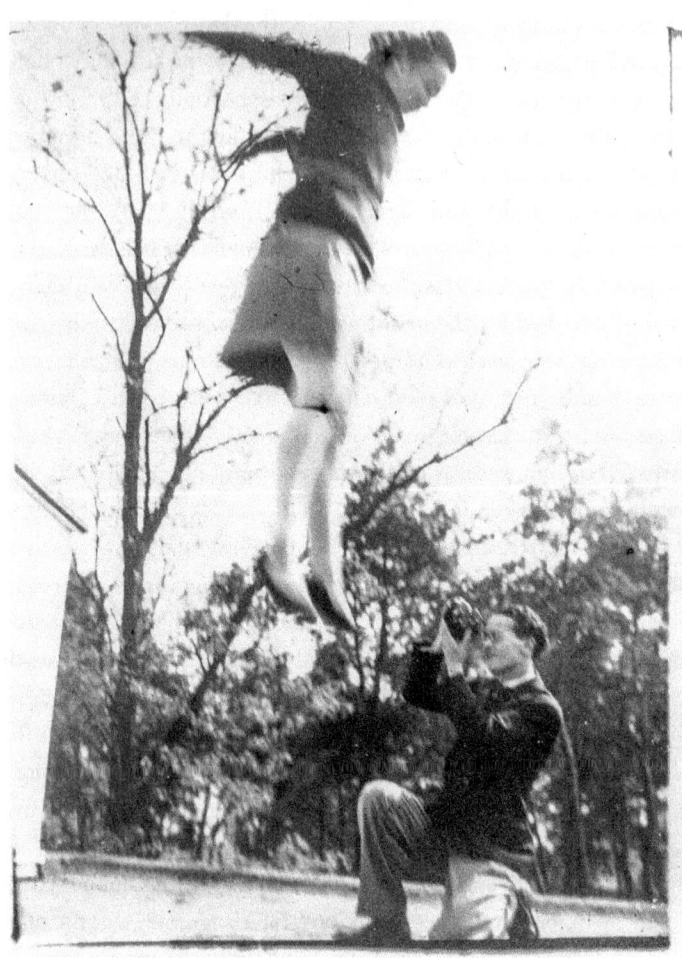

FIGURE 1.1 László Moholy-Nagy, the German dancer
Gret Palucca (1902–1993) while jumping on the roof of a Master
house at the Bauhaus in Dessau. The represented photographer might
possibly be Andreas Feininger. 1927–1928. Photograph on silver
gelatin paper, 11.8 × 8.8 cm. Inv. D 1981–359. Kupferstichkabinett,
Staatliche Kunstsammlungen, Dresden, Germany.
bpk, Berlin/Art Resource, New York.

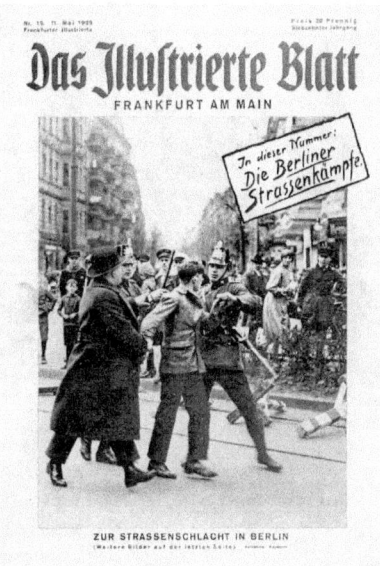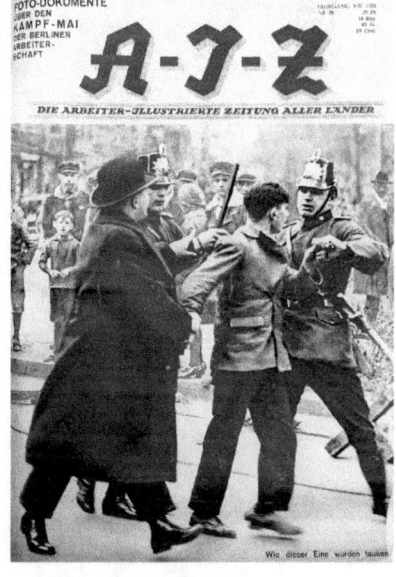

FIGURE 1.2 *left Das Illustrierte Blatt*, Frankfurt am Main, no. 19,
May 11, 1929. Polizei verhaftet Demonstranten am 1. Mai 1929
(nach einer Original-Kontaktkopie 13 × 18).

FIGURE 1.3 *right AIZ* vol. 8, no. 20 (1929). "Wie dieser Eine wurde wie tausende
Andere verhaftet und verprügelt." [How this one like thousands of others
was arrested and thrashed.]

"a combination of several pictures with their captions and accompanying text
. . . a skillful editor can reverse the significance of any photograph and influence a reader who lacks political sophistication in any direction he chooses."[7]
Of course, Münzenberg famously did this himself, as one can see in comparing
what the politically centrist *Das Illustrierte Blatt* in 1929 framed as a rioter was
depicted by the *AIZ* as a persecuted worker (figs. 1.2 and 1.3). A print drawn
from the full negative seems to offer yet another nuance by showing the larger
context of relative calm (fig. 1.4). As with others on the political extremes,
Münzenberg was even willing to engage in outright photo-fibs. An *AIZ* front
page from 1927 allegedly shows right-wing militia members participating in
shooting exercises on the property of then interior minister Walter von Keudell
(fig. 1.5). This picture raised such a stink that the magazine had to confess a few
weeks later that, naturally, it was a montage, "as any child could see." But as the

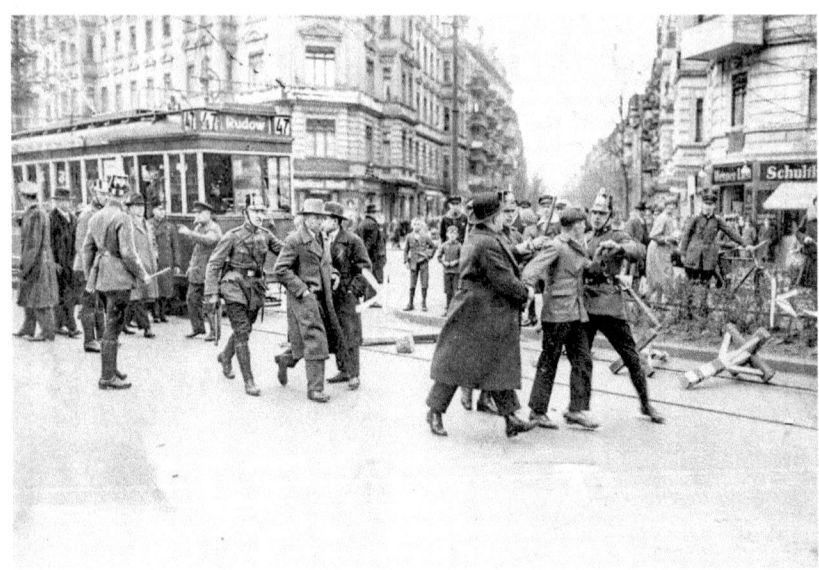

FIGURE 1.4 *above* Polizei verhaftet Demonstranten am 1. Mai 1929, nach einer Original-Kontaktkopie 13 × 18. Das Foto wurde von einem Pressefotografen der Firma "Keystone," vermutlich Paul Rudolf, aufgenommen. [A demonstrator arrested by the police on May 1, 1929, from an original contact print, 13 × 18 cm. Photograph taken by a photographer of the Keystone Company, presumably Paul Rudolf.]

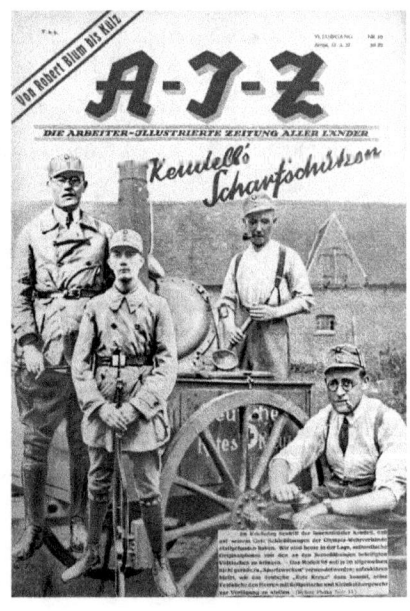

FIGURE 1.5 *right AIZ* vol. 6, no. 10 (March 3, 1927). *Keudell's Scharfschützen* [Keudell's marksmen].

feature inside the issue went on to explain, this picture told a higher truth by employing cut-and-paste manipulations to reveal a deeper reality hidden beneath the surface of mere appearances.

Exactly what constituted photo veracity in the *AIZ* came into sharp relief four years later when playwright Bertolt Brecht stated flatly in its pages that mass-printed "photography, in the hands of the bourgeoisie, has become a terrible weapon *against* truth."[8] Here was the dark underside of Weimar-era photo enthusiasm. While these commentators remained convinced of photography's liberating potential, they nonetheless identified two parallel phenomena that led to the hoodwinking and stultification of mass audiences at the very level of perception: too many images and too many meanings. For these observers, who used a photo and when it was taken mattered as much as what the image seemingly reported. No matter how objective these visions and their meanings seemed to be, and regardless of the irrefutability that this impartiality apparently confirmed, the photographic message was always contingent on the moment it was snapped and on the agenda of the person who delivered it. Moreover, its meanings were powered by mass-printed conveyances that assaulted in the form of a deluge.

In the following pages, I would like to suggest that Benjamin acknowledged these shortcomings when he published his "Little History of Photography" in 1931, the same year — not coincidentally — that Münzenberg and Brecht penned their now famous photo-misgivings. However, Benjamin chose not to stifle his burgeoning investment in photography's emancipatory potential for critical apperception. Instead he opted to nuance it. This he did by locating the revelatory agency of photography not just in the relationship between the camera and human perception made possible by the print, as Moholy had, but more specifically in the role played by the highly subjective realm of the unconscious, where contingency played the very most important role in perception. Like the more optimistic members of his Weimar-era cohort, Benjamin agreed that photography could access unseen worlds and report on the invisible to masses of people, thereby acclimatizing them to the shock experience of urban modernity. But he assigned this operation's unfolding to a realm where the conscious directives of ideology and reason held less immediate sway. Benjamin was therefore theorizing a deferral that saw photography's revolutionary disclosures work unencumbered on the raw — even primal — associations that make perception possible, much as he theorized for surrealism. Ultimately, he conceived this operation in part to help salvage, reclaim, and reinvent a medium whose emancipatory potential was being threatened by the twin blights of heavy proliferation and deep contingency in a modern environment already saturated with overpowering—even numbing—stimuli.

Photo-Inflation and Contingency

The context that helped drive Benjamin to his ideas about the optical unconscious was characterized by a surfeit of photographs that heavily determined everyday experience. Many at the time saw this phenomenon alternately as a flood, a marvel, a boom, a benefit, a shock, or a debilitating inflation. The advances in camera and image-printing technologies that made this excess possible had largely been developed before World War I. But confusing restrictions on the publication and mailing of pictures during the conflict, coupled with claims of paper shortages, largely sheltered Germany's everyday citizens from the practical implications of these advancements.

Not so after military defeat. Once Wilhelmine authority melted away in the Revolution of 1918–1919, vying political factions and commodity advertisers immediately pressed their points through innumerable magazines, leaflets, and postcards thickly larded with pictures. Many of these were photographs. Advertising commentator Ernst Bauer described this phenomenon as a colorful "papery flood" that swelled higher and higher as the revolution unfolded. "Berlin's streets," he explained, "debauched themselves in orgies of color while the buildings exchanged their gray faces for various excited masks. Every free space was ruthlessly covered up."[9] The heavy deployment of so many "mental weapons," as the government's information chief described this printed matter, often caused as much disquiet as the revolution itself.[10] In fact, for astute observers, the uprising to a large extent was its representation. Noting the plethora of political posters, banners, and postcards wallpapering Germany's urban corridors, commentator Hans Friedeberger concluded, "The street offers the picture of restlessness. It shines, luxuriates in colors, and appeals with a blood-warm expression of our turbulent times."[11] For Friedeberger, to experience the fervor was at best to see its picture, particularly in agitating fragments.

Berlin's Dada movement reveled in the photographic character of this cresting wave, and correspondingly recast the revolution one year after its defeat as a space rife with screaming prints. In the movement's 1920 trade fair (*Messe*), the first full-scale photo posters ever made yelled their slogans toward photomontages that recast this papery flood as a stormy sea of emulsion.[12] One of the most exciting things about Berlin's Club Dada was that it specifically saw the Weimar era's birth as a dizzying hail of representations, as much as bullets. And in this new sort of struggle, photography played a capital role in extending, enhancing, and agitating the human sensorium most effectively. It could shock audiences out of a wartime anesthesia induced, in large measure, by grand doses of soothing and reassuring images. Berlin's Dada movement sought to overturn this abuse of mass reproduction technologies by employing one of their most advanced forms, photography, to keep the revolution's pictorial assault alive.[13]

As the republic surmounted its early challenges, which included hyperinflation, political assassinations, and a right-wing putsch, photography increasingly proliferated in its progressively well-populated and expanding home: the illustrated magazine. These periodicals began to boom after the stabilization of the country's currency in 1924. By 1927, the photo editor of the high-circulation *Berliner-Illustrirte [sic] Zeitung* (Berlin illustrated magazine) could write that a reader "traveled the world" through the pictures of a single issue.[14] The summit of this photo-enthusiasm was reached with the famous *Film und Foto Ausstellung* (Film and photo exhibition) of 1929, which conclusively located photography's value in the medium's capacity to shape and extend perception.[15] Photographs were no longer prized as handcrafted rarities, for what Benjamin would refer to as their aura. Such had been the case in the now-defunct pictorialist movement. Instead, their new worth came from their ability to enhance visual awareness, a capability that the medium's availability for endless reproduction and dissemination strongly accelerated. The photo-boom was on.

Yet by the same time in 1929, critics complained of what they quickly began to call photo-inflation. By this reckoning, there were simply too many pictures, and they were overwhelming human perception. Paul Westheim, editor of the art magazine *Das Kunstblatt*, referred to the consequences of this phenomenon in 1932 as *Bildermüde* or "image weariness," while historian Wilhelm Hausenstein complained that too many experimental photographs repeating the same vertiginous or closely framed views had become formulaic and visually numbing.[16] As photo historian Olivier Lugon has explained, photo-inflation had led to a collapse in the photograph's value. Pictures had been overprinted like paper money and the presses now refused to stop spinning. Even vision itself increasingly seemed a devalued resource, susceptible to weakening or loss through overuse.[17]

In this heady context arose the parallel and sometimes countervailing worry that photographic meaning itself had experienced a dangerous profusion. Any one print could mean a number of things depending on its caption and context. By this other understanding, image abundance had not in fact devalued photography or exhausted human perception, but it had instead begun to shape the human mind in dangerously misguided and unmanageable directions. Münzenberg's comments and strategies are representative of this concern. Considering the heated nature of the enthusiasm and anxiety around photography, and taking into account the very urgency of human perception that seemed at stake, it is no wonder that Benjamin, a keen observer of "the relationship between the human senses, consciousness and the social world," chose to intervene.[18]

The Photographic Subject

As already noted, Benjamin's contribution to the highly public sounding off about photography worked with familiar notions of enhanced human perception. But it nevertheless offered something stunningly unique for its late Weimar time. To underscore its importance, I note one curious lacuna in all these discussions about the medium, be it about inflation or contingency. Despite the great and anxious loquaciousness about the relationship between photography and perception at this time, there was remarkably little writing that went beyond formulaic considerations, little thought that actually reflected on the consequences of photo-inflation for modern subjectivity. In other words, Weimar's tense photographic conditions failed to generate a comprehensive theory of the photographic subject. Such an account would have explained the medium's role in the formation of a radically altered human subjectivity, particularly as a mass or collective phenomenon. It is this, I believe, that Benjamin was on the verge of supplying when he broached the possibility of an optical unconscious in 1931.

To be sure, other commentators took small steps in this direction around the same time, and their efforts help reveal where Benjamin may have been heading with his "Little History of Photography." For example, before he condemned mainstream illustrated papers for reversing the meanings of the photographs they printed, Willi Münzenberg of the AIZ commented insightfully on how "photography works upon the human eye." According to his account, "What is seen is reflected in the brain without the need for complicated thought."[19] This notion touches on the problem of subjectivity in that the photographic message is understood to bypass the area of consciousness that produces rational thought. Instead the photographic message works directly on a more primal zone of unfiltered perception. Like Münzenberg, Paul Westheim also focused specifically on the psychological consequences of photography's profusion. In his 1932 "Bildermüde" essay, he noted that "the human eye today is *stuffed with image impressions* daily, hourly. . . . This kaleidoscope of constantly changing image impressions is altered so quickly that little in fact remains etched in our memory. Each image chases the next. . . . The result is . . . *overstimulation*. One might even say: the more contemporary man is given to see, *the less he experiences in seeing*. He sees far too much to be able to see consciously and intensely any more."[20] For Westheim, photo-inflation forced too many changing pictorial impressions on the mind and short-circuited the possibility of conscious vision. Instead, as one might surmise, stunned late Weimar viewers stood agog before this tide of emulsion and rotogravure ink. They could only process pictorial information in some other region beyond consciousness, if at all.

The other great gesture toward a theory of the photographic subject, aside from Benjamin's own, appeared in Kracauer's 1927 "Photography" essay.[21] In these pages the then-commentator for the *Frankfurter Zeitung* brilliantly anticipated the concerns that would arise more broadly in just a few years. As noted already, Kracauer worried that the "weekly photographic rations" of the illustrated papers threatened to overwhelm perception and operate as a strike against understanding. The mechanism that he saw behind this occlusion is insightful. As he explained, both the tremendous daily onslaught of pictures and, just as importantly, the great amount of visual information that even a single print conveyed worked to overwhelm and disable the natural workings of human memory. A photograph of his grandmother, for example, did not resemble his memory of her because it had not been passed through the subjective filtering that had left the few essential traits of her that his memory was able to record. Instead, the print teemed with extraneous information, all of equivalent weight. Kracauer deemed this information the photographic "garbage" that memory otherwise filters out to fashion a "monogram," the distilled and lasting imprint on the mind. This was something that photography, in its overabundance of information, could never produce.

In his "Little History of Photography," Benjamin took Kracauer's account of photography's relationship to perception and partly switched out memory for the unconscious. This move opened up a far more capacious psychological terrain that could permit a less negative assessment of photography's operations on subjectivity's formation, be it in the individual or collectively in the masses. Correspondingly, photography was not seen to overwhelm the capacity of subjective human memory, recollection being one of the mechanisms that allows unconscious sense perception to deliver unrepressed images to the conscious (among other things). Instead photographs could reveal the nearly invisible phenomena that only the unconscious could perceive at the actual unfolding of such events. Photography thus made these occurrences and their impact on the human sensorium accessible to the conscious "just as we discover the instinctual unconscious through psychoanalysis," to quote Benjamin's 1936 discussion of the optical unconscious. The camera, in other words, could serve as a seasoned Freudian analyst, ever vigilant before the "other nature" that the untrained eye could not capture. The photographic print was in turn the analyst's report, delivering the repressed optical sensation or memory that offered access to the pictorial agents and experiences that unconsciously form human subjectivity. By this conception, the photograph, itself contingent on time, context, and user, is significant for its very relationship to the contingency of human perception at the unconscious level. To a great extent, the photograph's contingency mirrored that of sense perception and could therefore be seen to house its own unconscious.

Benjamin, in fact, made notes along these lines in the sentences preceding his remarks on the optical unconscious in his 1931 "Little History" essay:

> Or you turn up the picture of [Karl] Dauthendey the photographer, the father of the poet [Max Dauthendey], from the time of his engagement to that woman whom he found one day, shortly after the birth of her sixth child, lying in the bedroom of his Moscow house with her veins slashed. Here she can be seen with him. He seems to be holding her, but her gaze passes him by, absorbed in an ominous distance. Immerse yourself in such a picture long enough and you will realize to what extent opposites touch, here too: the most precise technology can give its products a *magical value*, such as a painted picture can never again have for us. No matter how artful the photographer, no matter how carefully posed his subject, the beholder feels an *irresistible urge* to search such a picture for *the tiny spark of contingency*, of the here and now, with which reality has (so to speak) seared the subject, to find the *inconspicuous spot* where in the immediacy of that long-forgotten moment the future nests so eloquently that we, looking back, may rediscover it.[22]

What one finds here resonates with the punctum later articulated by Roland Barthes. In the photograph of an ill-fated couple, according to Benjamin, there is an emotional valence scarcely available to rational perception. Like the human unconscious itself, the picture harbors something "magical" that spurs the viewer's primal "urge" to search beneath the print's surface for an "inconspicuous spot" of scarcely restrained "immediacy." This involves the "tiny spark of contingency" signaling when a photographed moment meets the future beholder over the undefined zone of that beholder's unconscious. It is just this quality of contingency, shared by the photographic and human unconscious, that joins the two in a unique mode of perception not possible with painting. Notice that this is nearly the same conditionality that so worried Münzenberg and Brecht, the conditional nature of photographic meaning.

Such an interpretation, of course, involves reading Benjamin's short remarks on the optical unconscious literally and, therefore, leaving little room to understand his briefly articulated conception as a metaphor or allegory "with multiple and shifting meanings," as Miriam Hansen tells us.[23] This would be a metaphor, for example, that might laudably make the unconscious and photography available to rational analysis, even though both can never be fully known at the conscious level, if we follow Benjamin's logic. Neither does this literal explanation allow the unconscious to serve as an analogue for portions of the larger visual field before which the camera's lens stands and reports, or expand on the possibility that photography itself houses a dimension of a collective unconscious.

But it does, I believe, help clarify the historical urgency that Benjamin felt in conceiving a positive role for photography in 1931 and, more insistently, in the dire political climate of 1936. The medium, in its wealth of detailed information, in its grand profusion, and—most importantly—in its capacity to mean different things at the level of the unconscious, was heavily contingent on modern human subjectivity, particularly in a mass audience. As a consequence, it had increasingly moved from mediating human experience to constituting it. The modern subject as both an individual and collective was more than ever encountering the world with all its vagaries as, not through, a photographic representation. This made possible a unique relationship to the unconscious, surpassed only by film, that allowed a new reception of the external world. Benjamin gave this uniquely mediated experience the term sensorial "innervation." It forged "a porous interface between the organism and the world that would allow for a greater mobility and circulation of psychic energies."[24] Innervation through photography and film enabled audiences to dismantle the defensive shield of consciousness they built to shield themselves from capitalist and imperialist exploitations of modern technology, misuses that had led to the numbing of the sensorium and the impossibility of political action.[25] This conception is remarkably similar to what Berlin's Club Dada envisioned eleven years before Benjamin published his "Little History."

It is at this conceptual juncture where Benjamin, I believe, was preparing one of his most radical turns in proposing an optical unconscious, one stimulated and made accessible by photographic mediation. By laying the ground-work for a theory of the photographic subject in this way, he began combining the most important and fully formed theories of subjectivity that held purchase on the left at this time and that had earned Benjamin's fascination: those by Marx and Freud. Marx theorized a subjectivity that arose through the shaping and transforming of materials required for human survival or—more broadly—civilization, and the social relations that these activities with materials demanded. Problems arose when commodities in the shimmering realm of the superstructure were valued for their potential in exchange, rather than for their use or the actual labor put into them at the level of base manufacture. This was the phantasmagoria of capitalism that, like the photograph, bypassed the conscious part of the mind where rational decisions were made, and appealed instead to the unconscious. By Benjamin's view, it also defined the misuse of technology that numbed audiences to sensation. The chimerical world of commodity exchange alienated modern men and women from the true material base of the physical world and the more authentic forms of social relations that this realm fostered. Freud, in turn, offered a theory in which the subject was formed in the negotiation of his or her own drives with the restraints that civilization placed on these impulses. The unconscious served as a key mechanism in this mediation, albeit one that Freud repeatedly retheorized.

What Benjamin seems to have been preparing at this late Weimar moment is an updating of Marx's materialist critique into a theory of photographic mediation, one that he would soon move to film. Perhaps he recognized the degree to which both Marx and Freud used the camera obscura and photography as metaphors for ideology and perception, elements of their thought that Sarah Kofman discussed in 1973 and are reprinted in this volume.[26] But even if not, he recognized that subject formation in 1931 was being propelled less by problems around material relations than by the representation of those relations. An outmoded nineteenth-century manufactured object long ago sold in a Parisian arcade now bespoke not just its use value, the labor put into its manufacture, or its wavering exchange value, but the constellation of social relations, history, practices, and experiences through which it had circulated. Thus, Benjamin valued it not only for its material history or its place in commodity exchange. He also understood it as a social-historical mediator, a representation of lost or overlooked micromoments in history relished by the everyday collector and salvageable by the historian's discerning eye, generally as a facet in a montage-like historical constellation. It could reveal, in other words, the operations of the historical phantasmagoria of which it was a part. The photograph offered the same mediation and revelation, but of a sort available directly to the unconscious and the conscious simultaneously, once more: like a highly versatile Freudian analyst bridging the two realms with a single "spark," to use Benjamin's term from his "Work of Art" essay. It was through the photograph, therefore, that a materialist understanding of the subject's formation was joined with a Freudian one where drives and civilization played key roles. Crucial as well is that, for Benjamin, the photographic subject was also the revolutionary subject, capable of sensing the world around her or him more fully, and therefore better able to change it.

I need to emphasize that this is historically specific speculation, with a stress on speculation. Benjamin's ideas are hard to pin down because they continually worked in what Hansen calls "opposed valences," or opposite proposals that developed almost dialectically over time.[27] For instance, he soon moved on to formulate an even more radical take on subjectivity, seeing it as collective, rather than individual, and constituted through constellations of objects, images, and their histories as they circulated through communal zones of memory, consciousness, and unconsciousness to profound and liberating sensorial effect. Yet he did not completely abandon the notion of individual subjectivity. He articulated these new, nearly conflicting, ideas most thoroughly in his 1940 essay "On Some Motifs in Baudelaire," where he once again rethought photography, perception, and innervation.

But even with that moving target in mind, I would suggest that in reconsidering photography's Weimar-era condemnation as overabundant and dangerously contingent, Benjamin was using contingency itself to make the medium available to a new and historically specific understanding of modern subjectivity that operated in opposition to a burgeoning fascism. His fledgling notion of the optical unconscious therefore stood to offer a far more nuanced and potent explanation of how photography enhanced individual, and later collective, perception. The consequence for us was the birth of media theory that has since come to dominate our understanding of photography, film, television, and now the web. For we now find that the formation of our subjectivity, collective or not, unfolds within an ever more image-soaked environment, one in which the boundaries between reality and its representation have become blurred beyond conscious, and perhaps even unconscious, recognition.

Notes

1. Walter Benjamin, "Little History of Photography," in *Walter Benjamin: Selected Writings*, vol. 2, 1927–1934, ed. Michael Jennings, Howard Eiland, and Gary Smith (Cambridge, MA: Belknap, 1999), 510–512.

2. László Moholy-Nagy, *Painting, Photography, Film* (Cambridge, MA: MIT Press, 1973), 7. Second and third quotations from László Moholy-Nagy, "Photography Is Creation with Light" (1928), in *Moholy-Nagy*, ed. Krisztina Passuth (London: Thames and Hudson, 1985), 14, 28.

3. Johannes Molzahn, "Stop Reading! Look!," in *The Weimar Republic Sourcebook*, ed. Anton Kaes, Martin Jay, and Edward Dimendberg (Berkeley: University of California Press, 1994), 648.

4. Karl Nierendorf, "Preface," in Karl Bossfeldt, *Urformen der Kunst*, translated in *Germany: The New Photography, 1927–33*, ed. David Mellor (London: Arts Council of Great Britain, 1978), 18.

5. Albert Renger-Patzsch, "Photography and Art," in *Das Deutsche Lichtbild* (1929), translated in Mellor, *Germany*, 15.

6. Siegfried Kracauer, "Photography," in *The Mass Ornament: Weimar Essays*, ed. Thomas Y. Levin (Cambridge, MA: Harvard University Press, 2005), 58.

7. Willi Münzenberg, "Tasks and Objectives," in *Der Arbeiter-Fotograf* (1929), translated in Mellor, *Germany*, 51.

8. Bertolt Brecht, letter in "On the Tenth Anniversary of the *AIZ*," *AIZ* (1931).

9. Ernst Bauer, "Das politische Gesicht der Strasse," *Die Kultur der Reklame* 1, no. 2 (March 1919): 165.

10. Paul Zech, "Reichpropaganda," *Die Kultur der Reklame* 2, no. 2 (February 1920): 96.

11. Hans Friedeberger, "Das politische Plakat der Revolutionszeit," *Das Plakat* 10, no. 4 (July 1919): 276.

12. These posters were created by John Heartfield, born Helmut Herzfeld (1891–1968).

13. For more on this aspect of Berlin's Dada movement, see chapter 4 of Andrés Mario Zervigón, *John Heartfield and the Agitated Image: Photography, Persuasion and the Rise of Avant-Garde Photomontage* (Chicago: University of Chicago Press, 2012).

14. Kurt Korff, "Die Illustrierte Zeitschrift," in *Fünfzig Jahre Ullstein, 1877–1927* (Berlin: Ullstein Verlag, 1927), 280.

15. This exhibition was officially titled *Internationale Ausstellung des deutchen Werkbunds Film und Foto*.

16. Paul Westheim, "Bildermüde?," *Das Kunstblatt* 16, no. 3 (March 1932): 20–22; Wilhelm Hausenstein, "Photo-Inflation?," *Rhein-Mainische Volkszeitung*, January 29, 1930.

17. Olivier Lugon, "'Photo-Inflation': Image Profusion in German Photography, 1925–1945," *History of Photography* 32, no. 3 (autumn 2008): 219–234.

18. Douglas Nickel, "Three or Four Kinds of Indeterminacy," in *Photography and Doubt*, ed. Sabine Kriebel and Andrés Mario Zervigón (London: Routledge, 2017).

19. Münzenberg, "Tasks and Objectives," 51.

20. Westheim, "Bildermüde?," 20–22, emphasis in original.

21. Siegfried Kracauer, "Photography," 58.

22. Benjamin, "Little History of Photography," 510, emphasis added. Here Benjamin made a mistake in his account. The photograph in fact shows Dauthendey with his second wife, not his first. Furthermore, the family lived in St. Petersburg, not Moscow. This makes the long-forgotten moment he perceives in the photograph largely a matter of projection.

23. Miriam Bratu Hansen, *Cinema and Experience* (Berkeley: University of California Press, 2012), 156.

24. Hansen, *Cinema and Experience*, 137. See Hansen's larger section on Benjamin for a full explanation of his concept of innervation. I thank Michael Jennings for his encouragement to consider the significance of this concept.

25. Hansen, *Cinema and Experience*, 79–80.

26. Sarah Kofman, *Camera Obscura: Of Ideology*, trans. William Straw (London: Athlone, 1998).

27. Hansen, *Cinema and Experience*, 156.

——

CHAPTER TWO

"A HIDING PLACE IN WAKING DREAMS"

David Octavius Hill, Robert Adamson,
and Walter Benjamin's
"Little History of Photography"

——

SHAWN MICHELLE SMITH

Photography's demise began, for Walter Benjamin, with the pillar on the carpet. Such nonsense marked the decline of anything that could be called good taste. An accoutrement of those photography studios that were as much "torture chamber" as "throne room," the pillar took its place on the carpet alongside palm trees, framed by draperies, tapestries, and easels. All were arranged for "artistic" effect by the "businessmen" who "invaded professional photography from every side."[1] For Benjamin, the shame of the commercial, industrial age of photography (roughly beginning in the 1850s) is that the subject is overtaken by bourgeois pretensions, subsumed in its ornamental setting, and masked in its pose.[2]

The beginning of the end of photography comes quickly, within ten years of its advent. But in his "Little History" Benjamin reserves a brief early period from critique—a period before this "sharp decline in taste set in."[3] These early photographs belong to photography's first decade (the 1840s), to its "incunabula."[4] Importantly, this is the period before the industrialization of photography, before its rapid commercialization, before photographers were artists or professionals or businessmen or really even photographers per se. It was a moment when, Benjamin argues, photographer and camera, and camera and subject, were perfectly aligned—in which an emerging technology took aim at an emerging class, before the corruption of both.

But this early period was also something more—something magical. In it,

Benjamin recognized the distinguishing features of the new medium, characteristics that would be lost on later generations, and even overshadowed in his own shifting measure of photography over the course of five short years. In "Little History of Photography," Benjamin first articulates his ideas about the optical unconscious revealed by the new technology. Tracing his path through the history of photography, and considering the contemporary studies that helped shape Benjamin's reading of historical images in the 1930s, I return here to photography's early days, trying to discern in David Octavius Hill and Robert Adamson's photographs from the 1840s the "hiding place in waking dreams" that Benjamin discovered in them.

———

For Benjamin, the photographer whose work exemplifies the early, exceptional period of the new medium is David Octavius Hill.[5] In 1931, when Benjamin was writing his "Little History of Photography," he consulted Heinrich Schwarz's book of the same year, *David Octavius Hill, Master of Photography*.[6] Benjamin relied rather heavily on Schwarz in his discussion of Hill, seizing upon many of the themes celebrated by the art historian, and using some of the same language to assess the work. Specifically, Benjamin followed Schwarz in praising "the absolute continuum from brightest light to darkest shadow" in Hill's calotypes, noting "the way light struggles out of darkness" in the images.[7] For example, one might look to Hill's portrait of Reverend Mr. (John) MacKenzie (fig. 2.1). In the photograph, MacKenzie turns away from the camera to present himself in profile. His eyes are shadowed, and he seems to emerge out of the darkness that presses behind him. His coat is barely discernible as it blends into the blackness of the dark cloth background. In contrast, the whiteness of MacKenzie's face, framed by a stark white cravat, is almost ghostly. It is as if the darkness is just held at bay—as if it might subsume the man at any moment, pulling him back into an invisible netherworld.

Hill was not a photographer by profession, but a painter. His brush with photography was incidental. His photographs were, as Benjamin has said, "unpretentious makeshifts meant for internal use"; nevertheless, the photographs "gave his name a place in history, while as a painter he is forgotten."[8] Hill was a Scottish landscape painter who turned to photography as a means to an end, making photographic portraits as sketches for a monumental painting he conceived in 1843, called *The Disruption* (fig. 2.2). In a departure from his traditional landscape work, he set out to make a memorial painting to celebrate the First General Assembly of the Free Church of Scotland. From May 18 to May

SHAWN MICHELLE SMITH

FIGURE 2.1 David Octavius Hill and Robert Adamson, *Reverend Mr. (John) MacKenzie*, salt print from calotype negative. Courtesy of George Eastman House, International Museum of Photography and Film.

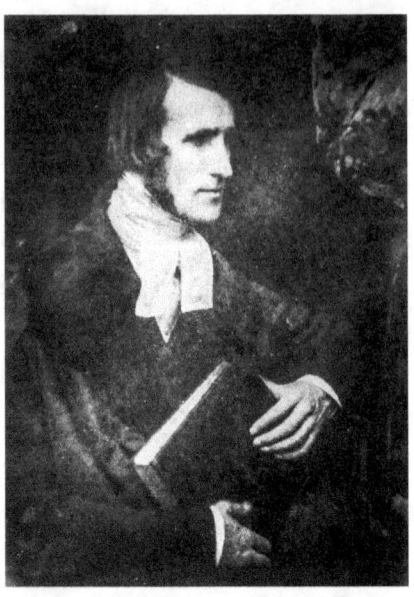

30, 1843, over two hundred ministers and elders (as well as hundreds of other interested parties), united in protesting the right of the monarch and nobility to select parish clergy, gathered in Edinburgh to finalize their withdrawal from the Presbyterian Church. Hill sought to represent the signing of the Act of Separation, and to do so he endeavored to combine over four hundred individual portraits in a single scene. He would build the painting of the group as a massive composite portrait. As one of Hill's first historians summarizes, "Hill was certain to founder on this theme, so disastrous from the artistic point of view. But the plan and development of the monstrous massing of several hundred portraits turned him forcibly towards photography."[9]

In pursuit of his monumental painting, Hill pursued photography. To do so, he needed a collaborator; indeed, he needed a photographer, and his friend Sir David Brewster introduced him to Robert Adamson, who would prove an essential partner.[10] Between 1843 and 1847, Hill and Adamson made approximately three thousand calotypes.[11] At first their subjects were largely limited to the participants in the General Assembly, those clerics and laymen who founded the Free Church, as well as the visitors who came to Edinburgh from France, Germany, Switzerland, and Holland to witness the convocation. But soon public interest in this prestigious parade to the studio in Rock House, and in the photographs themselves, began to grow, and members of aristocratic Scottish society also sought to have their portraits made.[12] Other foreign

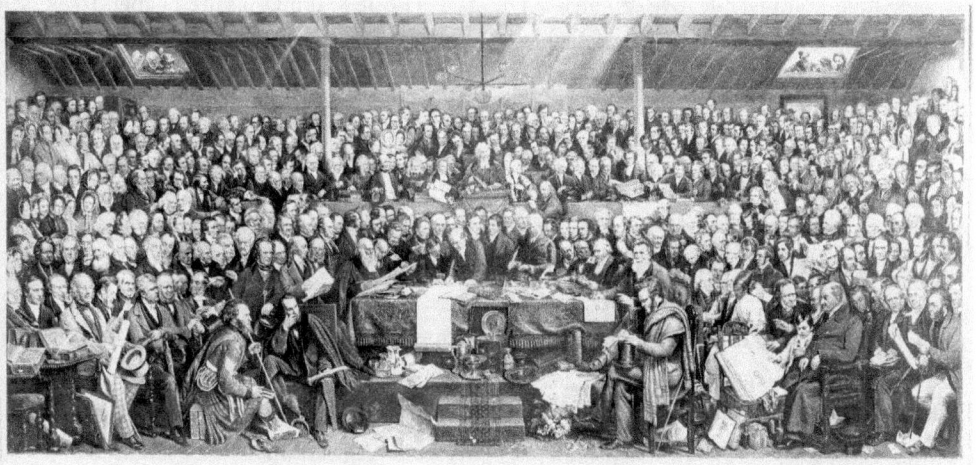

FIGURE 2.2 David Octavius Hill, *The Disruption* (signing of Deed of Demission painting); copy photograph by Thomas Annan, *The Signing of the Deed of Demission by the Ministers of the First General Assembly of the Free Church of Scotland.* Courtesy of George Eastman House, International Museum of Photography and Film.

visitors, including John Ruskin and Lady Elizabeth Eastlake, one of photography's early historians and wife of Sir Charles Eastlake, president of the Royal Academy and director of the National Gallery, also made appearances at the studio.[13] Further, within six months, Hill and Adamson had already branched out into other realms, exploring the aesthetic potential of the calotypes for landscapes and views of fishermen and women in nearby Newhaven.[14]

The calotype is a negative-positive photographic process invented by the Englishman William Henry Fox Talbot and introduced to Scotland by Talbot's close friend, Sir David Brewster, the prominent Scottish scientist (and friend of Hill) noted above. Brewster instructed Dr. John Adamson, his colleague at the University of St. Andrews, in the process, and John subsequently taught it to his brother Robert Adamson, who would become Hill's collaborator. The calotype is a paper negative from which salt prints on paper are produced. To make the negative, the photographer first sensitizes a sheet of paper with successive solutions of silver nitrate, potassium iodide, gallic acid, and silver nitrate. The paper is then dried in the dark before it is loaded in the camera. After an exposure of several minutes in the brightest sunlight, the negative is then developed in a solution of gallic acid and silver nitrate, fixed in a bath of sodium thiosulfate to remove unexposed silver salts, and finally washed. When dried, the typically high-contrast negative can be used to make a positive print on salted paper. To produce the printing paper, the photographer soaks a sheet of paper in sodium chloride (ordinary table salt), and then in a solution of silver nitrate. After it has been dried in the dark, the light-sensitive salted paper is exposed to the negative and contact printed in strong sunlight. The resulting positive print is then fixed in hypo, and toned with gold chloride, and finally washed and dried. Unlike later silver gelatin photographic processes, the paper calotype negatives and salt prints do not have an emulsion. Instead, the light-sensitive chemicals soak directly into the paper, and therefore "the image resides literally within the fibers of the paper." This gives the final print a textured look and feel, and softens the outlines of its details.[15]

The respective roles of Hill and Adamson in producing the calotypes is somewhat difficult to determine. In part, their collaboration is obscured by nineteenth-century understandings of art and debates about photography's relationship to art. In the nineteenth century, Hill, the painter and secretary of the Royal Scottish Academy of Painting, was deemed an artist; Adamson, the one-time engineer turned photographer, was considered a technician. An advertisement in the *Edinburgh Evening Courant* of August 3, 1844, announcing preparations for the publication of a series of volumes of calotypes by Hill and Adamson, notes that "the subjects" were "selected and arranged" by Hill, and the "Chemical Manipulations" were performed by Adamson.[16] Today we would understand Adamson to be the photographer and the artist primarily responsible for making the images. But in the mid-nineteenth century, the chemical and mechanical manipulations of the photographer, the use and mastery of the photographic technology, were not considered art. The artist was thought to be the orchestrator of the scene, the person who could arrange subjects for aesthetic effect and draw out the soul of a sitter, elevating the photograph from "mere [mechanical] likeness" to "true portrait."[17]

Although today we would acknowledge Adamson's mastery of the medium as the principal element of artistry distinguishing the calotypes, it is nevertheless also the case that Hill's talent for arranging subjects was salient in the process, and much of the charm of his contribution to the calotypes was lost in their translation to painting. For example, in *Four Members of the Free Presbytery of Dumbarton*, four men huddle around a tapestry-covered table (fig. 2.3). The setting is hard to identify: the carved wooden chairs and floral tapestry running down the middle of the background suggest a well-appointed interior space, but the viny branches in the far right corner could only cling to an outdoor wall. The men are posed in an indeterminate space, neither inside nor out (although

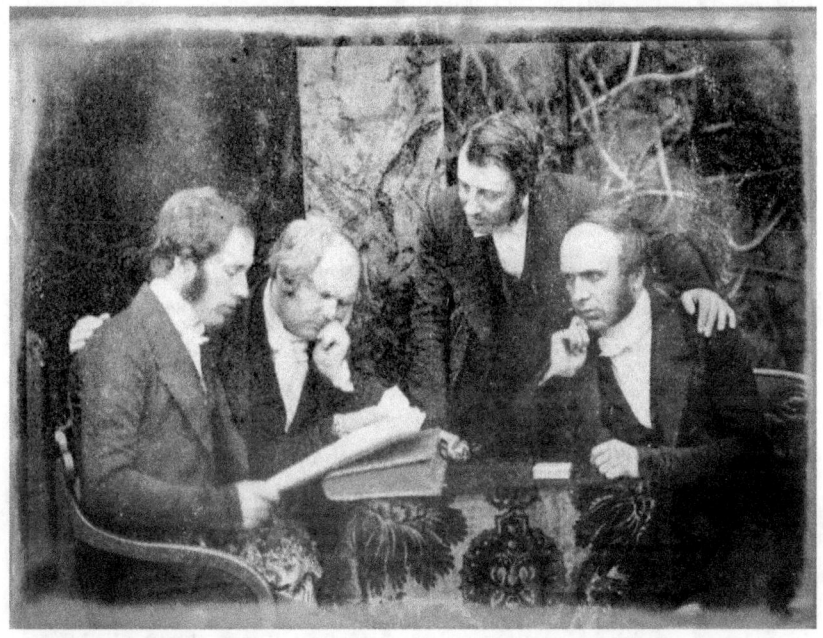

FIGURE 2.3 David Octavius Hill and Robert Adamson, *Four Members of the Free Presbytery of Dumbarton*, salt print from calotype negative. Courtesy of George Eastman House, International Museum of Photography and Film.

the exposures were certainly made outdoors). On the left, a man seated in profile holds a white document propped on a large book. His companion leans in to consider it with him, resting his arm around his shoulder. Their heads are bent together in contemplation. Beside them, on the right, another two men lean in, as if waiting to hear what their colleagues will say about the document they survey. One stands, hunched over in interest, his hand on the shoulder of his companion to the right. All of them wear dark suits and white shirts with stand-up collars and ties. They have brushed receding hairlines over tall foreheads, and sport long muttonchop sideburns. The men's dark suits blend together, making them seem literally unified, and highlighting by contrast the whiteness of their faces, shirts, and hands. The intensity of the stares and furrowed brows of the two men who mirror one another, bringing a folded hand to chin, mark the importance of the deliberations. The bright hands on shoulders left and right make it seem that the whole group is locked in a single embrace. Together they pose as if unified in solemn contemplation.

This beautiful formal photograph, balanced left to right and top to bottom, with its extremes of dark and light, was translated into a tiny grouping in the upper left corner of Hill's *Disruption* painting. The result is disappointing, to say the least. The man standing in the calotype has been squeezed behind his seated colleagues and is almost hidden from view in the painting. The only really recognizable figure is the man posed on the left in the photograph; his sharp profile is reproduced clearly in the painting, but here it stands out as discordant, as if tilted against the tide of his peers in the space of the auditorium.

Working with the calotypes he and Adamson produced, Hill labored on his monumental painting for twenty-three years, from 1843 to 1866. The painting depicts the signing of the Act of Separation and Deed of Demission on May 23, 1843, and presents 457 figures, including a few who were not present at the ceremony. It measures 12 feet by 4 feet 8 inches, and hangs in the Presbytery Hall of the Free Church of Scotland. Today the painting is regarded a failure largely due to its composite composition, which gives it what Michael Leja has called a "disjunctive perspective." As noted above, figures are uncomfortably crammed together, and some appear to have two or three heads where there was not room to fit another body. People posed in profile seem to turn away from the scene of the signing, creating awkward cameos, and individual figures are disproportionately large or small in relation to one another. The overall composition does not visually cohere.[18]

Several nineteenth-century viewers commented on the difficulty of Hill's task and the aesthetic problems inherent in composite paintings. Nevertheless, they found much to praise in the work. One reviewer, announcing the public viewing of the painting in the *Scotsman* of May 24, 1866, declared, "Most attempts at giving pictorial interest and expression, life and power, to a vast conglomeration of portraits of men engaged as spectators (or making as if they were) in some notable piece of business are generally . . . dead failures, bordering ofttimes on the idiotic." The same commentator averred, "Mr. Hill's picture of the Free Assembly in Tanfield signing the Deed of Demission is the reverse of all this: it is alive, and arrests."[19] A more critical reviewer writing for the *Glasgow Morning Journal* of November 1866 proclaims, "Pictures that contain masses of figures are liable to the censure that persons whose portraits are given are not in natural position: their faces are turned in one direction without obvious motive; the countenances are frequently blank and almost meaningless; the groups are not unseldom ranged together with little more taste than waxwork collections." Although not entirely praising Hill's painting, the same reviewer states, "Whilst Mr. Hill's picture does not altogether lack faults in this description—and it would simply be impossible to avoid them without giving rise to other and more serious defects, for some of the figures, although naturally placed, would be irrecognisable [*sic*]—he has succeeded, in a most astonishing measure, in combining tasteful, natural grouping, with vigorous, truthful expression of feeling, and, above all, strikingly correct and artistic portraiture."[20]

Hill's flawed painting is nevertheless fascinating, and it self-consciously points to the manner of its production. Hill and Adamson take their own place in the painting at the right-hand side: Adamson is depicted looking into a camera that he points toward the proceedings, and Hill sits just behind him, with sketch pad in hand. Their presence in the image draws attention to their explicit creation of the scene, but also subtly highlights the reconstruction of the scene after the fact. For, although Hill actually did attend the proceedings, it is unlikely that he or Adamson made any photographs within the chamber as the events unfolded because their typical exposures lasted several minutes and had to be taken outside in bright sunlight. The presence of the artists in the painting therefore figures a kind of retrospective prospect—it points forward to the construction of the painting after the event, out of photographic parts.

Remarkably, the monumental painting that began in photographs also ended in photographs. When the painting was finally complete (and after Adamson had prematurely passed away), Hill hired Thomas Annan of Glasgow and Hamilton to copy the work photographically, and to make carbon prints for sale and distribution. "The Disruption of the Church of Scotland," an 1866 pamphlet, announces, "Photographs now being made from Mr. D. O. Hill's Picture of the Disruption Assembly" in a variety of sizes and prices. The anonymous author of the pamphlet (or perhaps Richard Alexander, agent and manager, Office of the Disruption Picture) states, "It is a striking coincidence that, while the commencement of the Picture was thus marked by the elevation and higher application of Photography, its completion seems destined, by a combination of improved processes, to aid in the inauguration of a new era in the reproduction of Works of Art. And it may also be remarked that, long retarded as the completion of the Picture has been, its translation and multiplication by Photographs, so beautiful, and at the same time *imperishable*, could not, at an earlier date, by any means known to the Artist, have been secured."[21] Enabled by the introduction of the calotype process in the 1840s, and reproduced with the permanent carbon printing process of the 1860s, the *Disruption* painting is both the product and the marker of photographic invention. Although Benjamin does not seize upon the later photographic prints, it is remarkable (indeed, "a striking coincidence") that a mid-nineteenth-century commentator would so directly place *The Disruption* within the history of what one might call "the work of art in the age of its technological reproducibility." The intent of Annan's carbon prints was to bring the work of art into the hands of the Scottish masses, dispersing the image beyond its exalted place in the Presbytery Hall. In some ways, the circulation of the prints would seem to be the perfect example of the dissolution of aura inaugurated by photography that Benjamin describes in his essay of 1936, "The Work of Art in the Age of Its Technological Reproducibility." The original artifact, displayed under the controlled conditions of a religious hall, is brought closer to a large viewing public through its reproduction and circulation, dispelling its distancing aura.

———

Hill and Adamson's calotypes of the 1840s enjoyed a renaissance at the hands of the pictorialists in the late nineteenth and early twentieth centuries. J. Craig Annan, the son of Thomas Annan, who reproduced Hill's *Disruption* painting in the 1860s, collected the calotype negatives and reprinted them as carbon prints, sending copies to artists and curators throughout Europe. One enthusiastic recipient of the images was Alfred Lichtwark, who posed Hill (and also Julia Margaret Cameron) as historical precursors to the pictorialists, and included prints made from the Hill and Adamson calotype negatives in his exhibitions of pictorial photography in Hamburg in the 1890s.[22] Annan himself published an article on Hill and Adamson in Alfred Stieglitz's journal *Camera Work* in 1905, and as Martin Gasser has suggested, Hill, the painter of the Scottish Church's secession, may have particularly appealed to Stieglitz and those of his circle as a fellow "Secessionist."[23]

Thus, three decades before Benjamin wrote about Hill, those claiming photography for art had already begun to herald Hill and Adamson as early antecedents. Indeed, Hill and Adamson's work enabled the pictorialists to inscribe a long history for photography as art dating back to the very beginnings of the medium. The softness of Hill and Adamson's paper negatives and prints helped secure a tradition of pictorialist aesthetics, especially the preference for soft focus. The pictorialist predilection for platinum prints also correlated with Hill and Adamson's works on paper; in the platinotype process, platinum is absorbed by the paper, and sometimes the texture of the paper is visible in the pattern of the image, just as it is in Hill and Adamson's salt prints made from paper negatives. Even the religious themes that suffused Hill and Adamson's portraits, or at least provided the impetus for them, resonated with the sacred subjects that some pictorialists, including F. Holland Day, seized upon to elevate photography to fine art. Perhaps it was seeing the Hill and Adamson calotypes through the lens of the later pictorialists that snapped them into (diffuse) focus for Benjamin, enabling him to see in them something essential about photography.[24]

There is a considered solemnity to Hill and Adamson's photographs, and Benjamin attributes part of their magical quality to the technological constraints of making them: "The procedure itself caused the subject to focus his life in the moment rather than hurrying on past it; during the considerable period of the exposure, the subject (as it were) grew into the picture, in the sharpest contrast with appearances in a snapshot."[25] Hill and Adamson's long exposures compelled their subjects to sit absolutely still before the camera for several minutes. And so they composed themselves, bracing against the blaring sun. A number of them posed in a cemetery, where they might have been encouraged to contemplate the life of their portraits in relation to their own less permanent existence. And once again, the subjects might literally be said to grow into their images, as the light reflecting off them impressed their visages into the fibers of the chemically soaked paper of the calotype.[26]

Highlighting the technological constraints that required subjects to remain still for long exposures, Benjamin nevertheless expands and amplifies his argument, stating that the aura of Hill and Adamson's photographs is "by no means the mere product of a primitive camera."[27] It is also a characteristic of the subjects themselves, of the "member of a rising class equipped with an aura that ha[s] seeped into the very folds of the man's frock coat or floppy cravat."[28] Everything about these men and women would seem to represent them indexically: a man's coat reveals how he typically carries himself through its patterns of wear, its folds marking his presence and practice. A portrait of Reverend A. Capadose of the Hague provides a salient example (fig. 2.4). His vest shimmers at the waist, framing the bright white of a crisp shirt and cravat. The elbows and shoulders of his dark jacket are creased with regular wear. His lively, textured hair, mottled with gray, is swept forward and up from a striking profile. A look of concentration steadies his face behind small round spectacles. He rests his arm atop a large book, a *Biblia Sacra*, holding it spine toward the camera, and the volume seems to hold up Capadose as much as he does the book.

Neither Benjamin nor Schwarz was taken by the daguerreotype, the so-called "mirror with a memory." They did not celebrate its sharp, dazzling detail, which thrilled so many nineteenth-century commentators and twentieth-century historians alike. In fact, one of the things Schwarz most admires about Hill's work is that his camera seems to respect its subjects by leaving details in

FIGURE 2.4 David Octavius Hill and Robert Adamson, *Reverend A. Capadose of the Hague*, salt print from calotype negative. Courtesy of George Eastman House, International Museum of Photography and Film.

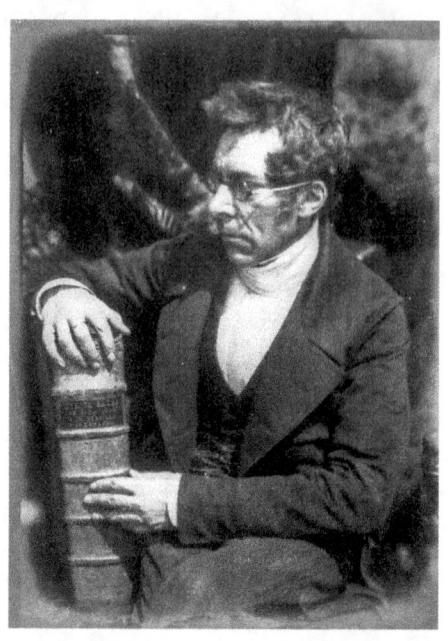

shadow: "It never drags people or things into a hard, merciless light that destroys every mystery. . . . Hill remained true to his primitive mechanical equipment, even when an advanced optics had already mastered instruments which completely vanquish darkness and which delineate phenomena as does a mirror."[29] The merciless light was already everywhere in the daguerreotype; darkness had already been put to flight, and appearances could be recorded "as faithfully as any mirror."[30] Nevertheless, Hill and Adamson chose to work with the calotype printing process, and Hill himself explicitly measured the success of his calotypes in relation to daguerreotypes by their relative lack of detail: "'The rough and unequal texture throughout the paper is the main cause of the calotype failing in details before the Daguerreotype . . . and this is the very life of it.'"[31] Hill initially suggested that sketches for his monumental painting would be made as both daguerreotypes and calotypes. Adamson, however, excelled in the calotype process, and his technical expertise probably helped to determine the choice of photographic technology they adopted. But as Hill makes clear, the choice was also based on an aesthetic preference for the soft rendering of the paper prints.[32]

Benjamin famously declared that "the first people to be reproduced entered the visual space of photography with their innocence intact."[33] Hill and Adamson's subjects were not yet visually scripted by an emergent visual culture; they were not yet practiced in the pose. They did not need to be propped up by an array of parlor tricks. Regarding the portraits, Benjamin states, "It has been said of Hill's camera that it kept a discreet distance. [And, in fact, Schwarz did say exactly that.] But his subjects, for their part, are no less reserved; they maintain a certain shyness before the camera."[34] The "shyness" that Benjamin finds in Hill and Adamson's subjects may be a result of their lack of familiarity with the pose, as Benjamin seems to suggest, but it may also be an effect of the constraints of the technology itself. Once again, given the slowness of the camera, Hill and Adamson's subjects had to be photographed in the brightest sunlight; blasted by the light, most turned away, shading their eyes in downward looks, or simply closing them tightly against the sun.

Among the many things that are remarkable about Benjamin's discussion of Hill and Adamson's calotypes is his celebration of aura in the work. In his later essay on photography, the famous "Work of Art in the Age of Its Technological Reproducibility" of 1936, Benjamin would condemn aura as the distancing effect of an art steeped in ritual. As many scholars have rehearsed, Benjamin would herald the elimination of aura introduced by photography's reproducibility. Aura is the essence of the original that photography, as a reproducible medium, dispels, making art newly available to politics. As the results of a negative-positive printing process, Hill and Adamson's calotypes were reproducible, and in this sense it is not surprising that Benjamin would seize upon them, rather than the nonreproducible daguerreotype, to begin his "Little History." And yet, it is not the reproducibility of the calotypes that interests him. Benjamin finds in the photographs an aura that he does not yet feel the need to condemn, an aura effected by the full tonal range of the calotypes, the stillness of their subjects, and an ineffable quality intrinsic both to the photographs themselves and to the men and women who populate them.

As Kathrin Yacavone has argued, the striking shift in Benjamin's evaluation of aura vis-à-vis photography "must be seen against the backdrop of twentieth-century history and the rise of fascism in Europe and Germany." By the mid-1930s, Benjamin was "viewing the medium through the perspective of an unprecedented cultural and historical crisis."[35] Yacavone encourages one not to regard this shift as a repudiation of his earlier thoughts about aura and photography, but rather to understand it as a response to shifting historical-cultural forces. A new photography was needed for a new era, but that does not discount or discredit the conception of an earlier, magical moment.

It is not only a dignified aura that Benjamin sees in Hill and Adamson's photographs. There is something further—something profound. Benjamin finds in the calotypes "something new and strange . . . something that goes beyond testimony to the photographer's art," something that exceeds the photographer and his intent. In part, this something is the felt presence of the subject, and it "cannot be silenced."[36] Looking at "Hill's Newhaven fishwife," Benjamin declares "the woman who was alive there . . . even now is still real." She "will never consent to be wholly absorbed in 'art.'"[37] Her presence fills Benjamin with "an unruly desire" to know her name, and he asks (using the words of poet Stefan George), "How did the beauty of that hair, / those eyes, beguile our forebears? / How did that mouth kiss, to which desire / curls up senseless as smoke without fire?"[38] In a notably affective response, a photograph fills Benjamin with a desire for the subject we are more accustomed to find in the work of Roland Barthes.[39] The "something more" of the photograph registers in Benjamin's affective excess. Here the radical presence of the photographic subject, what Barthes deemed "that-has-been," inspires Benjamin's desire and opens onto the optical unconscious.[40]

Benjamin lays out a subtle struggle between the photographer and subject. The photographic subject is not entirely subsumed in the photographer's art; something of the person remains unfiltered by the photographer to greet a later viewer. Benjamin marks that presence metaphorically as the subject's voice, which "cannot be silenced," suggesting a photographic resonance in sound as well as sight. Fred Moten has taught us to listen for the sound of the photograph, for the shattering cry of a heartbroken viewer who turns the photograph into an affective political tool.[41] Benjamin suggests that sound, at least metaphorically through the vehicle of the voice, might resonate through all photographs, even the most seemingly still and quiet.

The Newhaven Fishwife print, reproduced in Benjamin's "Little History" in its initial publication as "Kleine Geschichte der Photographie" in the German literary magazine Die Literarische Welt, is indeed beautiful (fig. 2.5).[42] Elizabeth Johnstone Hall sits, holding a large empty basket at her side. She is dressed in a simple white top and a striking striped apron. The round open rim of the basket she holds echoes the round open rim of her white bonnet. Beneath the bonnet, her smooth shiny hair, cleanly parted down the middle, further frames her face. She turns her head away from the camera, casting her eyes down, her brow furrowed slightly against the sun. Her hands, holding the textured basket, are tanned, her fingers calloused. She wears a band on her left ring finger.

Benjamin takes his reader on an incredible circuit from this photograph, into

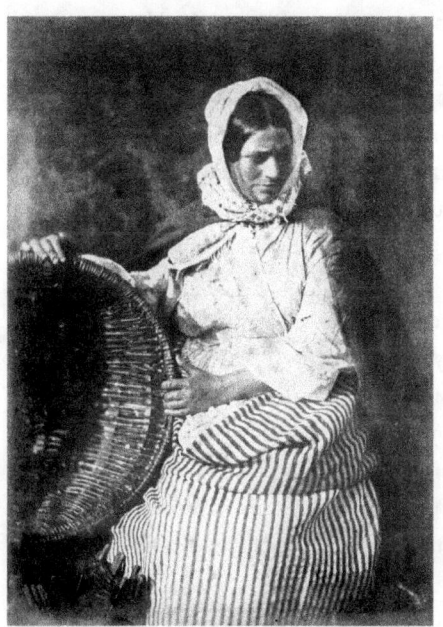

FIGURE 2.5 David Octavius Hill and Robert Adamson, *Newhaven Fishwife*, Elizabeth Johnstone Hall, salt print from calotype negative. Courtesy of George Eastman House, International Museum of Photography and Film.

magical, mystical realms, and finally into the optical unconscious, a "hiding place in waking dreams."[43] The passage bears quoting at length:

> No matter how artful the photographer, no matter how carefully posed his subject, the beholder feels an irresistible urge to search such a picture for the tiny spark of contingency, of the here and now, with which reality has (so to speak) seared the subject, to find the inconspicuous spot where in the immediacy of that long-forgotten moment the future nests so eloquently that we, looking back, may rediscover it. For it is another nature which speaks to the camera rather than to the eye: "other" above all in the sense that a space informed by human consciousness gives way to a space informed by the unconscious.[44]

Here Benjamin lays out another contest over the site of photographic perception, this one between photographer and viewer. Although one might assume that the photographer directs the image making and therefore comprehends it best, Benjamin and, later, Barthes pose the viewer as the locus of photographic understanding.[45] Indeed, Benjamin goes so far as to say that only the viewer might see all there is to see in a photograph, as well as the "something more." Regardless of his preparation and care, the photographer cannot fully control the photographic process, nor the response of later viewers. Despite his place behind the lens, the photographer does not necessarily see what the camera will record. Later viewers look back and see differently. In this subtle struggle over photographic discernment, it is the viewer, not the photographer, who truly sees and understands the photograph and its subject. What one might find in photographs is not only the optical unconscious of the viewer's desire, but also the optical unconscious of the photographer, what she did not see, but what was nevertheless present before the camera. The viewer sees through the photographer's blind eye.

This is the magical value of photography that "a painted picture can never again have for us."[46] The painting, by definition, presents only what the painter has put on canvas. The magic of the photograph lies in its accident—in what was unintended and even unseen by the photographer. It is intriguing, then, that one of the photographers Benjamin most admires was a painter who made photographs in the service of painting. But as Benjamin confirms, Hill's photographic subjects would not be subsumed or silenced; they would not be subordinated to his painting.

Benjamin's understanding of the optical unconscious recognizes the photograph's radically disruptive temporality. The "here and now," the present, exists in a past that holds the future. As Barthes and subsequent scholars including Eduardo Cadava have remarked, the photograph captures a moment always already past.[47] This is what lends the photograph a kind of ready-made nostalgia. However, Benjamin proposes that the photograph also registers a spark of futurity that it cannot fully contain.[48] Rather than always or only referring to a past moment, the photograph is future oriented, directed toward a moment the photographer cannot predict. As Ulrich Baer has argued, "Photographs compel the imagination because they remain radically open-ended"; "every photograph is addressed to a beyond that remains undefined."[49] Although made by the photographer and subject, the photograph always anticipates an unknown viewer and indeterminate moments of future viewing.

Here the revolutionary potential of photography seems more in line with the messianic moments of Benjamin's "On the Concept of History" (1940) than with the dissolution of aura he espouses in the "Work of Art" essay (1936). The tiny spark of contingency, of the here and now, might be analogous to the shards of messianic now-time that disrupt the flow of history.[50] A temporal revolution is at play in the contingent futurity of the photograph.

To explain further the optical unconscious, Benjamin turns to Karl Blossfeldt's close-up abstractions of ferns, foliage, and pods, and Eadweard Muybridge's human locomotion studies. In Blossfeldt's photographs new worlds are revealed in the minutest things: "Thus, Blossfeldt with his astonishing plant photographs reveals the forms of ancient columns in horse willow, a bishop's crosier in the ostrich fern, totem poles in tenfold enlargements of chestnut and maple shoots, and gothic tracery in the fuller's thistle."[51] In this way, "photography reveals in this material physiognomic aspects, image worlds, which dwell in the smallest things—meaningful yet covert enough to find a hiding place in waking dreams, but which, enlarged and capable of formulation, make the difference between technology and magic visible as a thoroughly historical variable."[52] Photography enables us to see what is hidden all around us, imperceptible to the naked human eye. The camera offers a prosthetic vision that extends the realm of the visible. But in so doing, the camera also makes us aware of how blind we are ordinarily, how much of the world around us we do not usually see.

The language of "waking dreams" suggests that the limited realm we perceive as the real world is deficient in other ways as well, that it is in fact a delusion. In Freudian terms, it might also suggest the flickering in and out of the unconscious in the process of conscious perception (more on this below). Even more profoundly, it might evoke the unconscious that is central to our conscious perception, suggesting that all of our waking moments are also dreams.

If Blossfeldt expands space with his enlargements, Eadweard Muybridge expands time by freezing motion in incremental steps. Muybridge's photographic studies still the discrete stages of movement usually imperceptible in the general flow. As Benjamin explains, "Whereas it is a commonplace that, for example, we have some idea what is involved in the act of walking (if only in general terms), we have no idea at all what happens during the fraction of a second when a person actually takes a step. *Photography, with its devices of slow motion and enlargement*, reveals the secret. It is through photography that we first discover the existence of this optical unconscious, just as we discover the instinctual unconscious through psychoanalysis."[53] Photography enables us to perceive what we otherwise cannot see, to consciously detect what passes before and through the eye unnoticed. The photograph freezes a moment usually lost to us in the rush of continuous movement; it enlarges fragments in the visual field to which we ordinarily cannot attend, making us newly aware of an extended visual universe.

Thus Benjamin seeks to explain the optical unconscious as an effect of the camera's ability to enlarge detail and to still movement. But Hill and Adamson's calotypes do neither of these things. Their exposures are slow and labored and, as Schwarz and Benjamin note, their camera keeps a discreet distance from its subjects. In other words, the optical unconscious of Hill and Adamson's calotypes does not accord with Benjamin's primary explanatory examples. What, then, is their "hiding place in waking dreams," and what is hidden there? The calotypes occupy uncertain spaces between inside and out, between darkness and light. The portraits are soft, not yet fast and forced. Men and women shade their eyes from the blinding light. Motionless in shifting time and blasted by the sun, fixed by chemistry and embedded in the fibers of fragile paper, they are also long dead. Some, perhaps, are buried in Greyfriars Cemetery, one of Hill and Adamson's otherworldly photographic places (fig. 2.6). The "hiding place in waking dreams" of the calotypes is a materialized dreamscape in which subjects are stilled in a time disrupted. As viewers we are invited to look back and behold the impossible presence of these long-gone people, and to search the prints for details recorded that may have evaded their photographers. We are made intensely aware of the photographic encounter between subject and photographers, and even between subject and sun, as all endeavored to draw out and fix an extended moment in time. During the long minutes of the exposure, as light permeated the chemistry-soaked paper, drawing with it human visages softened by the fibers of the paper negative, a strange new form of touch was captured, linking the light, the body, the image, the chemistry, the paper. All this happened under the photographers' (blind) eyes. Perhaps we can see what they saw, and perhaps we can see, like Benjamin, something more, the spark of futurity that defines the photograph's contingent time.

Turning back to the painting that started all these ruminations, ultimately we might read temporal rather than spatial discord in Hill's aptly named *Disruption*—the failed painting so indebted to photography. Working on the painting for over twenty years, Hill represented some figures as they looked at the time of the signing and some, including himself, as they looked at the time of his painting, two decades later.[54] The painting, then, like the photographs, is a testament to temporal disruption.

———

Benjamin's remarkable flight from the *Newhaven Fishwife* to the optical unconscious encourages an expansive critical exercise. In that vein, one might explore other resonances beyond those Benjamin explicitly names that lead from the materiality of the calotype to the optical unconscious. Given his later preference for reproducible photography, one can understand why the negative-positive calotype process might appeal to Benjamin over the daguerreotype, a nonreproducible single positive image. Once again, however, and somewhat surprisingly, he does not seize on the reproducibility of the calotype in

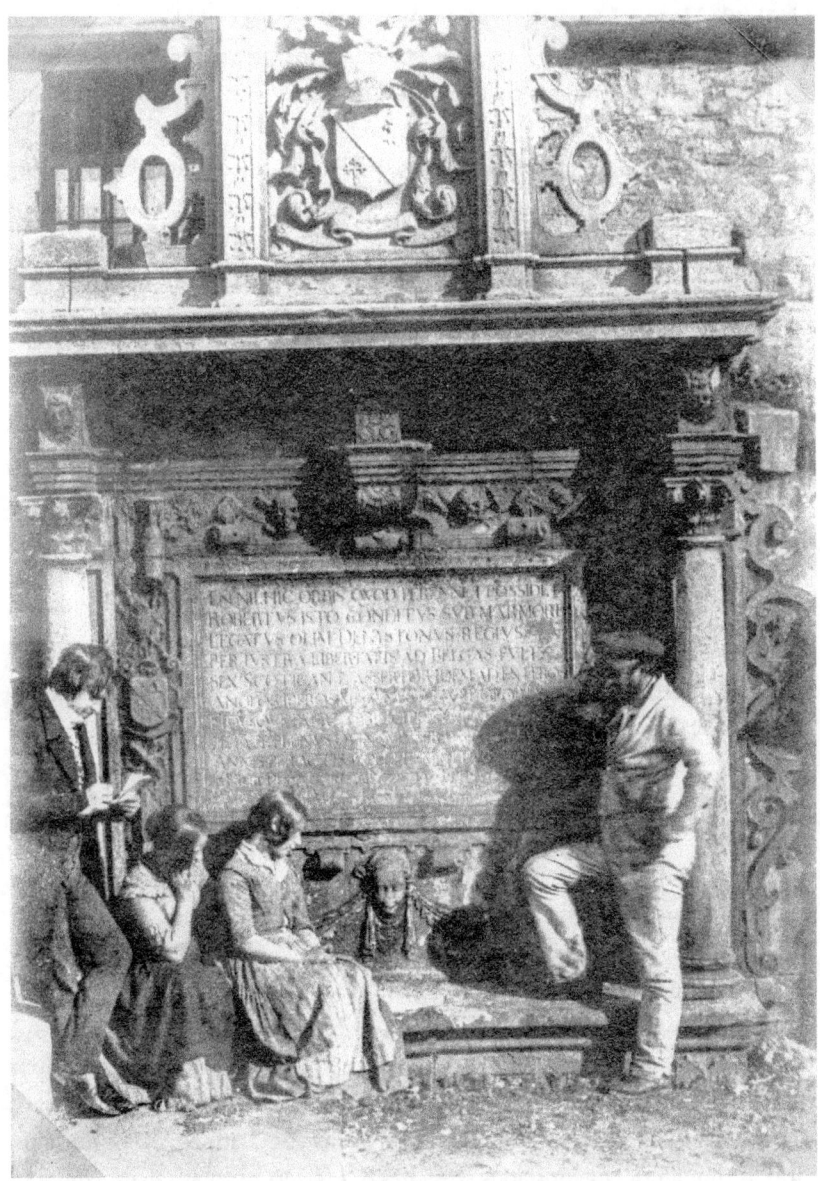

FIGURE 2.6 David Octavius Hill and Robert Adamson, *The Artist and the Gravedigger*, Greyfriars Cemetery, Edinburgh, salt print from calotype negative. Courtesy of George Eastman House, International Museum of Photography and Film.

his "Little History." Nevertheless, I would like to suggest that more expansive metaphoric qualities of the negative-positive calotype process might have inspired Benjamin's thoughts on the optical unconscious. As Sarah Kofman has argued in her discussion of Freud's *Moses and Monotheism*, Freud calls upon the metaphor of the photographic negative to explain the unconscious and memory in that text. Sense perceptions not initially made conscious can nevertheless be stored as negatives in the unconscious, developing into conscious thought at a later time (and for the first time). There is temporal disruption here as well, for what is remembered in this way is actually perceived for the first time. "In the psychic apparatus, the passage from negative to positive is neither necessary nor dialectical. It is possible that the development will never take place."[55] Kofman suggests that Freud draws on the image of the photographic negative to explain the unconscious, but might the comparison also work in reverse to tell us something about the photograph? Here it would seem that photography introduces an interpsychic dynamic, making the optical unconscious, in part, a social process. The photographer records things in a photographic negative that may only develop in the sight and mind of a later viewer.

One might take the resonance between Benjamin's optical unconscious, Freud's understanding of the perceptive apparatus of the mind, and the materiality of the calotype one step further. Soon after the invention of the paper calotype negative, photographers discovered that the negative could be made more transparent if it was waxed (fig. 2.7). This helped reduce printing time, allowing light to pass through the negative more efficiently.[56] If we take the negative as metaphor for thoughts recorded but unperceived in the unconscious and apply wax to this image, we might then recall another of Freud's famous figures for the perceptive apparatus of the mind, namely the "mystic writing pad." In his 1925 "Note upon the 'Mystic Writing Pad,'" Freud offers an extended rumination on perception focused on this writing device. For Freud, the mystic writing pad is analogous to the perceptual apparatus of the mind, in which conscious thought results from the interaction between perception, or the excitation of the senses by external stimuli, and unconscious stimulations. As he explains, "It is as though the unconscious stretches out feelers, through the medium of the system *Pcpt.-Cs.*, towards the external world and hastily withdraws them as soon as they have sampled the excitations coming from it."[57] The mystic writing pad provides an extended example of this process. The device itself is composed of a wax slab covered by a sheet of thin waxed paper, which is in turn protected by a sheet of clear celluloid. One writes on the celluloid with a stylus that transfers marks through the thin waxed paper to the wax slab beneath. At

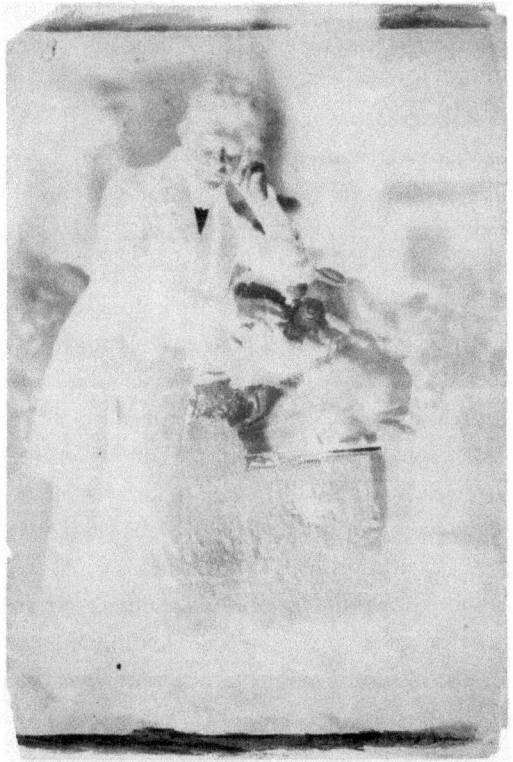

FIGURE 2.7 David Octavius Hill and Robert
Adamson, *George Meikle Kamp*, waxed calotype
negative. Courtesy of George Eastman House,
International Museum of Photography and Film.

the points where the two bottom layers connect, marks become visible through
the plastic. To clear the writing pad, one lifts the top two layers, separating them
from the wax slab. This erases the marks visible on the wax paper, readying it
for future use, while leaving impressions in the wax slab underneath. For Freud,
the plastic sheet and its closely connected thin waxed paper function like the
perceptual-consciousness system, and the wax slab is a kind of invisible storage mechanism tantamount to the unconscious. All three layers are put into
play when the perceptual apparatus of the mind is engaged. When the mind is
not engaged, it is cleared and ready to make new connections, but impressions
from previous perceptions remain in the unconscious.

We have in the calotypes first paper negatives that are then sometimes waxed to make them more transparent, from which soft paper prints can finally be made. The calotype begins, then, as a negative impression on paper made visible with wax. The wax added to the calotype might be considered analogous to the thin sheet of waxed paper in Freud's mystic writing pad that enables contact between the waxed slab underneath and the celluloid cover above, between the unconscious and the perceptual-consciousness system. But the analogy soon seems to fall apart, because the photograph is a permanent trace, without further receptive capacity in itself. And what most excited Freud about the mystic writing pad was its simultaneously "unlimited receptive capacity" and its ability to retain "permanent traces."[58] The calotype process might be endlessly repeatable, but the calotype itself must remain fixed. From the calotype negative any number of positive prints might be made, but they are always the same impressions. Nevertheless, if we return to the social aspect of photography's optical unconscious, we see that the photograph may provoke unlimited impressions in the receptive capacities of different viewers. If Benjamin's articulation of the optical unconscious suggests that a generic viewer might see captured in the photograph future possibilities unseen by the photographer, it is also the case that different viewers will see differently as they approach an image at different historical moments, and as their vision and perceptive capacities are shaped by disparate cultural and personal histories.

———

Over forty years after its original publication, Benjamin's "Little History" was translated into French to provide the central text for the November 1977 issue of the photography magazine *Le Nouvel Observateur.*[59] (Incidentally, the issue included a wonderful example of a pillar-on-the-carpet carte-de-visite.) The first photograph in the issue presents a full-page portrait of David Octavius Hill and the painter W. B. Johnston, made by Hill and Adamson, and it is, of course, an appropriate image to illustrate Benjamin's "Little History" (fig. 2.8). Here is a photographic portrait of two painters. They stand at a threshold, in the opening of a solid stone wall, its texture picked at by the harsh light. Behind them dark foliage is mottled by wind and sun. Johnston stands to the right, his prominent forehead bright in the light. He looks down at the ground before him, and tucks his right thumb into the small gap between buttons on his vest. Standing close beside him, Hill props his elbow on his companion's shoulder, bringing his fingers to rest on his face. In the crook of his other arm he holds a hat, its wide brim toward the camera. The bright white oval interior of the hat makes it seem like another face in this friendly grouping. Hill looks directly

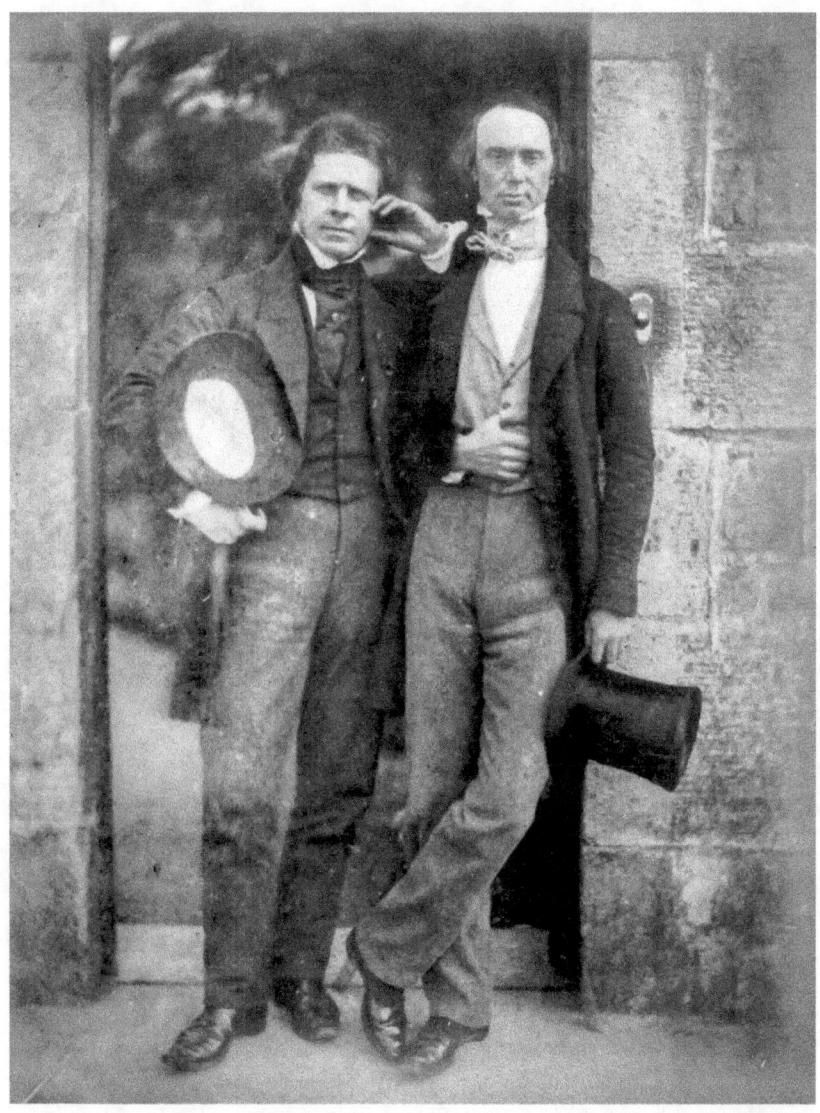

FIGURE 2.8 David Octavius Hill and Robert Adamson, *David Octavius Hill and W. B. Johnston*, salt print from calotype negative. Courtesy of George Eastman House, International Museum of Photography and Film.

back at the camera; his eyes are shadowed and squinting, but nevertheless they seem to meet our gaze. He looks forward into time and into the camera that will secure his place in history, as if searching for the unknown viewer who might find in his photographs, and even in this photograph of him, a spark of futurity that won't be silenced. Perhaps he understood, as Benjamin did, that photography won't stay in the past, and the temporal discord of photography's accidental futurity is the essence of its fundamental disruption.

Notes

1. Walter Benjamin, "Little History of Photography," in *Walter Benjamin: Selected Writings, vol. 2, part 2, 1931–1934*, trans. Rodney Livingstone et al., ed. Michael W. Jennings, Howard Eiland, and Gary Smith (Cambridge, MA: Belknap, 1999), 507–530, 515.

2. For Benjamin, a portrait of Kafka as a child "dressed up in a humiliatingly tight child's suit overloaded with trimming, in a sort of greenhouse landscape . . . in its infinite sadness" epitomizes the decline in photography ("Little History of Photography," 515). For Margaret Olin this portrait of Kafka is Walter Benjamin's Winter Garden Photograph, an inspiration for Barthes's own displaced (and more famous) Winter Garden Photograph in *Camera Lucida*. Margaret Olin, "Touching Photographs: Roland Barthes's 'Mistaken' Identification," *Representations* 80 (fall 2002): 99–118, 81–82.

3. Benjamin, "Little History of Photography," 515.

4. Benjamin, "Little History of Photography," 515.

5. According to Mary Warner Marien, the early historian of photography Lady Elizabeth Eastlake expressed a view of photography's early charms and subsequent decline similar to Benjamin's later assessment as early as 1857. According to Marien, "Her writing makes it appear as though Hill and Adamson lived in the golden age of photography, before the medium was cursed with scientific knowledge and a mediocre mass audience." Mary Warner Marien, *Photography and Its Critics: A Cultural History, 1839–1900* (Cambridge: Cambridge University Press, 1997), 97.

6. Schwarz studied art history in Vienna before and after World War I, and wrote his dissertation (1921) on the history of lithography in Austria. As Martin Gasser has argued, "For Schwarz, the invention of photography is essentially a logical extension of the invention of lithography." Martin Gasser, "A Master Piece: Heinrich Schwarz's Book on David Octavius Hill," *Image* 36, nos. 1–2 (spring/summer 1993): 32–53, 34–35.

7. Benjamin, "Little History of Photography," 517; Heinrich Schwarz, *David Octavius Hill: Master of Photography*, trans. Helene E. Fraenkel (New York: Viking, 1931), 38.

8. Benjamin, "Little History of Photography," 510. Heinrich Schwarz, one of Hill's early biographers and champions in the 1930s, outlines the history of his reputation as a photographer: Hill's contemporaries admired his work, and the London World Exposition of 1851 awarded an "Honourable Mention" to a large collection of calotypes by

Hill and Adamson; five years later, however, after the vogue of the carte-de-visite had taken hold in the 1850s, Hill was not included in the Photographic Society of Scotland. When Hill died in 1870, his obituaries failed to mention his work in photography. Not until the 1890s did Hill reemerge as a powerful presence in the history of photography. J. Craig Annan, a photographer from Glasgow, collected Hill's negatives and printed them with a pigment process, and then sent the images to famous artists throughout England, including Sargent and Whistler. In 1898, the Royal Photographic Society exhibited nearly seventy of Hill's portraits at the Crystal Palace in London, and the following year some of Hill's work was exhibited in Hamburg, where it was also collected. Schwarz, *David Octavius Hill*, 46–48.

9. Schwarz, *David Octavius Hill*, 25.

10. Schwarz, *David Octavius Hill*, 27, 33.

11. Sara Stevenson suggests that the bulk of the three thousand calotypes were likely taken in three short years, between 1843 and mid-1846. Sara Stevenson, *David Octavius Hill and Robert Adamson: Catalogue of Their Calotypes Taken between 1843 and 1847 in the Collection of the Scottish National Portrait Gallery* (Edinburgh: National Galleries of Scotland, 1981), 15.

12. Rock House was located on the slope of Calton Hill in Edinburgh. According to Sara Stevenson, the hill provided "clearer light and air" than other locations in the city. "The house was above sea level and avoided some of the city's smoke. It had a protected garden, facing south, to act as a studio and to gather the maximum sunlight for taking and printing . . . photographs." Robert Adamson leased the house in March 1843, and Hill joined him there in 1844. Sara Stevenson, "The Hill View: 'The Eye Unsatisfied and Dim with Gazing,'" *History of Photography* 30, no. 3 (autumn 2006): 213–233, 220.

13. Schwarz, *David Octavius Hill*, 30.

14. Stevenson, *David Octavius Hill and Robert Adamson*, 10.

15. William F. Stapp, then senior curator of photography at the George Eastman House, provides this technical and historical information in "Hill and Adamson: Artists of the Calotype," *Image* 36, nos. 1–2 (spring/summer 1993): 55–62, quotation p. 55.

16. Stevenson, *David Octavius Hill and Robert Adamson*, 11.

17. See my discussion of nineteenth-century discourses about the likeness and the portrait in Shawn Michelle Smith, "Superficial Depths," in *American Archives: Gender, Race, and Class in Visual Culture* (Princeton, NJ: Princeton University Press, 1999), 51–112. According to Larry Schaaf, it was not until the 1970s that historians of photography began to understand Adamson's central role in producing the Hill and Adamson calotypes. Schaaf attributes that recognition to Katherine Michaelson's *Centenary Exhibition of the Work of David Octavius Hill, 1802–1870, and Robert Adamson, 1821–1848* (Edinburgh: Scottish Arts Council, 1970). Larry J. Schaaf, "Science, Art and Talent: Henry Talbot and Hill and Adamson," *History of Photography* 27, no. 1 (spring 2003): 13–24, 23.

18. For Leja, such disruptive aesthetics were naturalized for viewers in the mass cul-

ture of the new visual print media of the 1840s and 1850s, prefiguring a visual disso-
nance that is usually associated with the later high-art experimentation of modernism.
Michael Leja, "Mass Modern," The Terra Foundation Lectures in Americanist Postmodern, March 8, 2012, School of the Art Institute of Chicago.

19. David Octavius Hill, *The Disruption of the Church of Scotland* (Edinburgh: Schenck and M'Farlane, 1866), 20.

20. Hill, *The Disruption of the Church of Scotland*, 28–29.

21. Hill, *The Disruption of the Church of Scotland*, 3–4.

22. Gasser, "A Master Piece," 38.

23. Gasser, "A Master Piece," 39, 40–41.

24. Such historical telescoping would correspond to one of Benjamin's primary critical tools—the "dialectical image" that, according to Susan Buck-Morss, informed Benjamin's Arcades Project, in which he looked to antiquated cultural forms and posed them in relation to current configurations to demonstrate and reveal, in a flash, capital-ism's changing sameness. Susan Buck-Morss, *The Dialectics of Seeing: Walter Benjamin and the Arcades Project* (Cambridge, MA: MIT Press, 1989). Even though that project was critical, seeking to expose and condemn capitalism's false and mystifying image of progress, Benjamin's dialectics also registered a desire and nostalgia for outmoded forms. Although Benjamin never celebrated the pictorialists, they may have enabled him to see qualities in Hill and Adamson's calotypes as fundamental to the nature of photography. In other words, he may have relied on the temporal telescoping dynamic of the dialectical image even without its devastating critique.

25. Benjamin, "Little History of Photography," 514.

26. Kathrin Yacavone, *Benjamin, Barthes and the Singularity of Photography* (New York: Continuum, 2012), 59.

27. Benjamin, "Little History of Photography," 517.

28. Benjamin, "Little History of Photography," 517. The tactility of the aura of the members of a rising class, impressed in clothing, is particularly lush in Schwarz's de-scription of it: "One can actually feel the surface textures in cravats of shimmering satin, waistcoats of dull-glowing velvet, collars of thick fur, and shawls made of soft Scottish wool" (*David Octavius Hill*, 39).

29. Schwarz, *David Octavius Hill*, 39. Schwarz also declares, "The products of Hill's camera are far from being a mirror-image of the visible world uninformed by the spirit" (39). See also Gasser, "A Master Piece," 36–37.

30. Benjamin, "Little History of Photography," 517.

31. D. O. Hill, letter to Mr. Bicknell, January 17, 1848, quoted in Stevenson, *David Octavius Hill and Robert Adamson*, 21.

32. As Mary Warner Marien suggests, "It seems likely that Hill and Adamson delib-erately chose a signature style," especially because technological information was widely available "had they found the blurriness of their images intolerable." Marien, *Photography and Its Critics*, 98.

33. Benjamin, "Little History of Photography," 512.

34. Benjamin, "Little History of Photography," 512.

35. Yacavone, *Benjamin, Barthes and the Singularity of Photography*, 96.

36. Benjamin, "Little History of Photography," 510.

37. Benjamin, "Little History of Photography," 510.

38. Benjamin, "Little History of Photography," 510, 528n6.

39. Kathrin Yacavone has made a strong case for Benjamin's "Little History" as a kind of affective precursor to Barthes's *Camera Lucida*. Yacavone, *Benjamin, Barthes and the Singularity of Photography*.

40. For more on affect in Roland Barthes's *Camera Lucida*, see Shawn Michelle Smith, "Photography between Desire and Grief: Roland Barthes and F. Holland Day," in *Feeling Photography*, ed. Elspeth H. Brown and Thy Phu (Durham, NC: Duke University Press, 2014), 29–46.

41. Fred Moten, *In the Break: The Aesthetics of the Black Radical Tradition* (Minneapolis: University of Minnesota Press, 2003).

42. Yacavone, *Benjamin, Barthes and the Singularity of Photography*, 36–37.

43. Benjamin, "Little History of Photography," 512.

44. Benjamin, "Little History of Photography," 510.

45. Victor Burgin argues that the significance of Barthes's *Camera Lucida* for theory is "the emphasis . . . placed on the active participation of the viewer in producing the meaning/affect of the photograph." Victor Burgin, "Re-reading *Camera Lucida*," in *The End of Art Theory: Criticism and Postmodernity* (New York: Macmillan, 1986), 88.

46. Benjamin, "Little History of Photography," 510.

47. Eduardo Cadava, *Words of Light: Theses on the Photography of History* (Princeton, NJ: Princeton University Press, 1997).

48. In her reading of Walter Benjamin and the optical unconscious, Miriam Hansen seizes upon arbitrary moments of chance, contingent moments that remain free from human intention and the narrative of history as progress. According to Hansen, "Benjamin develops the notion of an 'optical unconscious' from the observation that the temporality of some early photographs, despite all preparation and artistry on the part of both model and photographer, compel the beholder to seek the 'tiny spark of accident,' the 'here and now' by which the image is branded with reality, and thus to find the 'inconspicuous spot' which might yield, in the quality of that minute long past, a 'moment of futurity responding to the retrospective gaze.'" Miriam Hansen, "Benjamin, Cinema and Experience: 'The Blue Flower in the Land of Technology,'" *New German Critique* 40 (winter 1987): 179–224, 208.

49. Ulrich Baer, *Spectral Evidence: The Photography of Trauma* (Cambridge, MA: MIT Press, 2002), 24, 182.

50. Walter Benjamin, "On the Concept of History" (1940), in *Selected Writings, vol. 4, 1938–1940*, trans. Edmund Jephcott et al., ed. Howard Eiland and Michael W. Jennings (Cambridge, MA: Belknap, 2003), 389–400, 397.

51. Benjamin, "Little History of Photography," 512.

52. Benjamin, "Little History of Photography," 512.

53. Benjamin, "Little History of Photography," 510–512, emphasis added.

54. As Sara Stevenson notes, Hill updated some of the portraits of people he still knew in the 1860s, "with the uncomfortable result that some of the faces belong to the 1840s and others, like his own and Dr. George Bell's which have sprouted white whiskers, belong to the 1860s." Stevenson, *David Octavius Hill and Robert Adamson*, 31.

55. Sarah Kofman, *Camera Obscura: Of Ideology* (1973), trans. Will Straw (Ithaca, NY: Cornell University Press, 1999), 21–28, 27.

56. Although it does not appear that Hill and Adamson used the waxing technique extensively, Larry Schaaf demonstrates that they regularly retouched their negatives with ink and pencil, and they did occasionally use wax. Schaaf, "Science, Art and Talent," 18, esp. figure 4.

57. Freud, "A Note upon the 'Mystic Writing Pad'" (1925), in *The Standard Edition of the Complete Psychological Works of Sigmund Freud*, vol. 19, 1923–1925, trans. and ed. James Strachey in collaboration with Anna Freud (London: Vintage, 2001), 227–232, 231.

58. Freud, "A Note upon the 'Mystic Writing Pad,'" 228–230.

59. In 1978, Roland Barthes consulted that issue of the magazine extensively while writing *Camera Lucida* (published in 1980). Barthes does not cite Benjamin's essay in his bibliography, but he clearly attended closely to the issue that features the "Little History," taking from it nearly a quarter of the photographs for *Camera Lucida*. Margaret Iverson deems Benjamin's "Little History" an "important, though unacknowledged inspiration" for *Camera Lucida*. Margaret Iverson, "What Is a Photograph?," in *Photography Degree Zero: Reflections on Roland Barthes's* Camera Lucida, ed. Geoffrey Batchen (Cambridge, MA: MIT Press, 2009), 57–74, 61. In the same volume see also Geoffrey Batchen, "Palinode: An Introduction to *Photography Degree Zero*," 3–30, 10; and Geoffrey Batchen, "*Camera Lucida*: Another Little History of Photography," 259–273, 261, 271n10. In her reading of Benjamin's multiple written accounts of his response to the child portrait of Kafka that he owned, Kathrin Yacavone suggests that Benjamin's "existential phenomenology" of the "experience" of a photograph anticipates Barthes's *Camera Lucida* (*Benjamin, Barthes and the Singularity of Photography*, 89).

———

CHAPTER THREE

FREUD

The Photographic Apparatus

———

SARAH KOFMAN

The Photographer's Antechamber

Although Marx speaks more of an ideological consciousness than a class unconscious, the camera obscura functions, for him, much in the manner of the unconscious. Explicitly and repeatedly, Freud calls on this metaphor in his description of the unconscious. However, like the science of his time, he substitutes for the model of the camera obscura that of the photographic apparatus. The difference between these two models is minimal, the physical image in one becoming a chemical impression in the other. Still, through the mediation of the notion of the negative, the theory of vision remains the same: to see is always to obtain a double. The usage and principle remain identical.

The photographic metaphor returns several times, replacing those of the screen and of the sieve which are to be found in the "Project for a Scientific Psychology."[1] The *Three Essays on Sexuality* defines the neuroses as the negative of perversion.[2] A note specifies that, in the case of the perverse, the phantasm is *clearly* conscious.[3] Perversion is like a development of neurosis; it implies a passage from darkness to light, or from the unconscious to consciousness. Freud's use of the model of the photographic apparatus is intended to show that all psychic phenomena necessarily pass first through an unconscious phase, through darkness and the negative, before acceding to consciousness, before developing within the clarity of the positive. However, it is possible that the negative will not be developed.[4] The passage from darkness to light entails an ordeal, a test, and this is always a showdown of sorts. As well, Freud declares the photographic analogy to be crude and insufficient. To it, he adds other metaphors, making it clearly understood that, between the negative and positive phases, there intervene forces which enact a selection from among the negatives. The metaphor here is that of the watchman, the censor, present at the entrance to the dark antechamber, forbidding certain drives from entering into the clear room of consciousness.

Unconsciousness is a regular and inevitable phase in the processes constituting our psychical activity: every psychical act begins as an unconscious one, and it may either remain so or go on developing into consciousness, according as it meets with resistance or not. The distinction between foreconscious and unconscious activity is not a primary one, but comes to be established after repulsion has sprung up. Only then the difference between foreconscious ideas, which can appear in consciousness and reappear at any moment, and unconscious ideas which cannot do so gains a theoretical as well as a practical value. A rough but not inadequate analogy to this supposed relation of conscious to unconscious activity might be drawn from the field of ordinary photography. The first phase of the photograph is the "negative": every photographic picture has to pass through the "negative process": and some of these negatives which have held good in examination are admitted to the "positive process" ending in the picture.[5]

Not every negative, however, necessarily becomes a positive; nor is it necessary that every unconscious mental process should turn into a conscious one. This may be advantageously expressed by saying that an individual process belongs to begin with to the system of the unconscious and can then, in certain circumstances, pass over into the system of the conscious. . . . The crudest idea of these systems is the most convenient for us—a spatial one. Let us therefore compare the system of the unconscious to a large entrance hall, in which the mental impulses jostle one another like separate individuals. Adjoining this entrance hall is a second, narrower room—a kind of drawing-room—in which consciousness, too, resides. But on the threshold between these two rooms a watchman performs his function: he examines the different mental impulses, acts as a censor, and will not admit them into the drawing room if they displease him. . . . The impulses in the entrance hall of the unconscious are out of sight of the conscious,[6] which is in the other room; to begin with they must remain unconscious.

Now I know you will say that these ideas are both crude; and, more than that, I know that they are incorrect, and, if I am not very much mistaken, I already have something better to take their place. Whether it will seem to you equally fantastic I cannot tell. They are preliminary working hypotheses [and] are not to be despised. . . . I should like to assure you that these crude hypotheses of the two rooms, the watchman at the threshold between them and consciousness as a spectator at the end of the second room, must nevertheless be very far-reaching approximations to the real facts.[7]

The Stereotype

The metaphor of the photographic negative persists in *Moses and Monotheism*. Here, Freud uses it to describe the decisive influence of early childhood. The idea of the negative implies that an impression made may be retained without change, to be repeated within an image which will subsequently develop it. The metaphor is intended to show the constraining character of the past, and the compulsional force which determines its return, makes it dictate behavior, shape emotions, and so on. If the past repeats itself in this way, duplicating itself within representation, it is because the event has never been lived in the fullness of its meaning, in the positivity of its presence: "The psychic apparatus of the child was not yet completely receptive" to a certain number of impressions nor ready to endow them with meaning. Counter-proof: Hoffman's declarations, in which he "used to trace back the wealth of figures that put themselves at his disposal for his creative writings to the changing images and impressions which he had experienced during a journey of some weeks in post-chaise while he was still an infant at his mother's breast."[8] Freud then concludes: "What children have experienced at the age of two and have not understood, need never be remembered by them except in dreams; they may only come to know of it through psycho-analytic treatment."[9]

In *Moses and Monotheism*, then, the metaphor of the photographic apparatus is not used for the exact same ends as in other texts. This latter usage allows us to reevaluate the sense of the image of the negative and to suggest that the Freudian text is, at the very least, ambivalent.

The Development of the Negative

In effect, whenever Freud puts a metaphor in play, he always acts with great caution: he multiplies the images, declares them crude, provisional, or uses them for purely didactic ends. He will correct one metaphor with another, even though it is spatial metaphors which seem to him the most apt for describing the psychic apparatus. Images — of the censor, of the guard, of the watchman — will complete those of the photographic apparatus, unable to express, on its own, the conflictual character of the psyche. The camera obscura, a simple mechanical model, cannot give us a "good" picture of the unconscious: it fails to show that there are forces with an interest in producing or perpetuating ideological inversion. Such a model, with its emphasis on the necessity of inversion and on its mechanical character, obscures the class struggle and the relationship to desire. The precautions Freud takes, the fact that he questions his own methodological use of metaphors, shows the limits of the optical analogy in Marx.

Despite everything, despite the scientific character of his approach, Freud's text nevertheless fails to avoid the traditional system of mythical and metaphysical oppositions: unconscious/conscious, dark/light, negative/positive. A negative proof is "that which reproduces the model in inverted colours, the darks as light, the lights as dark. In order to obtain a positive proof, one applies the first negative drawing onto another sheet of paper possessed of the same properties and exposes the whole to light" (Littré). But the term "negative" has pejorative connotations: it is linked to darkness, to the antechamber, to the valet's backroom. As for consciousness, characterized by light, lucidity, the positive, it resides in a more noble place, the salon: it is the master. A text like this lends itself to the belief that psychism will submit to the same finality as the Hegelian dialectic: the passage from darkness to light. Photographic development would then suggest the development of the Spirit, becoming itself in the course of time, the positive taking over from the negative. Psychic time would therefore be linear: 1. the time of infancy, of the impression leaving a negative imprint; 2. the time of latency, the time of development or growth; 3. the time of the positive image, marked by the passage from darkness to light, from infancy to adulthood. The positive image, the double of the negative, implies that "what is at the end is already there in the beginning." Development adds nothing: it only enables the darkness to be made light.

In fact, even the first texts we have cited, but especially *Moses and Monotheism*, block such a Hegelian reading of Freud. In the psychic apparatus, the passage from negative to positive is neither necessary nor dialectical. It is possible that the development will never take place. Repression is originary, and there is always an irretrievable residue, something which will never have access to consciousness. The death drive, as a generalized economic principle, prevents us from confusing the negative in Freud with that in Hegel. What is more, when there is a passage into consciousness, it depends not on logical criteria, but on a selection involving conflicts between nondialectizable forces. Finally, to pass from negative to positive is not to become conscious of a preexisting meaning, light, or truth of a reason diverted from itself the better to be found, reappropriating itself in the course of its development. The passage to light takes place through a procedure which is not theoretical but practical: the analytic cure. As with Marx, only a transformation of the balance of forces leads to clarity. To pass from darkness to light is not, then, to rediscover a meaning already there, it is to construct a meaning which has never existed as such. There are limits to repetition inasmuch as full meaning has never been present. Repetition is originary. Hoffman's "creations" are the substitute memories of a past which never took place, of a presence which never existed. Substitutive procedures, whether normal or pathological, are originary repetitions which allow us to construct, after the fact, *post festum*, the meaning of experience, but as a hypothetical construction.[10] Thus, the photographic metaphor contains within it all we need to undertake a metaphysical reading of Freud, but also, and at the same time, what we need to undo these clichés. Provided that we read these texts with caution, we can see that a metaphor, like a concept, is not "metaphysical" in itself. Like that of Marx, Freud's text is heterogeneous.[11] It would seem, nonetheless, that the hypothesis of the death drive is that "more interesting thing," announced by Freud in the *Introduction to Psychoanalysis*, which would put an end to "fantastic" metaphors. The theory of the death drive dispels, then, any recourse to metaphysics, even though, in Freud's own words, that theory was the most speculative that he had ever advanced.[12]

Notes

1. "The sense-organs act not only as Q-screens, like all nerve-ending apparatuses, but also as sieves; for they allow the stimulus through from only certain processes with a particular period." Freud, "Project for a Scientific Psychology" (1895), in *The Standard Edition of the Complete Psychological Works of Sigmund Freud*, ed. and trans. James Strachey (London: Hogarth, 1966), vol. 1, 310.

2. Freud, "Three Essays on Sexuality" (1905), in *Standard Edition*, 1953, vol. 7, 165–167.

3. "The contents of the clearly conscious phantasies of perverts (which in favourable circumstances can be transformed into manifest behaviour), of the delusional fears of paranoics (which are projected in a hostile sense on to other people) and of the unconscious phantasies of hysterics (which psychoanalysis reveals behind their symptoms) — all of these coincide with one another even down to their details." Freud, "Three Essays on Sexuality" (1905), in *Standard Edition*, 1953, vol. 7, 165, note 2.

4. Freud, "Introductory Lectures on Psychoanalysis, Lecture XIX: Resistance and Repression," (1916–17), in *Standard Edition*, 1963, vol. 16, 295.

5. Sigmund Freud, "A Note on the Unconscious" (1912), in *Standard Edition*, 1958, vol. 12, 264.

6. On the conscious as sight, and the persistence of this image within the metaphysical tradition, see Jacques Derrida, *Margins of Philosophy*, trans. Alan Bass (Chicago: University of Chicago Press, 1982), 284.

7. Freud, "General Theory of the Neuroses: Resistance and Repression" (1916–1917), in *Standard Edition*, vol. 16, 295–296.

8. Freud, "Moses and Monotheism (III): The Return of the Repressed" (1939), in *Standard Edition*, vol. 23, 126.

9. Freud, "Moses and Monotheism," 126.

10. See Sarah Kofman, *The Childhood of Art: An Interpretation of Freud's Aesthetics*, trans. Winifred Woodhull (New York: Columbia University Press, 1988), especially chapter 3.

11. Another example of this heterogeneity: the metaphor of *arousal* for describing the return of the repressed. In his study of Jensen's *Gradiva*, Freud denounces Jensen's use of this metaphor: "'Arouses,' however, is certainly not the right description." Freud, "Delusions and Dreams in Jensen's Gradiva" (1907), in *Standard Edition*, vol. 9, 47. The criticism of this notion intervenes at precisely the moment when Freud opposes a philosophical and etymological understanding of the unconscious. The latter consider consciousness as a point of departure, and establish, between the conscious and the unconscious, a simple difference of intensity. The Unconscious, then, is the latent, the dormant, that which Freud will call the preconscious. The metaphor of arousal or awakening thus has the effect of confusing the preconscious with the unconscious or even the repressed. However, several pages later, Freud takes up this metaphor twice on his own account: "No mental forces are significant unless they possess the characteristic of aroused feelings" (49). "But as we have insisted with admiration, the author has not failed to show us how the arousing of the repressed erotism came precisely from the field of the instruments that served to bring about the repression" (49). Despite himself, then, Freud seems to yield to a metaphorical constraint, such that to speak of "a text by Freud" as a text of any other author, no longer makes sense. To the point, even, where it seems no longer relevant to know if Freud uses that metaphor "voluntarily or involuntarily" so soon after criticizing it.

12. See Freud, "Beyond the Pleasure Principle" (1920), in *Standard Edition*, 1955, vol. 18, 7–66.

CHAPTER FOUR

"TO ADOPT"

Freud, Photography, and the
Optical Unconscious

JONATHAN FARDY

Few concepts in photography studies are more intriguing and less understood than Walter Benjamin's concept of the optical unconscious. Benjamin glosses the idea in two essays, "The Work of Art in the Age of Its Technological Reproducibility" and "Little History of Photography." In the former he writes, "It is through the camera that we first discover the optical unconscious, just as we discover the instinctual unconscious through psychoanalysis."[1] In the latter he writes, "It is another nature that speaks to the camera rather than to the eye; 'other' above all in the sense that a space informed by human consciousness gives way to one informed by the unconscious."[2] That's it: a flash of illumination, but little else.

Many find Benjamin's idea powerful yet problematic. In *The Optical Unconscious*, Rosalind Krauss, for one, notes that she is "struck by the strangeness" of Benjamin's claim.[3] She asks, "Can the optical field—the world of visual phenomena: clouds, sea, sky and forest—have an unconscious?"[4] Krauss criticizes Benjamin for drawing a seemingly untenable analogy. But clearly Benjamin's claim is made not on the grounds of nature as such—the world of clouds, sea, sky and forest—but on the grounds of "another nature" made visible only through photography. Benjamin's claim speaks to the novel and complex ways in which photography and the unconscious may intersect.

This essay examines one such instance of intersection: the case of Freud's so-called "R is my uncle" dream, as recounted in *The Interpretation of Dreams*. Freud speculates that the face seen in his dream was psychically produced by means of compositing two faces in a manner akin to that employed by Francis

Galton (1822–1911) in his photographic studies of moral and racial types. I argue that this speculation raises a set of important questions on the nature of photography, the unconscious, and their intersections, as well as a wish to see and resist the specular construction of the figure of the Jew as envisioned in the fin de siècle discourse of anti-Semitism.

Dreaming Photography

The fin de siècle bore witness to the expression and expansion of two new ways of seeing and thinking: photography and psychoanalysis. Each promised to illuminate the dark corners of the world and mind. Nineteenth-century photography, as Allan Sekula memorably demonstrated, serviced the evidentiary demands of a newly emergent positivism in the social and psychological sciences.[5] By the mid-nineteenth century, the French psychiatrist Jean Martin Charcot (an early inspiration for Freud) was employing photography in his study of "hysterical" women. Photography provided Charcot with a means for documenting his patients as well as a ready-made model of visual empiricism to underwrite the science he believed he was forging. With all the confidence of naive empiricism he asserted, "You know that my principle is to give no weight to theory, and to leave aside all prejudice: if you want to see clearly, you must take things as they are. . . . Truth to tell . . . I am nothing more than a photographer, I record what I see."[6]

Freud followed Charcot and the empirical zeitgeist of turn-of-the-century psychology he represented. Freud's science centers on the "talking cure" unfolded through an immanent dialectic of speech and silence. What comes to light in the course of the psychoanalytic dialogue is less the speaker than the thing that speaks through speech and silence. And it is this thing, this "It" (*das Es* in German) that speaks. "What little we know of *it*," Freud writes, "we have studied from the dreamwork. . . . *It* is a chaos, a cauldron full of seething excitations."[7] Psychoanalysis is at once a theory of this It, the unconscious, and a therapy to negate its power by bringing it into the light of consciousness. But since the analyst too has an unconscious, It must also influence and distort the analytic process. It — the unconscious — can be theoretically represented and analyzed to an extent, but It can neither be the subject of a final theory nor a final analysis, for every analysis or theory will itself bear the distortions of the unconscious. This paradox according to which the unconscious can be represented yet not fully arrested makes It and photography strange bedfellows.

Photography is a form of seeing and knowing. But can photography itself be finally captured, seen and known? Barthes famously argued in *Camera Lucida* that photographs are indexical. They point to something. They say, "'Look,' 'See,' 'Here it is.'"[8] But can photography be indexed? One can point to photographs, to cameras, to photographers, and the like. But these are merely photography's representatives or "avatars," as W. J. T. Mitchell argues.[9] Barthes thus concludes, "Photography evades us."[10] Barthes's philosophical resignation is rhetorically underscored by his insistence on capitalizing the word photography throughout *Camera Lucida*. He transcendentalizes the term. The spectator only sees the shadows of this thing—this It—called photography. It is this unseen of photography as such and that of the unconscious as such that cross in the "R is my uncle" dream.

In *The Interpretation of Dreams*, Freud tells his readers of a strange dream he had while awaiting a momentous decision that would decide his academic future. Freud was up for promotion to the rank of professor extraordinarius (a rank roughly equivalent to that of associate professor in North America). He was worried. His colleague R (Freud keeps the name confidential) had been turned down when his turn for promotion came up. He speculates that R was denied promotion for what Freud discreetly calls "denominational considerations." By this Freud meant that R was denied promotion because he was Jewish. Anti-Semitism also threatened to rob Freud of his chance to become the academic equivalent of a "demigod," in his words.[11] At this precarious moment in his life, Freud says he dreamed of a man for whom he had a "great feeling of affection."[12] He continues, "I saw before me his face, somewhat changed. It was as though it had been drawn out lengthways. A yellow beard that surrounded it stood out especially clearly."[13]

Through analysis Freud discovers that the face in his dream was a composite image. The portrait was made of two faces: his friend R and his Uncle Josef. His uncle, Freud notes, had been convicted of a financial crime many years before. Freud's father always maintained that Josef was a "simpleton," however, and not a malicious criminal.[14] His crime was negligence, not fraud. Freud argues that the dream reveals an unconscious wish that R would have been denied promotion because he was a simpleton (which Freud secretly believes he is, despite his affection for him) rather than for "denominational considerations."[15] The face seen in the dream was thus an image composite of Uncle Josef and R as well as a character composite of criminal and simpleton. The figure that binds these composited faces and traits—Josef (criminal) and R (simpleton)—is the figure of the Jew. Framed in the visual and verbal matrix of anti-Semitism, this figure of the Jew is seen to be congenitally fated to deviance. It is this figure that stands out "especially clearly" in Freud's dream. As Lene Auestad points out in *Respect, Plurality, and Prejudice*, Freud's "dream presents us with a glimpse of the subjective anti-Semitism of the Vienna" of Freud's day.[16]

What I(t) Did

Why did Freud's psyche make this composite dream portrait? Perhaps this question is too leading. At the time of the publication of his dream book, Freud conceived the unconscious as a shadowy repository for thoughts too hard to face. To ask why Freud's psyche made a composite portrait would thus seem to wrongly figure the unconscious as an agent rather than a passive structure. Freud's passage from a static to an active, processual model of the unconscious developed in the 1920s, years after he published his masterwork on dreams. His later so-called "topographical model"—the now familiar id, ego, and super-ego—pictures psychic life as a dynamic interplay between primal drives, self-hood, and social norms.[17] To claim that Freud's unconscious made a composite dream image would therefore impute to the unconscious a form of agency theoretically at odds with Freud's pre-topographical model of the unconscious. Yet it is precisely a dynamic model of the unconscious—unconscious qua process—that shines in Freud's words. "What I *did was to adopt* the procedure by which [Francis] Galton produced . . . portraits: namely by projecting two images on a single plate."[18]

Who does "I" refer to in Freud's statement? Who or what was able "to adopt" Galton's procedure? To say that Freud adopted the procedure of composite printing used by Galton would be odd since Freud himself was unconscious while he dreamed the dream. But then who or what is responsible? The answer appears to be It: the unconscious. It made the composite. And It made a convincing composite, for it was only through analysis that the illusion was revealed. Freud's self-analysis reaches a two-fold conclusion: It did something and It did something seemingly photographic in nature.

Freud's interpretation of his dream theoretically images the unconscious as a productive and quasi-mechanical force—what Gilles Deleuze and Félix Guattari capture with their concept of the "machinic unconscious."[19] Deleuze and Guattari deploy the machine as model for the unconscious because it fittingly captures the idea of the unconscious as (in part) a set of automated and productive functions: the unconscious automatically produces dreams, fantasies, slips of the tongue, and the like, which is to say it produces symptoms. Freud's reading of his dream likewise accents a machinic dimension: the unconscious as a quasi-photographic process. The figuration of the unconscious as a machinic process recurs elsewhere in the dream book, as when Freud notes that "we should picture the instrument that carries out mental functions as resembling a . . . photographic apparatus."[20] The photographic process analogically captures Freud's sense of the psyche as a dynamic process leading from the capture of mental impressions through their development into dream images. But why was this machinic, quasi-photographic dimension of Freud's dream invisible in the dream itself?

Photography as a mode of imaging and thinking has "taught us a way of seeing," notes Celia Lury, which has "transformed . . . self-understanding."[21] Yet this transformational *way of seeing*, she argues, has been so thoroughly internalized and naturalized by seeing photographs that photography itself has, to an extent, been rendered optically unconscious. Confronted with a photograph of a tree, for example, and asked "What is this?" one could surely be excused for responding, "It's a tree" rather than "It's a photograph of a tree." By an unconscious act of metonymic substitution, the subject of the photograph comes to signify the photograph as such. Barthes calls this the problem of the "stubbornness" of the photographic referent. That which is pictured in the photograph can block from view the medium of photography. The photograph itself—apart from the subject of the photograph—is, Barthes concludes, almost "always invisible."[22] Likewise, the photographic dimension of Freud's dream was not visible in the dream itself. The photographic quality of the dream appeared in the dream as the medium of photography often does in waking life: it doesn't. It was rendered invisible or optically unconscious. It only became visible through Freud's self-analysis.

Galton (Self-Analysis)

I had wanted to keep this essay theoretical. I had hoped to keep the discussion focused on photography and its structural parallel with the concept of the unconscious. But Galton kept coming back like an intrusive thought—a stubborn symptom. I could not in good conscience ignore Freud's reference to Galton, a man whose life was stamped by his reading of his half-cousin's famous work—Charles Darwin's *On the Origin of Species*. Galton forged the field of eugenics—the term he coined to designate his new "science"—which held that moral character was determined by hereditary traits encoded in race and physiognomy.

Galton, like Charcot, saw photography as a means to shore up what he as-

JONATHAN FARDY

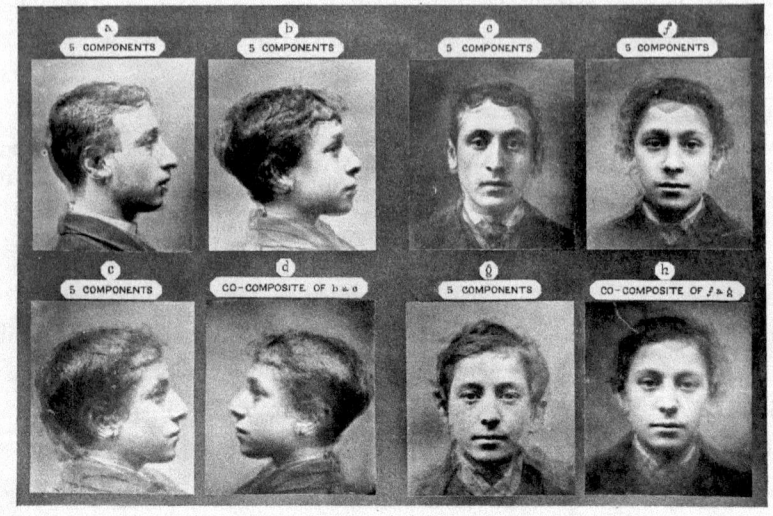

FIGURE 4.1 Francis Galton, *The Jewish Type*. Composite portraits. Reproduced from Karl Pearson, *The Life, Letters and Labours of Francis Galton*, vol. 2, *Researches of Middle Life* (Cambridge: Cambridge University Press, 1924).

sumed was empirically true, namely, that the visible, exterior body bears evidentiary traces of a person's inner psyche. Galton studied the faces of convicted criminals. He superimposed photographic portraits of such individuals over one another to create composites. He then observed, mapped, and cataloged those facial features that appeared to overlap in the composite studies. With these photographs, Galton sought to demonstrate that certain moral types share common facial and racial features. Galton saw his composites as scientific proofs of the veracity of eugenics. He was not alone in this conviction. Consensus was strong enough to see him made a fellow of the Royal Society in England.

In 1885, Galton published his photographic study of the Jewish type in *Photographic News* (fig. 4.1). There he describes his field research in a Jewish neighborhood in London. The composites he made there were, he said, "the best specimens . . . I ever produced." The subjects he selected for the composite studies were, in Galton's words, "children of poor parents, dirty little fellows." He continues, "The feature that struck me most as I drove though the . . . Jewish quarter, was the cold, scanning gaze of man, woman, and child." He concludes, "I felt, rightly or wrongly, that every one of them was coolly appraising me at market value, without the slightest interest of any other kind."[23]

Galton's description of the gaze of the men, women, and children of the Jewish neighborhood—a gaze he sees as rightly or wrongly fixed on "market value"—repeats the oldest of anti-Semitic prejudices: Jews care only for money. Galton saw "the Jewish type" as a social problem on the order of the problem of madness. Indeed the two figures—"the Jew" and "the mad"—were intimately linked in psychopathological theory of the time. Sander Gilman in *Freud, Race, and Gender* notes, "In Charcot's clinic there was an oft-stated assumption that Jews, especially Jews from the East, were at great risk for mental illness."[24] And both Charcot and Galton defended this view by deferring to the supposed objectivity of photography. The director of the photography department at Charcot's clinic, Albert Londe, summed up this sentiment precisely when he confidently noted that "the photographic plate is the scientist's true retina."[25] Seen in historical perspective, it is clear that "Galton's model of 'seeing' the Jew's gaze, of looking at the Jew looking, was part of the discourse of psychopathology during the late nineteenth century."[26]

The coolly dispassionate way in which Galton surveys the people of the Jewish neighborhood rhetorically represents his eyesight as objective because it is photographic, as if eye and camera are superimposed or composited into a singular, specular image. Galton claims not only to see the Jews, but to see behind their look, to see the intent behind their gaze. The figuration of photographic seeing in Galton's text takes the form of a psychic X-ray of sorts endowed with the power to see behind the face into the depths of the psyche or soul of the people of the Jewish quarter.

Simpletons and Swindlers

Freud came of age as a medical student at a time when anti-Semitism was not only popularly subscribed to but scientifically endorsed. Theories like Galton's were the norm, not the exception. Gilman notes that "racial models of the Jew" can be "found not only in the 'crackpot' pamphlet literature of the time; they are present in virtually all discussions of psychopathology published from 1880 to 1930."[27] Freud "had to conform," writes Gilman, "to these models of the Jew hidden in himself in order to function in this world."[28] Mary Bergstein has likewise noted that the "emphasis on determining types, racial or social, and the proofs of symptoms of illness, as represented in photography, seems to have imprinted" itself on Freud's thinking.[29] I want to build on Gilman and Bergstein's insights. The "R is my uncle" dream is a case of "seeing photographically," in Lury's poignant phrase.[30] But it is more than that. It is also a case of seeing the figure of the Jew in a photo-eugenic frame. This is not to imply that Freud's dream is a case of Jewish self-hatred. Indeed this is not really a case of Freud per se. It is a case of It—the unconscious—an unconscious trained to see the Jew as a psychopathological, social, and moral problem.

Consider these lines from a letter sent by Freud to his friend Emil Fluss. Here Freud describes a Jewish man he observed while sailing on a ship from Freiburg to Vienna. "Now this Jew talked the same way as I heard thousands of others talk before, even in Freiburg. His face seemed similar—he was typical. . . . He was cut from the cloth from which fate makes swindlers when the time is ripe."[31] Freud's letter repeats the two-fold thesis advanced by Galton, namely that Jews are fated to a destiny of financial corruption—the fate of born "swindlers"—and that this fate is written in the "typical face" of the Jew.

The dialectic of identification and disidentification with Jewishness marked Freud's intellectual and personal development. He was to later confess that as a young member of the medical faculty of the University of Vienna, he believed that he "was expected to feel inferior and alien because [he] was a Jew."[32] By 1926, however, he could say, "My language . . . is German, my culture, my attainments are German. I considered myself German intellectually, until I noticed the growth of anti-Semitic prejudices in Germany and . . . Austria. Since that time, I prefer to call myself a Jew."[33] Freud's statement suggests that his later identification as a Jew was a political as much as a cultural and ethnic identification, for it was in part a response to politically (and scientifically) sanctioned anti-Semitism. In 1938 anti-Semitism became official state policy in Austria when it was annexed by the Nazi regime. Anti-Semitism—given the veneer of legality and legitimacy by Nazi law—recast the figure of the Jew. To the charges of mental feebleness and criminality was now added that of enemy of the state.

Friend/Enemy

On December 9, 1930, Walter Benjamin sent the legal theorist Carl Schmitt a copy of his magisterial work *The Origin of German Tragic Drama*. Benjamin was convinced that the author of *Political Theology* shared with him a certain understanding of the concept of political sovereignty.[34] Benjamin's letter went unanswered. Shortly thereafter Schmitt published *The Concept of the Political*. There he famously argued that "the political" is an ontological condition that arises when conflict becomes existential.[35] With customary terseness, Schmitt writes, "The specific political distinction to which political actions and motives can be reduced is that between friend and enemy."[36] The moment a social antagonism becomes a matter of life and death, an existential struggle between friend and enemy, then and there, argues Schmitt, it becomes a truly political matter. One year later, Schmitt joined the Nazi party.[37] Until he fell out of favor, Schmitt's writings provided a justificatory veneer for Nazi jurisprudence. Benjamin's hope to establish an intellectual friendship with Schmitt was thus dashed the moment Schmitt's theory of friend and enemy found its concrete expression in the Nazi's political dichotomy of German and Jew. Seen in light of the Nazi terror that was to befall Germany, Austria, and much of Europe, Freud's "R is my uncle" dream is eerily prophetic. Freud's unconscious internalization of the figure of the Jew as a composite of criminal and simpleton prefigures the construction of the political figuration of the Jew as enemy of the state under the Third Reich.

Analytic Composite

Psychoanalysis is a science of incompletion. The unconscious can never be fully and finally grasped by analysis, for analysis itself is subject to the pressure and pull of the unconscious. As Sarah Kofman has pointed out, the telos of analysis is not to discover a "meaning already there, it is to construct a meaning which has never existed as such."[38] Meaning arises on the basis of associations formed between analyst and analysand. Meaning is made between the two, creating what Thomas Ogden has called the "analytic third."[39] The same is true of photographic meaning. It arises from social bonds that actually and virtually tie together photographs, photographers, subjects, and spectators in a dynamic meaning-making complex. Arguably no better visual analogy can be had for this analytic third of psychoanalytic and photographic meaning than composite photography. The overlaying of two subjects creates a novel third that exists only on account of the two, but cannot be reduced to either. Freud's self-analysis yields an analytic third, or even "another nature," in Benjamin's words. What comes to light is an optical unconscious — an It and an image — touched by a moment in technological modernity that presaged the coming of a new state terror, which was to fatally turn the figure of the Jew into an enemy of the state.

Coda (Wish)

If Freud's dream is a wish—the secret driver of every dream according to Freud—then perhaps it is ultimately a wish for a world where ambition and talent rather than race would be decisive. One might finally say that Freud's analysis of the "R is my uncle" dream was an act of unconscious resistance: the dream figure of the Jew, seen within the frame of Galton's procedure, exposes the specular and artificial fabrication of that figure, its reliance on a system of representations, which like It, the unconscious, necessarily produces a distortion—an illusion.

Notes

1. Walter Benjamin, "The Work of Art in the Age of Its Technological Reproducibility," in *The Work of Art in the Age of Its Technological Reproducibility and Other Writings on Media*, ed. Michael W. Jennings, Brigid Doherty, and Thomas Y. Levin (Cambridge, MA: Belknap, 2008), 37.

2. Walter Benjamin, "Little History of Photography," in *The Work of Art in the Age of Its Technological Reproducibility and Other Writings on Media*, 277–278.

3. Rosalind Krauss, *The Optical Unconscious* (Cambridge, MA: MIT Press, 1993), 178.

4. Krauss, *The Optical Unconscious*, 178.

5. See Allan Sekula, "The Body and the Archive," in *The Contest of Meaning: Critical Histories of Photography*, ed. Richard Bolton (Cambridge, MA: MIT Press, 1989).

6. Cited in Georges Didi-Huberman, *The Invention of Hysteria: Charcot and the Photographic Iconography of the Salpêtrière*, trans. Alisa Hartz (Cambridge, MA: MIT Press, 2003), 29.

7. Sigmund Freud, *New Introductory Lectures on Psychoanalysis*, trans. and ed. James Strachey (London: Penguin, 1989), 105–106, emphasis added.

8. Roland Barthes, *Camera Lucida: Reflections on Photography*, trans. Richard Howard (New York: Hill and Wang, 2010), 5.

9. See W. J. T. Mitchell, *What Do Pictures Want?* (Chicago: University of Chicago Press, 2005).

10. Barthes, *Camera Lucida*, 4.

11. Sigmund Freud, *The Interpretation of Dreams*, trans. and ed. James Strachey (London: Penguin, 1976), 217.

12. Freud, *The Interpretation of Dreams*, 218.

13. Freud, *The Interpretation of Dreams*, 218.

14. Freud, *The Interpretation of Dreams*, 217.

15. It should be pointed out that Freud, later in his analysis, reflects on his colleague N, who also had been denied promotion due to having been the defendant in

a suit brought against him by a woman. Thus Freud has yet more reason to interpret the figure of Uncle Josef as a composite of R (simpleton) and Josef/N (criminal).

16. Lene Auestad, *Respect, Plurality, and Prejudice: A Psychoanalytic and Philosophical Perspective* (London: Karnac, 2015), 26.

17. I am indebted to Sharon Sliwinski, who got me to see this.

18. Freud, *The Interpretation of Dreams*, 400, emphasis added.

19. See Gilles Deleuze and Félix Guattari, *Anti-Oedipus: Capitalism and Schizophrenia*, vol. 1 (London: Continuum, 2004).

20. Freud, *The Interpretation of Dreams*, 686.

21. Celia Lury, *Prosthetic Culture: Photography, Memory, Identity* (London: Routledge, 1998), 2–3.

22. Barthes, *Camera Lucida*, 6.

23. Francis Galton, "Photographic Composites," *Photographic News*, April 17, 1885, 243–245.

24. Sander L. Gilman, *Freud, Race, and Gender* (Princeton, NJ: Princeton University Press, 1993), 122.

25. Didi-Huberman, *The Invention of Hysteria*, 32.

26. Gilman, *Freud, Race, and Gender*, 122.

27. Gilman, *Freud, Race, and Gender*, 5.

28. Gilman, *Freud, Race, and Gender*, 5.

29. Mary Bergstein, *Mirrors of Memory: Freud, Photography, and the History of Art* (Ithaca, NY: Cornell University Press, 2010), 217.

30. See Lury, *Prosthetic Culture*.

31. Quoted in Gilman, *Freud, Race, and Gender*, 13.

32. Quoted in Gilman, *Freud, Race, and Gender*, 16–17.

33. Quoted in Gilman, *Freud, Race, and Gender*, 16.

34. Marc de Wilde, "Meeting Opposites: The Political Theologies of Walter Benjamin and Carl Schmitt," *Philosophy and Rhetoric* 44, no. 4 (2011): 363–381.

35. See Carl Schmitt, *The Concept of the Political* (1932), trans. George Schwab (Chicago: University of Chicago Press, 2007).

36. Schmitt, *The Concept of the Political*, 26.

37. See Gopal Balakrishnan, *The Enemy: An Intellectual Portrait of Carl Schmitt* (New York: Verso, 2000).

38. Sarah Kofman, *Camera Obscura: Of Ideology*, trans. Will Straw (London: Athlone, 1998), 28.

39. See T. H. Ogden, "The Analytic Third: Working with Intersubjective Clinical Facts," *International Journal of Psychoanalysis* 75 (February 1994): 3–19.

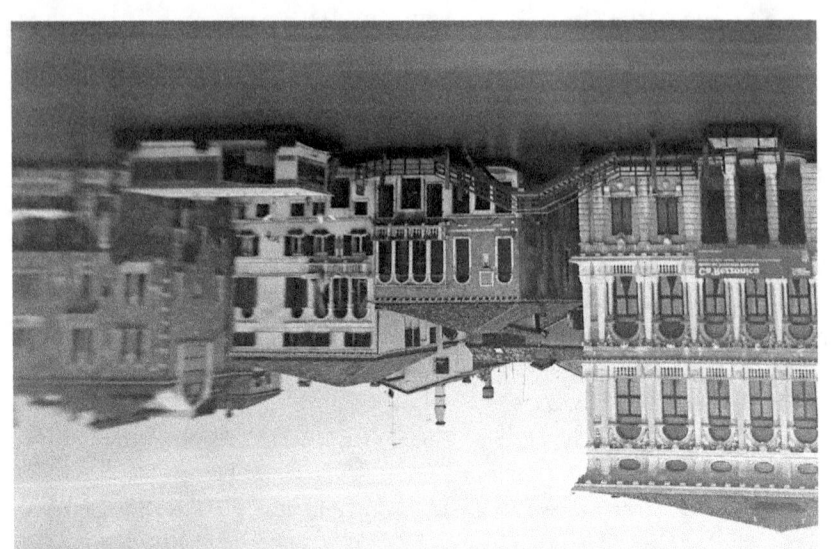

CHAPTER FIVE

THE POLITICS OF CONTEMPLATION

ZOE LEONARD AND

ELISABETH LEBOVICI

ELISABETH LEBOVICI: Here we are, talking before getting our words in written form, about the camera obscura you are installing in Venice. The camera obscura as an apparatus and an experiment has been written about extensively, but what often goes unexamined is the specific experience that each of us has in the space and time of a particular camera obscura. Can we talk, first, about this experience and about what it means?

ZOE LEONARD: Maybe we can start by talking about what a camera obscura is. The term *camera obscura* really describes a natural phenomenon: the principle that in a dark room, a small hole will let in light rays that will project an image of the outside world onto the opposite wall. Since light rays move in a straight line, the image comes in upside down and reversed (see plates 1–6).

There are written records of the observations of this phenomenon that date as far back as 400 BCE. Throughout history various tools have been built to utilize it in different ways; the camera obscura was employed by scientists to understand the physical laws of light. During the Renaissance, the camera obscura was instrumental in the understanding of perspective, and various apparatuses have been used by draftsmen, painters, and architects.

What is interesting to me is that photography has been separated from these other sciences and arts. And yet the camera shows us a kind of shared ancestry—that these various arts and sciences are deeply connected. Perhaps there is a way to think differently about these segregated practices—that there is a common ground, a desire to know and to understand the world around us and our place in it.

I think it's an interesting time to pick up this tool again. The field of photography is at a turning point, changing so rapidly, and we live in an incredibly image-saturated culture. My curiosity about the camera obscura involves asking questions about how we see, how we look, and what we take for granted about sight. The camera obscura offers us a way of seeing that does not have to result in a fixed image—such as a photograph or a film.

My iteration of the camera obscura offers photographic seeing as a spatial, temporal experience, a space that can be entered and inhabited. The inverted landscape inside the camera obscura is not a photograph; it is not an object. Rather, you are inside the camera and it becomes a space for observation and contemplation.

EL: I think the series of camerae obscurae that you have built—so far you have made three of these installations: the first in the Galerie Gisela Capitain in Cologne, the second in the Camden Arts Centre in London, and now, one in the Palazzo Grassi in Venice—represents a shift in your body of work, which spans thirty years. Could you describe, with a few shortcuts, what led you to these projects and to this form?

ZL: I began taking photographs when I was quite young. Right from the start I kept trying to find the limits of the medium. Back then, there were lots of different kinds of film, and I worked my way through as many as I could find: black and white, color, slide and print, infrared and ortho. I also tried to find the full range of my camera's capability. I tried shooting at every speed, pushing and pulling the film, playing with contrast and grain. When I learned to print, I experimented with various developers and papers. I often used outdated paper that was given to me or could be bought cheaply. I just wanted to see everything photography could do.

The subject was always part of it—I was aiming my camera at something, or someone—but the material was equally important. I was interested in the physical constitution of the photograph: what the print looked like, its size and tone, if it was dark or light, warm or cool, murky or crisp.

A few years into these experiments, I realized that most of this work was incredibly bad! I realized I needed to start all over again, to teach myself to make a decent picture. So I started in what I thought would be the simplest way, the most stripped-down elements: black and white, still life.

This led me down what turned out to be a long path, an extended exploration of different modes of representation, the different kinds of jobs a photograph can do. It can be a document, or a record; it can be used to transmit information, or employed as evidence, or proof. It can be a snapshot, intimately connected to memory and emotion. It can be a kind of blueprint of the world, or it can be completely abstract. Photographs can be used for both ordering and disordering the world.

I became interested in mapping and archiving. I liked the deadpan appearance of photographs used in science and cartography. I looked at war photographs, especially aerial reconnaissance photographs. I started experimenting with different kinds of situations, taking photographs from planes, in museums and libraries, of maps and books and displays. I was interested in the image as information, and equally in how that information was unreliable or subjective. Various ideas of classification and systems of interpretation created different versions of reality. This was much more interesting to me than the notion of a fine-art photograph.

I found myself questioning what constitutes knowledge: why things are ordered a certain way, what is accepted as fact, or truth, and how that categorization is connected to power, and to our lives. Photography seemed to be a kind of linchpin in this structuring.

Around the same time, I started playing with serial images, finding that sometimes it took multiple images to convey complexity. When I look back, I remember my own frustration: the great photographers seemed to be able to take a great picture—one image that says it all. You know, that's the myth with photography, right? The perfect moment, the decisive moment. But, usually, I couldn't take one perfect picture. I couldn't find the decisive moment, the ideal angle. I always seemed to miss it. My work often felt provisional, or even inadequate. I was frustrated with my pictures that seemed to be just to the side of the real action. My frame was somehow outside the frame. Now I realize that this is my work; that for me, the world, or my view of the world, is made of component parts, shattering and repeating, overlapping and simultaneous.

Around this period of time a lot of my friends and acquaintances—my community—began to get sick with AIDS. A couple of close friends got sick and a few people I knew died. I joined Act Up. I became politicized. In those urgent circumstances I started thinking about the political implications of how we organize our looking, how we gather and organize information in the world, and how we organize the way we make a picture of the world. Defining beauty or truth is never an absolute set of terms; there is a politics to it.

Those times were extreme. I became very aware of the very real cost of homophobia and sexism, and classism, and racism. I saw that the way we were defined and categorized translated into how we were valued. That valuation in turn determined if we would be cared for, if we would be recognized, if we would live or die. I got involved in direct action activism and also worked with two artist-activist collectives (GANG and fierce pussy). But my own art practice remained more idiosyncratic, and I struggled to find ways to talk about the institutionalized cruelty and prejudice I was encountering. I wanted to express this situation and to find my own voice within it. I began to photograph in medical museums, in history and science museums, in libraries and fashion shows, trying to look at the ways beauty was constructed, and also looking at how sexism and bias are built into the institutional framework of our society. I began to understand beauty as a construction, a set of rules and regulations. I became interested in how the frame of my camera could carry the attitude of my gaze. Calling these systems of order into question could be a way of upturning them or destabilizing them. I wanted to reframe the world so that we could consider alternative possibilities.

As I worked with different subjects, I began to think more about the place from which the picture is taken: my vantage point. Perhaps I could say this became the ground of my work. Rather than any one subject or genre (landscape, portrait, still life, etc.), I was, and remain, interested in engaging a simultaneous questioning of both subject and vantage point, the relation between viewer and world—in short, subjectivity and how it informs our experience of the world.

A few years ago I had a survey show, and in every conversation or interview around the exhibition, I was asked if I was still shooting analogue or if I had switched to digital. This persistent question seemed to come with a set of judgments. The implication seemed to be that analogue photography is beautiful, but nostalgic and old-fashioned, and conversely, that digital is not as pretty, but is faster and more contemporary. It felt as if I was being asked to say that one is better than the other—or rather, there seemed to be an expectation that I would defend analogue photography. The argument about which is better didn't make any sense to me. I find this binary confining and not very interesting. I'm still shooting analogue, but I think artists should choose whichever medium works best for them. Digital and analogue do different things; they have different qualities and different strengths. There's a larger question here about choosing to work with photography at all—a medium that is reliant on industrial production—but we can go into that later.

About a year after my survey show, I began teaching for the first time. The conversation around photography seemed to be framed in two binary oppositions: analogue versus digital and subject versus material. I found myself struggling to find a way to have a more expansive conversation about photography. I found myself asking the students: What is photography? Is it a print? An object? Is it a JPEG on your screen? Or does it only count if it's a TIFF? Or if you print it out? Is it a picture on your phone? Is it a projection? Is it a picture you see in your mind before you click the shutter? Is it that great image you missed? In short, is photography a thing, or a picture, or is it a way of seeing?

At the end of that first summer of teaching, this question followed me home. My first morning back home, I woke up thinking, "I want to make a camera obscura. Begin at the beginning, and see what happens from there."

EL: Psychoanalytic theory, such as the work of Jacques Lacan, uses the camera obscura as a model for the subject, or for the relations between the outside and the inside of the body — it is only through a pinhole that the world outside is represented and translated into images, which will, in turn, determine the psychic life of an inside surface — a place to stock "all that could be diversely called affects, instincts or drives."

ZL: The way that I approach these installations — making the entire space into a camera — creates a particular experience. You can walk around, sit down, lie on the floor; the image falls on all the surfaces of the room, so you are surrounded by the image. It's a spatial experience.

The camera obscura makes the mechanics of sight visible. It is a simplifed version, but what we see in the camera is like what happens inside our head: our eyes receive an image; light rays enter through the pupil; and the image lands on our retina, inverted and reversed. Then the brain, in turn, processes that image, and turns it right side up. There are a series of translations that allow us to comprehend the images we receive.

Inside the installation, you are experiencing images as they would be before they have been corrected: sight before comprehension. In this way, I think the space of the camera obscura is related to the space of the unconscious, to what happens inside the box of the head. Occupying this space allows us to engage with our own process of seeing, to actually track our process of seeing. We experience light, movement, color, contrast, and shape, and slowly we resolve these elements into a picture. In the camera, we can be present and conscious and observe ourselves as we go through this process.

Because the space is darkened, there is a certain mood, a kind of quiet. The room feels slowed down. The image is inverted; at first it is disorienting. And this allows for us to consider what it is we are seeing. Maybe it opens up space inside a process we take for granted.

These installations are also social spaces. You occupy this space with other people, and so this experience of looking and understanding is shared. You watch each other. And as the image moves and changes, it becomes a temporal experience. There is no beginning or end; you can stay as long as you want.

EL: This also connects with Jonathan Crary's theories of the observer, in *Techniques of the Observer: On Vision and Modernity in the Nineteenth Century,* that extract the camera obscura from the evolutionary logic leading to photography. Opposite many art practices — such as video — which produce a material record, even if they document an object or event that is already gone, this experience of the camera obscura produces the sense of a journey looking at things passing by.

ZL: The image in the camera obscura is not fixed. It is photographic seeing unhinged from the print, or even from the notion of a picture as a stable thing. Nothing is recorded; there is no way to repeat it or play it back, and no two people who visit the exhibition see the same artwork. The image changes constantly every minute and every day: a cloud goes by and the light shifts. You become sensitized to every small fluctuation.

A traditional camera obscura — an apparatus for drawing or one made in the nineteenth century as a tourist attraction — is designed for making pictures. There are a number of these tourist attractions still extant. Usually they are housed in small rooms, where the image is directed onto a small white table, which provides a kind of frame. A mirror is often used to flip the image right side up, so it is presented as a conventional picture.

In my installations, nothing is gathered into a coherent picture for the viewer. The image falls on the floor, on the wall, on the ceiling. The image is sharply in focus in some parts of the room and out of focus in others. In places it is distended and blown out. It is nonhierarchical: there is no privileged vantage point; no part of the image is more important than any other. This work questions the ways we gather images into a picture, or a fact, or a truth. The whole idea of a decisive moment dissolves here. Light comes in, hits the floor, and unpredictable things happen. It is fugitive and unstable, constantly unfolding. It relies on your body adapting to it: as your eyes adjust, you see more. A room that appeared completely dark at first is filled with an image.

For someone like me, who has made objects all their life, it feels liberating not to make an object, not to hang a thing on the wall. I come up with a set of conditions, and the work unfolds with its own logic.

In these installations there is another principle that is very important to me, which is that the room remains visible. I don't build out the space or conceal any of the existing architecture. I want viewers to be aware of where they are. The work becomes a kind of double exposure: an image of the outside world superimposed on an existing room.

EL: Art historian Nataša Petrešin Bachelez commented on this sort of exploration, which recalled for her the Light and Space movement associated with Robert Irwin, James Turrell, Maria Nordman, and Eric Orr, which was similarly concerned with the phenomenological experience of the moment of looking.

ZL: I love a lot of that work. Irwin especially has been inspiring for me. And I admire Orr and Turrell. But I think there is a real difference here in my approach. I don't think I can say that my explorations are about pure perception of color, light, and space. For me, this work is about locating oneself in the world, about social space and a consciousness of subjectivity and relationships to others, about histories of looking and picturing. There is an experiential component, which is great, but I think for me it is also tied to politics. Understanding that we inhabit this room together, yet differently — this is phenomenal to me. The idea of a space in which we can think about how we see and how we look — this is a profoundly political thing to do together.

EL: Could this site-specific installation be considered in relation to practices of institutional critique, which often reflect critically on their own place within art institutions? Many of these projects — by artists such as Hans Haacke, Michael Asher, or Andrea Fraser — have tried to "out" the institutions where they are embedded; they have sought to grasp the politics or structure of an institution by turning it inside out and making it visible. A camera obscura, on the other hand, pushes the outside world inside the gallery walls, queering it perhaps.

ZL: I love that question. What an idea, that a camera obscura can be an institutional critique!

I think of this work as a series. Each camera is a site-specific work, titled with the address of its location. But, as I make them, I also think about each site in relation to the others.

I was thrilled at the chance to make a camera obscura in Venice with a view onto the Grand Canal. This view is so layered. When I consider a site, I'm not really interested in pretty views. I'm more interested in views that are dirty or complex, contradictory views, views with layers of meaning. At the Camden Arts Centre in London, for instance, the space is a former library; it's a beautiful space and you could still see the architecture. I loved how the exterior and the interior overlapped. Across the street there was a construction site, and this construction site, the traffic outside, the vanishing point, the way the horizon meets the architecture, the way the sun coming through the lens hit the floor — all this was important.

There is a specific relationship to the camera obscura in Venice: it was a tool for many of the Vedutisti, and Canaletto is one of many artists known to have used camerae obscurae for rendering the city's architecture. But for me, this is only the beginning. The history of picturing here in Venice is also a nexus for thinking about the relationships between beauty, power, and art making, about the role of the picture in our society.

Venice is a mercantile city, a port, a place of exchange. Still a place of great wealth, it was a seat of economic power for several hundred years. It is a very beautiful city, considered one of the most romantic in the world, but simultaneously it is associated with death and decay. It is a city that is literally underwater.

One can't help but think of the great works of art which have used this city as material: from Shakespeare's *The Merchant of Venice* to Thomas Mann's *Death in Venice*, to Nicholas Roeg's *Don't Look Now*, and Jeanette Winterson's *The Passion*. For me the installation in Venice is a way to engage with this incredibly rich and complex history of drawing, painting, architecture, and film, as well as a long and complicated history of art patronage.

Palazzo Grassi, where I installed the camera, is an eighteenth-century palace directly overlooking the Grand Canal and facing the Ca' Rezzonico. The obvious wealth of the building is part of the installation — the image coming through the lens falls on the walls and floor, and onto the incredibly ornate carved and gilded ceiling. The histories of the palace — including its current incarnation as a space for a private collection of contemporary art — are all present. The space merges with the incoming images, each affecting the readability and the meaning of the other. I am interested in what this simple gesture can do. By placing a lens in the window of the Palazzo, I am asking us to look at both the interior and the exterior of the site.

While it is layered with historical references, it is a work that happens in the present, in the now. The boat traffic that goes by speaks to the quotidian: vaporetto and gondola, tourist boats and police boats, fireboats, work boats carrying equipment, cranes and machinery, boats for garbage collection. The water is an extraordinary color, both gorgeous and toxic.

EL: In the camera obscura, you have fluid, volatile, and simultaneous time. It isn't about duration. It's a "continuous project altered" all the time. Ian White says something which is beautiful about this continuous alteration in the camera obscura: that it is a space of tension at the intersection of accident and withdrawal.

ZL: You made a great point during our earlier conversation, that what happens in the camera obscura is not actually duration. Duration is what happens in cinema; it is a period of time that has been preset by the director: a film has a beginning, a middle, and an end, and you go through it. These installations do something else. They are constantly unfolding in a continuous present.

I appreciate John Cage's notion of chance as well as his idea of a continuous present. Photography is usually understood as a medium inextricably linked to the past — to memory, to history. But inside the camera, we are only in the now.

The viewer has a kind of democratic relation to the work: you come and go; you stay as long as you like. The piece is happening constantly, 24/7, for as long as it is installed. It is not a projection with a beginning, middle, and end. Nor is it a loop that repeats. Inside the camera obscura the piece is happening all the time and it is never the same. The only real duration is the length of the exhibition: when the show is over, I remove the lens, and the work is gone. In this way, the work is related to performance; it is ephemeral; there is no object to take away or preserve. It is an experience.

The aspect we haven't talked about yet is sound: in the installation, you hear what is happening outside. It becomes a soundtrack. The longer you stay in the space, the more you become conscious of the sound: the sounds of a small city in Cologne, the sound of a busy high street in London.

The work has a representational aspect, but at the same time it is abstract. I think sound is part of this. Obviously, the sound is in sync with the image, but at times it seems to be slightly delayed. There is a slow and quiet feeling in the camera that allows your listening and looking to be fully engaged. You know what you're looking at, but at the same time things feel a bit unfamiliar. The expectations of what things should look like are shifted and, at times, the light on the walls and ceiling forms abstract shapes and patterns. The sound provides a link to the outside world, a reminder that the image is of the street just downstairs, and somehow for me this presents a kind of interesting suspension: that reality can be understood as a simultaneous and parallel experience of both narrative representation and abstract sound and image.

As a viewer, I find that spending time in the camera allows me to move past the subject of the picture and into a deeper consideration of how an image is formed, or how I understand the image — what constitutes reality, or subjective experience.

I hope to create an extended state of observation.

EL: I perceive a twist in this work, which relates to the notion of authorship. By not signing the view or the image, but letting it happen and be altered continuously, you are conversing with a contemporary point of view, which relinquishes mastery or authorship, for instance of one's own image, one's own signature. I would call it a feminist point of view. What do you think of this argument?

ZL: When I print my photographs, I always leave the black frame from the film around the image. This can be the beginning of a conversation: "This is the way I see it. How do you see it?"

In the camera the image is framed, but what happens inside the frame is not fixed. It's a chance operation. The immersive quality of the work heightens your sense of your own presence, as a physical, social, political viewer. And you are not only a viewer, but also part of the subject, visible to others.

The experiential component is tied to a politics of viewership and subjectivity. I wouldn't say that the image itself is a feminist image, yet these questions of how we look are profoundly feminist questions. For me feminism is not only about content, but also about form.

EL: Can you describe this feminist questioning of form and your conversations around it?

ZL: I think a lot about Gertrude Stein's writing. She has characters. There is a story, but she never quite lets you get to the story. Or rather, she never lets you lose yourself in the story; she keeps you in the space of your own reading. You are aware of her writing and of the process of your reading — the words, their sound, their shape, the structure of the sentences, the repetition. So the story is there, but it's not the only thing.

Virginia Woolf also does something remarkable in her work in regard to subjectivity. Her work acknowledges subjective space. She fully describes the interior of a character's mind — what they are thinking, feeling, their internal dialogue, the reality of their consciousness — and at the same time, her characters move through the world; they interact. She doesn't give up the exterior world, the narrative, the social situation that's outside. She keeps us present in that moment of interaction — where your whole subjective interior meets and interacts with the outside world.

This is what I'm interested in, the way we live an interior and an exterior life, simultaneously and continuously.

CHAPTER SIX

FREUD, SATURN, AND THE POWER OF HYPNOSIS

MARY BERGSTEIN

The Twin Phenomena of Hypnosis and Hysteria

Psychosexual development and adult libido were among the major themes of Sigmund Freud's work. Therefore, it is pertinent to interrogate the erotic imagination of Freud's time and place in visual culture. Freud's notion that we dream in visual images, and that these images are never really forgotten, is an important assumption for the visual history of modernism and modernity.[1] In what we might call the photochemistry of psychoanalysis, then, images as agents of memory would never simply expire or disappear, even if they were consciously suppressed or repressed by a dynamic unconscious. Fugitive as such fragmented images may be, they could reconfigure and surface in manifest or latent content of memories (including screen memories), reveries, unconscious phantasies, and dreams.[2] As Freud maintained, and subsequent theorists have emphasized, the unconscious realm is a fertile storage place for representations of various kinds. When retrieved or reconfigured by way of psychoanalysis, previously unconscious visual content engenders deep feeling.

As light impressions, photographs and cinema closely mimic, at least in a metaphoric sense, the mental phenomena of memories and dreams. Because the carpentry (facture) of photography and film are more or less invisible (compared to painting and sculpture, for example) and both are considered truthful, if eerily deadpan, mediums of documentation, their content can operate in the minds of beholders without conscious critique, like unconscious or preconscious material.[3] In *Mirrors of Memory: Freud, Photography, and the History of Art* (2010), I explored the way photographs and films resemble dream images. Freud's *Interpretation of Dreams* (1900), for instance, uses abundant photographic and optical metaphors: microscopes, telescopes, photographic cameras, the refraction of light through lenses, and the latent and manifest states of photographic images (negatives and positives) to explain dream representations.[4] In Freud's first "Rome dream," a view of Ponte Sant'Angelo is observed from the framed window of a moving train. A concatenation of such views observed from a train slipping slowly out of the station unfolds as if it were cinema. Photos and films around the turn of the twentieth century were understood as kinds of living excerpts taken from the flow of reality, apart from (and yet uncannily self-similar to) the continuum of time and space, and therefore subject to infinite extendability and dynamism. The sensation of detachment experienced in looking at photographs and films, whether alone or in a social group, mirrors the Freudian concept of spectatorship within a dream.[5] Cinema has long been associated with Freud's notions of unconscious memory, vision, and desire. Laura Mulvey, in her famous essay "Visual Pleasure and Narrative Cinema" (1975), pointed to Sigmund Freud's *Three Essays on the Theory of Sexuality* (1905) and his later *Instincts and Their Vicissitudes* (1915), where *Schaulust* (scopophilia), or looking at an objectified other, plays a central role in the dynamics of eros.[6] In 2002, Luigi Malerba argued that every culture has its own style of dreamscape, and defined the mise-en-scène of twentieth-century dreams as cinematic—a kind of metaphysical limbo that is fluid and without horizon, a space of great mobility and subjectivity.[7]

The phenomenon of hypnosis, which had its origins in medical practice and theatrical spectacle, found a sympathetic agent in early film. A hypnoid state was an induced trance, which, like Freudian dream analysis, created a passageway in and out of the unconscious mind. Hypnosis rendered individual subjects unconscious and insensate, and was used in the treatment of hysterical women throughout Europe, where subjects were duly photographed and filmed. Cinema itself, of course, is a hypnotic medium; at the same time film, together with photography, was an effective means of representing hypnosis at the beginning of (and indeed throughout) the twentieth century. The themes that I have mentioned—hypnosis, cinema, photography, psychoanalysis, and dreams—overlay, intersect, and thicken one another in the following essay about the optical unconscious in Freud's Vienna.

In an attempt to call upon the erotic culture of Freud's environment, I consider the work of filmmaker Johann Schwarzer (1880–1914), physiologist Josef Breuer (1842–1925), and hysterical patient and social reformer Bertha Pappenheim (aka Anna O., 1859–1936). We shall see that the interrelated phenomena of hysteria and hypnosis produced an erotic (at times even violent) phantasy about the doctor-patient relationship. This, and related themes, including voyeurism, medical examination, and surgery, produced phantasms (imaginary productions or their cinematic corollaries) that operated in the visual territory of Freud's time and place.

Let us begin in Paris. The Gouffé affair (l'affaire Gouffé) was a sensational story of a young woman (Gabrielle Bompard) who committed murder while supposedly in a hypnotic trance induced by her devious lover, Michel Eyraud. Bompard claimed that it was under hypnotic suggestion that she lured the wealthy victim, Toussaint-Augustin Gouffé, to her home and seduced him, placing the sash from her peignoir around his neck, so that her hypnotist-accomplice could, by the mere tug on a hidden cord, strangle him. Bompard's defense was that because she suffered from fits of fainting and hysterical crises, she was especially vulnerable to suggestion and had virtually no power over her actions when in a hypnoid (and therefore unconscious) state.

This complicated, gruesome news story, with its forensic and psychological twists and turns, brought forth an effluvium of images, texts, and arguments as to whether a person under hypnosis was responsible for his or her actions. Tried in 1889, the case loomed large at the turn of the twentieth century among medical doctors and the general public. Ernest Clair-Guyot's illustrations of various episodes of the Gouffé affair (fig. 6.1) were published, for example, in *Le Petit Parisien* of June 15, 1890.[8]

The Gouffé case was representative of an expanded set of phantasies that prevailed in Freud's Vienna and throughout Europe. Such phantasies, rich with the thrilling possibilities of mind reading, telepathy, criminality, and the uncanny, took visual form in live performance, photography, cinema, and the human imagination. All of these salient forms of visual culture were to some extent saturated with the interlocking phenomena of hysteria and hypnotism around 1900.

Hypnosis was always a sex- and gender-laden practice. The idea of criminal hypnosis, including the seduction of women and fascination by women, was a matter of great debate in the medical communities of Paris and Vienna around the turn of the twentieth century. In Europe physicians and psychiatrists diagnosed certain hysterical women as seductive "coquettes," and receptivity to suggestion was likewise emphasized as a constitutive aspect of hysteria.[9] One fear was that hysterical women could be hypnotized easily and then raped when in a hypnoid state, but the inverse situation, that men could be entranced by seductive, manipulative women, was also at issue.[10]

Scientific culture had long acknowledged the criminal-erotic dangers of the hypnotism of hysterical subjects. Medical doctors routinely hypnotized

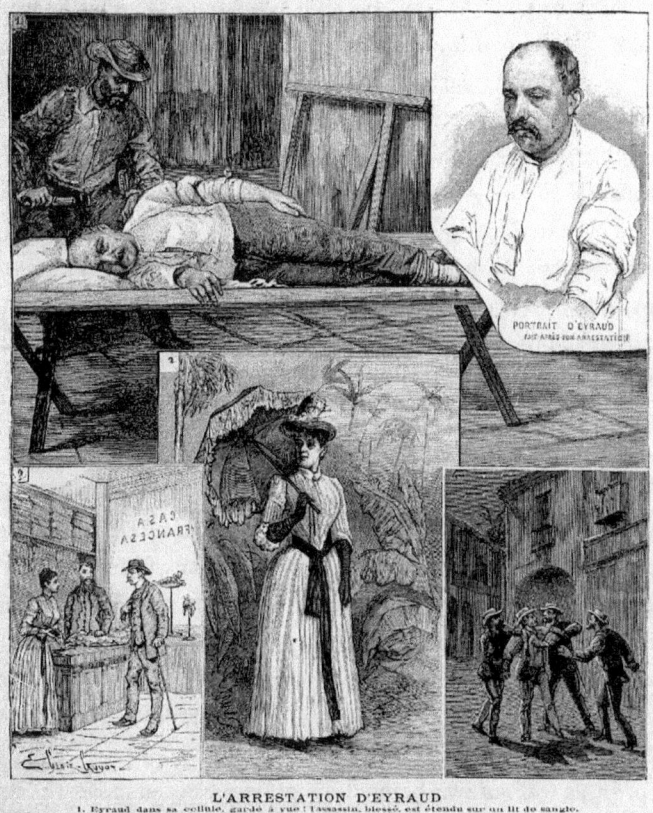

FIGURE 6.1 Ernest Clair-Guyot, *L'arrestation d'Eyraud*. Engraving.
Supplément littéraire illustré du Petit Parisien, June 15, 1890. Wikimedia
Commons, "File:PP 15-06-1890 Malle sanglante Arrestation d'Eymard.jpg,"
http://commons.wikimedia.org/wiki/File:PP_15-06-1890_Malle
_sanglante_Arrestation_d%27Eymard.jpg#/media/File:PP_15061890
_Malle_sanglante_Arrestation_d%27Eymard.jpg.

psychiatric patients, particularly women. Among the most prominent hypnotists were Freud's teachers, such as Hippolyte Bernheim (1840–1919), Georges Gilles de la Tourette (1857–1904), and Jean-Martin Charcot (1825–1893). Charcot's photographic team at the Salpêtrière Hospital, headed by Albert Londe (1858–1917), photographed hysterical women rendered unconscious by hypnosis in the 1880s, around the time of Freud's residency there (1885–1886). Men at the Salpêtrière hypnotized more or less abject young women, as we see in a number of arresting visual representations, and these images were published abundantly in the *Iconographie photographique de la Salpêtrière* of 1878 and the bimonthly journal, *Nouvelle Iconographie de la Salpêtrière*, which was published from 1888 to 1918. As performative as those hysterical episodes may have been—and even in their own time the hysterics at the Salpêtrière were considered actresses on par with Sarah Bernhardt—their now-famous representation in photography was dressed up as scientific documentation.[11] In 1982 Georges Didi-Huberman opened the eyes of late twentieth-century historians of visual culture with his important study, *The Invention of Hysteria*, about the Salpêtrière photographs and the context of their making, bringing medical and psychiatric photography to the forefront of feminist and visual studies.[12] Various photographs by Paul Regnard (1850–1927) and the neurologist-psychiatrist Désiré-Magloire Bourneville (1840–1909) were made familiar by Didi-Huberman (fig 6.2). The Salpêtrière photographs speak to us not only from the point of view of observant physician-photographers, but also from the minds and bodies of the represented subjects, who are photographed in (at least ostensibly) absent, unconscious states. Freud owned the *Iconographie photographique* and issues of the *Nouvelle Iconographie*, which are currently conserved in the August C. Long Health Sciences Library at Columbia University.

Apropos this well-known body of images, we are reminded of Freud's review of August Forel's *Hypnotism* of 1889, and his own writings on the subject from 1891 and 1893.[13] In those years, Freud himself invited a gendered reading of the technique. He stated that hypnosis worked best when conducted tête-à-tête, in a darkened room, with the subject's clothing loosened. And he stressed that women were more easily hypnotized by light and ocular fixation than men.[14] Freud theorized and practiced hypnosis to a limited extent. But he always warned against its potential abuses. One historical problem for Freud was the eighteenth-century Viennese physician Franz Anton Mesmer (1734–1815), who with his theory of animal magnetism was received by Viennese society as a would-be magician and miraculous healer. Even Wolfgang Amadeus Mozart spoofed Mesmer's techniques in the character of Despina in the final

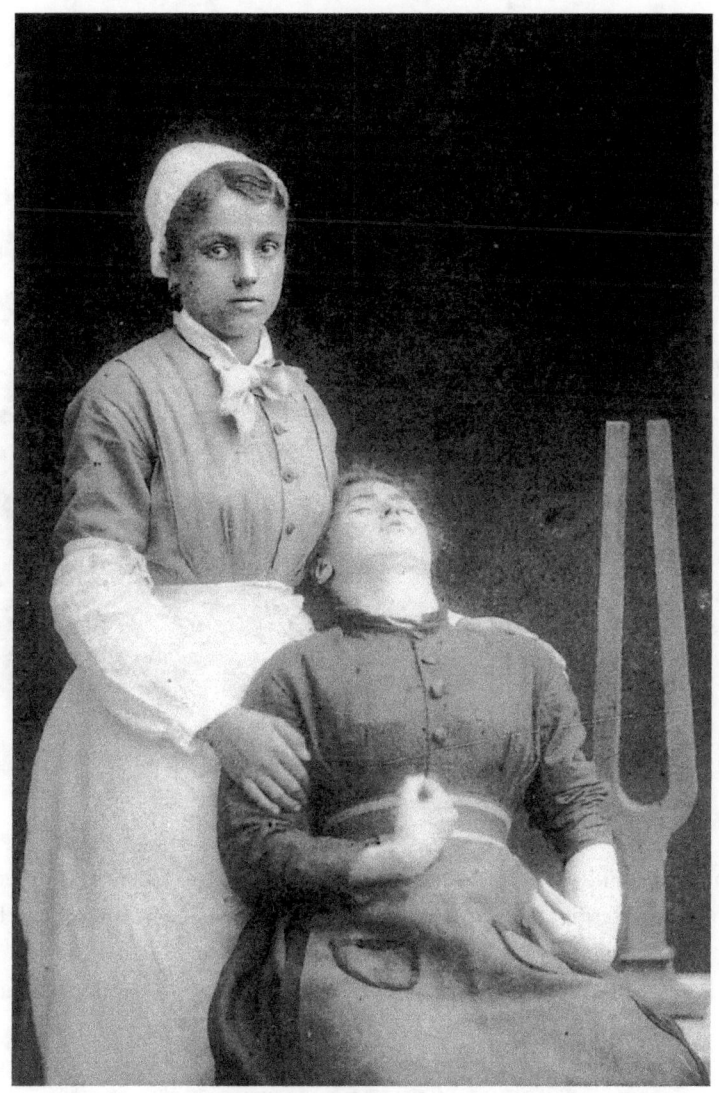

FIGURE 6.2 Désiré-Magloire Bourneville and Paul Regnard,
L'Iconographie photographique de la Salpêtrière, vol. 1, plate 21, *Lethargie:
Artificial Contracture in a Hypnotic State*. Courtesy Archives and Special
Collections, Columbia University Health Sciences Library, New York.

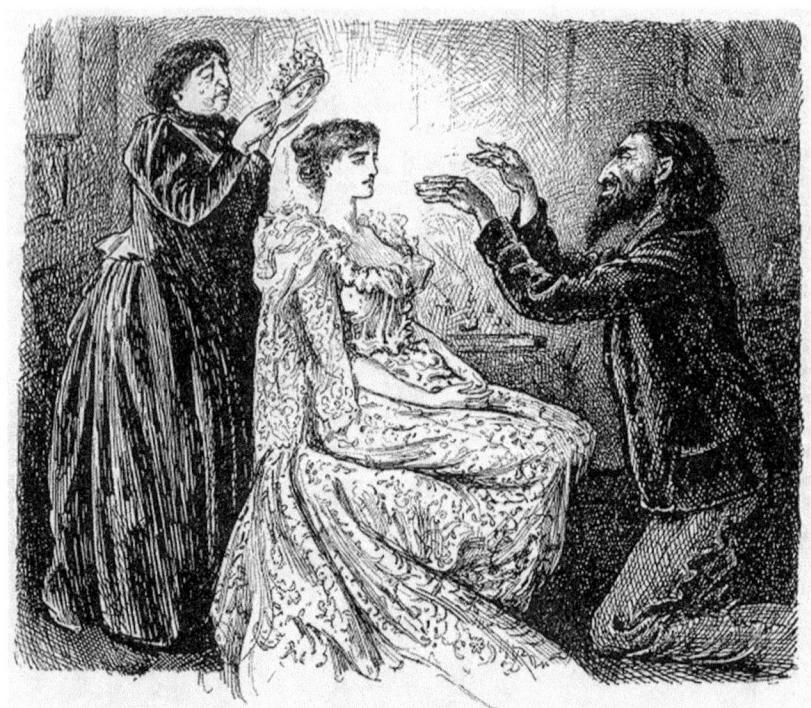

FIGURE 6.3   George du Maurier, *Svengali Hypnotizing the Innocent Trilby*. Engraving
for the first edition of *Trilby*, 1894. Image in the public domain.

act of *Così fan tutte*, where, disguised as a man, she revives sick people by way of
magnetism. Mesmer's dubious activities and association with illusionism left a
long trajectory of doubt about the validity of hypnotism in Vienna. Freud must
also have been cautioned by images of the fictional Jewish hypnotist Svengali
from the popular novel *Trilby* (1894) by George du Maurier (fig. 6.3), which
was also the subject of silent films made in Vienna by Jacob Fleck, *Trilby* (1912)
and *Svengali* (1914) under the label of Wiener Kunstfilmen, as well as several
other early *Trilby* films throughout Europe and America. But most importantly,
the philosophical concept of illusionism, as opposed to free will, troubled the
accepted precepts of religion, science, and ethics as they were practiced in
nineteenth-century Austria.[15] In any case, Freud rejected the technique of hypnosis in his own psychoanalytic practice in favor of inducing a relaxed state of
consciousness in the patient. This relaxation of consciousness was eventually
used for Freud's process of free association, in which recumbent patients spoke
about whatever came to mind without losing the dignity of their volition.[16]

Representation of Hypnosis in Popular and Medical Culture

The interlocking phenomena of hysteria and hypnosis were both spectacles verging on the supernatural that produced a voyeuristic frisson in their spectators. In *Medical Muses* (2011), Asti Hustvedt explored the way in which the hypnotized hysteric was represented in carnival acts, where nonmedical stage hypnotists reproduced Charcot's demonstrations at the Salpêtrière on the fairgrounds of Europe, for the delectation of the thrill-seeking public.[17] These presentations belonged to the tradition of stage magic acts and illusionism, but this time the hysterical subjects (who were highly suggestible and prone to surrendering their own agency) had a morbid attraction all their own.

Cinema was itself an illusory, hypnotic medium, and thus particularly well suited to the production of hypnotic illusions. Early silent cinema, which was shaped around a special repertoire of themes, thrived post-Gouffé on the drama of hypnosis and its thrilling dangers. Beginning with Georges Méliès in Paris, silent films were permeated with representations of hypnosis, and hypnosis was a vehicle for hysteria and predatory sex in these early moving pictures. It is significant that Méliès began his career as a magician or illusionist, and was therefore familiar with the public's fascination with sensational stage hypnosis. As early as 1897, he produced *Le Magnétiseur* (*The Hypnotist*).[18] At the same time, films of hypnosis were closely associated with medical cinema at the turn of the twentieth century. In one of Auguste and Louis Lumière's earliest films, *A Scene of Hypnotism*, the movements of a female subject under hypnosis bring to mind the photographs of hysterical women under hypnosis at the Salpêtrière.

Romanian neurologist Gheorghe Marinescu (1863–1938) made among the earliest of scientific films (1898–1901) about the difficulty of walking due to organic and hysterical hemiplegia. At the end of one of the films, men who had been hardly able to walk are seen in a posthypnotic state, skipping along like so many innocent children at liberty to play. The naive lyricism of the passage seems to anticipate Henri ("Le Douanier") Rousseau's hilarious *Football Players* of 1908 (New York, Guggenheim Museum). Marinescu was trained by Jean-Martin Charcot in Paris and had a sustained interest in the chronophotography of Albert Londe (1858–1917) and Étienne-Jules Marey (1830–1904). Marinescu's medical films (1898–1901) have a weird, awkward spirit about them in which footage of moving actors (patients) is integrated with documentary drawings to explain the symptoms and procedures. In *A Case of Hysteric Hemiplegia Healed through Hypnosis* of 1899, Marinescu's hypnotic suggestion reaches deep into the unconscious causes of a female patient's psycho-induced paresis and eradicates the symptoms. For a twenty-first-century viewer, odd, quaint, uncanny details, such as a nurse-assistant dressed in full Romanian folk costume and the whimsical wool knitted gym suit of the patient, which looks entirely fantastic, add to the optical dreamscape of this footage.[19]

So we see that medical films were as uncanny as fiction or still photography. In Italy, for instance, a 1908 film about hysteria, *A Hysterical Crisis* (one of a whole series of films about "La Neuropatologia" by the neurologist Camillo Negro and camera operator Roberto Omegna), portrays two doctors handling and eventually subduing a highly agitated woman patient, dressed in black and wearing a black mask over half of her face, who seems to be experiencing a hystero-epileptic seizure (fig. 6.4) as though her uterus had migrated toward her throat. This film is set in what can be recognized as a ward of the Cottolengo Hospital in Turin. It was ostensibly intended as medical instruction, and the action is all about the physical domination of a woman patient by two male doctors. During the course of treatment, the patient is thrown down and pinned to a hospital bed by the physicians, her ovaries compressed by a repetitive, somewhat violent pressing and pouncing on her belly by Camillo Negro while his assistant, Giuseppe Roasenda, looks on (fig. 6.5). Finally, her body is arranged immobilized in a restful position as though she has recovered. Whether this documentary is meant to be real or to look real (a sort of fin-de-siècle docu-drama?) is not clear.[20] However, the vigorous manipulation of a woman's reproductive organs as a cure for hysteria is "proven" in this documentary footage. Whatever else *A Hysterical Crisis* may represent, it expresses the male domination of a female body in a clinical setting, bridging misogynistic phantasy with what was apparently the accepted medical status quo. Following Marinescu, Negro, and Méliès, a spate of films about hypnotism and its effects followed well into the 1920s and beyond. These cinematic productions, which are too numerous to investigate in the present essay, have become a subject of study unto themselves.[21]

In refusing to countenance a silent film about psychoanalysis by Georg Wilhelm Pabst, *Geheimnisse einer Seele* (*Secrets of a Soul*, 1926), Freud tacitly announced his resistance to the new medium.[22] He was never enthusiastic about cinema as an art. Perhaps he intuited that movies, like the American popular music he so deplored, could ignite human emotions without fueling the intellect. However, as with Freud's famous indifference to André Breton and French surrealism, the cinema seems to have been his unwitting ally whether he liked it or not, especially in the familiar formula: film = dream = unconscious phan-

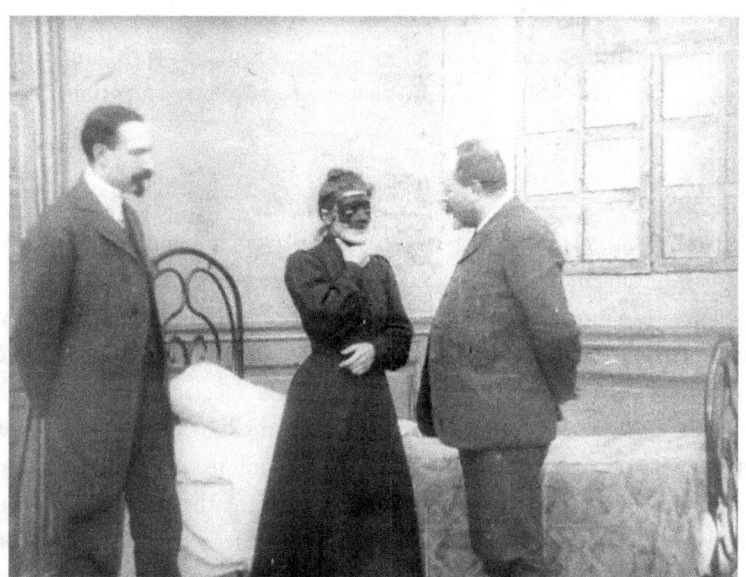

FIGURE 6.4 Camillo Negro, *A Hysterical Crisis*, still from *La Neuropatologia*, February 17, 1908, produced by Società Anonima Ambrosio, directed by Roberto Omegna. Courtesy Collection of Museo Nazionale del Cinema, Torino.

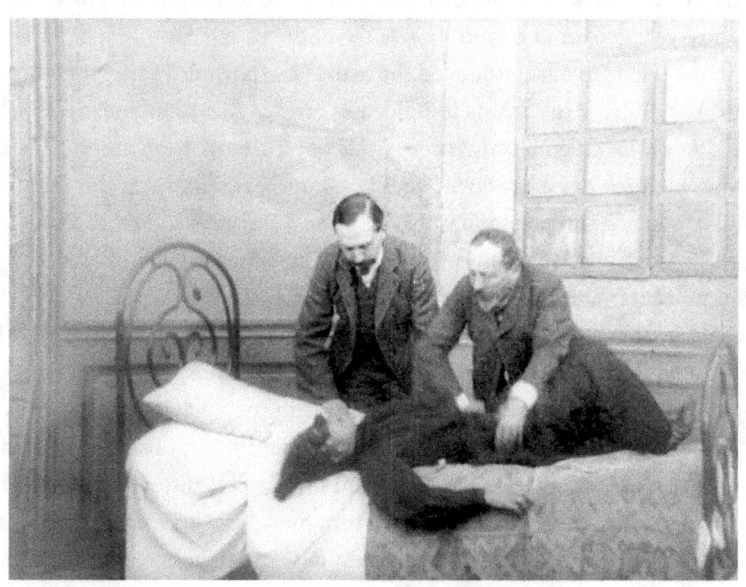

FIGURE 6.5 Camillo Negro, *A Hysterical Crisis*, still from *La Neuropatologia*, February 17, 1908, produced by Società Anonima Ambrosio, directed by Roberto Omegna. Courtesy Collection of Museo Nazionale del Cinema, Torino.

tasy. It is now taken for granted that cinema constitutes a dreamworld shared by members of the society at large, with luminous images springing from the unconscious depths of human individual and societal preoccupations.

Saturn!

The Saturn films of Johann Schwarzer, which played in Vienna and throughout the Austro-Hungarian Empire, consist of a series of erotic phantasies in which the viewer (as dreamer or audience) is protagonist. These imaginary erotic situations served as mise-en-scènes for scopic desires and their fulfillment. Schwarzer's narrative strategies, which frame the spectacle of female nudity, fulfilled a large market for erotica from 1906 to 1911. In their embodiment of obsessional visual phantasies, the Saturn films demonstrate the everyday reveries of the Viennese bourgeoisie, and as such they may be said to prove Freud's theoretical work in a low-culture production. In other words, Freud's ideas on statues come to life (Gradiva), hypnotism, transference and countertransference, and scopophilia, were hiding in plain sight in the Viennese visual culture of erotic comedy.

Johann Schwarzer (1859–1914) was from Javornik in Moravia (the same part of the world as Freud's hometown of Pribor), and he immigrated to Vienna as a twenty-year-old around 1900. The studio of the young photographer-chemist in Vienna seems to have produced the usual fare: portraits, genre scenes, local types, and nudes. Erotica was produced in printed format as well as glass lantern slides. His cinematically precocious Saturn films were among the first moving pictures to be produced in all of Europe, and among the first to be banned, officially suppressed in 1911.[23] But Schwarzer's season was in any case short; he was conscripted into the Austro-Hungarian army and killed on the Eastern Front in 1914, an early casualty of World War I.

On the surface, Saturn erotica typically stayed within the limits of a few predictable themes, and the images on screen are almost laughably manifest: women undressing to bathe, nude women dueling or playing croquet, wives betraying husbands, doctors examining patients, and statues come to life. These saucy little phantasies belong to the realm of popular culture rather than that of pornography per se. Although the Saturn films have little or no psychological depth, they resonate visually with certain themes that occurred in the early years of psychoanalysis. This overlay is not contrived; but rather, when we view them in a social cross-section, we see that certain themes were taken for granted in the society that produced them. Saturn images play in the preconscious mind just as cinema can speak to the fears or desires that haunt any particular culture. It is always pertinent to remember that visual culture (including the human imagination) and its most effortless understanding occur within the same society. In theoretical terms, however, psychoanalysis and visual culture can never mirror or explain one another. Nor should one closed system be marshaled to interpret another in a modernist plot, be it art historical or psychoanalytic. Perhaps the best approach with Saturn erotica is to let these early films and the beginnings of psychoanalysis resonate together in historical perspective.

The voyeuristic embarrassment of female flesh took on a novel dimension in the Saturn films because the medium was able to represent zaftig flesh in motion. Some of the movies are filmed outdoors, where chase scenes of nude women running away from predatory men show bouncy flesh in action as well as natural breezes animating the trees and water.[24] Notwithstanding the novelty of the film medium, a naked woman in nature, as nature, is perhaps one of the oldest ideas in the West, beginning with the biblical Eve and continued in high art by Corot, Courbet, and Manet, among others. The Saturn films adhere to essentially conservative themes, such as the romanticization of woman as nature, or, the idea that women are to nature as men are to culture.[25] For instance, a group of nude women in *Sklavenraub* (*Women Abducted as Slaves*) appear perfectly happy cavorting in the water of a pond; in spite of their fictional status as captives, they act playful and free when released into nature (fig. 6.6). The movements of water and flesh are visually absorbing, and Saturn films were truly photographs come to life, complete with jiggling, bouncy flesh, and captivating ripples of reflective water. In terms of vision, desire, and verisimilitude, Laura Mulvey's "male gaze" is at liberty to consume the buoyant scene from the detached viewpoint of the darkened theater.[26]

In a comedic manner, each Saturn phantasy was predicated on fully clothed bourgeois men looking at moving naked women. This sexual asymmetry presumed an adult male audience, and film showings were known as *Herrenabende*, or "gentlemen's evenings." Sometimes they were advertised as "black evenings" (in Trieste as *serate nere*) because men in the audience (as well as those on screen) were rigorously dressed in black formal wear. In a more poetic vein, "black evenings" may also refer to the darkness from which the collective gaze emanated, attracted to the radiant moving images before it. Saturn films were shown at traveling cinemas (*Wanderkino*), cinema booths at the Prater, or in large vaudeville theaters. An illustrated postcard advertising Leicht's Varieté at the Prater ("If you haven't visited Leicht's you haven't really seen

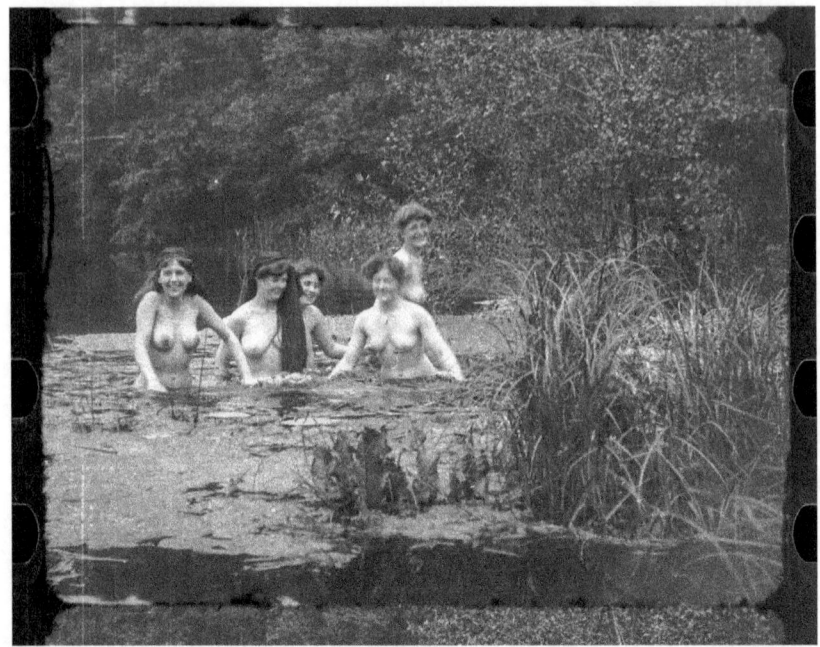

FIGURE 6.6 Johann Schwarzer, still from *Women Abducted as Slaves*, Saturn Films, Filmarchiv Austria, Vienna.

Vienna!") shows a supper-club theater crammed with crowds of people, suggesting large audiences for novelty acts and films (fig. 6.7). Saturn films were phantasies in which the imagining subject was the audience itself, doubling up, at times, with the films' protagonists. The male gaze was collective, focused, and self-referential in the reception of Saturn films. Let us keep in mind, too, that the male gaze was echoed by that of female viewers, and certain of the Saturn features were billed as *Pariserabende* (Parisian evenings) for men and women together. The conscious reactions of contemporary Austrian women to these films have not (at least not yet) surfaced in the historical record, but such films were (obviously) pertinent to their lives, as I explore in my discussion of Bertha Pappenheim.

The Power of Hypnosis

In *The Power of Hypnosis* (*Die Macht der Hypnose*), an erotic film comedy produced by the Saturn company in 1908, the act of voyeurism takes place on screen with the protagonist's gaze redoubled by that of the film spectators.

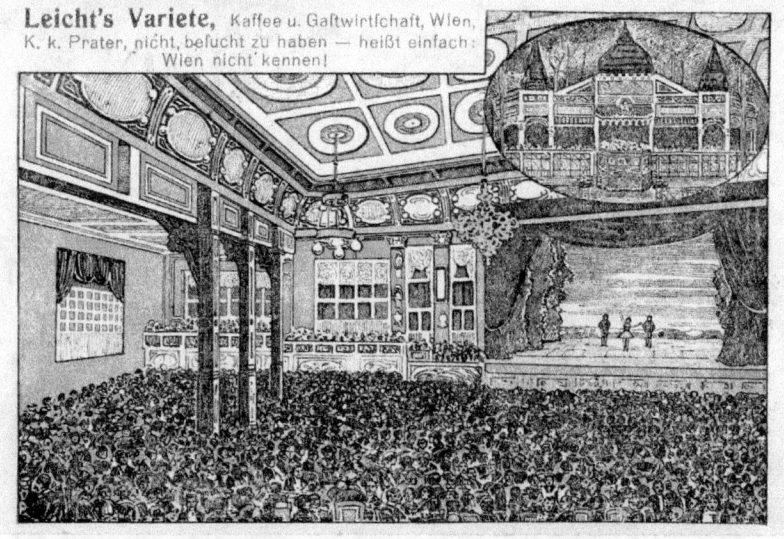

FIGURE 6.7 Anonymous, *Leicht's Varieté*. Viennese postcard, author's collection.

This film was clearly influenced by the Lumière brothers' *Scenes from a Hypnosis* and Alice Guy-Blaché's *Chez le magnétiseur* (1897). With the stilted furniture and lace curtains of a typical Biedermeier interior, Schwarzer's *Power of Hypnosis* is a good place to begin thinking about the vicissitudes of scopophilia. A middle-aged bourgeois visits a woman (presumably his mistress) in her sitting room wanting to make love to her. She proceeds to hypnotize her lover, and then undresses to a transparent black-trimmed net gown. Her attire (including the requisite shoes and stockings) is a costume of sexual display, but the gentleman-subject in question is unable to enjoy it, or even to realize his own scopic volition (fig. 6.8). Under her enchantment he has lost his agency for looking (or seeing), which has been turned over to the audience. In an inversion of the eroticized female controlled by the male hypnotist, the female character in *The Power of Hypnosis* prevails, and the gentleman's eyes are closed to his erotic object. But the erotic object is still available to the film spectator for his triumphal delectation.

This parody of voyeurism is a trick to be enjoyed, not by the male protagonist, but by the (presumably male) phantasizing audience, who laugh at a man who cannot perceive the carefully staged nudity that is in front of his own closed eyes, and in front of theirs. While he is under the influence of hypnosis, the woman plays humiliating tricks on him and steals his money. A young but-

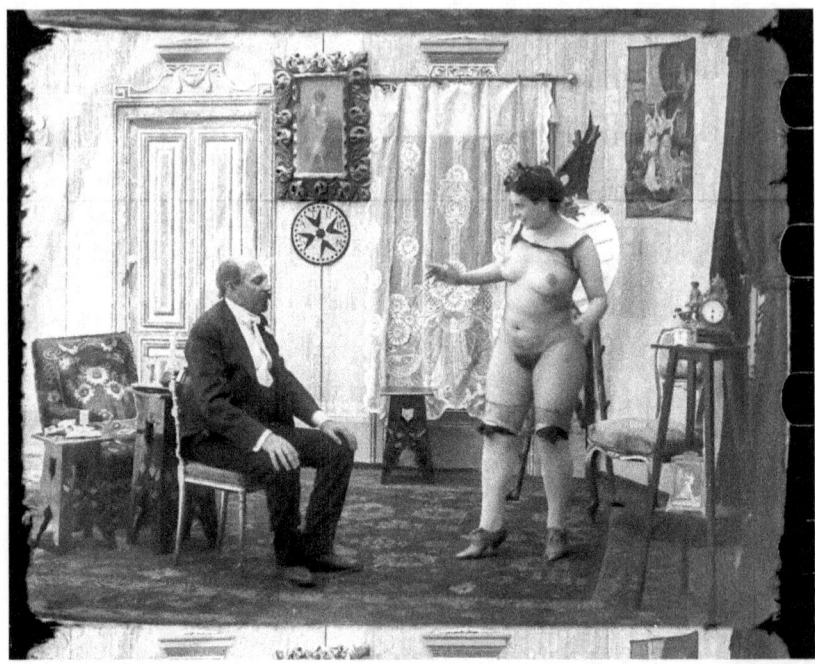

FIGURE 6.8 Johann Schwarzer, *The Power of Hypnosis*,
Saturn Films, Filmarchiv Austria, Vienna.

ler enters and exits the scene periodically to assist the woman with her trickery, implying that the hypnotized gentleman is also a cuckold. In an ironic moment when the subject is awakened from his trance, the lady appears dressed in a peignoir and the male victim takes leave of her in the customary courtly Viennese manner of *Küss die Hand*, that is, kissing her hand.

Schwarzer's *Power of Hypnosis* might be interpreted as a comment upon the extent to which an established turn-of-the-century man could be captivated by his mistress to his own detriment and be made to look ridiculous, or even ruined financially. Indeed, the only passage to actually be censored (cut) from this film relates to a comic reference to Phyllis and Aristotle, where the sexy hypnotist attempts to ride her victim like a horse, reversing the prevailing order of male dominance. Such an act (familiar to educated viewers of the time from Hans Baldung Grien's sixteenth-century print) must have been considered deleterious to society at large in the Austro-Hungarian Empire.[27] But whereas female flesh and sexuality have a malevolent power in works by Albrecht Dürer, Albrecht Altdorfer, and Hans Baldung Grien, the comedic shock of the war between the sexes in Saturn films portrays women as clever or bewitching rather than truly dangerous or evil. Women's bodies, including that of the hypnotist in *The Power of Hypnosis*, are to be enjoyed, even consumed, by the eyes of the spectators, according to popular culture, never really problematized or feared.

Anna O.

Besides serving as a code to the prevailing Zeitgesit, how can we relate Schwarzer's Saturn films to Freud and his patients in cultural history? Let us begin with Anna O. The Viennese physiologist Josef Breuer used hypnotism in the famous Freudian "Case of Anna O.," which for the first time (1880s) established hysteria and its treatment in the German-speaking world, and initiated the talking cure for psycho-induced paralyses and other neurotic problems. Certain of the Saturn phantasies can be connected to the life and work of Bertha Pappenheim, known in Freud's writing under the pseudonym "Anna O." Anna (Bertha) suffered from hysterical coughing, paresis, hallucinations, and language loss in the wake of her father's slow death from a tubercular tumor.

To the extent that Freud's case histories read like novellas or plays, the mise-en-scène for the case history of Anna O. was a sickbed after the fashion of the nineteenth century. And the young Anna's role in this complex drama was to be first her father's nurse and then her doctor's patient. Both of these roles required the enactment of disappointed or frustrated loves. The ingenue is abandoned twice: first by her father's illness and death and then by her doctor's withdrawal and dramatic return to his wife and family.

During the course of her treatment, Josef Breuer visited her at her home. House calls were the procedural norm in medical practice around 1900, and before Bertha fell ill Breuer visited her dying father, Siegmund Pappenheim, twice every day. Breuer, who considered the hypnoid state a basic predilection for or symptom of hysteria, believed that a person involved in prolonged nursing at the sickbed of a loved one was subject to some of the same conditions demanded by hypnotic procedures. Such conditions included crepuscular lighting, the nurse and her bedridden subject's concentration on a single object, such as a ticking clock or a lamp, and a focused attention to the sound and sight of the patient's deliberate breathing.[28]

Ten days after her father's death in 1881, the Pappenheim family called in a famous psychiatrist for a home consultation with Bertha: this doctor was none other than Richard von Krafft-Ebing (1840–1902), who was a noted expert on sexual disturbances.[29] Krafft-Ebing had written about melancholia and criminal psychosis in the years before his famous summa, *Psychopathia Sexualis* of 1886. Might Anna O.'s diagnosis appear hidden in the passages on hysteria in *Psychopathia*? There is no record of his interaction with Anna O. or his medical opinion of her case in 1881. We do know that Krafft-Ebing believed in general terms that the sexual life was very frequently abnormal and even perverse to the point of criminality in cases of female hysteria. Still, might he have diagnosed Anna O. not as a hysteric at all, but rather as a case of aggravated pathological melancholia, or hallucinatory melancholia, caused by grief, having lost two sisters and her father within a short period of time?[30] Anna O.'s sorrows may have included that of her emotionally detached mother, a suffering widow who had already lost two of her children. Distinctions between conditions such as hysteria and melancholia were not so clear-cut at the end of the nineteenth century. In fact, Freud's essay "Mourning and Melancholia" (1917) was an attempt to distinguish conditions of aggravated pathological melancholia from those of normal grief and its affects.[31] Anna O. may have slipped from a state of mourning into pathological melancholia complete with the refusal of nourishment and attendant self-torment.

During Breuer's lengthy visits, Bertha was frequently sedated with chloral hydrate (a sedative-hypnotic drug) among other hallucinogenic medications she took, including morphine, which may have induced toxic psychosis, yet another possible diagnosis for Anna O.[32] Under the power of drugs and hypnotic suggestion, Anna O. hallucinated images such as frightening black snakes. She saw death's-heads appear in the mirror, as if envisioning her father's future ghost. Mirrors, of course, are transformative, ghostly, protocinematic objects in everyday life. That topic deserves more analysis than the scope of this essay allows. Nevertheless, it's pertinent to remark here that the style of suspended oval mirror that was most common in nineteenth-century bedrooms (like that of Bertha's father, Siegmund Pappenheim) was called a Psyche. The reflective surface of the Psyche provided a cinema-like surface for the screening of hallucinations, particularly at night.

No one can forget that in the course of this intimate treatment Bertha (in the role of Anna O.) supposedly formed an amorous attachment (or transference) to her doctor, even hallucinating (and performing) that she was pregnant with Breuer's baby. At this point the doctor apparently demurred, leaving Vienna to go on vacation with his wife. He narrated the case to Freud, however, who published it in 1893 (articles) and 1895 (*Studies on Hysteria*).[33]

The literary and social culture of fin-de-siècle Vienna put great emphasis on "impossible" romantic love and its transformative power. In popular visual cul-

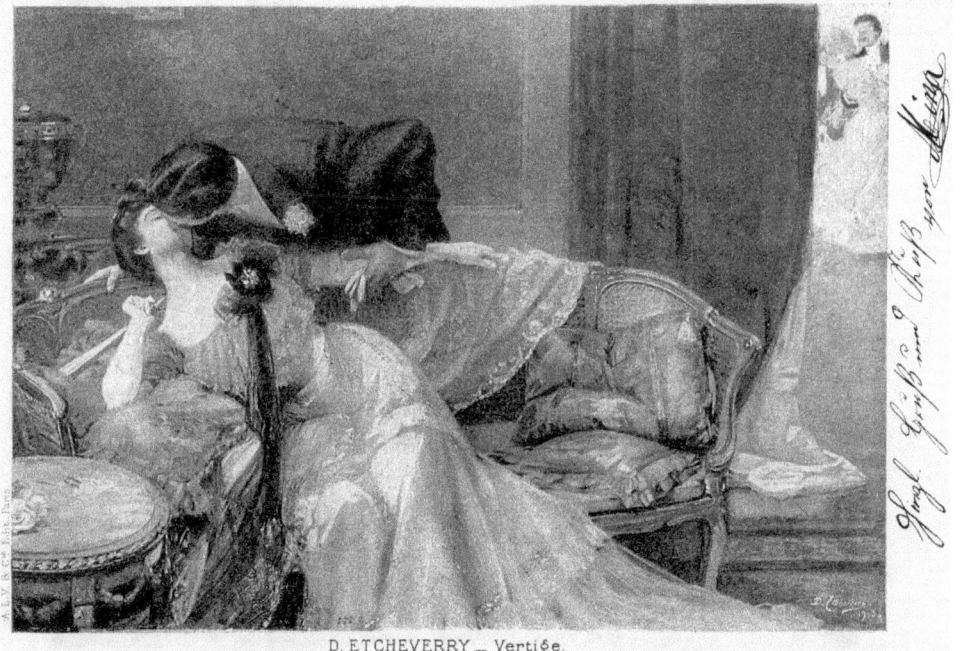

D. ETCHEVERRY _ Vertige.

FIGURE 6.9 Hubert-Denis Etcheverry, *Vertige*, A.L.V. & Cie Éditions, Paris.
Viennese provenance, author's collection.

ture, for example, Denis Etcheverry's highly romantic painting *Vertige* from the Parisian Salon of 1903 (Musée Carnavalet) was circulated as a favorite black-and-white postcard in Vienna, like the one addressed to Fräulein Hilda Hüttmann at Währingerstrasse 83, with "Grüss und Küss" from her friend Nina (fig. 6.9). It is likely that both Anna O. and Josef Breuer were susceptible to, or even protagonists of, this mentality. Their mutually mirroring cases of transference and countertransference became among the most accepted principles of Freudian psychoanalysis from this first instance of the talking cure to psychotherapy in the present day. The extent to which this melodramatic novella of Anna O. is fact or fiction in the medical record is less important than its resonance in cultural history as one of the founding narratives of psychoanalysis.

A doctor's romantic entanglement with a patient, which took place in a domestic setting, among nightclothes, chloral hydrate, morphine, and mirrors, could give rise to erotic phantasy in the visual imagination. Such imaginings are played out in a Saturn film of 1908–1910: *Der Hausarzt* (*The Family Doctor*) is a phantasy in which a malingering patient deliberately seduces her doctor dur-

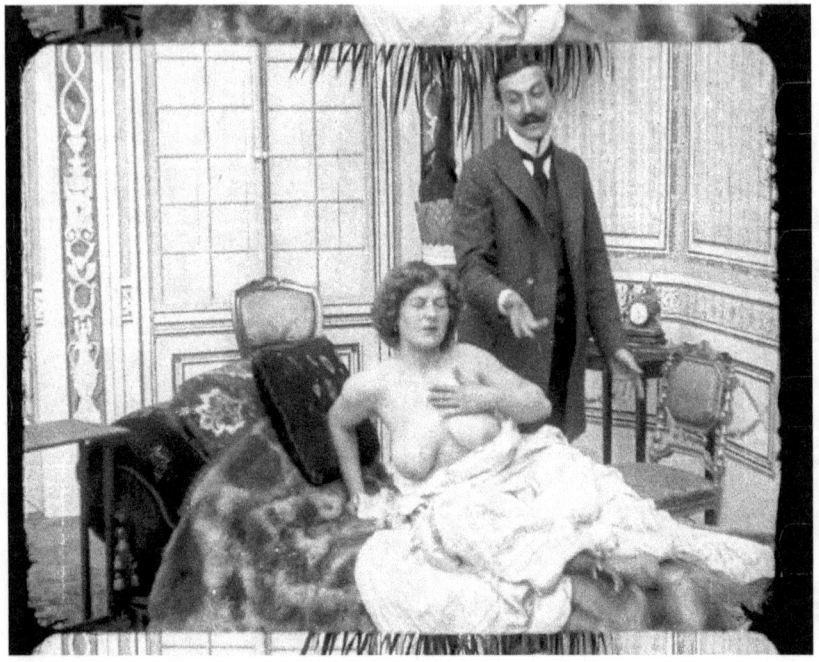

FIGURE 6.10 Johann Schwarzer, still from *The Family Doctor*,
Saturn Films, Filmarchilv Austria, Vienna.

ing a series of house calls. The patient reveals more of her body as the examina-
tions go on, all the while insisting to the doctor that she is not well and needs
further physical examination (fig. 6.10). The Saturn doctor's medical technique,
of course, like that of Freud and his contemporaries, consists of a morphologi-
cal (visual and tactile) examination of the patient. The seduction takes place
in two subsequent episodes in the patient's home: first on a couch in the parlor and then in a bed in the lady's boudoir. Next, after the family doctor reads
the lady's bedside diary, he realizes that she desires him, and they fall into each
other's arms. This phantasy provides a (popular) cultural context for Anna O.'s
psychological adventures with Josef Breuer.

Bertha Pappenheim recovered from her illness some years after her treatment, if not because of it. She became a social reformer who dealt with Jewish
issues and women's rights. If Anna O. was hysterical about sex in her youth,
she developed into an accomplished feminist in her later years. We may once
more tighten the Freudian association with Saturn films in terms of Pappenheim's further biography.

It is pertinent to my argument that in 1903 Pappenheim (the former Anna O.) visited Polish Galicia and western Russia to examine the abject condition of the Jewish population. And in 1911–1912 she traveled east to the brothels of Salonika, Istanbul, Jerusalem, Cairo, and Alexandria to find Jewish girls abducted from eastern Europe and rescue them from the sexual slavery into which they had been sold.[34] Here, one can turn to Schwarzer's Orientalist films of sexual slavery (*Sklavenschiksal, Sklavenraub, Am Sklavenmarkt, Im Harem,* and *Die Sklaverei im Orient*) for comparanda. These erotic film phantasies were contemporary with the campaign against white (Jewish) slavery by Bertha Pappenheim.

Pappenheim's volte-face from youthful hysteria to her eventual status as a highly esteemed social worker is legendary. In a facile, simplistic interpretation it might appear as though Bertha realized that what had ailed her as a girl was the patriarchal system. Her interest in women's issues was unprecedented in the German-speaking lands, and at the same time she was a practitioner of the noblest principles of Judaism. Meanwhile, Pappenheim's problematic personal biography seems to have a happy ending: she escapes from the stifling patriarchy of her father's sickroom and the sustained talking-cure attentions of Breuer and Freud. Her womanly know-how allowed Bertha Pappenheim to command the social horizon of Jewish life for others as well as herself. But, as wary of happy endings as all historians should be, I'd like to problematize Pappenheim's position a little further.

Apropos slavery and racialism, Pappenheim sometimes wandered onto a slippery slope: she applied one of the most common brands of Jewish Orientalism, claiming that Jews from Polish Galicia were "half-Asian," lazy, dirty, uncivilized, and depraved. And she was especially hard on the Jewish women from these regions, referring to their supposed "hot blood" and "moral insanity."[35] In blaming these victims for their own misfortunes, then, despite her conscious unwillingness to do so, Pappenheim designated western Europe as a colonial superego to be imposed upon the impoverished Jews of the East, who were, not unlike the hysterics of the Salpêtrière, amoral and out of control. Like hysterics, these eastern European Jewish women had been traumatized. Among the eastern Jewish women aided by Pappenheim were those rendered homeless by violent events, such as genocidal pogroms. Other women had acquired the marginalized status of *agunah*, still "shackled" to their marriage vows, having been abandoned by husbands who had emigrated to America or elsewhere. Bertha Pappenheim's particular style of Jewish Orientalism cast her as a quintessential protagonist of Austria and Germany, educated according to the precepts of her own society. A peculiar irony of Pappenheim's rescue work is that

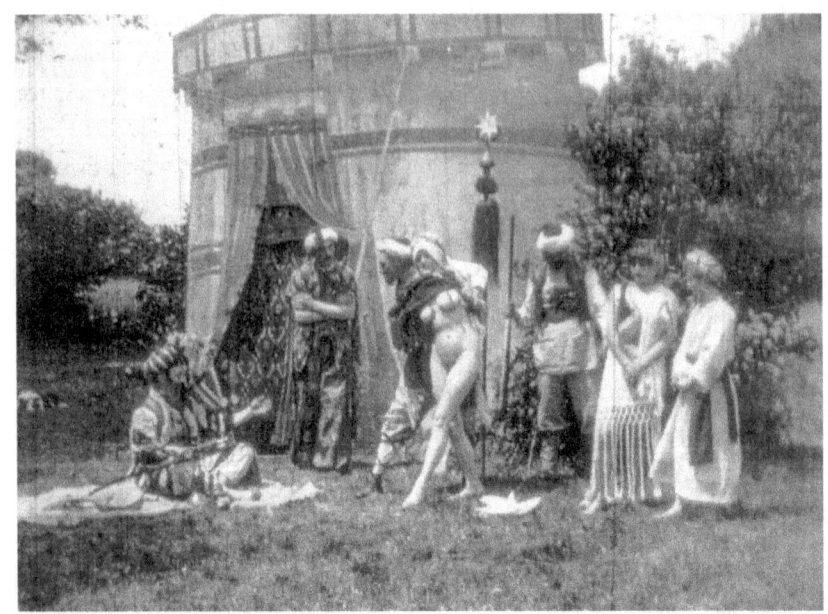

FIGURE 6.11 Johann Schwarzer, still from *The Slave Market*,
Saturn Films, Filmarchiv Austria, Vienna.

some of the Jewish girls who were abducted as slaves believed they were actually on their way to Germany or America to live as married women in a more modern, industrialized, bourgeois society.

In terms of Jewish Orientalism and sexual slavery, we may direct our attention to the *Slave Market* phantasies by Johann Schwarzer. These films reverted to Orientalist themes such as life in the seraglio and young women inspected for sale as slaves. Here the thrill of illicit looking was enhanced by the exotic lure of the East, at least in its fictitious European representation of a single sultan with numerous women in his entourage (fig. 6.11). Bertha Pappenheim probably did not see these movies, but she may well have known about them by way of her brother Wilhelm Pappenheim (1860–1939) or friends, and seen them advertised in the daily newspapers.[36] Freud, Breuer, and their fellow physicians may or may not have seen these phantasies at the Prater, a Wanderkino, or elsewhere. I am not suggesting any precise causality here, but rather I propose letting these phenomena resonate in the cultural moment.

It is well known that the Oriental harem and slave fantasy was an erotic staple of nineteenth-century European painting, as in Jean-Léon Gérôme's *Slave Market*, and that photography was the modern medium of colonial adventure.

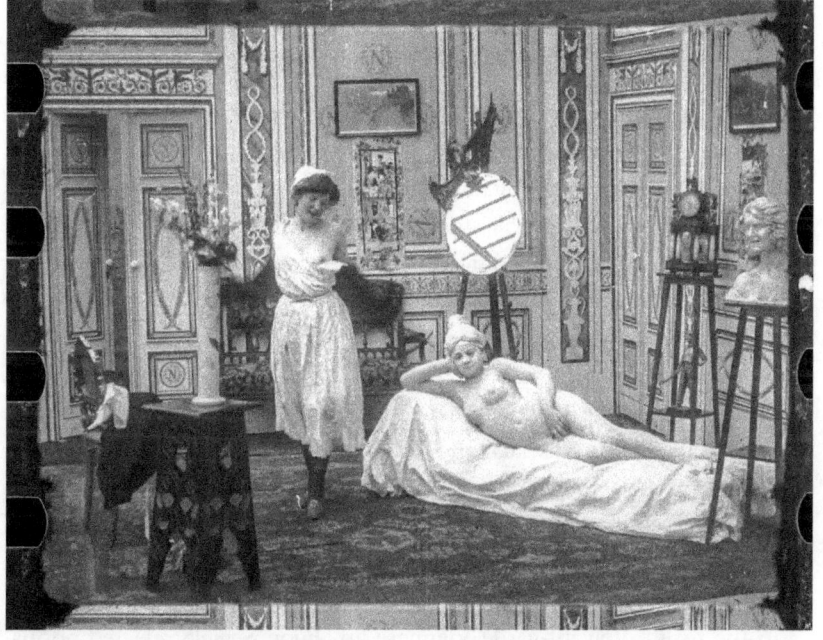

FIGURE 6.12 Johann Schwarzer, still from *The Vain Parlor Maid*,
Saturn Films, Filmarchiv Austria, Vienna.

The Orientalist phantasy undermined the bourgeois husband-wife relationship that prevailed as an ideal in newly industrialized Europe. The non-European women who were sexualized in exotic scenarios provided a reactionary phantasm for men whose wives, daughters, and even mistresses were evolving in a rapidly changing European society. The conjugal situation as such is satirized in Johann Schwarzer's *Modern Marriage* (*Eine Moderne Ehe*), in which a bourgeois husband, tricking his wife, goes to his mistress rather than to his office or his club. As soon as he leaves the house, however, the wife summons her own lover, who shows up immediately for an illicit tryst. As in *The Power of Hypnosis* with its accommodating manservant, the young parlor maid seems not altogether innocent, but rather complicit in the intrigues performed by both husband and wife. Young maids and manservants are rarely innocent in Saturn films, but rather coconspirators of the women or men wealthy enough to employ them. In Saturn's *Vain Parlor Maid*, the young servant takes the initiative to undress and mimic (or indeed compete with) a seductive recumbent marble sculpture. This episode seems to surprise the maid herself, who, ironically, comes from the same class of women who actually perform in the Saturn films (fig. 6.12).

Side by side with all of the visual material under discussion above, a single question hangs in the air: what about Viennese modernism? Modernist art in Vienna was contemporary art for Sigmund Freud and his circle. Although such art did not interest Freud, Johann Schwarzer, or Bertha Pappenheim, it lends itself, in an almost interminable stereotype, to psychoanalytic appreciation and critique. This cultural configuration of anxiety-ridden and highly expressive art comes under the umbrella term "Vienna 1900."[37] Paintings by Egon Schiele (1890–1918) and by the avant-garde atonal composer Arnold Schönberg (1874–1951) were radically modernist and anticlassical in their effect. Schiele's nudes, female and male, were awkward, anxious, physically afflicted, and ill at ease (fig. 6.13). His lovers (heterosexual and homosexual alike) are tormented rather than joyful in the act. Schönberg's images of the human visage, as in *Der rote Blick (The Red Gaze)* of 1910 (fig. 6.14) express the power of the gaze in terms of a stunned, horrified consciousness; the experience of scopophilia, or pleasure in looking, has gone awry and turned to absolute angst.

In the realm of avant-garde Viennese art, Egon Schiele rejected normative sexuality in favor of what art historian Gemma Blackshaw has called "the spectacle of the pathological body."[38] This documentary spectacle of disease was current in photographic illustrations of sick people in hospitals and departs greatly from the romantic concept of illness that is seen in films such as *Der Hausarzt (The Family Doctor)*. To this fact, the Saturn films were still old-fashioned in their treatment of the nude and in the psyche of the on-screen beholders, as well as the film spectators. Schwarzer's films do not disclose any real sexual anxiety, or dark side, or unhealthy alternative to the prevailing natural order. In fact, in one Saturn episode a female slave is actually rejected by the sultan for being too slender and adolescent looking—an aesthetic opposite to those of Kokoschka or Schiele.

A Difficult Treatment

I introduced this essay by way of early films on hypnotism and hysteria, and proceeded to analyze *The Power of Hypnosis* and other sexual phantasies from the Saturn films. Apropos pathology, I'd like now to complicate the issue and conclude by pointing out that Saturn erotica (innocent as it may initially seem) was compounded by serious humiliations of the flesh in the conditions of their reception. This is because Saturn screenings were not necessarily single fea-

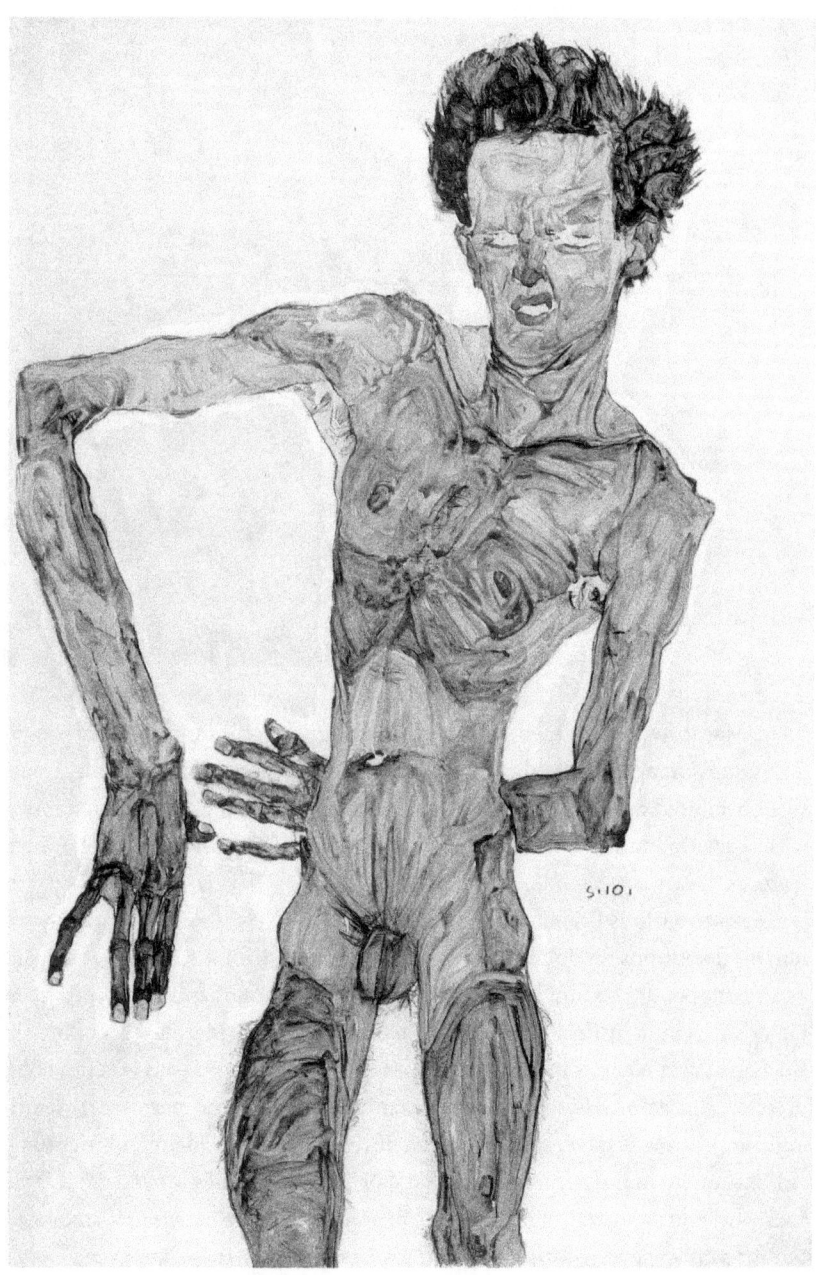

FIGURE 6.13 Egon Schiele, *Grimacing Self-Portrait*, 1910. Painting on paper, Albertina, Vienna. Wikipedia Wikicommons, work of art in the public domain.

FIGURE 6.14 Arnold
Schönberg, *The Red Gaze*,
1910. Wikipedia, work of art in
the public domain.

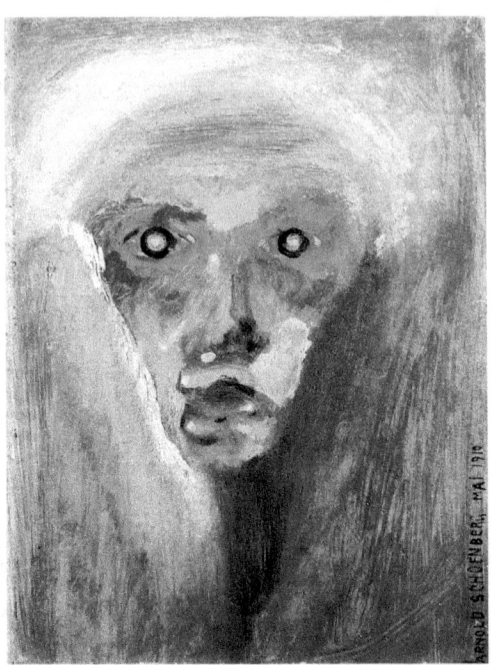

tures. Macabre slides of medical oddities and films of gruesome medical procedures and surgery frequently accompanied them.[39] In 1903, for example, Louis
Geni exhibited a traveling "anatomical museum" as well as cinematic erotica
with screenings and views designated for men only together with the Saturn
features.[40]

The ostentatious French surgeon Eugène Doyen (1859–1916) was the first to
film his operations for documentary purposes. In 1898, for instance, Doyen paid
a camera operator to film him performing hysterectomies and a craniotomy in
his private clinic in Paris. These films, which paralleled Marinescu's efforts in
Bucharest and Negro's in Turin, made a hero of the doctor, who was now film
director and actor. He was the physician-protagonist who performed seemingly impossible feats on screen. Doyen never meant such documentaries to be
entertainment in the fairgrounds of Paris or Vienna. But he enjoyed great fame
from these little movies, and Doyen's productions were eventually smuggled
out for public viewing for sensational entertainment.[41] They, like Louis Geni's
so-called Panopticon films, were commonly shown for gentlemen in tandem
with erotic films like the Saturn features in the Austro-Hungarian Empire. If
Vienna was the most medically advanced city in Europe around the turn of the
century, the scopophilia associated with medical procedures and anatomical
oddities thrived apace.

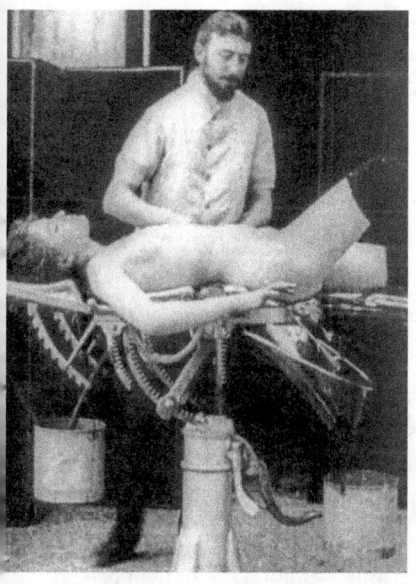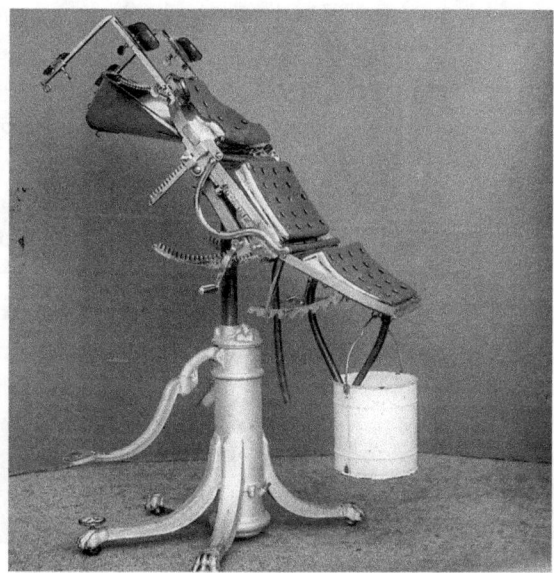

FIGURE 6.15 *left* Anonymous, *A Difficult Treatment*, possibly Saturn Films,
Filmarchiv Austria, Vienna. Image in the public domain.

FIGURE 6.16 *right* Doyen's operating table. Courtesy Archives Jean Doyen.

Such scientific medical documentaries seem to have inspired a film, *A Difficult Treatment* (*Eine Schwierige Behandlung*), which has been attributed to Johann Schwarzer, but may be by himself, or perhaps by an anonymous director, satirizing Doyen's surgical films (fig. 6.15). It features Doyen's patented operating table, known as Doyen's bed (*le lit de Doyen*) (fig. 6.16). Was this movie really an infomercial for a newly designed operating table? I would propose that it was probably not. In this film, of Austrian provenance and presently conserved in the Austrian Film Archive, the doctors and female surgical patient appear to be actors. Is the nude woman on the operating table to be understood as unconscious? Is she understood to be dead? Her body (nude except for shoes and stockings) is objectified, inspected, handled, and operated on by the pair of surgeons. Will they cut into her flesh? Will these doctors perform one of the vaginal or abdominal hysterectomies that were Doyen's specialties as filmed in 1898?[42]

Although it remains possible that this film was intended as a scientific introduction to the value of a new operating table, most twenty-first-century viewers, including a group of visually savvy students at the Rhode Island School of Design, see these images as darkly pornographic.[43] Apropos the humiliation of female flesh (as seen in the Saturn films), here we're introduced to a more morbid and intrusive kind of misogyny. The actress playing the patient was probably conscious in the filming of this episode, as certain aspects of her body posture would indicate. But in the cinematic representation, or phantasy, a woman's unconscious body becomes an object to be manipulated by men for a fetishizing (audience) beholder. The woman's body is looked at, examined, touched, and perhaps incised by the two male doctors. All the while she is (in the fiction of the film) in a state of oblivion induced by hypnotism, ether, or chloroform.

Are the images in *A Difficult Treatment* involuntary or unconscious by-products of scientific technical culture? No matter what the film's original purpose may have been, there is a perplexing slippage here between medical and pornographic cinema. The pathologized female body had a fetishistic lure as a focus for the male gaze. *Eine Schwierige Behandlung* (*A Difficult Treatment*) hovers between categories, and this condition of sliding between medical science and the phantasy realm of misogynistic sex may apply to many other art and nonart images in this culture, whether consciously or not. Due to the presence of certain photographs and films, be they imported or local, erotica did its cultural work in combination with medical voyeurism in Viennese society. Although such research is beyond the frame of this essay, it becomes pertinent for future study to look into the realm of factual, deadpan, documentary medical imaging and its relation to the subjective phantasy world of that which was visually forbidden.

Notes

I wish to thank Sharon Sliwinski for her generous advice in the reshaping of this essay.

1. Sigmund Freud, *The Psychopathology of Everyday Life* (1901), in *The Standard Edition of the Complete Psychological Works of Sigmund Freud* [hereafter SE], ed. and trans. James Strachey (London: Hogarth, 1953), vol. 6, 43–52, 47.

2. Sigmund Freud, *Screen Memories* (1899), SE, vol. 3, 301–322. "Phantasy," in the psychoanalytic context, refers to the subject's imagined scenes that are deeply influenced by unconscious desires and the processes of defense. See J. Laplanche and J. B. Pontalis's entry on the term in *The Language of Psychoanalysis*, trans. Donald Nicholson-Smith (New York: Norton, 1973), 314–315 (first French edition 1967).

3. Mary Bergstein, *Mirrors of Memory: Freud, Photography, and the History of Art* (Ithaca, NY: Cornell University Press, 2010), 8–9.

4. Bergstein, *Mirrors of Memory*, 9, 15, 18, 126–130, 146, 185, 189, 261–262, 273–274; and see introduction, this volume.

5. Bergstein, *Mirrors of Memory*, 130–135.

6. Laura Mulvey, "Visual Pleasure and Narrative Cinema," *Screen* 16 no. 3 (autumn 1975): 6–18; Sigmund Freud, *Three Essays on the Theory of Sexuality* (1905), *SE*, vol. 7, 123–243; Sigmund Freud, "Instincts and Their Vicissitudes" (1915), *SE*, vol. 14, 117–140.

7. Luigi Malerba, *La Composizione del Sogno* (Turin: Einaudi, 2002), 34, 54–55, 61, 77, 87.

8. *Le Petit Parisien* (*Supplément littéraire illustré*), June 15, 1890, 1. For the Gouffé affair, see Steven Levingston, *Little Demon in the City of Light* (New York: Doubleday, 2014).

9. Wilhelm Weygandt, *Atlas und Grundriss der Psychiatrie* (Munich: J. F. Lehmann, 1902), see case no. 26 and passim for "flirtatious hysteria."

10. Julien Bogousslavsky, Olivier Walusinski, and Denis Veyrunes, "Crime, Hysteria and *Belle-Époque* Hypnotism: The Path Traced by Jean-Martin Charcot and Georges Gilles de la Tourette," *European Neurology* (2009): 193–199.

11. See Alisa Luxenberg, "'The Art of Correctly Painting the Expressive Lines of the Human Face': Duchenne de Boulogne's Photographs of Human Expression and the École des Beaux-Arts," *History of Photography* 25, no. 2 (summer 2001): 101–112.

12. Georges Didi-Hubermann, *Invention of Hysteria: Charcot and the Photographic Iconography of the Salpêtrière*, trans. Alisa Hartz (Cambridge, MA: MIT Press, 2003), first published as *Invention de l'hystérie: Charcot et l'Iconographie photographique de la Salpêtrière* (Paris: Macula, 1982).

13. Sigmund Freud, "Review of August Forel's Hypnotism" (1889), *SE*, vol. 1, 91–102; Sigmund Freud, "Hypnosis" (1891), *SE*, vol. 1, 105–114; Sigmund Freud, "A Case of Successful Treatment by Hypnotism" (1893), *SE*, vol. 1, 117–132.

14. For an in-depth analysis of the transition from hypnosis to psychoanalysis, see Andreas Mayer, *Sites of the Unconscious: Hypnosis and the Emergence of the Psychoanalytic Setting* (Chicago: University of Chicago Press, 2013).

15. Perhaps brain science studies in the twenty-first, twenty-second, or twenty-third centuries will allow or necessitate people to revise those prevailing codes.

16. Mayer, *Sites of the Unconscious*, 158–59.

17. Asti Hustvedt, *Medical Muses: Hysteria in Nineteenth-Century Paris* (New York: Norton, 2011), 107–116 and passim.

18. Sharon Packer, *Movies and the Modern Psyche* (Westport, CT: Praeger, 2007), 55–67, 57; Stefan Andriopoulos, *Possessed: Hypnotic Crimes, Corporate Fiction, and the Invention of Cinema*, trans. Peter Jansen (Chicago: University of Chicago Press, 2008).

19. Marinescu's first film was *Walking Difficulties in Organic Hemiplegia* (1898). Marinescu had his patients walk before the camera against a black background in order to analyze their movements before and after treatment. He continued this work to 1901 with his assistants C. Parhon and M. Goldstein, employing camera operator Constantin Popescu, who shot *A Case of Hysterical Hemiplegia Cured through Hypnotic Suggestion* (1899) and *Walking Difficulties Due to Progressive Locomotary Ataxia* (1900). See Ramon Reichert, "Das Kino in der Klinik: Medientechniken des Unbewussten um 1900," in *Kino im Kopf: Psychologie und Film seit Sigmund Freud*, ed. Kristina Jaspers

and Wolf Unterberger (Vienna: Bertz + Fischer, 2007), 23–29, 26; Luke McKernon, "Dr. Gheorghe Marinescu (1863–1938)," in *Who's Who of Victorian Cinema*, 2014, http://www.victorian-cinema.net/marinescu.

20. Reichert, "Das Kino in der Klinik," 25, 26.

21. See Andriopoulos, *Possessed*. In my view, the erotic and criminal undertones of hypnosis, suggestion, and hysteria have never been dissociated in the popular imagination. In the mid-twentieth century, for example, Federico Fellini continued this idea in *Le notti di Cabiria* (*The Nights of Cabiria*, 1957), where a heartbreaking Giulietta Masina, as a young Roman prostitute named Cabiria, is preyed upon, seduced, exploited, robbed, and abandoned by a man who has seen her hypnotized in a cheap stage act. The unctuous seducer, who calls himself Oscar, is most certainly an accomplice of the carnival hypnotist rather than the accountant he claims to be. His trickery and violence are predicated upon Cabiria's unconscious revelations (while in a hypnotic trance) that she longed for intimacy and marriage. Cabiria's life is one of poverty and vulnerable abjection, but as we learn from her continuous good-natured will to survive (resilience is a positive aspect of the stereotypical Italian female character), she cannot be classified as hysterical.

22. Packer, *Movies and the Modern Psyche*, 43–48. Karl Abraham and Hanns Sachs served as consultants for this film.

23. Michael Achenbach and Paola Caneppele, "Born under the Sign of Saturn: The Erotic Origins of Cinema in the Austro-Hungarian Empire," *Griffithiana: La Rivista della Cineteca del Friuli* 65 (1999): 126–139, 135.

24. Leigh Goldstein, "Review of Michael Achenbach, Paolo Caneppele, Ernst Kieninger, *Projektion der Sehnsucht: Saturn, Die erotischen Anfänge der österreichischen Kinematografie* (Vienna, Filmarchiv Austria, 2000)," *Moving Image* 9 (spring 2009): 253–256, 253.

25. See the now-classic essay by Sherry Ortner, "Is Female to Male as Nature Is to Culture?," in *Woman, Culture and Society*, ed. M. Z. Rosaldo and L. Lamphere (Stanford, CA: Stanford University Press, 1974), 67–87.

26. Laura Mulvey, "Visual Pleasure and Narrative Cinema," *Screen* 16, no. 3 (autumn 1975): 6–18; Freud, *Three Essays on the Theory of Sexuality*; Freud, "Instincts and Their Vicissitudes," and see note 5, above.

27. Michael Achenbach, Thomas Ballhausen, and Nikolaus Wostry, eds., *Saturn: Wiener Filmerotik 1906–1910/ Viennese Film Eroticism 1906–1910* (Vienna: Verlag Filmarchiv Austria, 2009), 79, 174.

28. Laplanche and Pontalis, "Hypnoid State," *The Language of Psychoanalysis*, 192–194.

29. Max Rosenbaum, "Anna O. (Bertha Pappenheim): Her History," in *Anna O.: Fourteen Contemporary Reinterpretations*, ed. Max Rosenbaum and Melvin Muroff (New York: Free Press, 1984), 1–25, 6.

30. For a typical turn-of-the-century view of melancholia, see Archibald Church

and Frederick Peterson, *Nervous and Mental Diseases* (Philadelphia: W. B. Saunders, 1899), 700–710.

31. Sigmund Freud, "Mourning and Melancholia" (1917), SE, vol. 14, 243–258.

32. Elizabeth Loentz, *Let Me Continue to Speak the Truth: Bertha Pappenheim as Author and Activist* (Cincinnati: Hebrew Union College Press, 2007), 210.

33. Sigmund Freud, *Studies on Hysteria* (1893–1895), SE, vol. 2, 1–47.

34. See Edward J. Bristow, *Prostitution and Prejudice: The Jewish Fight against White Slavery, 1870–1939* (Oxford: Oxford University Press, 1983), 4, 6, 39, 51, 70, 72, 102, 218–219, 232–235, 253, 257, 260–261, 263–264, 266, 269, 273, 276, 279–280, 284, 299–391, 304–305, 323.

35. Loentz, *Let Me Continue to Speak the Truth*, 123–156, 133–134, 141, 143.

36. See Elizabeth Loentz, "The Problem and Challenge of Jewishness in the City of Schnitzler and Anna O.," in *A Companion to the Works of Arthur Schnitzler*, ed. Dagmar C. G. Lorentz (Rochester, NY: Camden House, 2003), 79–102.

37. For "Vienna 1900," see Eric Kandel, *The Age of Insight: The Quest to Understand the Unconscious in Art, Mind, and Brain from Vienna 1900 to the Present* (New York: Random House, 2012).

38. Gemma Blackshaw, "The Pathological Body: Modernist Strategising in Egon Schiele's Self-Portraiture," *Oxford Art Journal* 30, no. 3 (2007): 377–401.

39. Achenbach and Caneppele, "Born under the Sign of Saturn," 131.

40. Achenbach and Caneppele, "Born under the Sign of Saturn," 131.

41. See Thierry Lefebvre, *La Chair et le Celluloïd: Le Cinéma Chirurgical du Docteur Doyen* (Paris: Jean Doyen, 2004).

42. Transactions of Societies, British Gynaecological Society, meeting held December 14, 1899, "Dr. E. Doyen of Paris gave a Cinematic Demonstration of Gynaecological Operations," *London Medical Press and Circular*, January 3, 1900, 8–9; and see Jacques H. M. Cohen, "The Scandalous Dr. Doyen, or the Solitary Tragedy of a Prodigy," trans. Karine Debbasch, Histoire de la santé, Bibliothèque numérique Medic@, January 2006, http://www.biusante.parisdescartes.fr/histoire/medica/doyen-en.php.

43. My most sincere thanks to all my students in Visual Culture in Freud's Vienna from 2013 and 2014 for their valuable feedback on the issues addressed in this essay.

CHAPTER SEVEN

ON THE COUCH

MIGNON NIXON

The setting is like the darkness in a cinema,
like the silence in a concert hall.
Federico Flegenheimer

There is a scene in Nanni Moretti's film *The Son's Room* (2001) in which a prospective patient, a middle-aged man making his first visit to a psychoanalyst,
pauses upon entering the consulting room to examine the couch. It is a fine
couch, he remarks, "simple, comfortable, even elegant in its way. . . . But I have
no intention of lying on it."

Still, the analyst's marine-blue couch receives many visitors over the course
of the film. One woman spends the hour calculating her losses. How much does
the analyst really understand—20 percent of what she is saying, or 30? There
have been 460 sessions, she chides, and after every one, to assuage her disappointment, she shops. A male patient gushes dreams. They pour from him in
unbroken succession, filling the analytic hour like water flowing noisily into a
bath. A woman suffers from obsessional thoughts. Her time on the couch is
measured as metronomically as her daily routine, in a recitation of the rituals
that mete out her hours. The analyst's thoughts drift across to the cupboard
where he stores a private collection of objects, a treasury not of antique figurines such as Freud favored, but an extensive array of running shoes—fetishes
not of Eros but of Nike—stacked in precisely ordered rows.

While the patients talk, the tall, bearded analyst, his long limbs folded into
an armchair classically positioned behind the couch, smiles, sighs, takes notes,
drops and lifts his eyes, flexes his fingers, makes the occasional tactful observation, but mostly abides. In one session, he mentally counts the seconds until

the patient departs. For these visitors are sufferers in need of his help, but also intruders, whiners, time wasters, and bullies. He needs his space. At the end of the day, Giovanni Sermonti closes the doors of his office and, in unmistakable emulation of Freud at Berggasse 19, in turn-of-the-century Vienna, enters the adjoining rooms, the scene of his apparently contented bourgeois life.

Then, one Sunday morning, amiable Oscar, the dream gusher (whose stream of consciousness, however, is punctuated by fleeting fantasies of suicide), telephones in a state of distress. It is a blow for the analyst, who has just persuaded his son to join him for a run. The moody adolescent boy has been much on his mind. But Oscar persists, and the analyst finally agrees to meet him. He drives to the countryside, where he finds Oscar padding disconsolately about his untidy house, crumpled by the discovery of a spot on his lung. Returning to town that afternoon, the analyst learns that his son has been killed in a diving accident. Now he can no longer endure the talk of the patients, their trivial worries, their inconsolable sadness, and, even worse, their joy. Tears flow as he struggles to listen from the lap of his chair. As for Oscar, whose distress call took the analyst to the countryside while his son was dying in the sea, Giovanni cannot resist dashing the man's wishful fantasies, blotting his hope. Yet the cancer has deepened the patient's insight; it may be his cure. At last, Oscar breaks off the analysis. Soon Giovanni expels all the patients from his life. He closes his practice and asks his patients to leave him alone.

Imagine you are lying on Freud's couch. What can you see?
John Forrester

From my reclining yet propped-up, somewhat Madame Récamier–like position on the couch, I face the wide-open double door. At the foot of the couch is the stove. Placed next [to] the stove is the cabinet that contains the more delicate glass jars and the variously shaped bottles and Aegean vases. In the wall space, on the other side of the double door, is another case or cabinet of curiosities and antiques; on top of this case there are busts of bearded figures—Euripides? Socrates? Sophocles, certainly. There is the window now as you turn that corner, at right angles to the cabinet, and then another case that contains pottery figures and some more Greek-figure bowls. Then, the door to the waiting room. At right angles again, there is the door that leads through the laboratory-like cupboard room or alcove, to the hall.
H. D.

Freud's original conception of the psychoanalytic setting is commemorated in two museums, one at Berggasse 19 in Vienna, where he lived and practiced medicine and then psychoanalysis from 1891 to 1938, and another in Hampstead, north London, in the house where he took refuge at the end of his life, and to which his extensive collection of antiquities, his library, and his couch were spirited through the intercession of well-placed friends. For some forty years after Freud's death in 1939, his psychoanalyst daughter, Anna Freud, continued to live and work in the house at 20 Maresfield Gardens, preserving Freud's rooms exactly as he had left them, as if in anticipation of the moment when, upon her own death in 1982, the house would be officially converted into a museum, or, as John Forrester has observed, "a museum within a museum: a museum of precious ancient objects, within an ordinary house in Hampstead where a great man died."[1] London's Vienna counterpart opened earlier, in 1971, with no collection to display. Here there are no antique statuettes, no vases, no bowls, no books, and no furnishings beyond the waiting-room chairs and a few minor items that Anna Freud, already planning the museum in London, would subsequently deliver into the empty hands of the Sigmund Freud Society of Vienna. In contrast to the diorama of discipleship in London, the centerpiece of Vienna's museum, with its bare walls and uncarpeted floors, is a panoramic display of life-sized photographs of Freud's consulting room and study. These pictures, which were taken on the eve of the family's departure in 1938, stimulate a reflection on the historical forces that shaped psychoanalysis as a diasporic culture. As Forrester has written of his own visit to the museum in 1975: "It had a derisible atmosphere, perhaps one deliberately induced to remind visitors of yet one more loss that the war had visited on Vienna; but it still prompted the thought that a museum of fake souvenirs is a fake museum — a screen museum, the Freudian might say."[2]

The photographic history of the psychoanalytic consulting room begins with a young engineer-photographer, Edmund Engelman, summoned to Berggasse 19 by August Aichorn in May 1938. Working in secret and using only natural light for fear of alerting the Gestapo, Engelman produced some 150 negatives, including a complete photographic record of Freud's consulting room and study (fig. 7.1).[3] At the Freud Museum in Vienna, the enlarged photographs wrap around the walls at wainscot level so that the visitor entering the consulting room will be facing the carpet-draped couch and Freud's chair tucked discreetly behind it. In her psychoanalytic memoir, H. D., one of Freud's more devoted analysands and a devotée also of the couch, leads us ceremoniously to the scene. After passing up a curved stone staircase to a landing, and being ushered

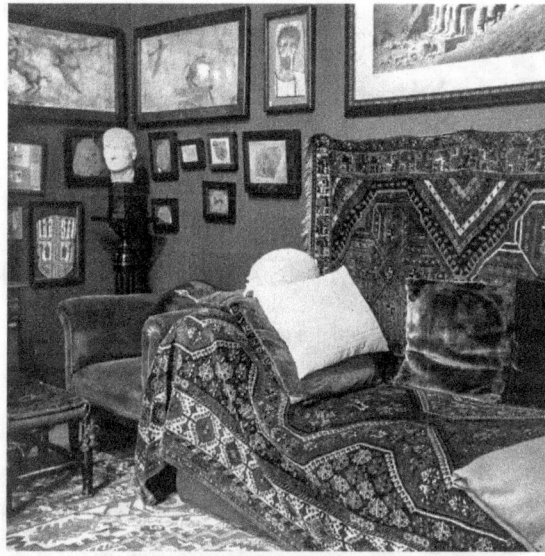

FIGURE 7.1 Edmund
Engelman, Freud's
couch, 1938. Library of
Congress, Prints and
Photographs Division.

137

ON THE COUCH

in through the door to the right (the one to the left leads to the family apartment); after possibly meeting the previous patient on the stairs; after crossing
the carpeted waiting room and depositing one's coat on one of the pegs in a
narrow corridor reminiscent of a laboratory or school; after being invited into
the consulting room itself, beyond which lies the book-lined study filled with
antiquities; after tracing this path, one will find "tucked into the corner, in the
three-sided niche made by the two walls and the back of the couch," the Professor. "He will sit there quietly, like an old owl in a tree. He will say nothing at
all or he will lean forward and talk about something that is apparently unrelated
to the progression or unfolding of our actual dream-content or thought association. He will shoot out an arm, sometimes somewhat alarmingly, to stress
a point. Or he will, always making an 'occasion' of it, get up" and light a cigar.[4]

An early plan for the Vienna museum would have placed a replica couch
and armchair, each in its assigned position, in an otherwise empty consulting
room.[5] By instead relying on photographic documentation, supplemented by
letters and memorabilia arranged and numbered in shallow glass vitrines—
by "eschewing reconstruction, which would suggest historical continuity,"[6] in
favor of an archival presentation—the architects chose instead to present the
history of Freudian psychoanalysis through the medium of "a screen museum"
(a "screen memory" being, in psychoanalytic terms, a false form of remembering that covers desire) (fig. 7.2). At the Freud Museum in Hampstead, For-

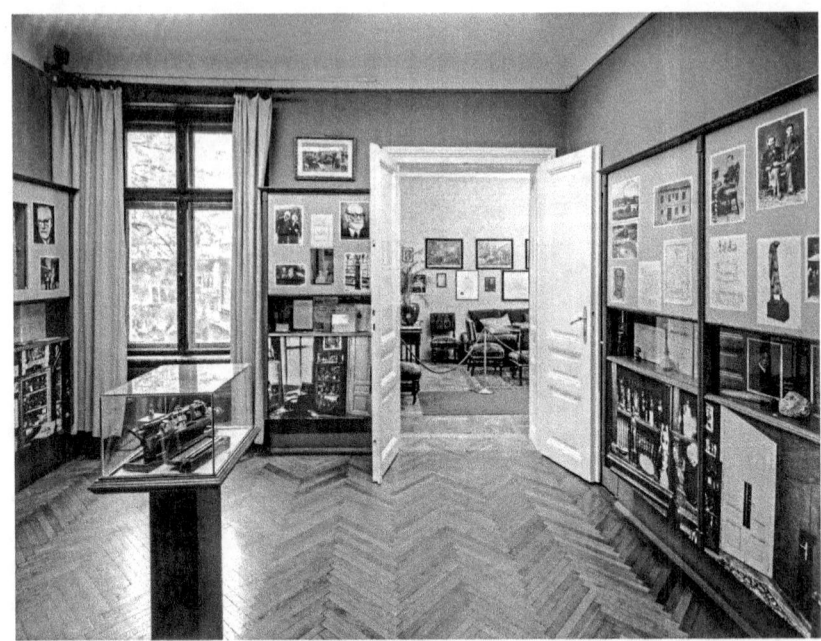

FIGURE 7.2 Gerald Zugmann, view from the consulting room into the waiting room, taken from approximately the position of the couch, Freud Museum, Vienna. Photo copyright Gerald Zugmann (www.zugmann.com).

rester observes, the visitor encounters by contrast "a meticulously conserved milieu: the real furniture, the books, the little objects useful in everyday life and useless anywhere else," most notably the couch.[7]

Continuously on display at the Freud Museum in London since 1986, Freud's own couch, that sacred relic of psychoanalysis — that "flying carpet for unconscious voyaging," as Marina Warner describes it in the museum's guidebook — now lends itself to the scopophilic curiosity it was charged with frustrating in the treatment itself, in which the patient was prevented from observing the analyst (fig. 7.3).[8] By Freud's own account, the couch had "a historical basis," being "the remnant of the hypnotic method out of which psychoanalysis was evolved."[9] The couch was apparently the gift of a patient, one Mrs. Benvenisti, who presented it to her doctor in 1891.[10] In his 1913 essay "On Beginning the Treatment," following a detailed discussion of what he deemed the crucial factors for initiating analysis — "arrangements about time and money" — Freud offers "a word about a certain ceremonial," the relative positions of analyst and analysand, in which the patient lies on the couch while the analyst sits behind

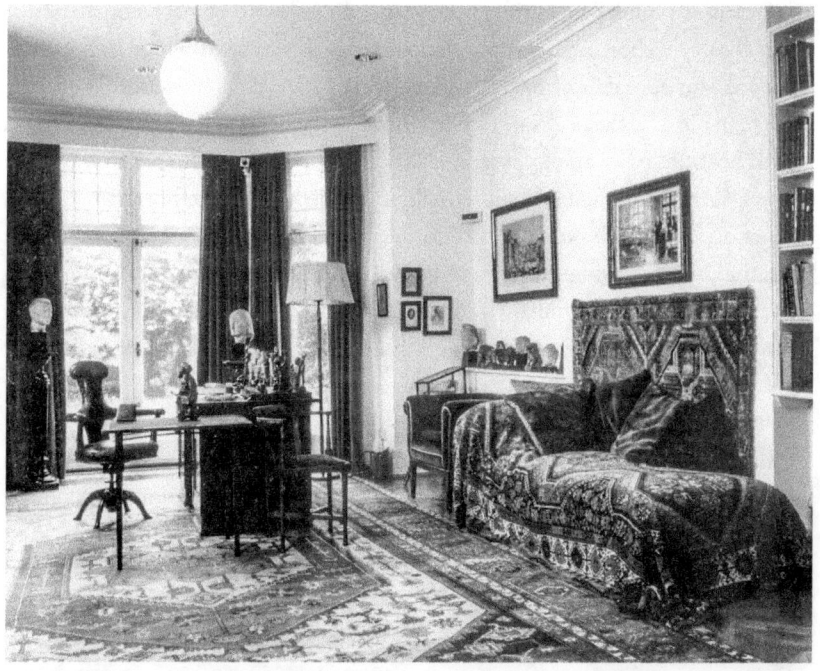

FIGURE 7.3 Freud's couch. Freud Museum London.

her or him and out of sight.[11] The first consideration is "a personal motive" —
"I cannot put up with being stared at by other people." Second, "since while
I am listening to the patient, I, too, give myself over to the current of my unconscious thoughts," Freud observes, there is a danger that the analyst will be
interfered with in this process by the patient, who may also be influenced by
the other's facial expressions. Freud's brief note concludes: "The patient usually
regards being made to adopt this position as a hardship and rebels against it,
especially if the instinct for looking (scopophilia) plays an important role in his
neurosis."[12] And this may perhaps go some way toward explaining the notable
fact that the cultural and phantasmatic history of the psychoanalytic scene, the
setting or frame, has been constructed preeminently in the privileged arena of
modern scopophilia and voyeuristic desire — in cinema.

Freud himself rejected such "plastic representation" of psychoanalysis, at
least on the one occasion when the idea was put to him.[13] That was in the summer of 1925, when Karl Abraham, founder of the Berlin Psychoanalytic Institute, relayed a proposal from Hans Neumann, an independent filmmaker in
Berlin, for an "educational film" about psychoanalysis.[14] Abraham described the

project as a "popular, scientific, psychoanalytic" film, to be based on an actual clinical case. A short treatise on psychoanalysis was to be provided to the audience "like an opera libretto."[15] Freud demurred. "My chief objection," he wrote Abraham, "is . . . that I do not believe that satisfactory plastic representation of our abstraction is at all possible" (this film about the talking cure would be silent).[16] Abraham died of a sudden illness in December, the break with Freud unmended, but not before he and another of Freud's disciples, Hans Sachs, had seen the project through to filming. Taken over by the German UFA film company, Neumann's Lehrfilm (a genre of the time, with others being produced on subjects including gynecology) became the commercial offering *Secrets of a Soul*, directed by G. W. Pabst and featuring Werner Krauss and Pawel Pawlow as patient and psychoanalyst.

The consulting room in which the treatment unfolds is a capacious salon richly appointed with flowered carpet, heavy draperies, lace curtains, and a wide couch that thrusts diagonally into the room, facing away from a bank of windows against which the analyst is seated. The case concerns a chemist whose symptoms include a knife phobia and fantasies of killing his wife, with whom he is impotent. The treatment begins with the two men facing each other across a low table, but the patient soon transfers to the couch. Dwarfed by its great size, he rolls around, tormented by the memory of violent dreams, at times adopting a quasi-fetal position and frequently turning to face the analyst, who answers these signs of distress by reaching over to pat the younger man gently on the arm, gestures charged with the affective resonance of speech in the talking cure. In the absence of sound, the spatial setting assumes an exaggerated significance, posing a question that remains largely unspoken in the literature of psychoanalysis: "What state does lying on a couch induce?"[17]

> Points of importance at the beginning of the analysis are arrangements about time and money.
>
> *Sigmund Freud*

The psychoanalytic couch is an icon of modern culture. Yet "Freud hardly wrote anything on the subject after his original recommendations," notes the editor of a recent special issue of *Psychoanalytic Inquiry* devoted to this neglected point of technique, the use of the analytic couch. This reticence on the part of the founder, the editor suggests, is enough to ensure that the couch is "a topic that is perhaps the least controversial in psychoanalysis." For even if "using the couch in psychoanalytic treatment constitutes the sine qua non of the whole enterprise," the editor observes, the clinical literature studiously avoids discussing it. Or rather, he contends, because the couch is the sine qua non of the whole enterprise, it must be taken for granted and ignored.[18] "How droll," then, remarks another practitioner, "that one of psychoanalysis's two clinical fundamentals" (the other being free association) "should receive more attention as an icon than as a technical dimension."[19]

The scene of psychoanalysis is commonly referred to as the frame.[20] The frame unites the time and space of psychoanalytic experience, regulating the frequency and duration of the sessions, the arrangement of the consulting room and its furnishings, and the postures of analyst and analysand. Deviations from the established pattern break the frame. A patient who misses appointments, neglects to pay the fee on time, or refuses to lie on the couch breaks the frame, as does an analyst who fails to keep to time, miscalculates the fee, or interrupts the session by answering the telephone, for example. Breaking the frame is seen to signal unconscious resistance to the analysis. And because resistance is valued in psychoanalysis as a part of the transference (or, in the case of the analyst, the countertransference), these minor actions assume a heightened significance. Transference—the displacement onto the analyst of emotions originally associated with central figures in the patient's life—is brought into focus by the frame.

Psychoanalysis, writes Jean Laplanche, "leads to the dissolution of all formations—psychical, egoic, ideological, symptomatic" but, crucially, also "offers the constancy of a presence, of a solicitude, the flexible but attentive constancy of a frame."[21] The function of the frame is to contain. "It is because the principle of constancy, of homeostasis, of *Bindung* is maintained at the periphery, that analytic unbinding is possible."[22] He compares the role of the frame to that of the ego in dreaming. In its desire for sleep, the ego assumes a "peripheral place . . . leaving the field open to the primary process."[23] Just as sleep is the medium of the dream, for Laplanche the frame supports the process of analysis.

Writing in the 1960s, the Argentine psychoanalyst José Bleger also proposed a distinction between the "process" of analysis and the frame, "made up of constants within whose bounds the process takes place."[24] Bleger compared the frame to an institution. The analysand may experience a particularly strong transference to the frame itself, he points out, "instead of the therapist," and this may enable her or him to "share in the prestige of a great institution"—or, conversely, by negative transference, may lead the patient to disparage (or break) the frame.[25] In much the same way that, for a student, the university setting itself may hold greater importance than the faculty or fellow students, an individual analysand may experience analysis primarily as an effect of the frame.[26] For Bleger, the conventions that structure analysis and guarantee its constancy are institutional features. "A relationship which lasts for years, in which a set of norms and attitudes is kept up, is nothing less than a true definition of institution," he observes, concluding: "The psychoanalytic situation is an institution in itself, especially the frame."[27]

The institutional conventions of psychoanalysis—hours and fees, carpets and cushions, the chair and the couch—support the task of unbinding. That is, psychoanalysis is an institution paradoxically devoted to dissolution. Even the frame, Bleger maintains, must ultimately become an object of analysis, or unbinding, and "here we are likely to find the strongest resistance."[28] For when the analysis turns to the frame, it touches on the "catastrophic situation" of infantile vulnerability, the fear of change.[29] "The analyst modifies the furniture of the consulting room, changes the couch, moves. . . . As is well known, in these circumstances very intense reactions can be noticed, which can be real, even if only temporary, psychotic episodes, as if the change that has taken place mobilizes very primitive anxieties, of a symbiotic type, that are normally contained by the familiar set up."[30] So writes Luciana Nissim Momigliano, the Milanese psychoanalyst to whom Nanni Moretti refers his audience for a theoretical understanding of the proposition that, as Momigliano puts it, psychoanalysis is an encounter between "two people talking in a room."[31] The strange dynamic between analyst and analysand, however, is also a ritual that unbalances social intercourse through a series of calculated discrepancies: one speaks while the other listens in silence; one reclines while the other sits upright; one is charged with the exercise of singular self-restraint, while the demand on the other is to speak as freely as possible. As Laplanche explains, the work of analysis depends on this "essential dissymmetry in the relation" in order for the transference to develop and to evolve.[32] The distance rigorously maintained between analyst and analysand, the scopic and social estrangement of the two people talking in a room, and the admonition to avoid contact outside the ritual space all contribute to the atmosphere of an encounter Laplanche describes as enigmatic, as contracted in an "enigmatic dimension."[33] "What is offered," observes Laplanche, "is a place for speech, for free speech, but not, properly speaking, the place of an exchange."[34] Analysis offers a place for speech within the enigmatic dimension of the frame.

In a published discussion between Moretti and a group of analysts, one audience member objected that, "in Germany, psychoanalysts would not go to visit a patient on a Sunday" as Sermonti does in *The Son's Room*. To which the film-maker testily replied, "Perhaps in another country an analyst would never go and visit his patient on a Sunday; instead, in Italy, in a film of mine, he would!"[35] This in turn prompted another panelist, the psychoanalyst Stefano Bolognini, to announce, in his closing remarks: "I just want to reassure our colleague who spoke earlier about the Italian analyst's methods of practice: yes, usually they are human and affective, but they do not go to the home of the patient!"[36] To one rule — psychoanalysts don't pay house calls — the analysts of Germany and Italy, if not the filmmakers, apparently can agree, but the century-long debate over the proper distance between analyst and analysand, or the institutional limits of the frame, is not yet at an end.

Films about psychoanalysis routinely deviate from the rules, breaking the frame so as to motivate the plot. Moretti, however, is insistent about his fidelity to the analytic situation. "I wanted to respect the setting," he remarks. "I wanted the analyst's work to be carried out in his consulting room." While an American screenwriter might, Moretti claims, "tend to feel that this might be a boring thing to represent . . . I wanted my film, the work in my film, to be carried out within those walls, within the consulting room."[37] Turning to a lead-ing theoretical voice on the setting, he mentions the work of Momigliano, who contrasts the rigid adherence to orthodoxy in psychoanalysis in America to analysis in Europe. In the "hyper-rigid technique" once "popular in the United States," she observes, "the principle of abstinence becomes the 'rule' of absti-nence; in an effort to follow the rules of impersonality and anonymity, con-sulting rooms were left bare, so that none of the analyst's personality or taste could be seen."[38] In America, it seems, filmmakers find the setting boring, and analysts make it so.

Such asceticism is contrary to Freud's own invention, the consulting room as a repository of past civilizations embodied in the serried rows of so many statu-ettes, figured vases, reliefs, textiles, and objets d'art of every description. For Freud, as Forrester has observed, the very model of psychoanalysis is collect-ing: "Freud opened up a whole set of related fields of phenomena, whose scien-tific study would require assiduous and painstaking collections: dreams, jokes, parapraxes, early memories."[39] And it is "alongside these distinctively Freudian collections," he observes, "that we should place his contemporaneous collec-tion of antiquities," a treasury displayed exclusively in the consulting room and study as one index of "its intimate connection with his psychoanalytic work."[40]

Freudian psychoanalytic technique, however, did demand a renunciation of visual contact between analyst and analysand, effecting a displacement of scopic desire from the face of the analyst to the milieu of analysis. Freud recommended that the two people talking in a room look away from each other, the analyst seated behind and at right angles to the couch; and unlike H. D., who relished the view of Freud's collection (and claims to have impressed her analyst by inspecting first the room and only then turning her gaze to the doctor himself), some patients balk at the couch. "It's a fine couch. . . . But I have no intention of lying on it," Giovanni's prospective patient assures him. "A particularly large number of patients . . . ask to be allowed to go through the treatment in some other position," Freud acknowledged, "for the most part because they are anxious not to be deprived of a view of the doctor." He persevered. "I insist on this procedure," Freud explained, in order "to prevent the transference from mingling with the patient's associations imperceptibly, to isolate the transference and to allow it to come forward in due course sharply defined as a resistance."[41] One function of the couch, therefore, is to keep analyst and analysand apart, to prevent them from becoming visually, or reflectively, entangled.

His original "recommendations on technique," Freud observed, "were essentially of a negative nature," cautioning the prospective analyst about "what one should not do"—above all, the analyst must not reciprocate the patient's demand for love—without requiring that the would-be analyst emulate Freud's clinical technique in every particular. As the culture of psychoanalysis calcified into the institution of psychoanalysis, however, "the docile analysts did not perceive the elasticity of the rules that I had laid down, and submitted to them as if they were taboos."[42] In short, "the institutionalization of psychoanalysis," as Moustapha Safouan trenchantly observes, "was carried out as if psychoanalysis had never existed"—through repression.[43]

In repression, "the subject effaces her- or himself as a subject who knows what is going on."[44] "Elided as the subject of her or his own utterance," the "docile" analyst is content to "present her- or himself purely as an interpreter of the Text," obedient to the word of Freud as to dogma. And "an institution founded on dogma," Safouan observes, "is repression personified."[45] For Momigliano, the hardening of the principle of abstinence into law, characterized by a clinical sterility in which the consulting room was left bare and the "analyst always wore the same clothes," amounts to a repression, an effacement of the analyst as a subject who is capable of responding creatively to the patient.[46] So if, to extend Momigliano's suggestion, the frame of psychoanalysis is a symptom of the institution that underpins it—a repressive institution founded on dogma—a critique of the institution of psychoanalysis might begin in the consulting room itself.

The couch was slippery, the headpiece at the back was hard. I was almost too long; if I were a little longer my feet would touch the old-fashioned porcelain stove that stood edge-wise in the corner. . . . There was the stove, but there were moments when one felt a little chilly. I smoothed the folds of the rug, I glanced surreptitiously at my wristwatch. . . . I tucked my cold hands under the rug. I always found the rug carefully folded at the foot of the couch when I came in. Did the little maid Paula come in from the hall and fold the rug or did the preceding analysand fold it, as I always carefully did before leaving?

H. D.

Then there is the couch itself, which may be low, broad, comfortable, or quite the contrary; the chair of the analyst; the arrangement of the consulting room — shall it be furnished as a study or as a drawing room? Or shall it be left totally unfurnished apart from the couch and the chair?

Alice and Michael Bálint

The room had the harsh and anguished modernity of the rooms in the paintings of Francis Bacon; in its motel-like detachment from the things of this world, it was like analytic abstinence itself. The couch was a narrow foam-rubber slab covered with an indifferently chosen gold fabric; over its foot, where the patient's shoes rested, a piece of ugly black plastic sheeting was stretched. The room was like an iconoclast's raised fist: this analyst's patients didn't come here to pass the time of day, it told you.

Janet Malcolm

Dr. Schrift had two Utrillo prints and one Braque. (It was my first shrink, so I didn't realize these were the standard APA-approved prints.) He also had a Danish-modern desk (also APA-approved), and a brownish Foamland couch with a compulsive little plastic cover at the foot and a hard wedge-shaped pillow, covered with a paper napkin, at the head.

Erica Jong

In Buenos Aires in 1999, the Boston-based photographer Shellburne Thurber began a project to document psychoanalysts' offices. Returning to Boston the following year, she continued the series, photographing consulting rooms, studies, and waiting rooms. The photographs' subjects range from plush private suites to cluttered institutional cells. Most concentrate on the business end of the couch, showing the relative positions of the head of the sofa and the analyst's chair. On the evidence of this series at least, Freud's rug-draped convalescent bed, or its cousin, the vintage claw-foot fainting couch, continues to be used by some analysts. More often it is replaced by daybeds, camp beds, cots, or even ordinary living room or bedroom furniture equipped with odd-sized pillows. Some analysts remain ensconced behind the couch, while others seem to have migrated into positions alongside the analysand, nestled noiselessly in deep, soft armchairs, keeping their feet raised on broad ottomans. Others sit upright in straight-backed chairs, swivel, or rock.

On the evidence of Thurber's photographs, overdetermination is the design strategy par excellence of the psychoanalytic consulting room. The walls are often lined with books, gaps opening to betray a little of the analyst's "personal taste." A scattering of rugs, busts, wall hangings, paintings, and, most common of all, prints (these last being mostly abstract compositions of the landscape-of-the-mind type) complete the look. Rows of figurines, strategically placed for optimal visibility — on a shallow shelf beside the couch, for example — pay tribute to Freud's own collection of antique statuettes. The founder's fascination with cultural syncretism also finds echoes in the selection of prominently displayed artifacts, a Native American wall hanging or an African mask (fig. 7.4). Less poetic symbols of contemporary culture occasionally infiltrate the scene. In one Buenos Aires office, a picture of Freud keeps company with a television set (fig. 7.5). Inside the door of a Framingham, Massachusetts, office, the corner is filled with file cabinets and an untidy stack of boxes containing, according to Thurber, prescription drugs.

Thurber's project began serendipitously in Buenos Aires when, as the houseguest of an elderly psychoanalyst, she was given the use of the consulting room one afternoon to read. "Struck by how intense and energetic" the analytic setting was, she asked to photograph it. The analyst "not only agreed but offered to contact her friends to see if they would like their offices photographed as well," and Thurber returned to Boston with a series of a dozen or so pictures. Continuing the project there, she traded on a prestigious fellowship to gain the entrée granted more casually in Buenos Aires. "I encountered some resistance getting into the oldest and biggest institution, Boston Psychoanalytic," the artist recalls, but "I managed to break through, thanks to the Harvard letterhead."[47] Back home, Thurber assembled a more extensive series of some seventy-five consulting-room pictures that testify to the significance, more specifically the transferential significance, of the setting for the analyst.

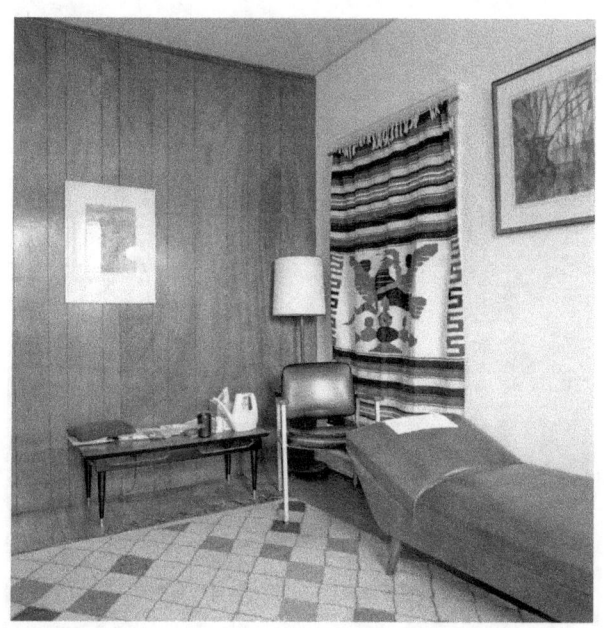

FIGURE 7.4 Shellburne Thurber, *Brookline, Mass.:*
Office with Native American Wall Hanging.

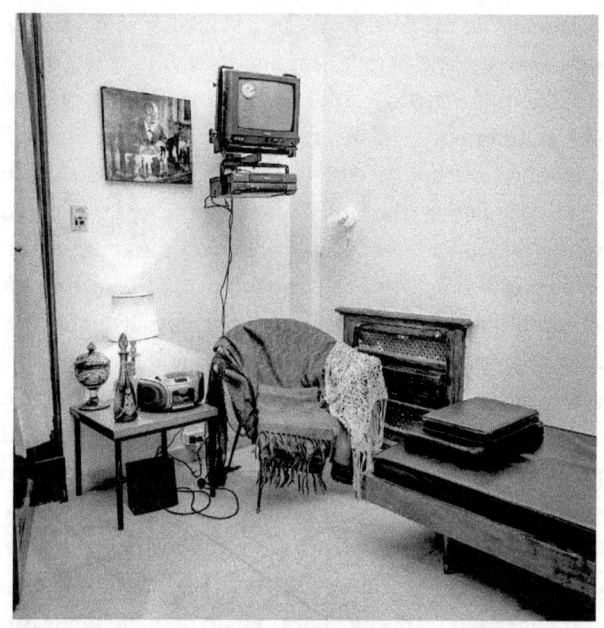

FIGURE 7.5 Shellburne Thurber, *Buenos Aires: Analyst's*
Office with Television and Picture of Freud.

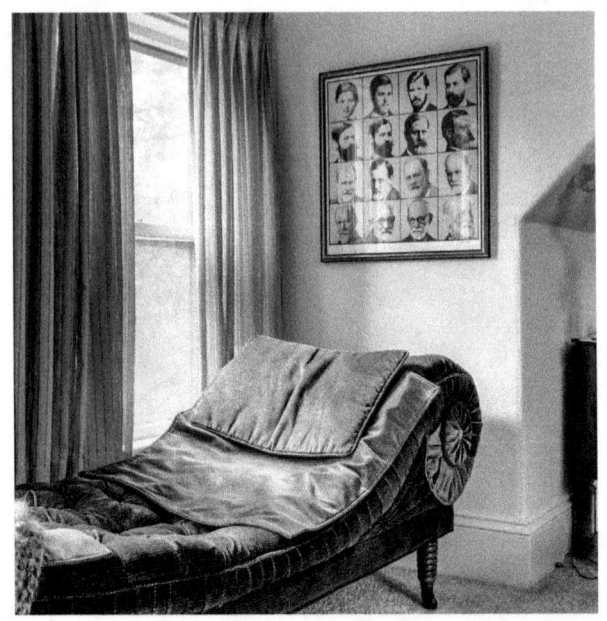

FIGURE 7.6 Shellburne Thurber, *Newtonville, Mass.:*
Blue Couch with Multiple Portrait of Freud.

"Having patients 'on the couch' may be a source of pride, supporting one's identity as an analyst," one practitioner admits.[48] And if the presence of the couch itself stakes this claim to legitimacy, busts and images of Freud, a fixture of the rooms Thurber photographs, reinforce it. In one, a blue velvet couch, its soft lap spooned out by the settling-in of so many backsides, its creased, rumpled upholstery the proof of frequent and sustained use, is gently illuminated by a floor-length curtained window. Behind the couch is the analyst— not the occupant of this actual consulting room, but Freud. Or rather, sixteen Freuds, his bearded visage repeated in a multiple portrait arranged in a Warhol-esque grid of photographic portraits made at different moments in his life (fig. 7.6). The desire of the analyst to occupy the place of the master, Safouan has noted, is the fantasy with which psychoanalysis as an institution has always had to contend. From the outset (in Freud's own time), the institutionalization of psychoanalysis was, writes Safouan, "a piece of acting out, a staging of desire at its most stubbornly resistant to signification: that is, of desire as essentially bound to (not to say effectively identical with) the defense which forbids each and every one of us from enjoying a certain quotient of pleasure held out or 'promised' by the place of the master."[49] The desire to occupy the place of the master is repressed, and with it theoretical curiosity about its surrounding space, which is the setting.

How, then, do we even know what contemporary psychoanalytic consulting rooms look like, apart from those we might pay to see? Turning from Thurber's photographs to the pages of a professional journal, *International Psychoanalysis*, the bulletin of the International Psychoanalytic Association, we find it — confirming José Bleger's prescient observation that it is important "to consider the psychoanalytic situation as an institution in itself, especially the frame" — illustrated with a locally inflected global survey of analytic interiors. A Seattle consulting room is dominated by a Native American wall hanging, a patterned couch, and a geometric rug; in Hamburg, a parquet floor is warmed by a Turkish rug; in Paris, a Mies-type couch is illuminated by a wall of light-flooded windows. The June 2003 issue, however, also offers, on its Letters page, a comment from one analyst, Willem Linschoten, objecting to the disappearance of cartoons in favor of the waiting-room and consulting-room pictures. To illustrate his complaint, Linschoten provides a photographic caricature of his own "ivory tower" cell. A first attempt to produce this (digitally manipulated) image was, he reports, busy with the paraphernalia of the electronic office — computer equipment, cables, and adapters. "The first version of my 'room full of insight' was blurred with the seemingly useless trivia of our digital age." A second effort, cleared of this "abundant chaos," was instead "too sparse," an effect rectified by the "cunning placement" of a few objects: guitars propped in the corner, a "gaudy" abstract painting, a volume of Freud's *Interpretation of Dreams* on the analyst's chair, a female figure on a pedestal, a statuette of Michelangelo's *Moses* and a "coffee-table book," in the form of Edmund Engelman's 1976 monograph, *Berggasse 19*, with Freud's picture emblazoned on its cover, and a framed diploma over the couch.[50]

The issue of *International Psychoanalysis* in which this parody of the frame appears, highlighting the analyst's own transference to the couch, examines a "crisis in psychoanalysis." As measured by indices such as numbers of new patients and training candidates, psychoanalysis, it reports, is in decline. "The model of the typical analysis, handed down from generation to generation through the mythical image of the armchair and couch, is now restricted to the privileged," Elisabeth Roudinescou has observed in a recent manifesto for a "renewal of Freudianism."[51] "Soon psychoanalysis will only be of interest to an ever more restricted fringe of the population," Jean-Bertrand Pontalis has predicted, asking: "Will there only be psychoanalysts left on the psychoanalysts' couch?"[52] In this light, the photographic portfolio of consulting rooms in

International Psychoanalysis might be seen as compensatory, securing the identity of the analyst as one who (still) has patients on the couch, even if they are only other analysts.[53]

Until recently even the clinical literature has been reticent on the matter of the frame. "I shall not waste many words on the question of the furnishing of the consulting room," remarks Henrik Carpelan—in an article entitled "On the Importance of the Setting in the Psychoanalytic Situation." The furnishing of the room, the author continues, "is decided by functional necessities, and the analyst's personal taste," as if neither factor was worth the trouble to explore in the kind of depth that is devoted to other elements of the frame, the timing and frequency of sessions, for example, or the length of the analysis—or payment. "The consulting room should not be an art museum or an exhibition hall," he advises. On the other hand, "this does not mean that it should necessarily be spartan and cold." Above all, it should not elicit "excessive envy" from the analysand.[54] The brittle tone of these recommendations persists when it comes to managing patients who sometimes "complain about the hardness of the couch, or the cushion being too high or too low, too hard or too soft," or about the upholstery being irritating or causing them to sweat. "Most of these complaints are accessible to analysis"—meaning that they are transference responses that can be integrated into the analysis itself. Some patients, however, preferring "material well-being to psychic balance and internal satisfaction," present a "serious problem in this regard."[55]

Exasperation with patients who complain about the couch is a recurrent theme in the literature that touches on the topic, and is in marked contrast to analytic attitudes toward actions that break the frame in other ways. Even when patients use the couch uncomplainingly, the analyst may criticize the way this is done. One analysand of Carpelan, for example, "had the habit of moving the cushion and folding it double. He pretended it was more comfortable in this way. Only after analyzing his narcissistic need of making the analysis on his own conditions was he able to leave the cushion as I had put it."[56] One is left to wonder whether the unstated demand to leave the cushion as the analyst has placed it is simply a matter of respecting the frame of the analysis, consistent with Freud's original demand that patients lie on the couch, or might also betray some frustrated professional fetishism. Or, to think of it another way, perhaps the analyst fears that the patient absorbed by creature comforts is soft, a descendant of the nineteenth-century salon-dweller that Walter Benjamin described as a somnambulant whose "gaze was enveloped in billowing curtains and swollen cushions."[57]

For psychoanalysis does not consider itself a soft option. The silence of the analyst, the strict routine, the scopic and social deprivations of the ritual, and of course the fee, all underpin a stringency that, as Roudinescou observes, may now be its undoing:

> When it comes to contemporary patients, they bear little resemblance to those of earlier periods. Generally speaking, they fit the image of this depressive society in which they live. Impregnated with contemporary nihilism, they present with narcissistic or depressive disturbances and suffer from solitude or loss of identity. Often lacking either the energy or the desire to submit to long analyses, they have trouble with regular attendance at analysts' consulting rooms. They often miss sessions and can often no longer stand more than one or two a week. Lacking financial means, they tend to suspend the analysis as soon as they realize there has been an improvement in their condition, even if that means taking it up again when the symptoms reappear. This resistance to entering into the transference setup indicates that if the market economy treats subjects like commodities, patients too have a tendency in their turn to use analysis as a form of medication and the analyst as a receptacle of their sufferings.[58]

If, as Freud observed, "points of importance at the beginning" of analysis are "arrangements about time and money," these remain points of cardinal significance at its historical end. The institutionalization of psychoanalysis, predicated on the multiplication of the setting into so many private rooms where the couch and the chair would meet at right angles to make the frame, is now dominated by the very "medical order" in which, as Safouan has observed, institutional psychoanalysis also, at its cost, sought to enlist.[59] In Freud's own time, his followers had already "consolidated the one trend that Freud wanted to avoid: the shrinkage of psychoanalysis into an annex of psychiatry."[60] In a series of photographs of clinical settings, including the disused furniture of the Royal Psychiatric Society—hard, flat, overused couches in stark contrast to Thurber's homier surrounds—the British artist Sarah Jones documents the particular demise of the couch as a psychiatric accessory.

In vanishing, however, the couch has become newly visible. While psychoanalysis, psychotherapy, and seemingly any therapy involving "talk" have lost currency—both in the psychotropic drug culture of contemporary psychiatry and in that most discursive of cultural spaces, the university—a surprising number of artists have repaired to the couch. Two trends of thought about psychoanalysis seem to be at work in these recent projects. One extends an interest of some Conceptual art in the Freudian logic of collecting and is materialized particularly in photographic and object-based compendiums. Another seeks to explore, within the medium of video, the "dynamics of transference" in psychoanalysis.[61]

> Plush—the material in which traces are left especially easily.
> *Walter Benjamin*

Susan Hiller's *After the Freud Museum* (1995) investigates Freud's habits of collecting (fig. 7.7). Each of fifty brown cardboard boxes, of the type used by archaeologists for storing and sorting samples, contains a selection of specimens—potsherds in polythene bags, toys, chemists' vials filled with the waters of ancient rivers, a miniature television monitor—each piece artfully arranged, titled, and accompanied on the inside lid by a supplementary text or picture. Box 021, "Joy," for example, contains a set of thirty-six mounted slides, duplicates of the glass slides Hiller discovered in the Freud Museum in London. "I sorted and catalogued the remnants and found there were four types: scientific specimens, miniature curiosities, traditional magic lantern slides, and early Disney cartoon strips."[62] Echoing both the cabinet of curiosities and the Fluxbox, *After the Freud Museum* makes the heterogeneity of Freud's collections its organizing principle and connects with Freud as, in Forrester's description, "a collector of farts and grimaces, an archaeologist of rubbish *avant la lettre*, as well as a collector of the fading yet precious detritus of Western civilization."[63]

In 1995, Cornelia Parker, too, made a pilgrimage to the couch, extracting a souvenir, a few feathers plucked from the pillow on which the heads of analysands once rested. From this trace of the talking cure she produced another, a photogram. Parker also collected samples of nicotine. Taking custody of rags used to clean the tarnish of cigar smoke from articles in the museum, she harvested Freud's exhalations as a material for drawing. For Parker, Freud's feathers, and Freud himself, were to be part of a larger set of historical figures, whose physical traces (including, for example, a feather found floating through the air in Benjamin Franklin's attic) are incorporated into her oeuvre.

Hiller and Parker explore Freud's principle of collecting, Hiller by assembling a heterogeneous collection of objects "after" Freud, Parker by taking her specimens "from" Freud. Both reflect on "the spirit of 'scientific' acquisition pervading Freud's collections."[64] Thurber and Jones, too, participate in Freud's propensity to collect. None of these artists produces anything like a compre-

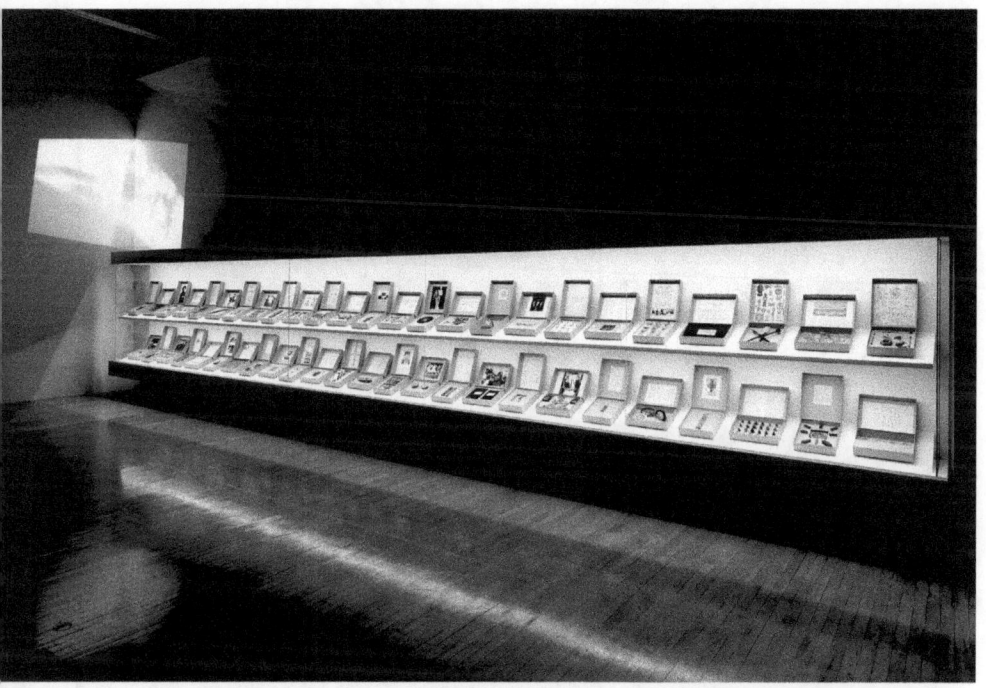

FIGURE 7.7 Susan Hiller, *From the Freud Museum*, 1991–1997, collection Tate, London.

hensive archive. Nor did Freud. "This was never meant to be a visual catalog comparing and contrasting different offices from various parts of the globe," Thurber says, but a limited series, in keeping with the artist's other projects documenting site types, motel rooms and abandoned houses, for example.[65] Freud's model of collecting is expansive but selective, aspiring to initiate new collections — dreams, parapraxes, and jokes — and to combine these with the collection of antique objects that represented, for him, civilization itself. In the antique setting of psychoanalysis, the ancient collection and the psychoanalytic one rub elbows in a dialectical fashion: "The model of the dream consistently subverts the model of permanence offered by the ancient statues in their cases, standing guard over desk and couch."[66]

Mary Kelly's *Post-Partum Document*, begun in 1973, is a psycho-conceptual museum of maternity commemorating, from the maternal subject position, the early childhood of the artist's son (figs. 7.8 and 7.9).[67] At one level, this exhibition of the maternal-infantile relation both extends and counters Freud's collection of antiquities, which Forrester describes, paraphrasing Marx, as "a concise compendium of his version of civilization" — a collection in which "every piece or item . . . represented a paternal figure standing guard over the myste-

FIGURE 7.8 Mary Kelly, detail of *Post-Partum Document*: "Documentation I, Analysed Faecal Stains and Feeding Charts," 1974. Perspex unit, white card, diaper linings, plastic sheeting, paper, ink. Seven units: 28 cm H × 35.5 cm W. Image courtesy of the artist, Susanne Vielmetter Los Angeles Projects, and Pippy Houldsworth Gallery. Copyright Generali Foundation. Photo: Werner Kaligofsky.

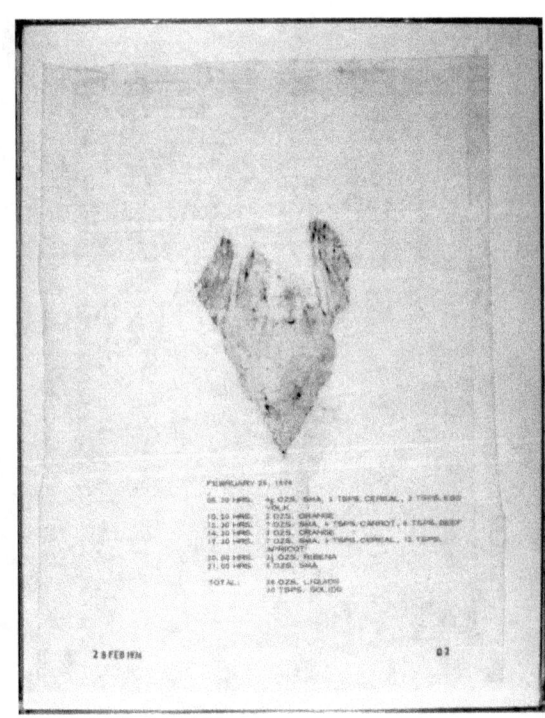

FIGURE 7.9 Mary Kelly, detail of *Post-Partum Document*: "Documentation IV, Transitional Objects, Diary, and Diagram," 1976. Perspex unit, white card, plaster, cotton fabric, string. Eight units: 28 cm H × 35.5 cm W. Image courtesy of the artist, Susanne Vielmetter Los Angeles Projects, and Pippy Houldsworth Gallery. Copyright Generali Foundation. Photo: Werner Kaligofsky.

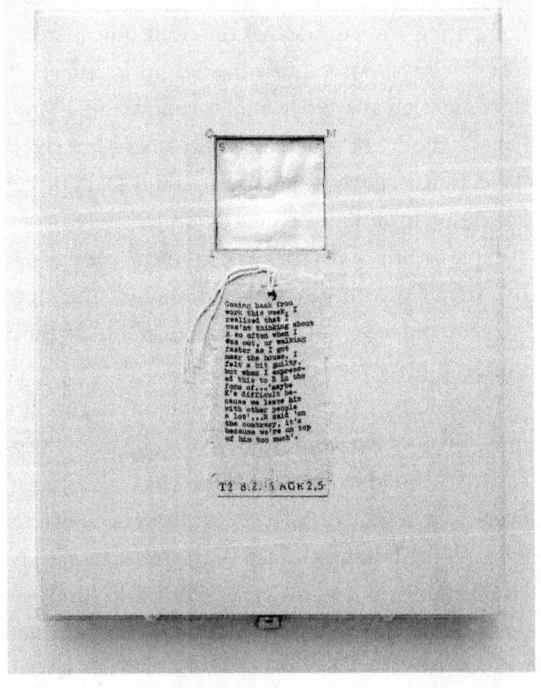

rious feminine."[68] For *Post-Partum Document* offers its own set of fragmentary relics — textiles, casts, tablets engraved with mysterious characters — a collection in which every element refers to the maternal figure Freudian psychoanalysis overlooks. It adopts Freud's own habits of collecting to constitute the maternal subject both materially and linguistically, in things and in words. It partakes of Freud's ambition to turn dreams, jokes, and slips of the tongue into the "serious stuff of science," extending that logic to the "covert objects of shame" associated with the maternal role.[69] To the archive of "farts and grimaces" assembled by Freud, Kelly adds fecal stains, baby talk, and maternal fetishism, incorporating the maternal subject and placing its objects, too, into the public discourses of psychoanalysis and of Conceptual art.

First exhibited at the Institute of Contemporary Art in London in 1976, *Post-Partum Document* was received with indignation by the British tabloid press. The perceived scandal of a mother contaminating the maternal-infantile bond and the aesthetic autonomy of the gallery at once was predictably in keeping with the cultural anxiety that has attended psychoanalysis and the art it has inspired throughout its history. The Freud Museums of both Vienna and London, accordingly, have more recently welcomed the involvement of artists and the display of contemporary work as a means to demonstrate, in their different ways, the continuing cultural resonance of psychoanalysis.

In London, the museum has presented installations by Hiller, Sophie Calle, Sarah Lucas, and Valie Export, among others. For Lucas's exhibition, *Beyond the Pleasure Principle* (2000), the artist was given the run of the house, and trashed it. In a series of savagely humorous interventions, she occupied the rooms with installations of overturned furniture, cast-off underwear, and, assigned pride of place above the couch, an enlarged photograph of the artist's own headless torso, one nipple shown slyly protruding from a hole in her shirt. Caricaturing the Anna Freudian diorama of discipleship, Lucas "played out her role as bad-girl rebel . . . with singular relish and inventiveness," Linda Nochlin has observed — a transgression against the setting, a spectacular splintering of the frame, which the museum readily accommodated.[70] For by taking out her defiance of the master on the setting — by enacting her negative transference to psychoanalysis in its own milieu — Lucas also claimed psychoanalysis for her own. Borrowing the title of a work by Freud in which the master himself laid siege to his own theories, *Beyond the Pleasure Principle* uses psychoanalysis as an object that, in Juliet Mitchell's formulation, survives through our very efforts to destroy it: "The artist or critic is helped by the theory of psychoanalysis to develop the capacity to destroy that theory so that she or he can make use of it."[71]

In Vienna, the involvement of Joseph Kosuth in an exhibition to commemorate the fiftieth anniversary of Freud's death resulted in the formation of a foundation to create a permanent collection of work, donated by the artists—including John Baldessari, Jenny Holzer, Ilya Kabakov, Sherrie Levine, Haim Stainbach, and Franz West—and displayed in the former family apartment at Berggasse 19, rooms now used by the museum as library and exhibition space. The mission of the foundation, according to Kosuth, is to assemble "an art collection in which post-Freudian thought would actually be manifested internally in the work."[72]

Freud himself, however, was little interested in the effect psychoanalysis began to exert on art in his own time. "The interpreter of dreams," writes Forrester, "would never have dreamed of adding a Picabia or a Duchamp to his collection of antiquities."[73] It is in Freud's writings that "we encounter the typical modernist objects—the readymade, the found object, the bit of detritus, the god as a shout in the street, the Surrealist transvaluation of values," not in his artistic tastes. Visiting Vienna on his honeymoon in 1921, André Breton called on Freud, intending to alert him to the role his theories might play in the Surrealist revolution to come—only to find that the inventor of psychoanalysis was a fatherly doctor who didn't "much like France" and was indifferent to modern art.[74] Breton's recollections of that afternoon are a study in negative transference to the master, expressed as bitter disappointment in the analyst's style.

A modest plaque at the entrance: "Dr. Freud, 2–4"; a not very attractive servant girl; a waiting room whose walls are decorated with four mildly allegorical engravings—Water, Fire, Earth, and Air—and with a photograph depicting the master among his collaborators; a dozen or so patients of the most pedestrian sort; and once, after the sound of a bell, several shouts in succession—not enough here to fill even the slimmest of reports. This until the famous padded door cracks open for me. I find myself in the presence of a little old man with no style who receives clients in a shabby office worthy of the neighborhood G.P.

André Breton

Glenn Ligon's *The Orange and Blue Feelings* (2003) is an edited video recording of three meetings with his therapist (fig. 7.10). Its total length, about an hour, is that of a single session. Through the technique of dual-channel pro-

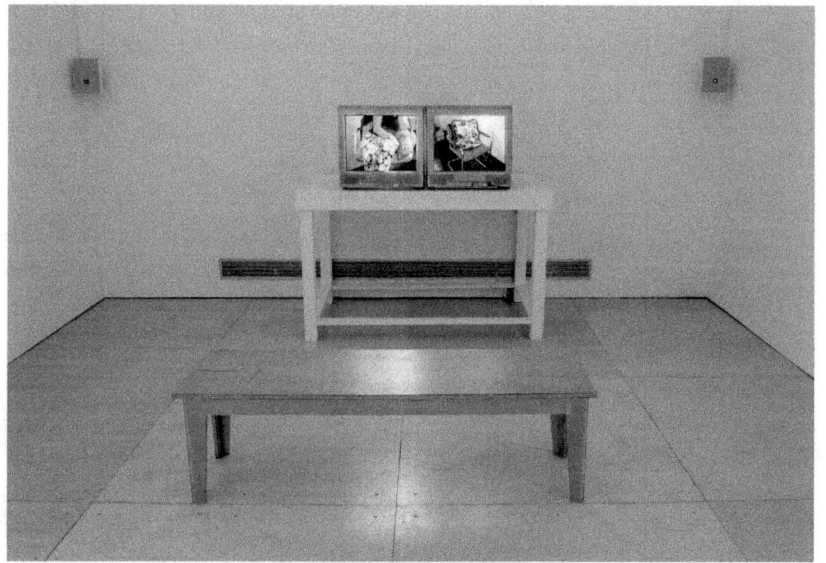

FIGURE 7.10 Glenn Ligon, *The Orange and Blue Feelings*, 2003. Copyright Glenn Ligon; courtesy of the artist, Luhring Augustine, New York, Regen Projects, Los Angeles, and Thomas Dane Gallery, London. Installation view Gallery 400, University of Illinois, Chicago, 2009. Photo: Tom Van Eynde. Original in color.

jection, therapist and patient are relegated to discrete frames, their respective scenes playing slightly out of sync. The therapist, a middle-aged woman partial to flowered prints and bangle bracelets, twirls in her swivel chair. Her foot in its kitten-heeled shoe rests delicately on a cushion. Stroking her bare arm rhythmically, she stirs the bangles. Her face is never seen. A pillow tucked into the chair cradles her body to this "habitual seat, a sort of nest padded with accustomed objects," as Janet Malcolm has described the analyst's armchair, comparing it to "a chronic invalid's chair."[75]

The patient, Ligon himself, remains offscreen, his frame filled by the unoccupied end of a couch. Camera movements are small and desultory, mimicking the glassy gaze of a patient undergoing the talking cure, eyes sliding aimlessly over a prosaic assortment of props. The camera lingers on a box of tissues in front of an open window. Catching the breeze, the paper ruffles. An untidy pile of bags sunk on the floor, a houseplant, a shelf lined with books, bric-a-brac, a Freud doll, a corner of patterned carpet, a vase of flowers, a row of framed photographs, a diploma, and a desk piled with papers provide the camera with other vignettes. Once, it jerks unexpectedly toward the window, briefly training its lens on the street below. For almost an hour we listen in as the invisible patient and his Gena Rowlandsesque therapist explore Ligon's anxieties about some recent work.

Transference, writes Laplanche, is "the very milieu of analysis, in the sense of its surrounding environment."[76] The milieu of the transference, he observes, is most perceptible when change is in the air, for "one notices a milieu less when one is plunged in it; more so when it is rather briskly altered or when one leaves it."[77] Ligon's video portrays an analysis in medias res. The figure of the analyst, with her husky voice, coquettish wriggling, and flamboyant dress, is recorded with detachment. If the camera's gaze falls on the foot resting on the pillow, this seems to be as much because, in face-to-face therapy such as this, the patient cannot always be staring back at the therapist and must find relief from the other's gaze somewhere, as because the shoe seems flirtatious. The setting, too, is presented with scant curiosity, like the accustomed environment of a neighbor's living room in which a vase or a picture is occasionally moved but without altering the overall effect. And if the camera wanders around the room from time to time, poking into corners and grazing objects, its investigation is perfunctory. The long, static shots do not probe, highlight, or inventory the room's appointments so much as confirm their familiar presence. Bad taste and comfortable clutter have become the institutional furniture of the frame.

What returns attention to the milieu of psychoanalysis, according to Laplanche, is change. When the milieu is altered, it attracts fresh notice. This occurs especially when the analysand "acts out" by committing "an infidelity to the analytic relation."[78] The patient actualizes desire, goes outside the relationship, acts on an impulse (to have an affair, in the classic scenario) rather than bringing this wish to analysis. Freud called this lateral transference, an action that sidesteps the analyst. In *The Orange and Blue Feelings*, Ligon agonizes over the possibility that therapy will vitiate his art, that "a more balanced life makes for banal work." Preferring to keep his art separate from his therapy (for reasons that become evident as the recorded session's crash tutorial in postmodernism falters), he recognizes the threat to the analytic relation this withholding represents. His solution is to make his therapy the subject of his art, to turn the consulting room into a set, actually to move in. This gesture, however, goes beyond infidelity to the analytic situation and dissolves it.

The acting out that is the real drama of *The Orange and Blue Feelings* is Ligon's shattering of the frame. He nullifies the analytic contract by taking over the role of the analyst as "the director of the method."[79] The video begins with Ligon informing the analyst that overnight he has listened to the recording of a previous session. ("I thought my voice sounded really faggy," he tells her. "That's another thing I have to deal with in therapy, why I hate my voice"—to which the therapist weakly replies, "Oh dear.") Presently, in response to Ligon's account of a childhood memory he holds in his mind as a photograph, uncertain when or even if the event ever occurred, the therapist, recovering her authority, announces, "It's called a screen memory, in fact." By this time, however, the analyst has become the star of the show, the body on the screen, and it is the patient who is directing the analysis.[80]

The analyst must be "director of the method," contends Laplanche. Failing this, "there is no analysis."[81] In Ligon's video, analysis dissolves. Yet the situation suggests another possibility. According to Laplanche, the patient's acting out does not lead inevitably to rupture. An act of infidelity, he proposes, "may be drawn back into that relation, interpreted, in sum, as a transference of transference: 'What you could not, did not wish to tell me, you have signified, enacted, outside.'"[82]

The Orange and Blue Feelings extends over three sessions and concerns the mysterious disappearance of a painting. A portrait of Malcolm X, based on an image copied from a children's coloring book and intended for an exhibition at the Walker Art Center in Minneapolis—"the most interesting painting in the show"—turned up missing from the shipment, stirring anxieties of loss and longing that Ligon associates in therapy with early childhood experience. The portrait was actually produced with the help of a child, he explains to the therapist. As an artist-in-residence at the Walker, he was asked to take part in the museum's educational programming, an obligation he discharged by inviting local schoolchildren to "color in" motifs from his archival source material: vintage coloring books featuring black heroes of American history—figures such as Harriet Tubman, George Washington Carver, and Malcolm X. When one child responded with a vision of Malcolm X resplendent with rouged cheeks and pink lipstick, Ligon, captivated by the fearlessness of "the little queer child who puts lipstick on the image of the father," translated the motif into a large-scale painting that was to be the centerpiece of the Walker exhibition.

"A little boy did that?" the therapist asks. "I'm assuming it was a he," Ligon answers uncertainly, sounding suddenly curious about what the therapist is saying, "unless I'm just projecting myself backward." Up to then, the therapist has been hung up on the act that Ligon copies. Even as a child, he acknowledges, he "never drew from imagination," preferring to copy from source material. "Maybe it's time," she urges, adding, "Maybe it's long past time." "Throw your stencils onto the fire, so to speak?" he demands. "Mmm, I don't know." "I have a lot of anxiety about talking about art work in therapy." He tells her instead about making art in school as a small child, about being ridiculed by a teacher for painting a papier-mâché ocean liner orange and blue. "You'd think art class would be the one class where anything would be fine, where there wouldn't be rules," she replies. "Everybody has an agenda," he reminds her. "I ended up painting the boat black." "You don't like my colors. Fuck you!" she cheers. "I was just thinking about people in the gallery listening to this," he remarks. "It's embarrassing."

Ligon showed *The Orange and Blue Feelings* alongside the original portrait of Malcolm X. He recovered the rolled canvas from the trash after inadvertently—unconsciously, to say the word—discarding it in a studio sweep-up. "I found it between the first session we recorded and the second," he announces to the therapist toward the end of the tape, adding, "I was thinking about the fact that I didn't tell you." Ligon's infidelity, his lateral move—what he "could not, did not wish to tell" his therapist and has instead "signified, enacted outside"—cycles back into the analysis as the ending of the story. His disclosure is timed to conclude the work, the video-analysis he is directing. Ligon broke off therapy shortly after the work was first shown.[83] But if the video records the dissolution of the analysis, it also enacts what Laplanche calls "a transference of transference" from one locus to another: "In other places—during analysis, outside analysis—other possibilities of 'transference' are available to the analysand, other poles for the elaboration of an individual destiny."[84]

> Video's real medium is a psychological situation, the very terms
> of which are to withdraw attention from an external object—an
> Other—and invest it in the Self.
>
> *Rosalind Krauss*

Critics reviewing *Going There*, the 2003 New York gallery exhibition in which Ligon first presented *The Orange and Blue Feelings*, expressed surprise and disappointment at its apparently confessional mode. In contrast to Ligon's previous work, including stenciled word paintings, in which passages of text are applied to white canvases—works that, as one critic observed, "managed to address subjectivity and its politics by way of elegantly conceived formal frameworks"[85]—*The Orange and Blue Feelings* instead seemed self-centered, seemed to summon Rosalind Krauss's early critique of video as producing "an aesthetics of narcissism."

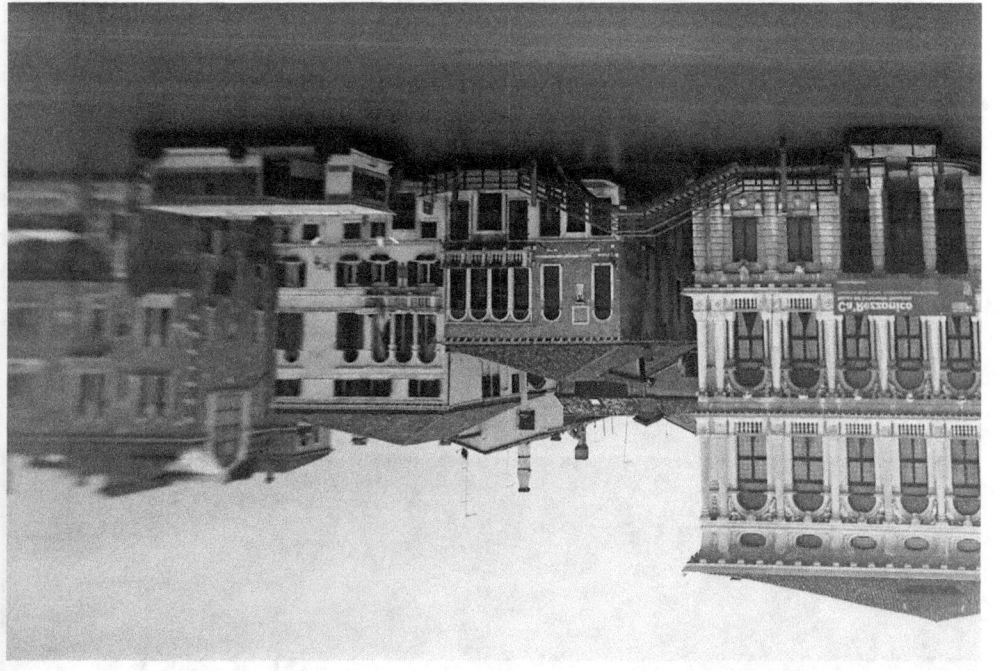

PLATE 1 Zoe Leonard, *Campo San Samuele*, 3231. Photograph by Lothar Schnepf.

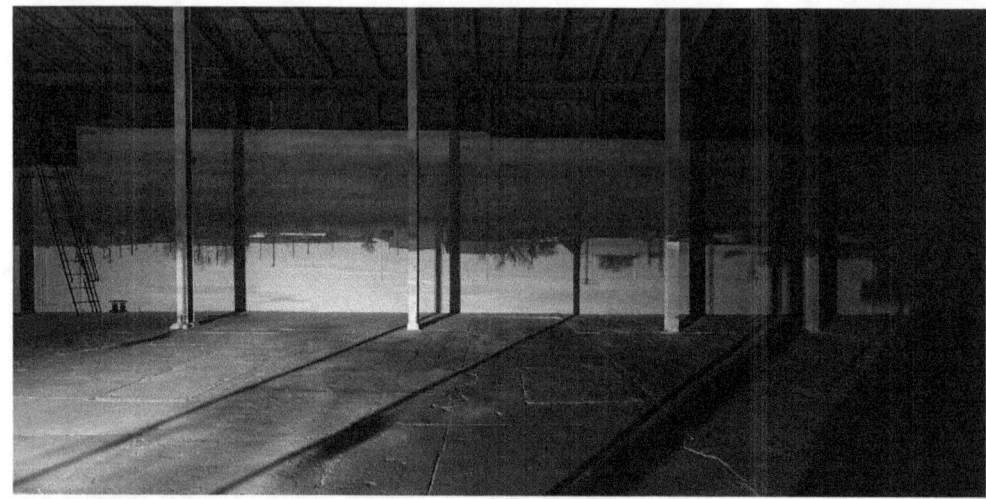

PLATE 2 Zoe Leonard, *100 North Nevill Street*. Photograph by Fredrik Nilsen.

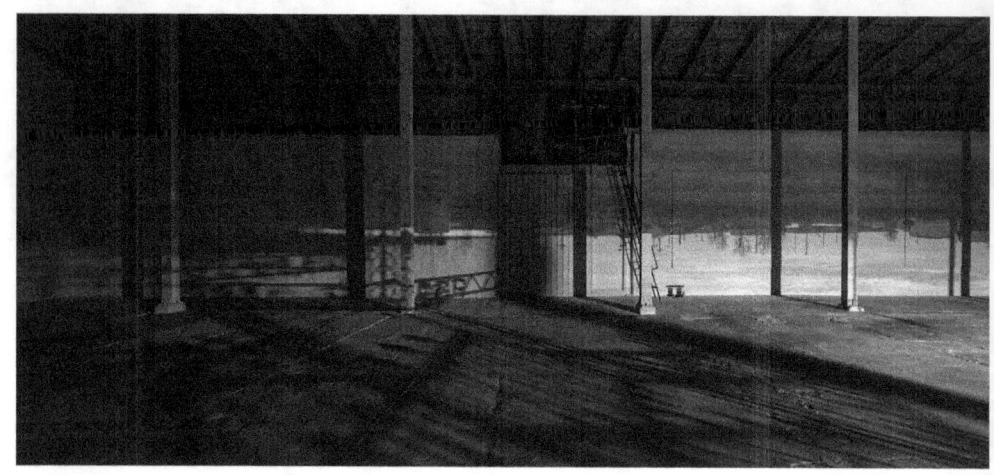

PLATE 3 Zoe Leonard, *100 North Nevill Street*. Photograph by Fredrik Nilsen.

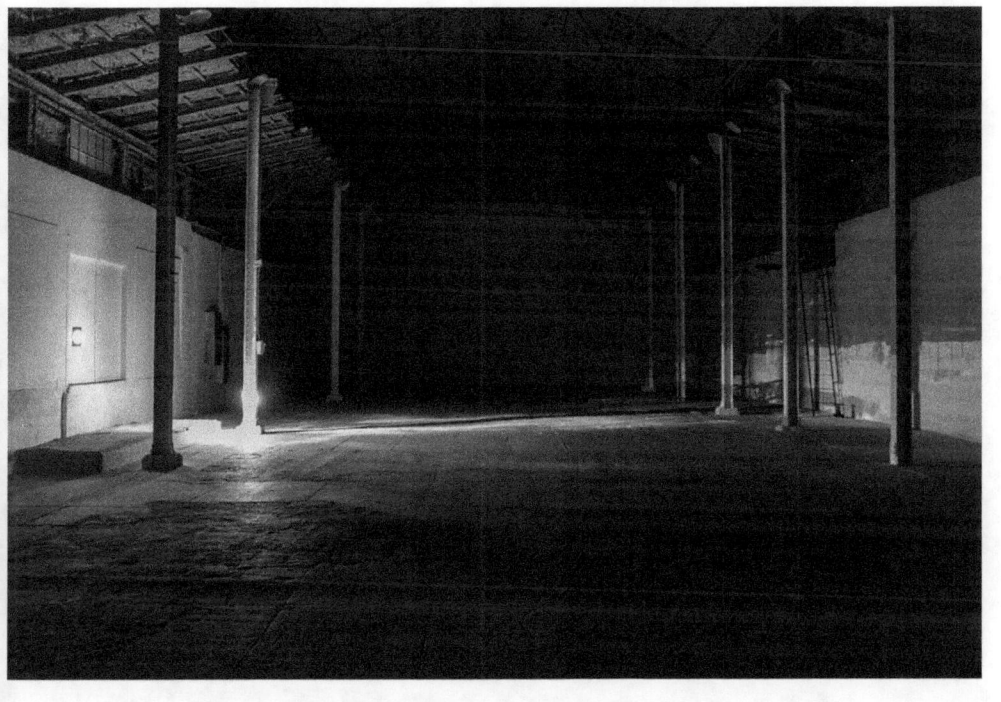

PLATE 4 Zoe Leonard, *100 North Nevill Street*. Photograph by Fredrik Nilsen.

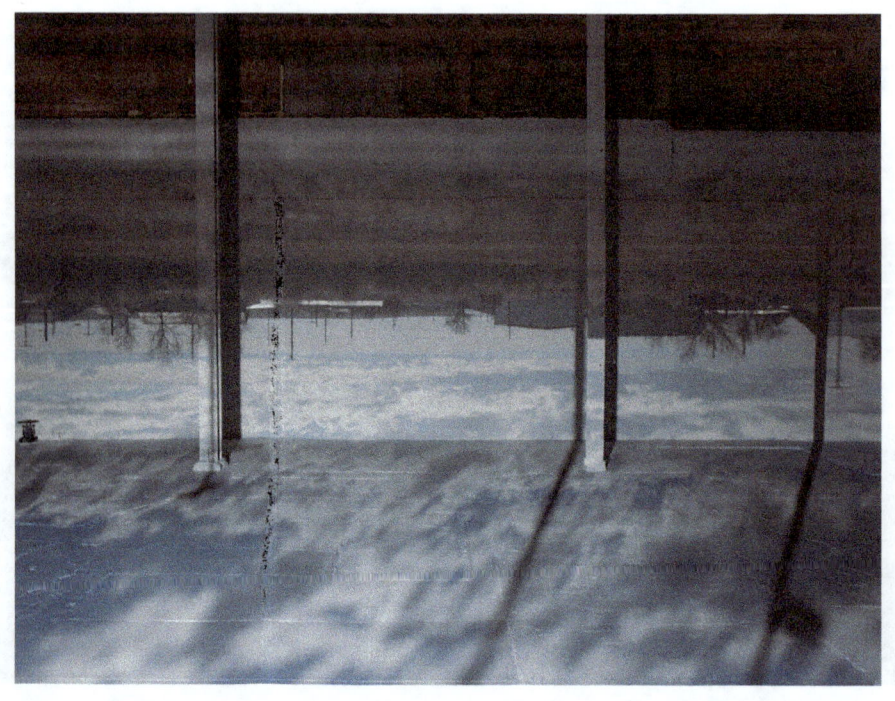

PLATE 5 Zoe Leonard, *100 North Nevill Street*. Photograph by Fredrik Nilsen.

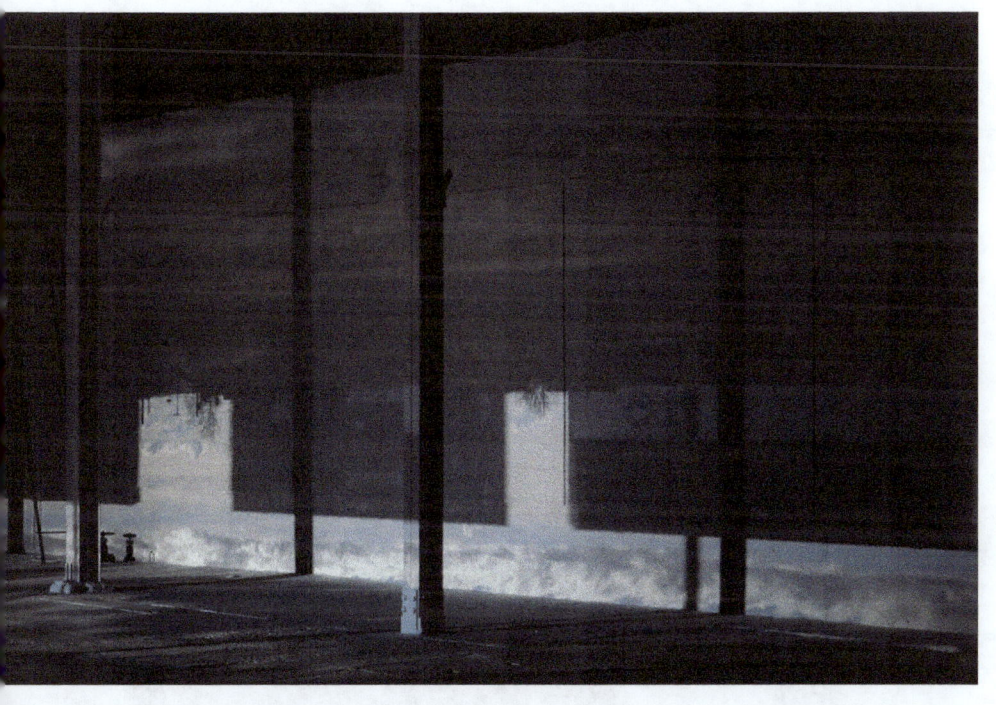

PLATE 6 Zoe Leonard, *100 North Nevill Street*. Photograph by Fredrik Nilsen.

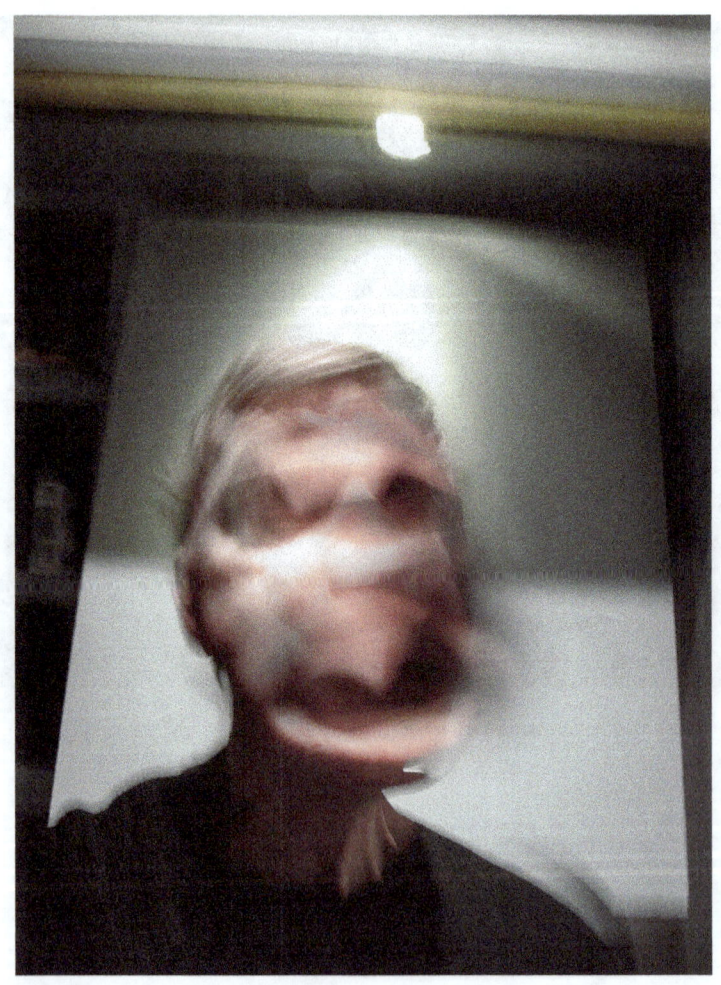

PLATE 7 Kristan Horton, *Sligo Heads, Beak,* 2012.

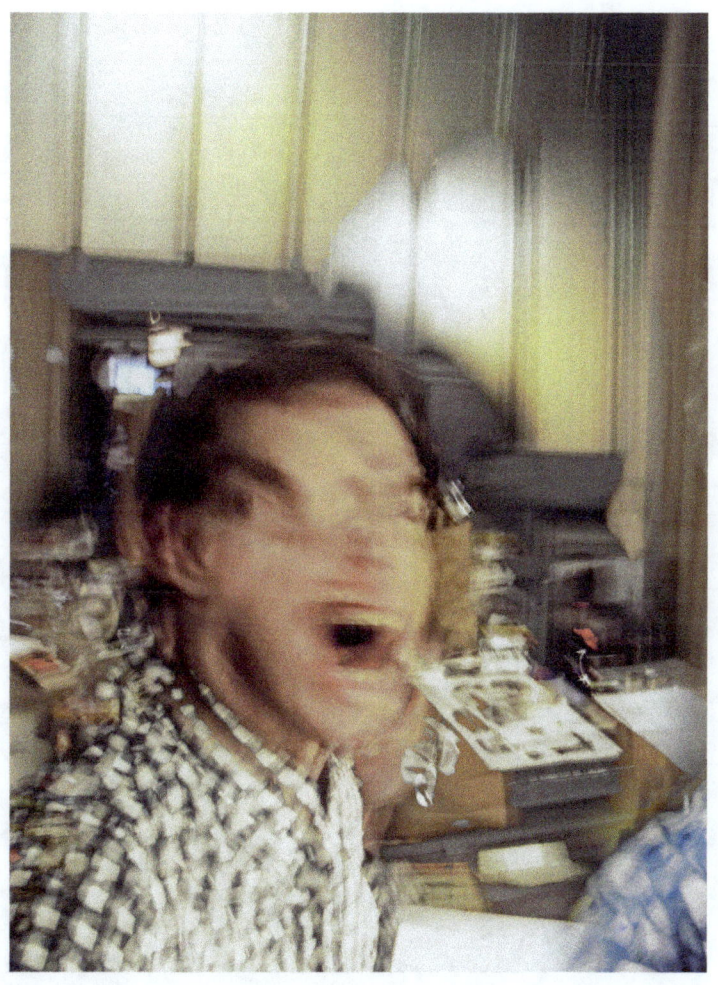

PLATE 8 Kristan Horton, *Sligo Heads, Chatter*, 2012.

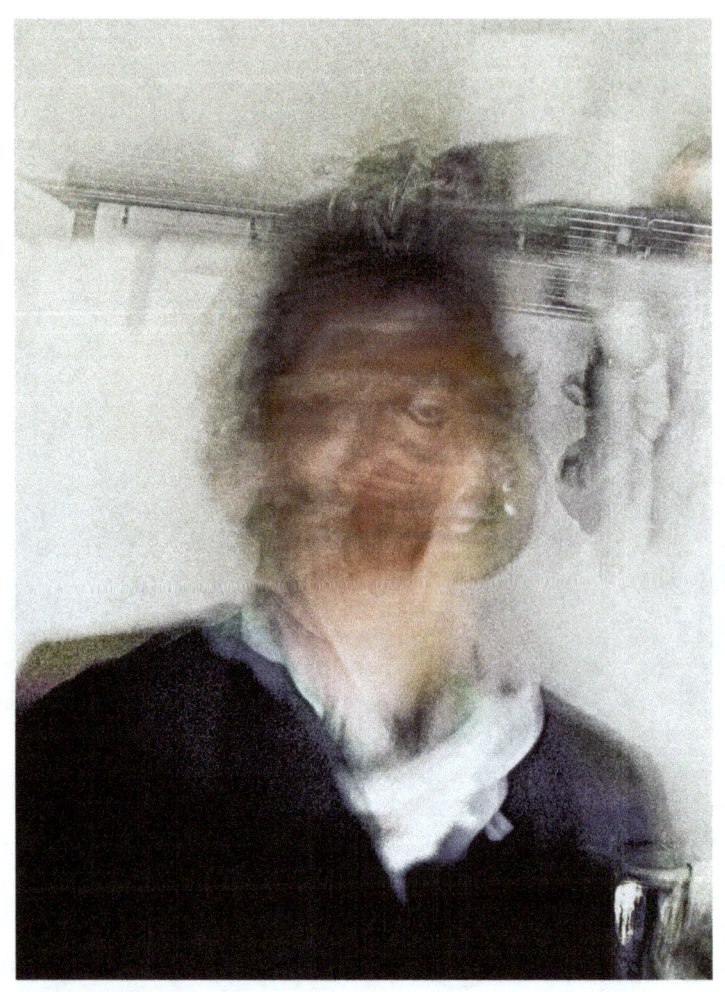

PLATE 9 Kristan Horton, *Sligo Heads, Octavious*, 2012.

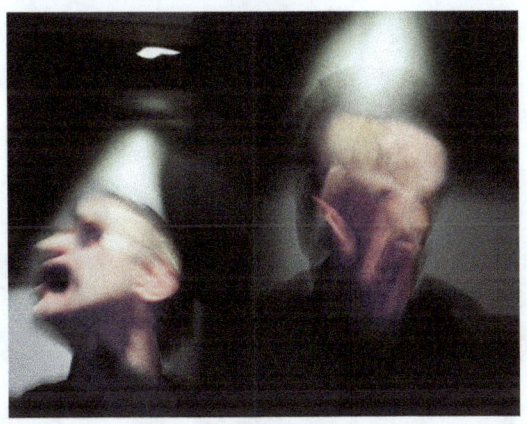

PLATE 10 Kristan Horton, *Sligo Heads,
Old Master Heads*, 2012.

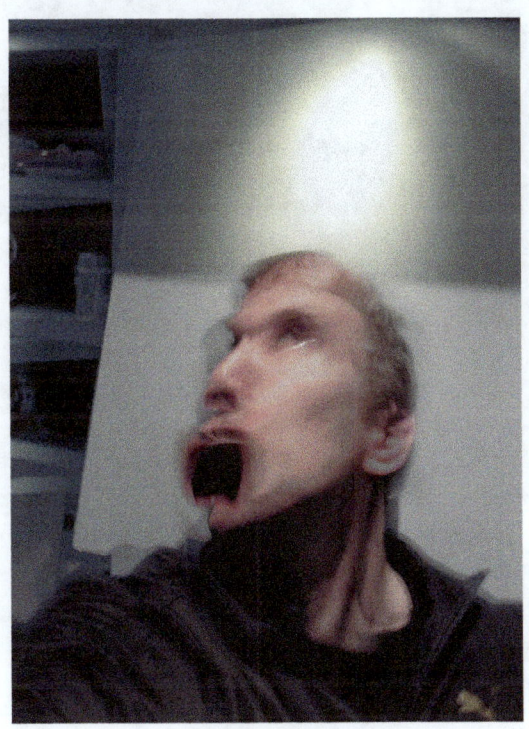

PLATE 11 Kristan Horton, *Sligo Heads,
Werewolf*, 2012.

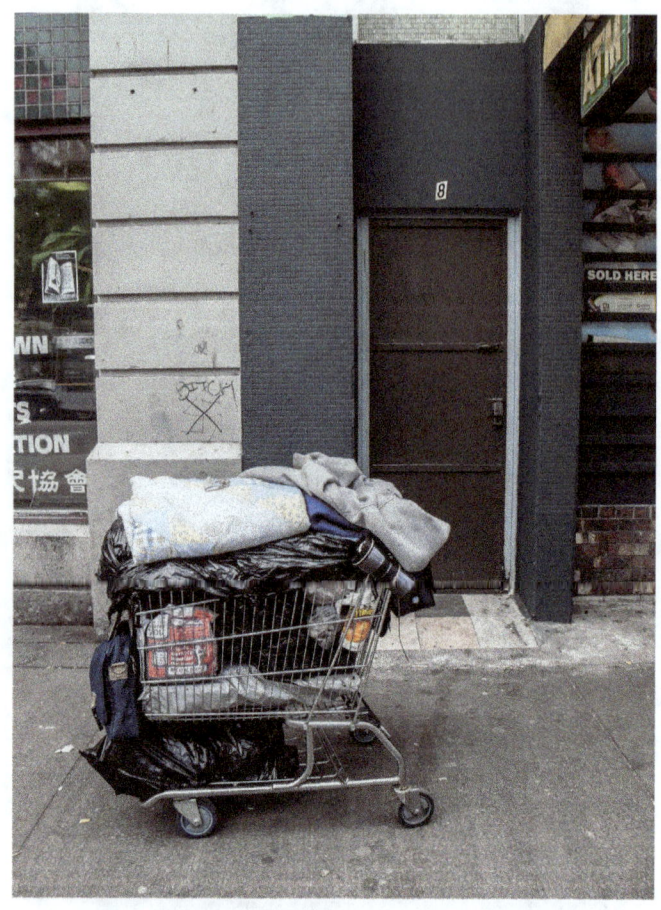

PLATE 12 Kelly Wood, *Vancouver Cart (No. 22)*, 2011.

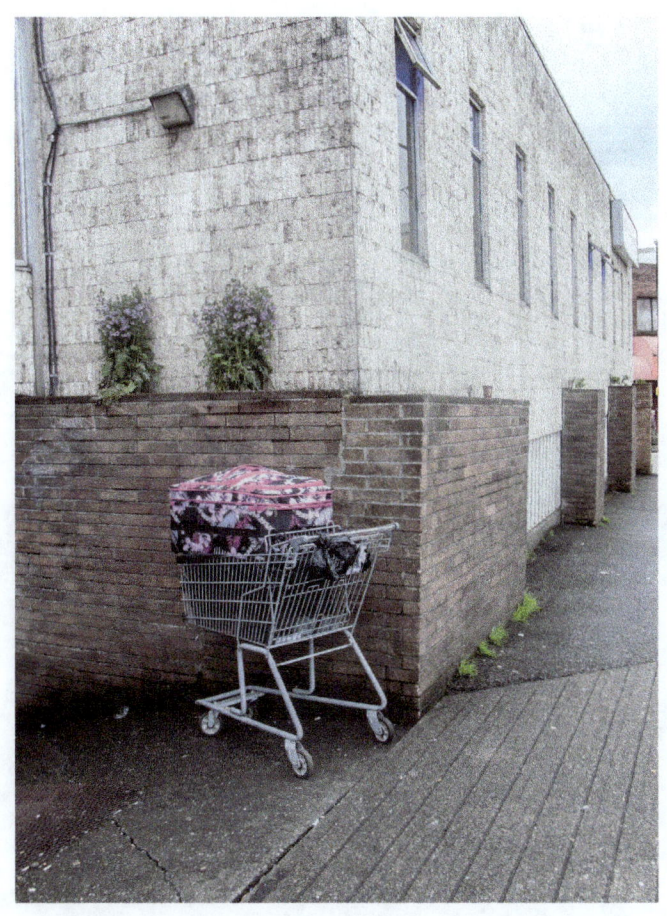

PLATE 13 Kelly Wood, *Vancouver Cart (No. 31)*, 2011.

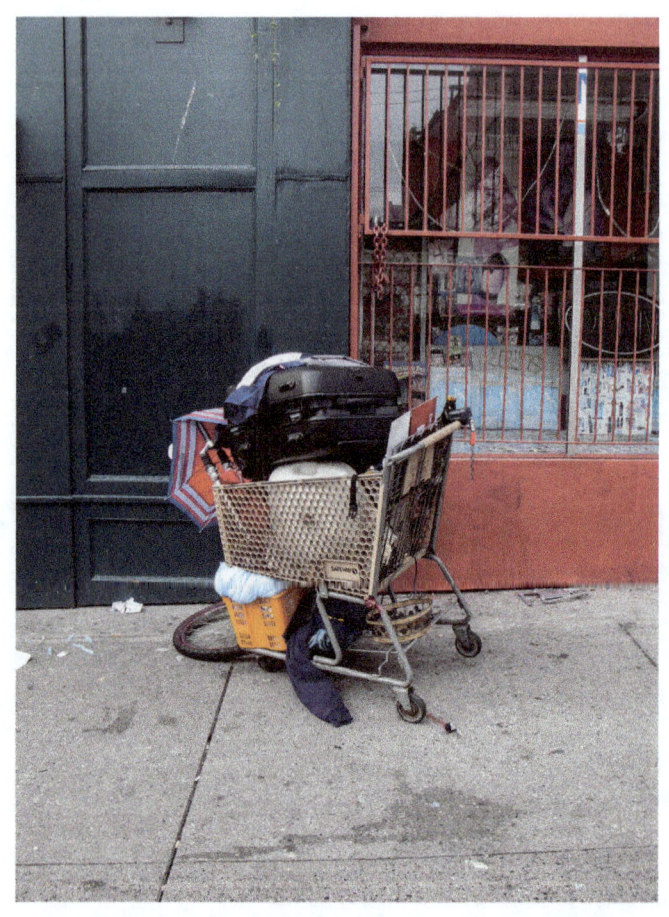

PLATE 14 Kelly Wood, *Vancouver Cart (No. 47)*, 2011.

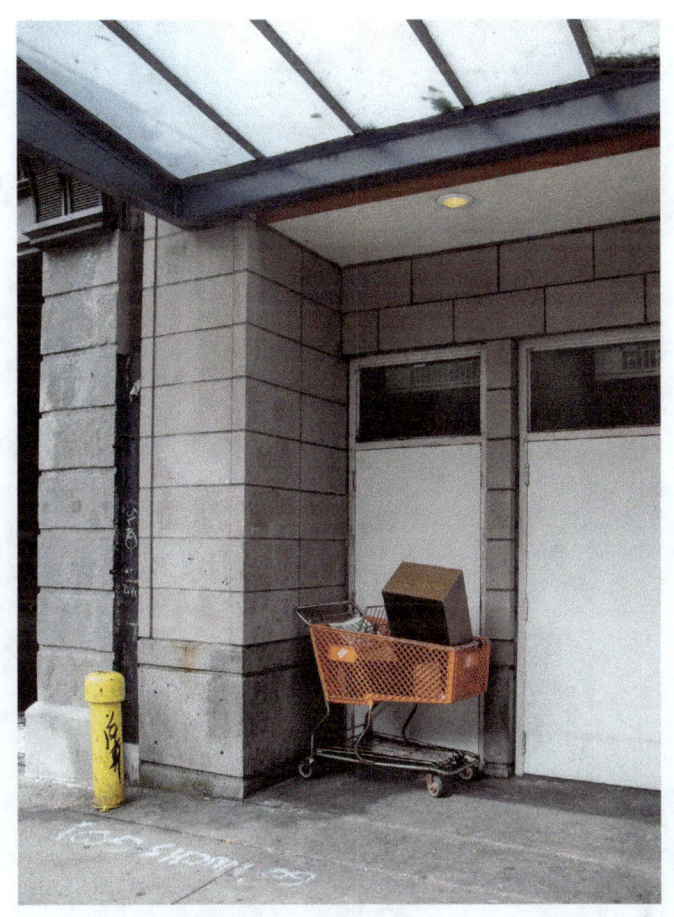

PLATE 15 Kelly Wood, *Vancouver Cart (No. 48)*, 2011.

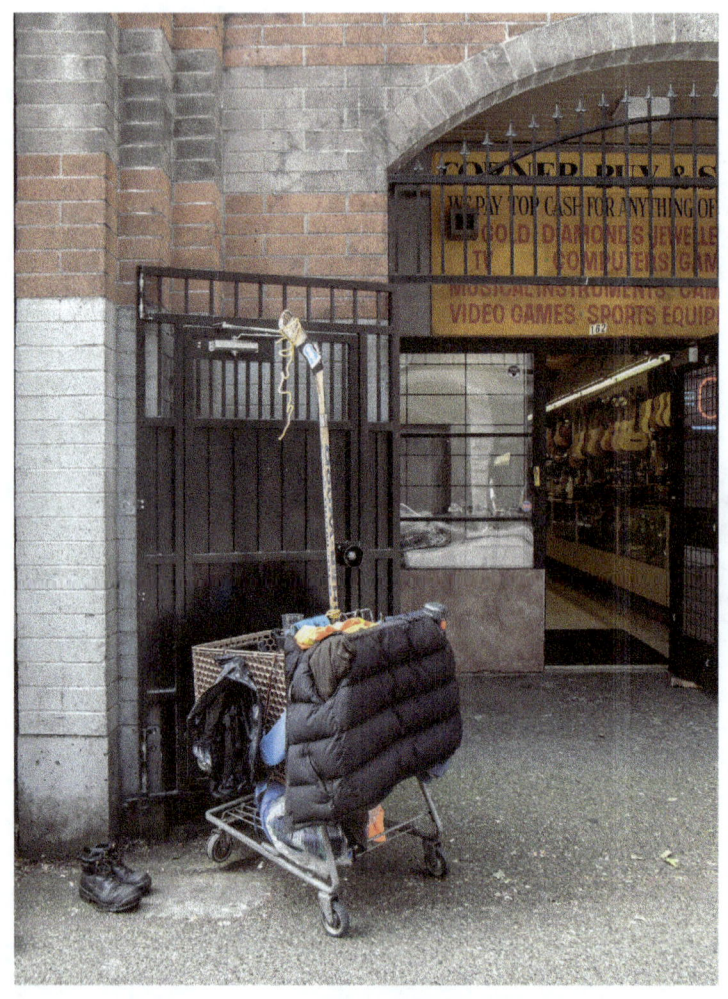

PLATE 16 Kelly Wood, *Vancouver Cart (No. 62)*, 2011.

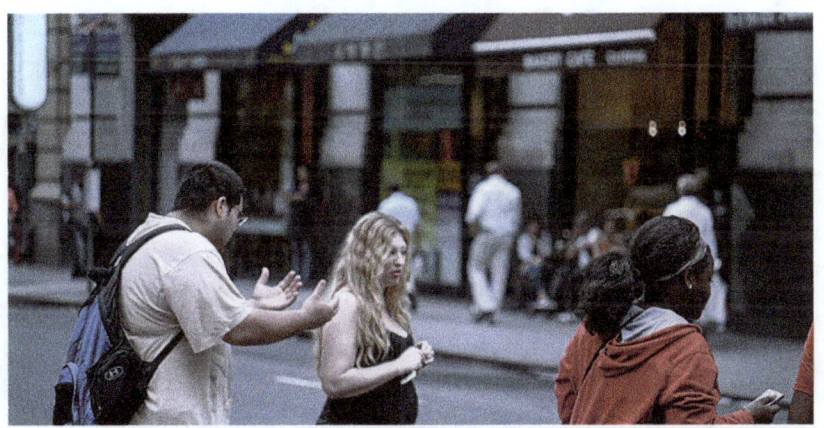

PLATE 17   James Nares, still from *Street*. Courtesy
of James Nares and Paul Kasmin Gallery.

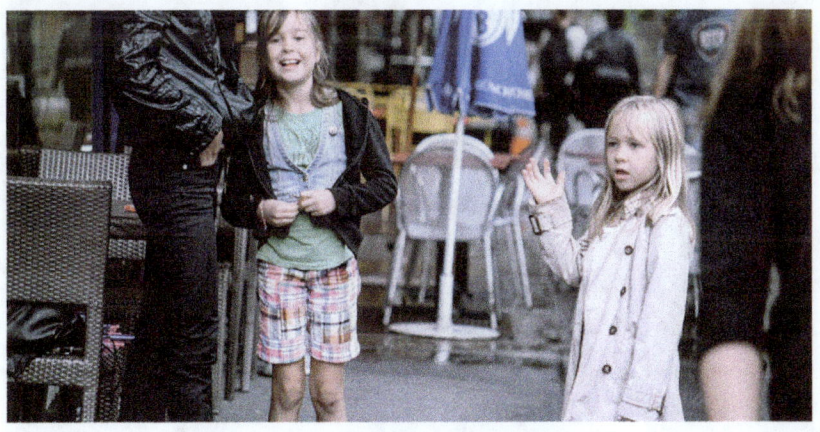

PLATE 18   James Nares, still from *Street*. Courtesy
of James Nares and Paul Kasmin Gallery.

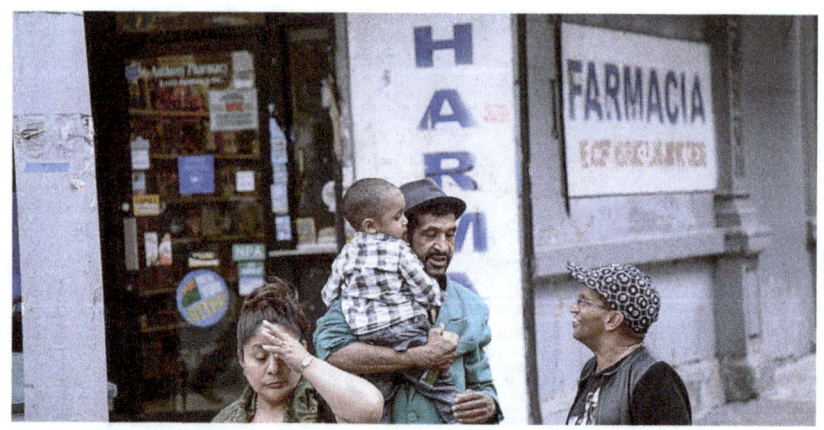

PLATE 19 James Nares, still from *Street*. Courtesy
of James Nares and Paul Kasmin Gallery.

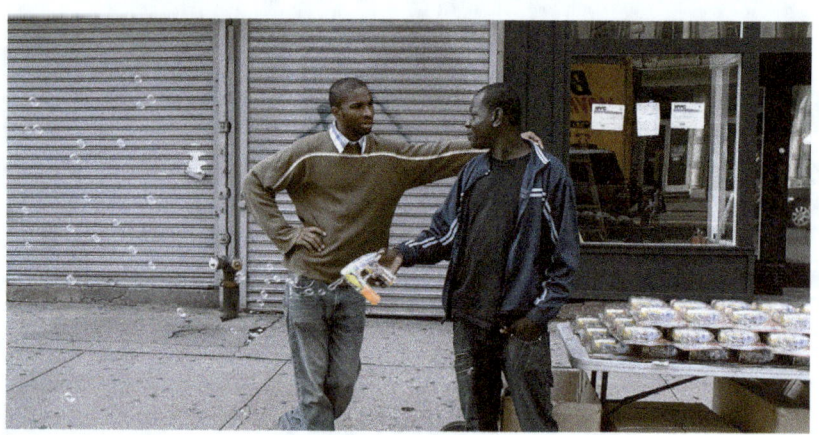

PLATE 20 James Nares, still from *Street*. Courtesy
of James Nares and Paul Kasmin Gallery.

By connecting the medium of video and the condition of narcissism, Krauss observed, "one can recast the opposition between the reflective and the reflexive into the terms of the psychoanalytic project. Because it is there, too, in the drama of the couched subject, that the narcissistic re-projection of a frozen self is pitted against the analytic (or reflexive) mode."[86] The reflexive mode of analysis facilitates alienation from a self-image that encapsulates the subject. "The process of analysis is one of breaking the hold of this fascination with the mirror."[87] Or, as Laplanche expresses it, there is a primordial split at the heart of transference, "which means quite simply that the other is the other. . . . He is other than me because he is other than himself. External alterity refers back to internal alterity."[88]

As Laplanche observes, there is an "essential dissymmetry" in the analytic situation, a distance, or difference, that is preserved especially by the silence of the analyst. In Ligon's video, dissymmetry is the organizing principle. Therapist and patient are relegated to separate screens. One is visible, the other is not. One is a woman, the other a man. One is white and the other, as we know, is black. For Ligon's work has often referred, indirectly, to the identity and subjectivity of the artist. His early paintings quote from literary texts. In one particularly well-known work, *Untitled (I Feel Most Colored When I Am Thrown Against a Sharp White Background)*, 1990–1991, this sentence written by Zora Neale Hurston is stenciled in black oil stick on a door-sized white panel. The writing is crisply legible at the top but, like a newspaper passed from hand to hand, becomes smudged and murky from overuse toward the bottom. Gummed and clotted, the stencils transfer the inky oil from one application to the next down the panel so that each line is less distinct than the one above. Toward the bottom end, the text fades out into illegibility.

Continuing to investigate the medium of printing in *Runaways* (1993), a lithographic series, Ligon solicited physical descriptions of himself from ten friends and typeset the texts in the format and graphic style of his archival source, mid-nineteenth-century posters designed to track down fugitive slaves. One read: "Ran away, Glenn Ligon. He's a shortish broad-shouldered black man, pretty dark-skinned, with glasses." Throughout his work, Ligon mines text to represent the historical and cultural construction of identity, using the figure Glenn Ligon as a frequent, but not exclusive, point of reference. He returns to this strategy in *The Orange and Blue Feelings*, at one point handing over to the therapist a school evaluation report in which the child, Glenn Ligon, is described as a moody boy who sometimes withdraws. When he brought the report home, he recounts, "My mother did a dramatic reading of that," warning him, "This will go on your record"—meaning, he elaborates, "my record with a capital R." As she saw it, "That's how black kids get labeled."

Text, Krauss observes, is what is missing from performance-based video. Its absence is what renders the medium narcissistic. For performance, she notes, conventionally relies on some form of text, "whether that is a fixed choreography, a written script, a musical score, or a sketchy set of notes around which to improvise."[89] By contrast, video performance, centered on the body of the performer before the camera, produces the effect of a "collapsed present" equivalent to the space-time of mirror reflection, or the patient on the couch—the very task of analysis being to convert the "fascination with the mirror," or reflective mode, into a reflexive one. "The analytic project," Krauss observes, is one in which "the patient disengages from . . . his reflected self, and through a method of reflexiveness, rediscovers the real time of his own history. He exchanges the atemporality of repetition for the temporality of change."[90] In short, psychoanalysis is not a confessional mode, in which self-image is nurtured, but a gradual process of alienation from the sovereign self.

Ligon has consistently relied on thick citation to represent the historical construction of identity through transference. "Making a painting, for me," he explains, "is akin to making a film adaptation of a text: it's just one possible way out of many of responding to a given text."[91] His experiment with video-analysis appears to be a departure from this practice of citation because the text it adapts, or interprets, is an autobiographical narrative. But if we understand psychoanalysis as a reflexive mode, opening onto the dimension of alterity, then its task is to render the subject, to borrow a term favored by Ligon, "opaque."[92] "Yes, you can take me for an other, because I am not what I think I am; because I respect and maintain the other in me."[93] This, writes Laplanche, is the statement the analyst addresses to the analysand. It also offers a possible description of how the work of Glenn Ligon attempts to address its audience.

> I don't remember if he asked me to kiss him. I don't remember at all.
> *A contributor to an inadequate history of conceptual art*

"Sometimes artists rush in where critics refuse to tread," Yvonne Rainer once remarked.[94] So in 1998, the artist Silvia Kolbowski wrote to sixty artists, inviting them to take part in an oral history project she would call *an inadequate history of conceptual art*.[95] Each artist was asked to select a Conceptual work— "not your own, of the period between 1965 and 1975, which you personally wit-

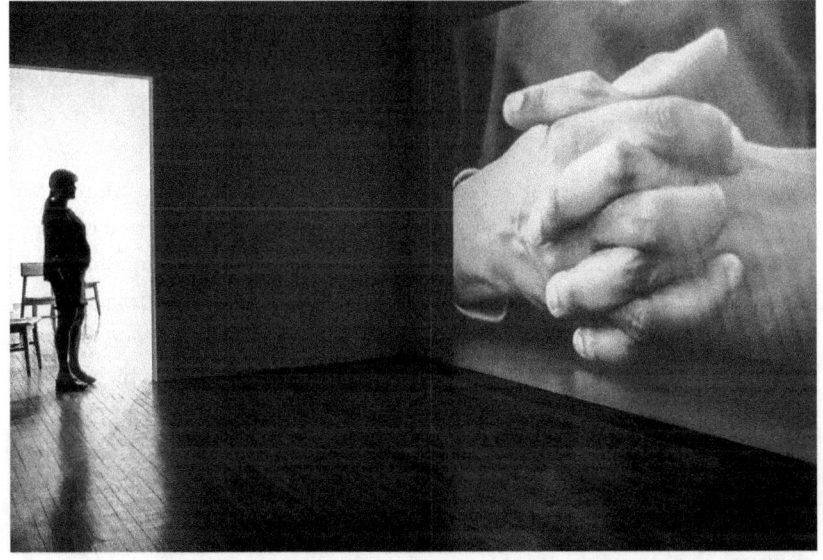

FIGURE 7.11 Silvia Kolbowski, *an inadequate history of conceptual art*,
1998–1999. Installation view.

nessed/experienced at the time"—and to attend a taping session with Kolbowski. Prospective participants were admonished to refrain from refreshing their
memories by conducting research and, in the taping itself, to avoid disclosing
their own identities or those of the artists whose works they described. Twenty-
two artists ultimately participated in face-to-face sessions with Kolbowski, who
recorded their statements and videotaped their hands as they spoke.[96] In the
resulting installation, projected images of the speakers' gestures played in a
darkened room while their voices could be heard in an adjoining space (fig.
7.11). The two recordings were deliberately run out of sync so that an "essential dissymmetry" between the hand and the voice, or the video and the audio
components of the piece, was strictly maintained.

By asking artists to describe a work from memory, and in her presence, and
by imposing a set of rules on the procedure, Kolbowski set up, loosely speaking, a psychoanalytic situation. "I thought that if I asked artists to speak from
memory about Conceptual projects from the past, the recountings would include both valuable recollections and the fallacies of human memory," she has
commented.[97] "I'm somewhat resisting your original request that it has to be
something that I experienced," one contributor begins, setting the psychoanalytic tone of the piece. "I guess I should ask myself why this stuck in my mind

all these years, over thirty years," reflects another. "I guess the reason I'm talking about it is that it stuck with me for a long time as to what this was about," one acknowledges. "It's easy to remember, it's easy to remember, it's easy to remember," chants another speaker, as if to will the act.

"An inadequate history" might be another name for psychoanalysis itself, for the subject of psychoanalysis is constructed in resistance and repression, in forgetting as much as in remembering. "Freud's analysis of the collection of screen memories revealed how memories are tendentious, how their function as witnesses is a false function, a false form of remembering instead of desiring," Forrester observes.[98] "A screen museum" is his description of the Freud Museum in Vienna, "a museum of fake souvenirs," tokens of the kind by which we purport to remember what we actually desire. It is worth remembering, too, that this screen museum was conceived in 1971, the midpoint of the time period, from 1965 to 1975, that brackets *an inadequate history*. And it is important to observe that certain of the strategies informing the installation of the Freud Museum are also characteristic of Conceptual art. These include the displacement of the object by the photograph and the text and the concomitant frustration of scopic desire, as well as the reorientation of the museum or gallery from an exhibition space, or space of display, to an archive.[99] The Freud Museum, with its "derisible atmosphere," its photographic record of the rooms in Freud's time, its research library, its carefully labeled and indexed "minor memorabilia"— and, ultimately, its art collection curated by Kosuth—is a screen museum on the Conceptual art model.

In particular, it invites comparison with Kelly's *Post-Partum Document*, a pivotal work of Conceptual art that is often omitted from that history. One aim of *an inadequate history*, according to Kolbowski, is to contest exclusionary histories by reconceiving Conceptual art in terms that, as the artist has noted, "allow for the inscription of women artists," some of whose work (unlike Kelly's) still is not well known, into an alternative art history.[100] For *an inadequate history*, Kolbowski therefore invited participants to employ a notably inclusive definition of the term:

> For the sake of the project, the definition of conceptual art should be broad enough to encompass such phenomena of that period as actions documented through drawings, photographs, film, and video; concepts executed in the form of drawings or photographs; objects where the end product is primarily a record of the precipitant concept, and performative activities which sought to question the conventions of dance and theater.[101]

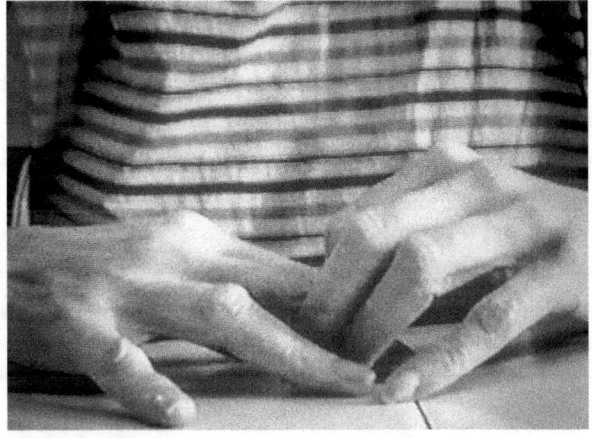

FIGURE 7.12 Silvia Kolbowski, still from *an inadequate*
history of conceptual art, 1998–1999.

Such an elastic description, as Alexander Alberro has observed, privileged "the most transitory manifestations of the movement, those most likely to have left 'inadequate' traces and thus most dependent on the memory of direct witnesses for insight into their initial receptions" — those, in short, that are most likely to reveal a screen history.[102] One contributor highlights this very possibility by observing of her own recollection, "I like telling people about it, because I like it a lot. But I don't think I actually saw it." A male speaker, describing a video work that addressed viewers by solicitation, reports: "I don't remember if he asked me to kiss him. I don't remember at all."

As well as expanding the history of Conceptual art, *an inadequate history*, as Rosalyn Deutsche has observed, "forges a link between history and psycho-analysis."[103] For the manner in which speech and gesture are combined in the work is, as she points out, evocative of the hybrid discourse that constitutes one of Freud's principal clinical discoveries: that the words and gestures of the analysand may not carry the same message. In *an inadequate history*, visual attention falls on the small gestures of the body, particularly on the hands (fig. 7.12). The subjects sit facing the camera. Sometimes the camera is trained directly on the body, so close that the rhythm of breathing becomes part of the action; more often a table occupies the middle ground between the camera and the speaker. Fingers twist and pinch, tap the table, fidget. Hands stir the air, fly out of the frame, or fold together. Gestures, creasing and unfolding pockets of space, betray the effort of recollection as memories are traced, gathered in, and pinned down. Concentrating almost forensically on the hand of the artist—famously canceled as a marker of the artist's presence in Conceptual work—the videotape excludes the facial image. The stutters of memory to which Kolbowski refers consume the body as much as the voice.

Kolbowski's own voice is never heard. Her role in eliciting and collecting these oral histories is marked only by the texture of a silent and invisible presence, a presence that structures the work as, in Krauss's terms, a reflexive situation rather than a reflective one. As in psychoanalysis, the listener establishes the parameters. The speaker is asked not to research the work to be described (a rule that resonates with Freud's instruction to patients not to prepare material for sessions), not to reveal her or his own identity, and not to disclose the authorship of the work described. Some participants break the frame. A few have obviously researched their contributions, delivered with a fluidity and factual accuracy that betrays them by comparison with others who, struggling to remember, piece together stories that are full of holes. Kolbowski's *an inadequate history* interrogates the history of Conceptual art psychoanalytically by demonstrating that those who witnessed it, even those who produced it, cannot exactly remember it.

> If we interpret a transferential movement, it is not to attack it as a defense, nor to resolve it; it is in the end to make it evolve, to help in its evolution.
>
> *Jean Laplanche*

An earlier postmodernism expanded the compass of psychoanalysis beyond the confines of the consulting room to embrace a broader culture. The current return to the analytic scene instead reconnects with the history of psychoanalysis as a practice and, even more, an institution in dissolution, making historical psychoanalysis visible in its vanishing. "Even in its failing," Roudinescou observes, psychoanalysis has a role to play in waking the depressive society from its dreamless, drug-induced torpor.[104] "Less theoretical and more clinical," more eclectic in technique and "detached from the conflictual passions that marked the preceding period," the contemporary psychoanalysis of Roudinescou's description shares something in common with contemporary art.[105] Both have reached the point of "greatest resistance," which is the analysis of the frame.

The survival of the artist as a pivotal figure in postmodernism, beyond the putative death of the author—a central tenet of much Conceptual art—in itself evidences the role transference plays in establishing, and sustaining, a dynamics of transference in art. In *an inadequate history of conceptual art*, Kolbowski reflects on the role of the artist, even the most self-effacing Conceptual artist, as a figure of transference. An unidentified artist describing an unidentified work by another unidentified artist elicits transference on the part of the audience—through the enactment of transference itself. The presence in the scene of a listener, even (or especially) one who is silent and invisible, stimulates this dynamic. What is of even greater concern to the histories of Conceptual art and institutional critique, however, is transference to the frame. The vaunted austerity of Conceptual art concentrated attention on "matters of time and money," and of setting—on opening and closing hours, the duration of an exhibition or a work, the function of captions and catalogs. These seemingly neutral elements showed the frame itself to be, as Laplanche writes of analysis, "situated in transference."

Yet despite being, as Joan Copjec observed in 1984, "coextensive with the very field of psychoanalysis," transference is a pointedly neglected dimension of its history.[106] In cultural criticism, those who invoke psychoanalysis give a wide berth to transference—wary, perhaps, of the concept's association with a clinical practice that is seen to be outmoded. It is a given of contemporary criticism that the theory and practice of psychoanalysis are separable, that psychoanalytic theory has achieved autonomy from the frame. But this division (in psychoanalytic terms, this splitting) has given rise to an academic psychoanalysis that is often dismissed, with some justification, as institutionalized, docile, and dogmatic—a form of cultural criticism in which the critic effectively "effaces her- or himself as a subject who knows what is going on."

Psychoanalytic criticism, like art that explores psychoanalysis, has a responsibility, in Laplanche's terms, to "evolve." "Perhaps we are looking the wrong way round" in seeking to apply psychoanalysis to culture, Laplanche proposes. "Maybe transference is already, 'in itself,' outside the clinic."[107] For Laplanche, transference is always already extramural, beyond the clinic, and the ultimate aim of psychoanalysis is a "transference of transference," returning transference to the world. How, then, does psychoanalysis end? "Briefly," writes Laplanche, "this problem of ending replays, precisely, the whole problem of analysis."[108]

Notes

First published in *October* 113 (summer 2005): 39–76. © 2005 Mignon Nixon. Permission to reprint granted by the author.

I wish to thank Judith Batalion and Uschi Payne for research assistance with this article and the Research Committee of the Courtauld Institute of Art for research support.

1. John Forrester, "Collector, Naturalist, Surrealist," in *Dispatches from the Freud Wars: Psychoanalysis and Its Passions* (Cambridge, MA: Harvard University Press, 1997), 132.

2. Forrester, "Collector, Naturalist, Surrealist," 132.

3. Engelman left Germany for the United States in 1939. The negatives remained in London with Anna Freud. See Edmund Engelman, *Berggasse 19, Sigmund Freud's Home and Offices, Vienna 1938* (New York: Basic Books, 1976). For a systematic and illuminating analysis of Engelman's photographs, see Diana Fuss, "Freud's Ear: Berggasse 19, Vienna, Austria," in *The Sense of an Interior: Four Writers and the Rooms That Shaped Them* (New York: Routledge, 2004), 71–105.

4. H. D., "Writing on the Wall," in *Tribute to Freud* (1970; reprint, Manchester: Carcanet Press, 1985), 22.

5. Christian Huber, Freud Museum Library, Vienna, e-mail communication to the author, May 27, 2004.

6. Lydia Marinelli and Georg Traska, "Besuch einer Wohnung: Zur Architectur des Sigmund Freud-Museums," in *Architektur des Sigmund Freud-Museums* (Vienna: Freud Museum, 2002).

7. Forrester, "Collector, Naturalist, Surrealist," 132.

8. Marina Warner, preface to *20 Maresfield Gardens: A Guide to the Freud Museum* (London: Freud Museum, 1998), viii.

9. Sigmund Freud, "On Beginning the Treatment (Further Recommendations on the Technique of Psychoanalysis I)," in *The Standard Edition of the Complete Psychological Works of Sigmund Freud*, vol. 12, ed. and trans. James Strachey (London: Hogarth, 1958), 133.

10. *20 Maresfield Gardens*, 54.

11. Freud, "On Beginning the Treatment," 126, 133.

12. Freud, "On Beginning the Treatment," 134.

13. Sanford Gifford, "Freud at the Movies, 1907–1925: From the Piazza Colonna and Hammerstein's Roofgarden to *The Secrets of a Soul*," in *Celluloid Couches, Cinematic Clients: Psychoanalysis and Psychotherapy in the Movies*, ed. Jerrold R. Brandell (Albany: State University of New York Press, 2004), 147.

14. Hans Neumann to Karl Abraham, quoted in Gifford, "Freud at the Movies," 151.

15. Karl Abraham to Freud, June 7, 1925, quoted in Gifford, "Freud at the Movies," 151.

16. Freud, quoted in Gifford, "Freud at the Movies," 151.

17. Steven J. Ellman, *Freud's Technique Papers: A Contemporary Perspective* (Northvale, NJ: Jason Aronson, 1991), 204. As Ellman is one of the few analytic practitioners to write on the use of the couch, it is worth quoting him more fully: "From my perspective, the important question is whether or not lying on the couch more easily induces a state that is difficult to replicate while sitting up or being in any other position in an

analytic office. One might then ask what state does lying on a couch induce? The answer to this question is crucial, if one maintains that lying on a couch is a necessary condition for an analysis. The alternative to this position would profess that complying with the analyst's conditions is a necessary condition for analyzability. This is an untenable position if one also wants to provide a condition in which the patient is able to freely say what is on his mind."

18. George Moraitis, "Prologue," *Psychoanalytic Inquiry* 15, no. 3 (1995): 275.

19. Alvin Frank, "The Couch, Psychoanalytic Process, and Psychic Change: A Case Study," *Psychoanalytic Inquiry* 15, no. 3 (1995): 324.

20. See Luciana Nissim Momigliano, "The Analytic Setting: A Theme with Variations," in *Continuity and Change in Psychoanalysis: Letters from Milan*, trans. Philip P. Slotkin and Gina Danile (London: Karnac, 1992), 33.

21. Jean Laplanche, "Transference: Its Provocation by the Analyst," in *Essays on Otherness* (London: Routledge, 1999), 227.

22. Laplanche, "Transference," 227.

23. Laplanche, "Transference," 227.

24. José Bleger, "Psycho-Analysis of the Psycho-Analytic Frame," *International Journal of Psycho-Analysis* 48 (1967): 511.

25. Bleger, "Psycho-Analysis of the Psycho-Analytic Frame," 514.

26. Donald Winnicott observed, "In some cases, it turns out in the end or even at the beginning that the setting and the maintenance of the setting are as important as the way one deals with the material." D. W. Winnicott, "The Importance of the Setting in Meeting Regression in Psychoanalysis," in *Psychoanalytic Explorations*, ed. Clare Winnicott, Ray Shepherd, and Madeleine Davis (Cambridge, MA: Harvard University Press, 1989), 96. Winnicott describes the setting as the "environmental provision" in the analysis, commenting that "the patient is not there to work with us except when we provide the conditions which are necessary" (97). These conditions, he observes, vary from one patient to another, and the analyst may sometimes be unable to create, or sustain, the necessary environment. A patient may, for example, demand absolute constancy in the placement of objects in the room, or insist that the curtains be always drawn. Here is another scenario:

> Let me a take a very crude example. A patient of mine went to an analyst and very quickly she got confidence in him and therefore she began to cover herself over with a rug and lie curled up on the couch with nothing happening. The analyst said to her "Sit up! Look at me! Talk! You are not to lie like that doing nothing; nothing will happen!"

According to Winnicott, "the patient felt that this was a good thing for the analyst to do" since it was obvious by his response that he could not meet her needs. "She got up and talked and got on very well with the analyst on the basis of a mutual interest in modern art" — until another analyst could be found (97).

27. Bleger, "Psycho-Analysis of the Psycho-Analytic Frame," 512, 514.

28. Bleger, "Psycho-Analysis of the Psycho-Analytic Frame," 517.

29. Bleger, "Psycho-Analysis of the Psycho-Analytic Frame," 515.

30. Momigliano, "The Analytic Setting," 59.

31. Momigliano, "The Analytic Setting," 59.

32. Laplanche, "Transference," 228.

33. Laplanche, "Transference," 228.

34. Laplanche, "Transference," 228–229.

35. Nanni Moretti, Paola Golinelli, Stefano Bolognini, and Andrea Sabbadini, "Sons and Fathers: A Room of Their Own, Nanni Moretti's *The Son's Room* (2001)," in *The Couch and the Silver Screen: Psychoanalytic Reflections on European Cinema*, vol. 44 of *The New Library of Psychoanalysis*, ed. Andrea Sabbadini (Hove, U.K.: Brunner-Routledge, 2003), 69.

36. Bolognini, quoted in Moretti et al., "Sons and Fathers," 72.

37. Moretti, quoted in Moretti et al., "Sons and Fathers," 65.

38. Momigliano, "The Analytic Setting," 39. See also R. P. Fox, "The Principle of Abstinence Reconsidered," *International Review of Psycho-Analysis* 11 (1984): 227–236.

39. Forrester, "Collector, Naturalist, Surrealist," 118.

40. Forrester, "Collector, Naturalist, Surrealist," 118, 116.

41. Freud, "On Beginning the Treatment," 134. Adam Phillips has remarked that "in the first psychoanalytic setting—the paradigm of every psychoanalytic consulting room—the patient could not see the analyst but could see his idols," his collection of figurines. Adam Phillips, "Psychoanalysis and Idolatry," in *On Kissing, Tickling and Being Bored* (London: Faber and Faber, 1993), 117.

42. Freud to Sándor Ferenczi, 1928, quoted in Momigliano, "The Analytic Setting," 37. Among the not-so-docile were Ferenczi, who treated his more disturbed patients with marked affection; Melanie Klein, inventor of the psychoanalytic play technique; Donald Winnicott, author of the influential idea that the setting is "the summation of all the details of management"; and Jacques Lacan, who experimented with variable lengths, including the short session, from which a patient might be dismissed after five minutes or sooner.

43. Moustapha Safouan, *Jacques Lacan and the Question of Psychoanalytic Training*, trans. Jacqueline Rose (London: Macmillan, 2000), 63.

44. Safouan, *Jacques Lacan*, 67.

45. Safouan, *Jacques Lacan*, 66–67. Or, as Adam Phillips observes, "the one thing psychoanalysis cannot cure, when it works, is belief in psychoanalysis. And that is a problem" (Phillips, "Psychoanalysis and Idolatry," 130).

46. Momigliano, "The Analytic Setting," 39.

47. Shellburne Thurber, conversation with the author, October 13, 2004. Some analysts from Boston Psychoanalytic were receptive and helped facilitate the project, she adds. The artist held a Bunting Institute fellowship from Radcliffe College at the time.

48. Roy N. Aruffo, "The Couch: Reflections from an Interactional View of Analysis," *Psychoanalytic Inquiry* 15, no. 3 (1995): 370.

49. Safouan, *Jacques Lacan*, 62.

50. Willem Linschoten, "Letter," *International Psychoanalysis* 12, no. 1 (June 2003): 4.

51. Elisabeth Roudinescou, *Why Psychoanalysis?*, trans. Rachel Bowlby (New York: Columbia University Press, 2001), 140, 141.

52. Jean-Bertrand Pontalis, quoted in Roudinescou, *Why Psychoanalysis?*, 16.

53. One contributor, Hamburg-based author and photographer Claudia Guderian, has recently published an illustrated book on the subject, trumpeted as the first global survey of the setting, a volume whose very existence attests to the threatened disappearance of the couch. See Claudia Guderian, *Magie der Couch: Bilder und Gespräche über Raum und Setting in der Psychoanalyse* (Stuttgart: Verlag W. Kohlhammer, 2004). See also Claudia Guderian, *Die Couch in der Psychoanalyse: Geschichte und Gegenwart von Setting und Raum* (Stuttgart: Verlag W. Kolhammer, 2004).

54. Henrik Carpelan, "On the Importance of the Setting in the Psychoanalytic Situation," *Scandinavian Psychoanalytic Review* 4 (1981): 152.

55. Carpelan, "On the Importance of the Setting," 153.

56. Carpelan, "On the Importance of the Setting," 153.

57. Walter Benjamin, "I [The Interior, the Trace]," in *The Arcades Project*, trans. Howard Eiland and Kevin McLaughlin (Cambridge, MA: Belknap, 1999), 213.

58. Roudinescou, *Why Psychoanalysis?*, 140.

59. Safouan, *Jacques Lacan*, 63. See also Jean Clavreul, *L'ordre médical* (Paris: Seuil, 1978).

60. Siegfried Bernfeld, "On Psychoanalytic Training," *Psychoanalytic Quarterly* (1962): 467, as cited in Safouan, *Jacques Lacan*, 62.

61. Sigmund Freud, "The Dynamics of Transference" (1912), in *The Standard Edition*, vol. 12.

62. See Susan Hiller, *After the Freud Museum* (London: Book Works, 2000).

63. Forrester, "Collector, Naturalist, Surrealist," 122.

64. Forrester, "Collector, Naturalist, Surrealist," 136.

65. Thurber, conversation with the author, October 13, 2004.

66. Forrester, "Collector, Naturalist, Surrealist," 130.

67. See Mary Kelly, *Post-Partum Document* (London: Routledge and Kegan Paul, 1983).

68. Forrester, "Collector, Naturalist, Surrealist," 137.

69. Forrester, "Collector, Naturalist, Surrealist," 125, 126.

70. Linda Nochlin, *Sarah Lucas: GOD IS DAD* (New York: Gladstone Gallery, 2005), 8.

71. Juliet Mitchell, "Theory as an Object," *October* 113 (summer 2005): 27–38, 33. Mitchell cites Mary Kelly's *Post-Partum Document*, of which she observes, linking her own history to Kelly's: "I hope we have been destructive of psychoanalytic theory (though I know I have very often only related to it); it has obviously survived our, and

other, more powerful attacks not only in the generic sense that it is bigger and stronger than we are. It has survived in the sense that matters: its survival can only be assured by the fact that it has changed, though certainly not utterly."

72. Joseph Kosuth, "Text for the Sigmund Freud Museum," *Foundation for the Arts, Sigmund Freud Museum Vienna*, vol. 2 (1998), 13.

73. Forrester, "Collector, Naturalist, Surrealist," 125.

74. André Breton, "Interview with Doctor Freud" (1921), in *The Lost Steps*, trans. Mark Polizzotti (1924; reprint, Lincoln: University of Nebraska Press, 1996), 70–71. I am grateful to David Lomas for drawing my attention to this text.

75. Janet Malcolm, *Psychoanalysis: The Impossible Profession* (London: Granta, 1983), 47.

76. Laplanche, "Transference," 216.

77. Laplanche, "Transference," 217.

78. Laplanche, "Transference," 217.

79. Laplanche, "Transference," 227.

80. Apropos of matters of time and money, Ligon reports that he paid the therapist a location fee for the use of the consulting room for filming, including footage of the empty office shot after hours. Glenn Ligon, conversation with the author, March 9, 2005.

81. Laplanche, "Transference," 227.

82. Laplanche, "Transference," 217.

83. Glenn Ligon, conversation with the author, March 7, 2004.

84. Laplanche, "Transference," 231.

85. Johanna Burton, "Glenn Ligon, D'Amelio Terras," *Artforum*, March 2004, 184.

86. Rosalind Krauss, "Video: The Aesthetics of Narcissism," *October* 1 (spring 1976): 57.

87. Krauss, "Video," 58.

88. Laplanche, "Transference," 221.

89. Krauss, "Video," 53.

90. Krauss, "Video," 58.

91. Glenn Ligon, interview by Byron Kim, in *Glenn Ligon: un/becoming* (Philadelphia: Institute of Contemporary Art, 1998), 53.

92. As Lacan puts it, "In this labor, which he undertakes to reconstruct this construct *for another*, he finds again the fundamental alienation which made him construct it *like another one*, and which has always destined it to be stripped from him *by another*." Jacques Lacan, *The Language of the Self*, trans. Anthony Wilden (New York: Delta, 1968), 11. Cited in Krauss, "Video," 58.

93. Laplanche, "Transference," 228.

94. Yvonne Rainer, "Looking Myself in the Mouth," in *A Woman Who . . . : Essays, Interviews, Scripts* (Baltimore, MD: Johns Hopkins University Press, 1999), 89.

95. Silvia Kolbowski, "an inadequate history of conceptual art," *October* 92 (spring 2000): 53.

96. Of the sixty invited artists, forty agreed to take part, of whom twenty-two were recorded.

97. Kolbowski, "an inadequate history," 53.

98. Forrester, "Collector, Naturalist, Surrealist," 130.

99. See Benjamin H. D. Buchloh, "Conceptual Art 1962–1969: From the Aesthetics of Administration to the Critique of Institutions," *October* 55 (winter 1990): 105–143.

100. Silvia Kolbowski, conversation with the author, May 12, 2003. Kolbowski cites, for example, the exhibition *L'art conceptuel: Une perspective*, organized at the Musée d'Art Moderne de la Ville de Paris in 1989, and its catalog, as an official history from which work by women was largely excluded, noting that this show "set the tone for the 'return'" of Conceptual art in contemporary practice.

101. Kolbowski, "an inadequate history," 53.

102. Alexander Alberro, "Silvia Kolbowski: American Fine Arts Co.," *Artforum* 38, no. 4 (December 1999): 148–149.

103. Rosalyn Deutsche, "Inadequacy," in *Silvia Kolbowski: inadequate . . . Like . . . Power* (Vienna: Secession, 2004), 77–78.

104. Roudinescou, *Why Psychoanalysis?*, 143.

105. Roudinescou, *Why Psychoanalysis?*, 142.

106. Joan Copjec, "Transference: Letters and the Unknown Woman," *October* 28 (spring 1984): 68.

107. Laplanche, "Transference," 222.

108. Laplanche, "Transference," 218.

———

CHAPTER EIGHT

VISION'S UNSEEN

*On Sovereignty, Race,
and the Optical Unconscious*

———

MARK REINHARDT

> For it is another nature that speaks to the camera
> rather than to the eye: "other" above all in the sense that a space
> informed by human consciousness gives way to a space informed by the
> unconscious. Whereas it is a commonplace that, for example, we have
> some idea what is involved in the act of walking (if only in general
> terms), we have no idea at all what happens during the fraction of a second
> when a person actually takes a step. Photography, with its devices of slow
> motion and enlargement, reveals the secret. It is through photography
> that we first discover the existence of this optical unconscious, just as we
> discover the instinctual unconscious through psychoanalysis.
> *Walter Benjamin, "Little History of Photography"*

> Images are neither on the wall (or on the screen) nor in the head
> alone. They do not *exist* by themselves, but they *happen.*
> *Hans Belting, "Image, Medium, Body"*

> The world of vision captures us due to what we do not see.
> *Darian Leader,* Stealing the Mona Lisa

With the "optical unconscious," Walter Benjamin bequeathed to visual and political studies something at once alluring and elusive. Exploring how photography and film capture details that escape the eye in the course of daily life, he promised a revelatory turn in theory and criticism while treating the two media as themselves revelations, pathways into previously inaccessible or uncharted territories of human being and social experience. Yet neither the turn's angle nor the paths' destination is easy to determine. It is not surprising, then, that Benjamin's concept, analogy, metaphor, or poetic gesture — and the elusiveness stems, in part, from uncertainty over which applies — has been more often invoked than analyzed or employed.[1] Is his promise empty? I believe not. The optical unconscious was generative for Benjamin's thinking and, despite all that has changed since his time, can remain so for ours. This essay attempts to put his term to work. My wager is that exemplifying and reflecting upon the different senses one might give the optical unconscious can alert us to complexities and perplexities often overlooked in analyses of certain important features of politics and visual culture.

One of these features is race, a visual artifact carrying a singularly powerful charge. Whether as ideology, institution, or lived experience, race is of course not made only by visual means, but its inequities and indignities remain tightly bound to ways of seeing human difference and organizing the perceptual field. To the rich critical tradition arising from that insight, Benjamin's optical unconscious offers at once a contribution and a potentially destabilizing challenge. On the one hand, stressing the unseen elements in visual experience may broaden our sense of how race is constructed. On the other, it poses the puzzle of how the invisible can be part of visual construction. What might this puzzle tell us about racialized perception? How, in turn, can such perceptions help understand the role of the unconscious in shaping what we see and our encounters with photography?

Though I will take up such questions, I first engage another aspect of politics, sovereignty. That may not seem an obvious point of departure. Certainly, one can read widely in the political science literature on sovereignty without encountering much in the way of visual analysis. While reflecting the constraints of a discipline rarely willing to engage the visual domain, the omission involves a matter more intrinsic to the topic: still less than race is sovereignty a wholly optical affair. Yet in warding off challenges and forming collective subjects, sovereignty, too, has always relied upon the orchestration of gazes and theatrical displays of power, from royal spectacles to televised presidential addresses to the walls erected at so many contemporary state borders.[2] Susan Buck-Morss captures a key feature of this reliance when arguing that "the sovereign is an icon in the theological sense" and, as such, "demonstrates the power of the visible image to close the circle between constituting and constituted power."[3] The issues at stake in understanding that power are large and difficult, and my engagement with them will be limited. Still, Benjamin's enigmatic notion may shed some light on how a sovereign, as Buck-Morss writes, "embodies an enigma — precisely the power of the collective to constitute itself."[4] At the very least, the image of sovereignty examined below should make some sense of what Benjamin was offering us and how to construe the relationship between what he called the optical and the instinctual. Thinking through that relationship, furthermore, reveals how thoroughly race and sovereignty are imbricated with each other: exploring the optical unconscious makes clear how hard it is to think through the visual construction of race without examining the problem of sovereignty, and how often and deeply the theory and practice of sovereignty require the making of racial others. (That making, as we will see, also left its mark on Benjamin's own conceptualizations.)

How do the links among race, sovereignty, and the optical unconscious emerge in particular images, genres, media, or scopic regimes? Attending to cinema only in passing, devoting much space to cases that appear to be either pre- or postphotographic, turning to familiar forms of photography only in the essay's final two sections, my response builds slowly. I believe, however, that such an approach can sharpen the analysis of photography — in the strictest sense — while blurring that category's boundaries in useful ways. In that, I aim to follow Benjamin: clearly, he sought to show how photography exposed layers of experience of which we might not otherwise be aware, but in pursuing his promptings we also discover how engaging the unconscious, following its links, alters our sense of where and when photographs can be found. Yet recognizing those promptings is not so easy, and so it is difficult to know which kind of engagement to pursue. Before turning to sovereignty, then, it's worth pausing over the difficulties.

Parallel Lines?

Benjamin introduced the optical unconscious in his 1931 "Little History of Photography" and then, borrowing language from that text (but emphasizing cinema more than still images), reintroduced it in "The Work of Art in the Age of Its Technological Reproducibility," of which he wrote three distinct versions in the mid- to late 1930s.[5] The passage from the "Little History" that stands as one of my epigraphs reappeared, with no more than minor variations and a few additional clauses, in the artwork essay's long-canonical third version:

> Clearly it is another nature which speaks to the camera as compared to the eye. "Other" above all in the sense that a space informed by human consciousness gives way to a space informed by the unconscious. Whereas it

is a commonplace that, for example, we have some idea what is involved in the act of walking (if only in general terms), we have no idea at all what happens during the split second when a person actually takes a step. We are familiar with the movement of picking up a cigarette lighter or a spoon, but know almost nothing of what really goes on between hand and metal, and still less how that varies with different moods. This is where the camera comes into play, with all its resources for swooping and rising, disrupting and isolating, stretching or compressing a sequence, enlarging or reducing an object. It is through the camera that we first discover the optical unconscious, just as we discover the instinctual unconscious through psychoanalysis.[6]

This returns us to the perplexity with which I began. How is a space "informed by" the unconscious? What kind of space? What kind of unconscious? And how do the optical and the instinctual bear on each other? Merely by way of analogy? Or are they entwined? The text fails to give readers much assistance.

Some claim failure is inevitable, the passage a dead end. Even while appropriating Benjamin's term for her work as an art historian, Rosalind Krauss finds his discussion's "strangeness" unhelpful. How, she asks with some exasperation, can "the optical field . . . *have* an unconscious?" Noting that Freud would have found Benjamin's remark "simply incomprehensible," she swiftly leaves the latter's work behind.[7] Shawn Michelle Smith finds the passage more instructive, drawing on it in her shrewd study of photography and the unseen, but shares Krauss's sense that Benjamin's concept cannot intelligibly be given a psychoanalytic cast. His work is useful for visual analysis, Smith argues, if we stay on "the optical side of this equation," the side Benjamin was inviting us to explore: "If psychoanalysis discovers the (instinctual) unconscious, a psychic process the conscious mind cannot know, photography discovers the optical unconscious, a visual dynamic the eye cannot see. As the (instinctual) unconscious remains unknown, so the optical unconscious remains unseen. Just as Freud took recourse in visual metaphors to explain the unconscious, Benjamin borrowed the language of psychoanalysis to explain the unseen that photography makes us aware of in its invisibility."[8] Benjamin was, on this account, noting a parallel, describing lines of inquiry that do not cross.

Is this right? There is no doubting that photographs make available for inspection much that we would not otherwise see. As the neuropsychiatrist Eric Kandel observes, "the eye does not work like a camera" and the brain filters out much information captured by our sensory organs while adding visual elements not obtained through them.[9] Something may be gained by proceeding as if Benjamin's response avoids giving vision's unseen a strongly psychoanalytic character. Perhaps there are cases one can render more accurately; certainly one is enabled to say particular things. (Smith's readings of photographs, from Niepce's pewter plates to Abu Ghraib's digital horrors, are impressive examples.)

Still, trying to say them raises questions about what it means to read Benjamin this way, where to draw the boundaries of "the optical side." Given the nature of his preoccupation with technology and the political hopes and fears he repeatedly attached to photography and film, the optical unconscious must be understood as part of an account of the work performed by vision's unseen. Even a preliminary response to his invitation must note more than that we routinely miss much of what unfolds in our visual field — screening out things unimportant to the task at hand as so much flotsam and jetsam — and more even than photography's ability to reveal interesting patterns and logics to those oversights. In addition, we need to understand Benjamin as underscoring the frequency and power of cases in which what we encounter visually but not knowingly shapes somatic response, mood, even behavior. The question, then, is how the shaping happens and with what effects. Will a compelling response silence or amplify the psychoanalytic resonances of Benjamin's term? At stake is not merely the meaning of a difficult moment in a text already too often given over to hieratic criticism but how we make political sense of images and visual experience. In working through the issues, let us first turn, in a Benjaminian spirit, to an instance of sovereignty and photography from the seventeenth century (fig. 8.1).

Sovereign Seeing, Wayward Glances

The picture serves as portal to a theory that gives visual performance a crucial role in generating political order. The theory presents sovereignty as the solution to the problems of nature as war, an argument that turns on nature's lack, and sovereignty's provision, of a "*visible* power to keep [people] in awe."[10] The "Artificiall Man" or "*Mortall God*" dominating the illustration's upper half, sword grasped in one formidable hand and crosier in the other, is that power.[11] By making visible the components and scale of the sovereign body politic, the picture aims to inspire at once awe and submission. *Leviathan*'s famous frontispiece, then, is itself a kind of performance: it not only depicts sovereignty established but also enacts the sovereign's visible power. And the enactment turns on what we might call the power of the visible, for, as pictured, the Leviathan em-

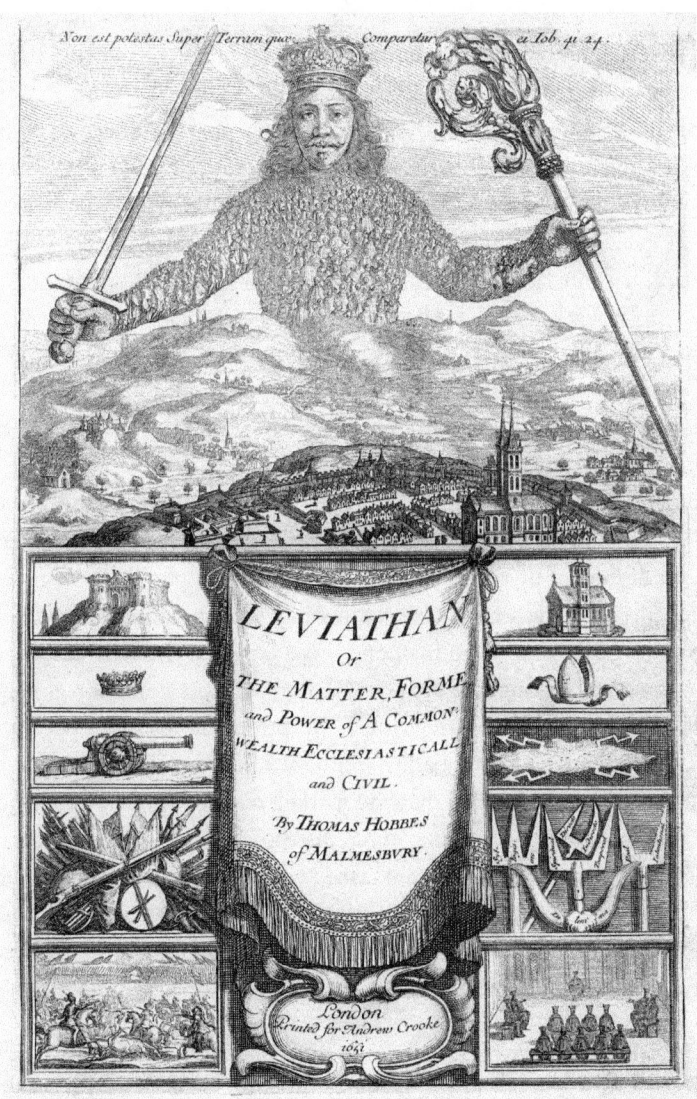

FIGURE 8.1 Abraham Bosse (attributed), *Leviathan* frontispiece, 1651.
Courtesy of the Chapin Library, Williams College, gift of Donald S.
Klopfer, Class of 1922.

bodies what Krauss characterizes as "the two qualities onto which the optical sense opens uniquely: the infinitely multiple, on the one hand, and the simultaneously unified, on the other."[12]

The theory, however—and this is its conceptually innovative core—construes our submission as consensual. The idiom of contract treats sovereign power as legitimated, indeed created, only through the choice of each individual to alienate his or her own rights and powers. Knowing we are power's artificers chastens rather than emboldens us as we confront the product of our alienation: *Leviathan* explains how we emancipate ourselves from nature's insecurity and terrors by authoring our own subjection.[13] Here the image again plays a crucial role, showing sovereign and subjects to be mutually constitutive visual artifacts: only sovereignty binds together the hundreds of tiny bodies that bring it into being.

Chapter 16 of the text explicitly argues that a multitude cannot become a people before accepting a sovereign, but the frontispiece extends and complicates the argument by revealing that the eye, too, is a portal. Through the eye, the enactment of sovereign power reaches into the inner sources of subjectivity as a play of gazes unfolds both among those depicted and between engraving and its viewers. Although we are asked to think of our submission as voluntary and the resulting state as pure artifice, the authorship pictured here troubles the idea that contract leaves behind, without residue, the paradoxical or mystical union of ruler and ruled that had marked medieval political theology. On Hobbes's account, it seems as if the representative shapes—must always already have shaped—those who are tasked with forming him, for "the subject," in Christopher Pye's words, "first comprehends himself figured in the external and irreducibly theatrical person of the 'Artificial Man.'"[14] If that seems paradoxical, Pye argues, so is the presentation of spectatorship in the frontispiece:

> The sovereign form, then, represents the viewing subject in a double and contradictory fashion. He mirrors our gaze directly, his ample and singular presence the narcissistic reflection of our own. But the spectator's activity is also represented *en abîme* in the subjects . . . whose collective gaze invests [the sovereign's] eye with its singular power. . . . Through our doubled gaze, we are able to see in the eye that looks directly at us, not just a secondary reflection of our eye, but the fully distinct and objective embodiment of our sight. In a sense, we are made the spectators to our own powerful vision.[15]

This analysis of the paradoxes and reflexivity of the Hobbesian spectacle of power depends on a simple pictorial detail: "Each of those subjects who constitute the king's body stands, with his back to the viewer, gazing up at the sovereign's eye."[16] Pye, one of the frontispiece's most acute analysts, is not alone in insisting on the point: indeed, without exception scholars who discuss the glances portrayed within the image claim all sight lines run upward, converging on the face.[17] Capturing the engraving's most obvious features, the claim also fits the written text's larger theoretical argument about how to understand the body politic. *Leviathan*'s argument aspires to inescapability: every subject should be represented by a sovereign who will, once constituted, brook no dissent.

The problem with these commentaries, and with the frontispiece's visual enactment of Hobbes's written account, is that the image harbors dissonant or dissident elements. Despite its pervasiveness, the observation that all subjects gaze at the head of the sovereign simply is not accurate. Attend to the little faces, map the sight lines, and you will see that many do not reach the sovereign's eyes or face but instead pass below or to the side. In most cases, certainly, deriving much from these errant angles would be a form of simple-minded literalism. Abraham Bosse, the engraver, has rendered some faces in profile, his aim obviously to humanize the subjects and generate visual variety and interest, enlivening the image without altering the argument it makes.[18] Presumably, we should treat these figures as if they were gazing more directly upward. But other cases elude that explanation: as pictured, the body politic incorporates bad subjects. In the crook of the right arm, the arm grasping the sword charged with ensuring docility and compliance, a few heads swivel well off course. One youthful-seeming, shaggy-headed fellow looks—unmistakably—right at us. One or two others appear to join him. While the latter cases are murkier, this much is clear: the sovereign neither receives all gazes nor is the only figure whose gaze engages ours when we look at the frontispiece (figs. 8.2 and 8.3).

What to make of these wayward glances? I have used the language of clarity and unmistakability, yet countless viewers have been mistaken, have scrutinized the image without consciously registering what lies before them. I assume, at least for the sake of argument and the issues it can raise for us, that the overlooked faces nevertheless register, making our reception of the image a moment in which a kind of optical unconscious is at work. The other eyes watching beneath the threshold of conscious perception may subtly disturb our viewing, mattering affectively even though not recognized cognitively. (Fear of being watched secretly is an elemental form of paranoia, one reason why the eyes of painted portraits feature in a certain kind of horror movie.) Is there not something unnerving, perhaps uncanny, about this famous image? We should not be surprised, given the way it aims to produce visually the very fear of

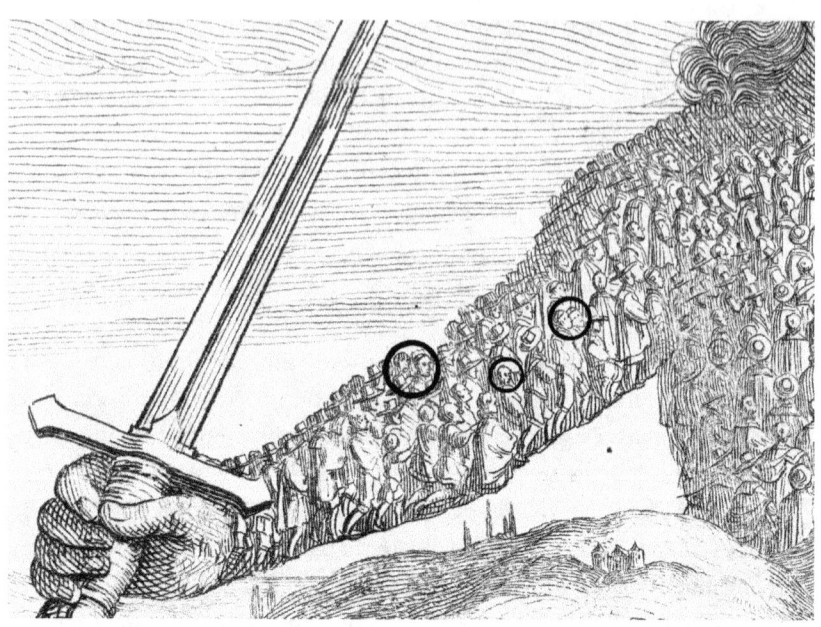

FIGURE 8.2 Frontispiece detail. Courtesy of the Chapin Library, Williams College, gift of Donald S. Klopfer, Class of 1922. The faces in the circle on the right are among the many intended to be taken as looking at the face of the sovereign, even though the sight lines pass well below the chin. Perhaps something like this applies to the man on the right side of figure 8.2's left circle. The swivel over the shoulder in the center circle renders such a reading far-fetched. And the shaggy-haired figure in the upper left of the circle on the left? There is no doubt that he is looking outward, right at us. Figure 8.3 makes that clearer.

FIGURE 8.3 Frontispiece detail. Courtesy of the Chapin Library, Williams College, gift of Donald S. Klopfer, Class of 1922.

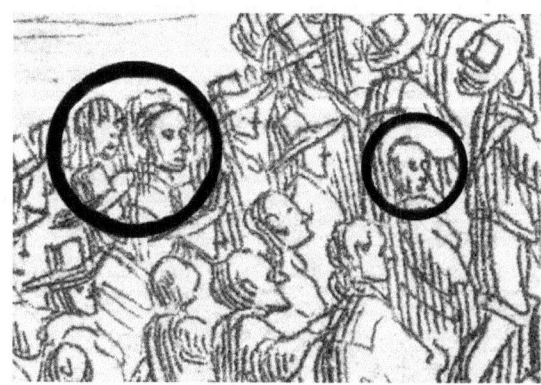

sovereign authority that the book describes and explains — and given, too, the odd temporal structures or paradoxes marking moments of founding and thus efforts to inaugurate a social contract.[19] So let us imagine that although those figures swiveling toward us diverge from the official program, undermining (if in small ways) the theory's logic of universal submission, they also intensify the anxiety propelling (Hobbes hopes) acceptance.

To pursue the conjecture, though, first note the ways imaging technologies shaped how the frontispiece was created, circulated, and received. As Noel Malcolm has shown, Hobbes's encounters with the dioptric anamorphoses of Jean-François Niceron's innovative perspective glass (encounters informed by his own deep engagement with optical theory) helped inspire *Leviathan*'s distinctive theory of representation, sovereignty, and the body politic.[20] And as is well known, before *Leviathan* was published, Hobbes presented the exiled Charles II with a manuscript copy of the text featuring a drawn frontispiece (in which the question of whether subjects gaze upward does not arise, as all face the viewer).[21] In 1651, however, when the typeset book entered the public sphere of an England at the end of a prolonged and bloody civil war, it bore the engraved version, with its subtler and more complex enactment of the Hobbesian theory of sovereignty. As a convention of book design, the engraved, emblematic frontispiece, understood as an integral part of the author's argument, was at the apex of its historical importance, and Hobbes stands out among political theorists for his preoccupation with the form.[22] Like Benjamin, he sought to make the most of the political opportunities provided by mechanical reproducibility.

Engraving and the printing press are not, however, the only technologies shaping our encounter with the wayward figures lurking in *Leviathan*'s picture of the body politic: by allowing me to scan the frontispiece, enlarge whatever caught my eye, and embed the enlarged details here, contemporary digital imaging made it easier to present my claims to you. Furthermore, it was only through using the digital zoom to examine the JPEG I had made for other purposes that, contrary to everything written about the subjects' gazes, I first discovered the faces staring back at me. Before then, I too had failed to see them.

Though personal, that history of viewer response is not unique. When I made a passing reference to the unexpected swiveled heads while speaking to a room full of political theorists who know Hobbes's work, they seemed startled. Part of what they knew was that all eyes gaze into those of the sovereign. Yet just weeks after those discussions, I watched other readers make the discovery without any prompting. As my undergraduate seminar gathered around a first edition of *Leviathan,* students jostled for space. Denied an adequate view, several at the periphery of the group whipped out their iPhones, found the image on the Internet, and—fusing the optical and tactile in ways undreamed of by Benjamin, but perhaps still in keeping with his speculations in the artwork essay—began enlarging it with their touch screens. Soon enough, one of them exclaimed, "Some of the little guys in the right arm are looking out at us." Other students promptly echoed her. True, some were art history majors—but they found what eminent art historians had missed.

Encounters of this kind fit the Benjaminian pattern of photographic revelation. That's because, though engraved in the mid-seventeenth century, the frontispiece the smartphone users saw and I present here is essentially a photograph. The ease of enlarging made ubiquitous by digital imaging informs other writing about Hobbes and the frontispiece. In the walled town at the image's center, for instance, Francesca Falk recently identified two plague doctors. Found in both the drawn and engraved versions, they are clearly visible (though not so legible) to the unassisted eye, and their implications for the meaning of the image are far from trivial, but they have scarcely been noted in the literature (fig. 8.4).[23] More recently still, Magnus Kristiansson and Johan Tralau have argued that, contra a host of commentaries, Hobbes's Leviathan is indeed the sea monster invoked by the book's title: magnification, they claim, reveals the tips of the sovereign's fishy tail (fig. 8.5).[24]

Where does all this photographically mediated poring over visual details leave the image of Hobbes's day? Return to the swiveled heads. If they could be seen only when digitally magnified, then that would make a Benjaminian point—but at the cost of finding nothing odd or surprising about the long-running failure to notice the little bodies' rebellious acts. We would have no reasonable basis for thinking those acts could have effects on the book's readers. One could not treat the original, 1651 edition of the *Leviathan* frontispiece as if it exemplifies a kind of optical unconscious, a form of potentially unnerving hiding in plain sight. But the picture at the front of the first edition—and presumably, most scholars who discuss the frontispiece have taken the trouble to examine this version—is relatively large (9 7/16 × 6 1/8 inches), its rendering delightfully sharp. Examining the engraving with the naked eye, it is possible, if one looks closely at the tiny figures, to see the wayward glances. It's of course easier still with a magnifying glass, a technology available to people of means at the time of the book's publication.

Photography, furthermore, plays a more ambiguous role in this problem of the (un)seen than my story so far has allowed. Reproductions of the whole

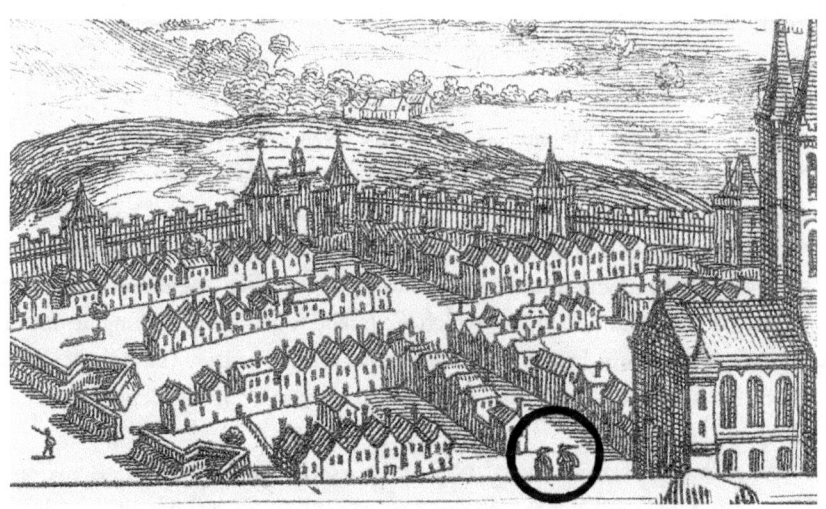

FIGURE 8.4 Frontispiece detail. Courtesy of the Chapin Library, Williams College, gift of Donald S. Klopfer, Class of 1922. Although curiously out of scale with the rest of the town, the two circled figures are clearly wearing the beak masks that were the mark of plague doctors in Hobbes's time.

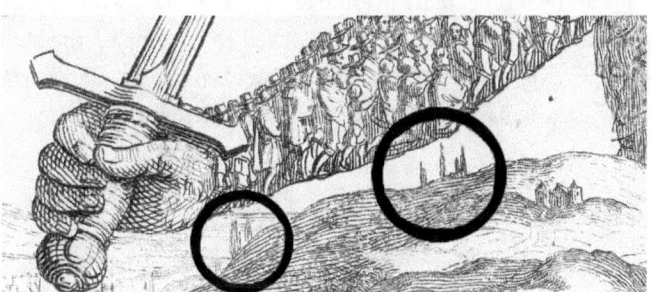

FIGURE 8.5 Frontispiece detail. Courtesy of the Chapin Library, Williams College, gift of Donald S. Klopfer, Class of 1922. Kristiansson and Tralau's spiky tail ends, which have elsewhere been referred to as "trees." Note the ocean visible in the upper right edge of the circle on the left, though the tail seems to be on land.

frontispiece in scholarly commentaries or assorted contemporary editions of Hobbes's text don't reveal the subjects' faces in much detail, and in such cases one must doubt the outward gazes register at any perceptual level. Scholarly writings on the frontispiece, however, as well as the covers of inexpensive paperbacks, often enlarge the upper half of the engraving, making the faces in question visible again.[25] Yet the figures still go unnoted; still writers insist on the uniformity of the subjects' gazes. Even Kristiansson and Tralau, despite their scrutinizing of enlarged minutiae, report that "the monarch's body is constituted by human bodies which are linked together, all looking up at the sovereign"—a claim belied by one of the illustrations they provide.[26] All of which returns us to the question: how to understand this particular instance of vision's unseen?

What kind of instance is it? Not, of course, precisely the type Benjamin has in mind. He underscores the camera's capacity to record details that elude the eye and to present a reality or nature we will exit when we look away from the photograph. (Even after examining a Muybridge study of a running horse, we will not perceive horses' movements in the world in the way they were revealed by the photographic series.) I, in contrast, have discussed details visible in an image and yet repeatedly overlooked even by those who have studied it. Yet just as the term may usefully be stretched to encompass the strange case of Hobbes's wayward subjects, the Hobbesian case, in turn, allows us to puzzle through some of Benjamin's photographic and cinematic claims.

Affect and Allegory

We might pursue those claims by taking the overlooked details as examples of what some contemporary affect theorists call "side perceptions." As William Connolly stresses, because "the eye takes in more than it registers explicitly," such perceptions affect us even as, indeed because, they slip beneath the threshold of recognition.[27] Drawing his examples from Hitchcock's *Vertigo*, a classic site of psychoanalytic criticism, Connolly explores fleeting filmic experiences, unrecognized by most viewers, better described as agitations and intensities than as matters of "ideological politics, narrative form, or cultural message."[28] Affective shifts induced by visions unseen, they do not rise to the level of consciousness but are neither repressed by spectators nor part of the unconscious in a Freudian sense. Such side perceptions, Connolly argues, are obscured by the psychoanalytic quest for deep interpretation but color our responses to film. Film can thus help us grasp how the "layering of culture" unfolds in daily life, where side perceptions are also part of the process in which "cultural habits, skills, memory traces, and affects" are at once shaped by and folded into "muscles, skin, gut, and cruder brain regions" amid what he calls "the body/brain/culture network."[29] As Connolly's language suggests, this notion of nonconscious perception extends well beyond the optical, engaging our embodiment in all its sensory modes.

Benjamin anticipated much of this. He, too, theorized layering and nonconscious perception. (Think of his attention to the moment when hand meets cigarette lighter.) For decades, he sought to understand how capitalism, new technologies, and distinctively modern forms of shock had transformed the human sensorium and the nature of experience. Not long before his "Little History" introduced the optical unconscious, he concluded his essay on surrealism by envisioning—dreaming of and yearning for—an interpenetration of "body and image space" in which "all revolutionary tension becomes bodily collective innervation, and all the bodily innervations of the collective become revolutionary discharge."[30] (Though such moments were the stuff of Hobbes's worst nightmares—he hoped sovereignty would render them impossible—he, like Benjamin, stressed the circuits linking image, nerves, bodies, and body politic. *Leviathan*'s frontispiece asserts visually what Benjamin's surrealism essay declares textually: "The collective is a body, too."[31]) The artwork essay's account of the optical unconscious is surrounded and inflected by analyses of habit, distraction, cinema's tactile qualities, and, above all (in one version of the essay), innervation, Benjamin's term for exchanges among affective energy, bodily movement, and external stimuli—and, hence, his key to exploring the prosthetic extensions of the senses and *"the tasks which face the human apparatus of perception at historical turning points."*[32]

If we start with this Benjamin, we find a line of thought running both backward (through Bergson, for instance) and forward in intellectual history, and (though Benjamin seems to have borrowed innervation from Freud, for whom it was a key term) we could choose to do so without treating psychoanalysis as more than the source of a generative analogy—without, that is, placing particular emphasis on Freudian topography or on notions such as sublimation, repression, and the like.[33] Brian Massumi positions Benjamin in just this way when, right before invoking him as a precursor, he describes images as "the conveyors of forces of emergence . . . vehicles for existential potentialization and transfer."[34] Understanding the optical unconscious in this spirit casts those disobedient Hobbesian subjects as exemplars of the side perception, unseen but nevertheless taken in when one looks at (some versions of) the image. When hidden in plain sight, they are not merely overlooked: infolded noncognitively but consequentially, they shape not only sensation and sentiment but our acts of meaning making, even though we do not absorb them at the level of meaning. The particular nature of the hidden details makes the shaping all the more likely, for the human brain devotes more space to face recognition than to any other visual object, attending especially to the direction of gazes, and a large experimental literature shows not only that subliminal pictures of human faces can influence viewers' "thoughts, memories, and feelings" but that anxiety is intensified when facial perception is unconscious.[35] Digital and other photographic enlargements of the frontispiece thus enable us to notice consciously what otherwise would most likely register without our awareness.

We could, however, certainly object to this characterization from within psychoanalysis and perhaps from Benjamin's project as well (for the question is precisely how much the latter is a psychoanalytic enterprise). To see why, we might begin by asking whether it is so clear that the perception of the swiveled heads should be stripped of semantic, allegorical, or ideological significance, registering nothing more than a kind of intensity or inchoate unease. What of the details' meaningfulness? Do they not figure forces and questions haunting the project of Hobbesian sovereignty? Beneath its confident tone, *Leviathan* is suffused with anxiety about subjects indifferent to the sovereign's inducements and threats. What the wayward glances allow us to see but not register is the incompleteness of the sovereignty we are nonetheless instructed to obey. Their presence in the frontispiece is fortuitous, but surely the imperfection thus revealed is necessary, not contingent. We thus might even read the shaggy-headed man and any fellow dissidents as figures of the psychoanalytic insight that, in Eric Santner's words, "when bodies are joined to language, one is always stuck with an uncanny remainder," a dynamic leaving the sovereign in "a fundamentally precarious position . . . subject . . . to a radical ontological vulnerability where a form of life can become horribly *informe*."[36] Enacting truths we must never avow lest our own actions swerve off course, they embody what Slavoj Žižek calls the "'unknown knowns,' the disavowed beliefs, suppositions, and obscene practices we pretend not to know about, although they form the background of our public values."[37] Read in this way, the optical unconscious exists in part *within* the frontispiece as a space for lodging what can neither be dispensed with nor explicitly affirmed or argued.[38]

Stressing the barriers to acknowledgment leads us to ask why details that (once one has noticed them) seem so easy to see have been so often missed. How do the faces come to register only subliminally? Can the oversights be utterly unmotivated? As the interplay of gazes in the *Leviathan* frontispiece suggests, an image of sovereignty is not just a theatrical or intimidating display but a screen onto which we project — something we create as we project — fears and fantasies, longings and aversions. Believing that all eyes look into the sovereign's fulfills, perhaps, a fantasy of sovereignty's agency and completeness, its ability to protect us — and, though the potency of the sovereign and the unanimity of subservience diminish us, they may, through the fantastical and transitive workings of the wish, feel to us like testaments to our own powers.[39] Or, at least, the belief that all gaze upward allows us to admire the magnificent totality of Hobbes's theoretical achievement, the perfection of his model. The wish to do so may motivate even those many scholars who oppose his political project — just as, relatedly, theorists of mass society, including some of Benjamin's colleagues in the Frankfurt School, often obscured dissent and the limits of incorporation, giving too seamless and totalizing a picture of the social forms they condemned.

Pondering motive and oversight leads to one more way in which the image and responses to it act out psychoanalytic insights into the failures and distortions inherent in looking. Every commentary on the frontispiece, mine included, identifies the sovereign with the giant head sitting atop the composite body. Hobbes's text, however, does not support that gloss. The extended mapping of the body politic that makes up *Leviathan*'s introduction provides a different metaphor: because it gives "life and motion to the whole body," sovereignty is "an Artificiall *Soul*."[40] Substituting head for soul in the frontispiece must have felt like a pictorial necessity (and spared Hobbes, the materialist, the embarrassment of beginning his book by illustrating the "incorporeall body," an idea on which he later showers scorn).[41] Taking the head as incarnating sovereignty is, of course, not a mistake but rather the only competent response to how the picture signifies. Still, the switch reminds us of — even figures — the constitutive role of misrecognition.

Hobbes obviously knew that in practice sovereignty could never be perfectly complete or frictionless. Did he know the friction found expression in his cover image? Since he was (most scholars assume) intimately involved in the design, one could suppose he asked Bosse to include someone like the shaggy-haired man as a small, difficult-to-locate reminder of important but unspeakable truths. Despite Hobbes's robust sense of humor, however, that he supervised these particular details seems improbable. Why would he have found even an obscure image of refused incorporation, indifference, or unpunished disobedience helpful to his project?[42] Does it not make more sense to assume the humor is the engraver's, employed with a knack for visual detail but without much recognition of the import for the theory? Of course, without textual evidence of a kind that seems not to exist in this case, one can do no more than speculate about knowledge and intentions, but resolving the question is less important than recognizing its stakes. Understood as escaping the awareness and defying the explicit intentions of the book's author, the little men in the crook of the right arm offer allegories of the unconscious not merely in their being so often overlooked while hidden in plain sight but also for their unexpected swerves. Without them, the towering mass pictured in the upper half of the *Leviathan* frontispiece endures as a figure of sovereign subjectivity—the very kind of ego later pushed from its position by Freud's Copernican decentering. However modestly, those swiveled heads also perform that displacement, combating authoritarian politics just as Benjamin hoped mechanically reproduced images would. Disrupting sovereign control—of both state and author—they exemplify but exceed the limits of techno-phenomenological conceptions of the optical unconscious, crying out for a more direct engagement with psychoanalytic senses of the unconscious as a structural aspect of psyche and subjectivity. In that, too, it turns out, they are joined by Benjamin himself.

Mellerdrammers in Black and White

Does he leave the relationship between the optical and the instinctual wholly indeterminate? One can believe so only by ignoring evidence that is, like the frontispiece's wayward glances, visible on the surface. For efforts to understand the optical unconscious, the long predominance of the artwork essay's third version is unfortunate, since the text represses—not merely overlooks but omits in a manner amounting to denial or motivated forgetting—some of Benjamin's most interesting remarks on the topic. He originally specified the relationship in the artwork essay's first iteration and refined his account in the second. Both texts contain the same line that concludes the discussion of the optical unconscious in the third version—"it is through the camera that we first discover the optical unconscious, just as we discover the instinctual unconscious through psychoanalysis"—but then, unlike the more widely discussed variant, add, "Moreover, these two types of unconscious are intimately linked." Benjamin sketches the connections in fascinating detail:

> For in most cases the diverse aspects of reality captured by the film camera lie outside only the *normal* spectrum of sense impressions. Many of the deformations and stereotypes, transformations and catastrophes

which can assail the optical world in films afflict the actual world in psychoses, hallucinations, and dreams. Thanks to the camera, therefore, the individual perceptions of the psychotic or the dreamer can be appropriated by collective perception. The ancient truth expressed by Heraclitus, that those who are awake have a world in common while each sleeper has a world of his own, has been invalidated by film—and less by depicting the dream world itself than by creating figures of collective dream, such as the globe-encircling Mickey Mouse.[43]

Benjamin's later omission is significant, then, for here, obviously, psychoanalysis is far more than a parallel. The camera also turns out to have a privileged relationship to such stuff as psychoanalysis was made on: the dreamwork impinges upon it, thereby letting us see visions previously unseen by most people. Benjamin makes clear, too, that the psychic materials informing the optical unconscious shape life in "the actual world." How to understand that shaping? Read with a narrow emphasis on the restrictions mentioned in the final sentence, his discussion seems to concern only energies and affects produced in responses to cinema. Benjamin indeed goes on to stress how films can trigger a potentially therapeutic "collective laughter" and "release of unconscious energies."[44] But I think the narrow reading is mistaken. To make the most of what Benjamin is saying, we need to press further, pursuing his suggestion that the relations between the unconscious and the camera are intimate and complex, that films and photographs also *register* psychic forces—eruptions of the unconscious—we might not otherwise be capable of perceiving.[45] To take a cue from the essay's second version when exploring the optical unconscious, we must understand "the other nature that speaks to the camera" as including both the world of dreams and the broader complex of forces and terms—desire, drive, fantasy, condensation, displacement, repression—crucial to Freud's mapping of psychic life.

Benjamin's language and examples urge us forward. As Miriam Hansen argues, he grasps Mickey Mouse as a "dialectical image," one that "embodies the disjunctive temporalities of human and natural history," entering "the uncanny" through a "utopian" blurring of identity boundaries.[46] If we take his invocation of psychoanalytic terms and forces seriously, however, we must recognize how the visual construction of race has shadowed the idea of the optical unconscious at least since Benjamin first drafted the artwork essay. The very passage that fatally undermines the ego's sovereignty also introduces the problem of racialization. It scarcely needs saying that murderous racism was at the heart of the political projects that Benjamin, by elaborating concepts "completely useless for the purposes of fascism," explicitly intended the artwork essay to re-sist.[47] What calls for commentary, rather, is the legacy of visual construction en-coded in the global icon to which he often turned when thinking about film and mass culture and that he here uses to exemplify the optical unconscious and figure mass-mediated dream life: cavorting across the screen, Mickey Mouse is an emblem of not merely commercial fantasy but also racial spectacle.

An early and serial reenactor of *Uncle Tom's Cabin*, created when Walt Disney drew inspiration from the image of a blacked-up Al Jolson in *The Jazz Singer*, Mickey was the bastard offspring of new technologies of mechanical reproduction and the historical tradition of blackface minstrelsy.[48] In the in-augural Mickey Mouse cartoon, *Steamboat Willie* (1928), the roots in black-face are evident not only visibly but audibly, when Mickey leads an extended, wordless performance of "Turkey in the Straw," which is to say — as the melo-dies are the same — the minstrel song "Zip Coon." In *Mickey's Mellerdrammer* (1933), Mickey plays both Topsy and Tom during a performance of *Uncle Tom's Cabin*.[49] As he prepares for the roles by blacking up in his dressing room, he reenacts one of *The Jazz Singer*'s iconic scenes. Warbling "Mammy," he studies himself in the mirror, spoofing the moment in which Jolson's Jackie Rabino-witz encounters his black double in the looking glass and thereby, as Michael Rogin argues, sheds Jewishness to lay claim to an unmarked whiteness — and, we might add, a greater share of national sovereignty.[50]

That moment is no anomaly. Blackface's representational and performance practices had proved crucial to the nineteenth-century invention of a dis-tinctively American mass culture and remained important to the shaping of racial order through the first decades of the twentieth century. Rooted in ridi-cule, blackface comedy was a genre of disdainful domination, but the theater of racial impersonation was also fueled by disavowed desire. Minstrelsy gave whites access to the corporeal and libidinal freedom they had projected onto the black bodies they were subordinating. The optics of racial masquerade dis-played what Kobena Mercer calls "the constitutive ambivalence that structures whiteness as a cultural identity."[51] Whites' ambivalent play with the color line proved transformative: throughout its heyday, as Rogin shows, the application of burnt cork not only facilitated politically charged negotiations and recon-figurations of identity and difference but also featured in the films responsible for key formal and technological breakthroughs.[52] Furthermore, as Nicholas Sammond demonstrates, blackface was fundamental to the invention and rise of animation.[53]

Although Benjamin did not say so, the icon he used to epitomize the rise of the new dreamscape spooling round the globe in celluloid strips of black and white was thus also circulating the visual conventions and fantasy life, the fears and desires, disavowals and displacements, of the much older tradition of burnt cork. Not only Mickey's look but also his conduct and character, including, crucially, what Sammond calls his "resistance to regulation," did that cultural work. The unruliness that led Benjamin to construe the cartoons as potential sites of resistance to fascism and capitalism carried on the long lineage of white fantasies about black bodies and desires. Benjamin seems not (consciously?) to have recognized that (perhaps because, by the 1930s, Mickey and similar characters had become *"vestigial* minstrels, carrying tokens of blackface minstrelsy in their bodies and behaviors, yet no longer signifying as such").[54] There is little evidence that even his most serious readers have made the connection, either: just as his links between optical and instinctual have gone largely unexplored, the visual-racial entailments of his use of Mickey Mouse are almost entirely unnoted in the scholarly commentary.[55] It is perhaps symptomatic that even *The Optical Unconscious*, Krauss's psychoanalytically informed critique of art historical accounts of modernism as a practice of visual mastery, both balks at Benjamin's insistence on the connections between psychoanalysis and the camera and finds no space for investigating, or even mentioning, European modernism's entanglements with colonial and racial imaginaries.[56] Mickey embodies, then, at once the work of visual construction and the role of the unacknowledged and unseen in that work. Attending to blackface undermines some of the utopian hopes the artwork essay's second version lodged in Disney's creation but reinforces Benjamin's psychoanalytic turn. If we wish to stress the intertwining of the instinctual and the optical, on the one hand, and race and sovereignty, on the other, his seemingly casual example turns out to be a very good place to start.

No Mere Words

One person who would appear to understand this is Kara Walker. Early in her career, she fitted a statuesque Lady Liberty with Mickey Mouse ears, all rendered in black against a lighter background (fig. 8.6).[57] The move is obvious enough, and could be considered merely an easy dig at some more generalized "Disneyfication" of the American cultural landscape. But that seems an odd response given the iconography of the scene in which that irreverent detail is set (fig. 8.7), and no one is more attuned to the historical resonances of such a visual gesture than Walker, whose entire oeuvre bears on (though is not ex-

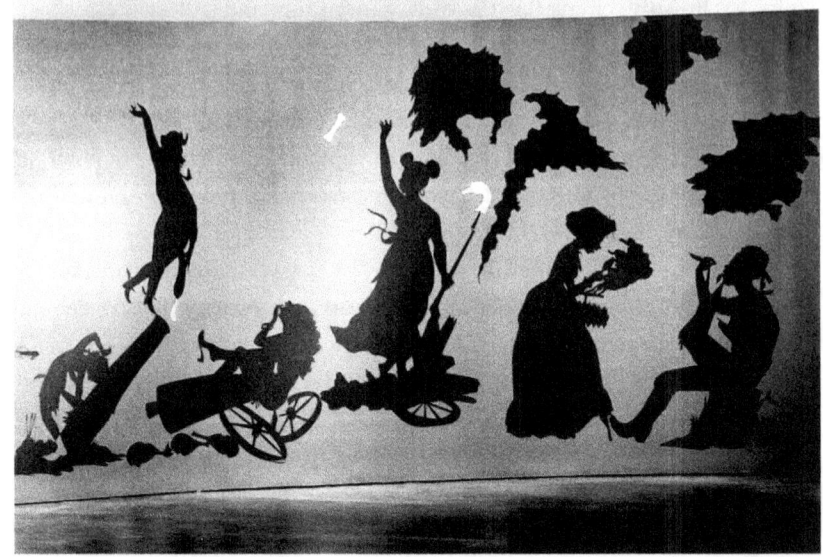

FIGURE 8.6 Kara Walker, detail of *No mere words can Adequately reflect the Remorse this Negress feels at having been Cast into such a lowly state by her former Masters and so it is with a Humble heart that she brings about their physical Ruin and earthly Demise*, 1999. Cut paper and paint on wall. Installation variable; approx. 132 × 780 inches (335.3 × 1981.2 cm). Artwork © Kara Walker, courtesy of Sikkema Jenkins and Co., New York. Installation view: California College of Arts and Crafts, Oakland, 1999. Photo: Ian Reeves (detail).

clusively preoccupied with) race and its optical unconscious. We might thus take *No Mere Words* as, among other things, an engagement with how racial subordination and fantasy-rich, denigrating forms of cross-racial desire such as blackface have helped to shape (white) American national identity. At least if we limit ourselves to her silhouettes, as I will for the moment, Walker keeps us at a remove from the media at the center of Benjamin's considerations, but in a way that may prove productive.

Walker's visual strategies in the silhouettes bring together aspects of the optical unconscious my discussion so far has tended to hold apart. One is the problem of the overlooked, the missed or misrecognized detail—the more literal sense of vision's unseen. The other is the way unconscious forces shape what and how we see. The interplay of the two creates much of her art's psychic and political charge. That charge is considerable, the silhouettes often a riot of violent and highly sexualized racial psychodramas (though often one might

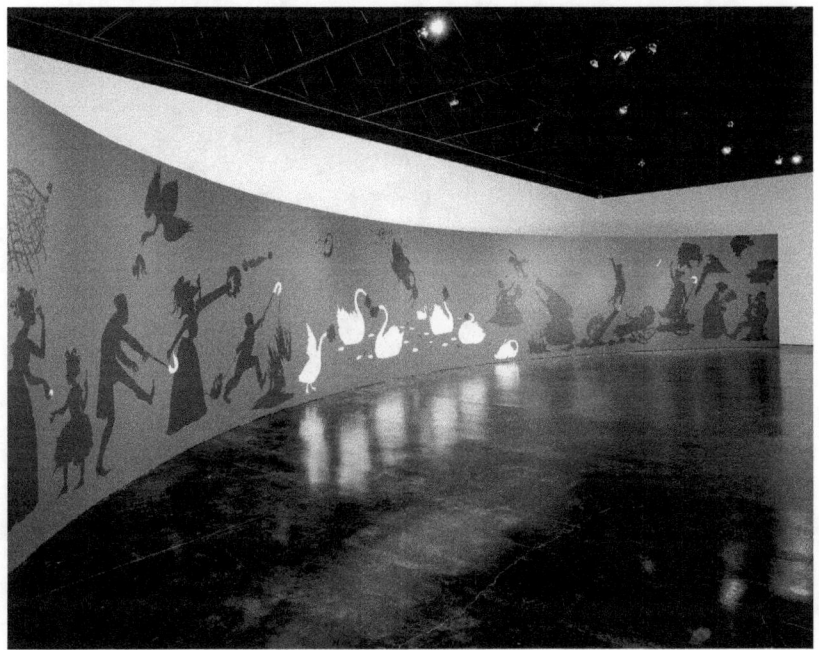

FIGURE 8.7 Kara Walker, *No mere words can Adequately reflect the Remorse this Negress feels at having been Cast into such a lowly state by her former Masters and so it is with a Humble heart that she brings about their physical Ruin and earthly Demise*, 1999. Cut paper and paint on wall. Installation variable; approx. 132 × 780 inches (335.3 × 1981.2 cm). Artwork © Kara Walker, courtesy of Sikkema Jenkins and Co., New York. Installation view: California College of Arts and Crafts, Oakland, 1999. Photo: Ian Reeves.

as well say violent and conspicuously racialized sexual psychodramas), with dramatis personae and settings that conjure (a certain version of) the antebellum, plantation South. However anarchic its appearance, there is method to the mayhem. The acts depicted are scandalous, grotesque, at times surprising in matters of detail, but certain characters or character types, settings, scenes, objects, and acts recur. In this brief encounter, let us focus on just one of the artist's common maneuvers, an important part of what I have elsewhere referred to as her art of racial profiling—the use of doubling.[58]

Consider a detail from a work called (to abridge considerably) *Presenting Negro Scenes*: a woman runs away from something distressing her (fig. 8.8)—and not surprisingly, given the scene swirling around her (fig. 8.9). Angled forward, this white woman (for she has been rendered to read that way, socially, even though her cutout figure has the deep black typical of silhouettes) holds

FIGURE 8.8 Kara Walker, detail of *Presenting Negro Scenes Drawn Upon My Passage Through the South and Reconfigured for the Benefit of Enlightened Audiences Wherever Such May Be Found, by Myself, Missus K.E.B. Walker, Colored*, 1997. Cut paper on wall; watercolor on paper. Installation variable; approx. 144 × 1,860 inches (365.8 × 4,724.4 cm). Artwork © Kara Walker, courtesy of Sikkema Jenkins and Co., New York. Installation view: The Renaissance Society at the University of Chicago. Photo: Tom van Eynde (detail).

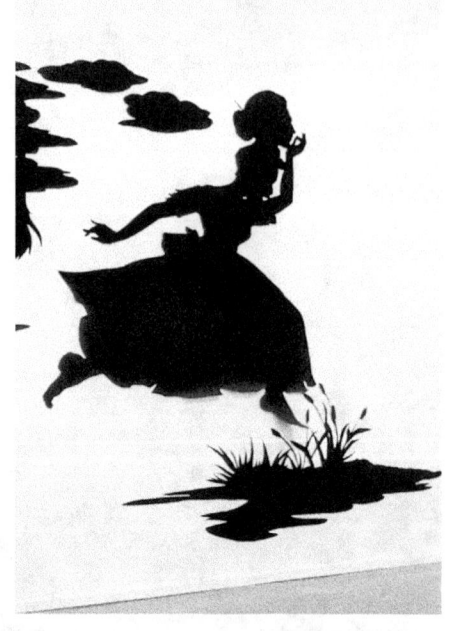

her hand to her mouth, perhaps merely a demure gesture of dismay, more likely a soon-to-fail attempt to keep herself from vomiting. Preoccupied with the scene she's fleeing and how it has made her feel, she seems not to see the boggy, mucky ground on which her forward foot is about to land. And yet she is, too, looking at that ground, for she is in fact two: just beneath the first head lies another, legible as socially black, of a woman whose gaze, features, and expression differ from the one sitting atop her. The lower expression is hard to read, but this woman seems more aware of the ground beneath her feet. With such works, our conscious perception is likely, if just for a moment, to err: a viewer may read the image one way, only to discover details upending that reading, inducing disorientation, forcing reconsideration. Repeatedly—for the example can be multiplied many times—Walker's art plays in that gap between eye and mind. Side perceptions abound.

Yet it is not enough to say that those visions impinge upon us, shaping conscious experience even when not consciously seen, or that they do so once more, differently, when viewers realize their initial oversight—though all this is true and important. The game of the hidden figure, the missed or misrecognized shape, packs a wallop because of the origins, character, and stakes of the material in question. One dark body with two heads, two thoughts, and thus

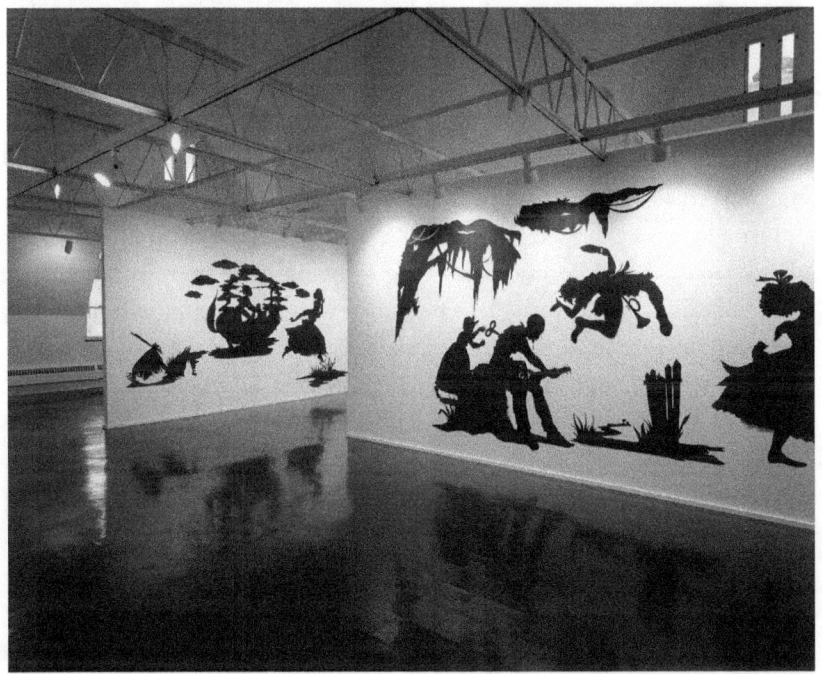

FIGURE 8.9 *Presenting Negro Scenes Drawn Upon My Passage Through the South and Reconfigured for the Benefit of Enlightened Audiences Wherever Such May Be Found, by Myself, Missus K.E.B. Walker, Colored,* 1997. Cut paper on wall; watercolor on paper. Installation variable; approx. 144 × 1,860 inches (365.8 × 4,724.4 cm). Artwork © Kara Walker, courtesy of Sikkema Jenkins and Co., New York. Installation view: The Renaissance Society at the University of Chicago. Photo: Tom van Eynde.

perhaps two souls, two unreconciled strivings, two warring ideals: one can't fully feel the two-ness of *Presenting Negro Scenes* without engaging the material and psychic lives of power.[59] Time after time, Walker's double takes lay bare and intervene into the cognitions, emotions, affects, desires, fears, and fantasies with which American perceptions of race are imbued. In her work, as for Freud, the figure of the double draws us into the realm of the uncanny.[60] The psychodramas she stages are deeply shaped by history—she borrows her material from a vast archive of racist literary and visual fantasy, advertising, pornography, and so on—but the resulting images reflect and invite impulses that well up from within, exceeding the grasp of empirical historiography. They engage the unconscious in the strongest of Freudian senses, showing that though racializing vision seeks social control, structures hierarchies, and is often tied to state power, it is not a domain in which the ego can be in charge. Yet even that third-person description fails to capture the force of the work, which does not so much articulate a proposition as thrust upon the spectator a feeling, a shudder of recognition: "I am not in control." Entering the domain of racial fantasy, giving the optical unconscious a psychoanalytic cast, Walker's art invites viewers to experience the limits of psychic sovereignty.

Like Hobbes's engraved frontispiece, Walker's silhouettes are of course not photographs, and as portraits they tend to be no more representations (let alone indexical traces) of actual sitters than were, I trust, those little figures gathered together in/as the sovereign's body.[61] Unlike the *Leviathan* image, however, which photography touched only in later dissemination and reception, her works have a formal relationship to the medium. In the period more or less suggested by Walker's characteristic *topoi*, the silhouette still hung on as a form of portraiture while already, as Lisa Saltzman observes, rapidly being "supplanted by ensuing techniques and technologies of visual representation, photography foremost among them." Walker's art is crucially, Saltzman's analysis suggests, shaped by the temporality of after—after the moment her chosen form was current and, of course, after the period that provides so many themes and visual motifs for her work.[62] That temporality, however, is part of the work's engagement with the present, with the weight of accumulated images, narratives, and historical fantasies now. The engagement is abetted by the way in which Walker's silhouettes come after—in the sense of being informed by, not supplanting—photography, too. They show the influence of what Benjamin calls photography's "dynamite of the split second," its "accentuation of hidden details," its "far flung debris."[63]

Although the laborious, intention-directed work of cutting silhouettes is unlikely to produce the kinds of visual accidents often found in photographs, Walker's art has its own dynamite and debris—at times, literal explosions, often bits and pieces of broken bodies—and its revelations borrow from what the camera has wrought and how it has taught us to see. Trading on those learned perceptual skills, her images deliberately insinuate into contour and line aspects of, as Benjamin would say, "another nature." In provoking thought about the place of the optical unconscious in the visual construction of race, Walker's work thus helps us understand how that construction proceeds in not only the aspects of everyday life captured by photography but also photographs themselves.

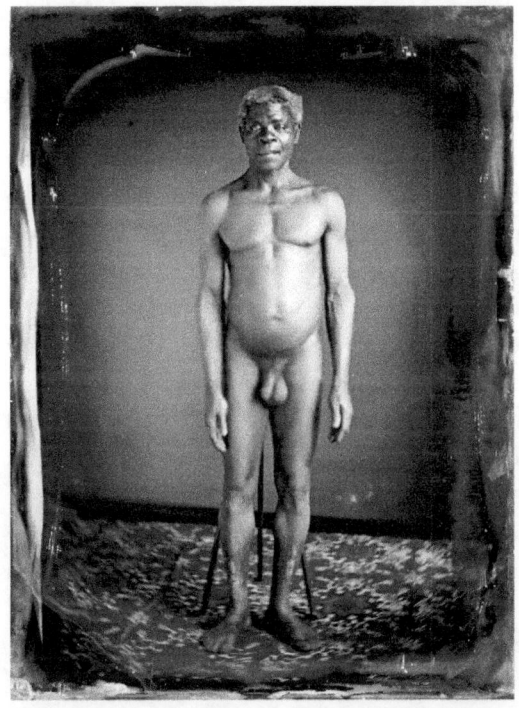

FIGURE 8.10 J. T. Zealy,
"Jem, Gullah, belonging to
F.N. Green" (Gibbes's label),
3.25 × 4.25 inches. Courtesy
of the Peabody Museum of
Archaeology and Ethnology,
Harvard University, PM#35-
5-10/53046 (digital file
no. 101260010).

Science and Dream

Consider a picture of the man we know only as Jem, a photo drawn from a series now notorious for the purpose it was intended to serve, the circumstances of its making, and its manner of representation (fig. 8.10). Taken in the medium's early days, this daguerreotype returns us to the moment and milieu so often revisited by Walker. Though cruel, it appears to be cool, sober, and far from the silhouettes' formal strategies and fantastical dreamscapes. If, however, we examine it for traces of the optical unconscious, reflecting on not only race but also sovereignty, what do we find? We might begin with how Jem came to be photographed.

In 1850, while visiting Columbia, South Carolina, Louis Agassiz, a Harvard professor then considered the nation's preeminent scientist, commissioned daguerreotypes of seven enslaved men and women.[64] Seeking evidence to support his recently publicized view that blacks and whites derived from separate origins, Agassiz toured slave plantations in the area and selected subjects he considered to be of pure African birth or heritage. The seven were later taken to the Columbia studio of photographer Joseph T. Zealy, who produced fifteen daguerreotypes, each portraying one person. No one pictured is fully dressed. All are topless; two of the men wear nothing. Local slave owner and fellow polygenesist Dr. Robert Gibbes collected the photographs from Zealy, labeled them, and forwarded them to Agassiz for use in continuing and publicizing his research. Yet few people saw them in Agassiz's lifetime or for many years afterward. Long forgotten in the attic of Harvard's Peabody Museum, the daguerreotypes came to light again in 1976 and have since been exhibited, published, and analyzed, making them "perhaps some of the best-known" photos ever taken of enslaved people.[65]

While thus exposed to the world, the five men and two women on display remain obscure. Only Gibbes's labels reveal that the man in the photograph reproduced here was named (or called by whites) Jem. Only the labels reveal the (first) names of the other subjects—Alfred, Delia, Drana, Fassena, Jack, Renty—and the kinship ties within the group (listing Delia as "daughter of Renty," Drana as "daughter of Jack"). Gibbes also indicated the African group or place of origin Agassiz assigned to each, and the names of the white men who claimed these human beings as property. Beyond this, the lives of the men and women in the daguerreotypes remain largely irrecoverable.[66]

Without seeking an impossible recuperation, we can still gain a better understanding of the images' interplay of seen and unseen by following Ariella Azoulay as she investigates "the photographic situation to which [the slaves] were subjected."[67] Even before we look, the facts of slavery make clear that Zealy's studio was a theater of white control, but the images add visual proof. Given the long exposure time required by a daguerreotype, the still poses on display suggest that all seven slaves obeyed the instructions they were given when posing.[68] (By Jem's legs, one can see the legs of the brace helping him keep still.) But whoever gave those instructions, we should, as Azoulay argues, view the photographs as the product of an agreement among Zealy, Gibbes, Agassiz, and the legal owners of the photographed subjects, treating each of those men as in a sense present in the studio.[69] Although already home in Massachusetts when the pictures were taken, even Agassiz was there. Especially Agassiz: the initiator of the photographic encounter, he was the one who needed the studio to prove a scientific theory by staging, in Azoulay's words, "an acting out of the white man's supremacy" before the camera's lens.[70]

So far, stressing the multiple agencies operating in the photographic situation seems to deny the sovereignty of any one party while underscoring the control exercised by whites as a group. Without minimizing the violence of the slaves' material subordination or their concomitant lack of control of the means

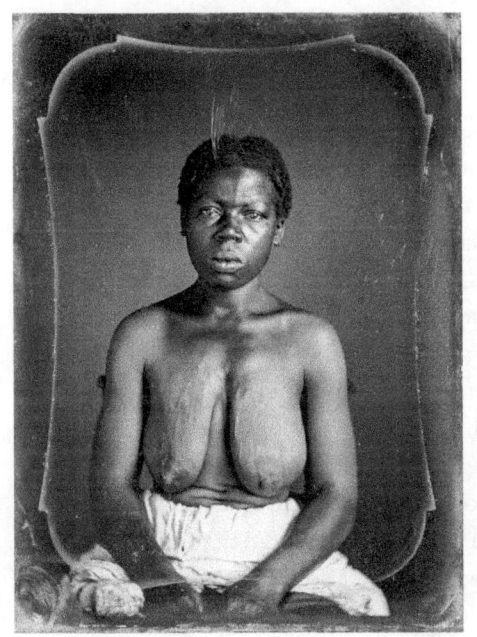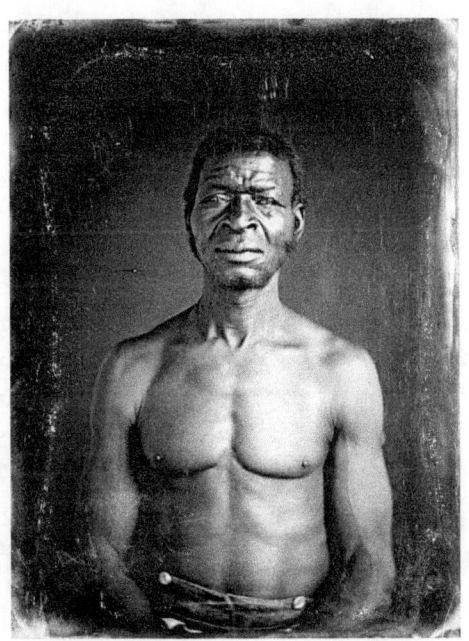

FIGURE 8.11 *left* J. T. Zealy, "Drana, country born, daughter of Jack Guinea. Plantation of B.F. Taylor, Esq." (Gibbes's label), 3.25 × 4.25 inches. Courtesy of the Peabody Museum of Archaeology and Ethnology, Harvard University, PM#35-5-10/53041 (digital file no. 101260005).

FIGURE 8.12 *right* "Jack (driver), Guinea. Plantation of B.F. Taylor, Esq." (Gibbes's label), 3.25 × 4.25 inches. Courtesy of the Peabody Museum of Archaeology and Ethnology, Harvard University, PM#35-5-10/53043 (digital file no. 101260007).

of representation, however, Azoulay argues that they, too, nevertheless shaped the encounter and the image: "even as merely photographed persons," subjects "take part in the power play on which they leave their mark."[71] Agassiz's desire for illustrated racial types required pictures that were uniform and impersonal, but despite the enforced stillness of each man and woman photographed, the intended similarity and typological exemplification he sought are, in Azoulay's reading, "disrupted by the different looks in the eyes of each subject."[72] In the frontal photographs, Delia appears "frightened," while "Drana's gaze is tougher, more seasoned, grudging and scornful toward those seeking to photograph her look," and Jack's squint seeks to "turn the tables" on those who thought they controlled his image (figs. 8.11 and 8.12). Issuing "an address extending beyond total subjection and suspending it," the subjects of these photographs do not look only at those in the room: by staring directly into the lens of the camera, they "address someone who is not present, an addressee who opens the space in which they are placed, who undoes—albeit very slightly—its oppressive limits."[73]

Such claims about the thoughts and feelings conveyed by the looks of people caught in so constrained a setting risk a kind of ventriloquism (born perhaps of a feeling that respecting the dignity of the enslaved requires us to find ocular proof of their humanity or courage). I can imagine very different readings.[74] Yet even if some of her specific attributions warrant skepticism, Azoulay's analysis helps us see how, in bearing visible traces of the violence that produced them, the pictures display the failure of Agassiz's demonstration, defying his desire for typology and subverting his "presumption to use [photography] for showing the blacks in their purity." Indeed, she reveals the project to be undermined even by the signs of its success: just as Agassiz sought to stage "scientific proof" of black inferiority, "photography exposed the performative content" of the effort, documenting "the cyclic manner in which it produced the required results."[75] While one might wonder for whom this performativity fails—white, antebellum viewer or twenty-first-century critic?—we have reason to think the pictures indeed faltered on some level in their own time: Agassiz showed the daguerreotypes at one meeting of the intimate and exclusive Cambridge Scientific Club, but never otherwise displayed them in public, not even when illustrating his subsequent writings on race.[76]

What failed? A more satisfying answer requires further inquiry. Following Azoulay, I have so far approached the photographs primarily as windows onto conditions. Though important as they are horrifying, neither the circumstances of the daguerreotypes' production nor how the subjects navigated them can tell us all we need to know about the images' workings and solicitations. If they engage the optical unconscious at all, the questions Azoulay would have us ask stay strictly on "the optical side," casting vision's unseen in nonpsychoanalytic terms. While making clear that the photographs are always "excessive with regard to any sovereign representation that one side or another . . . wishes to impose," these inquiries fall short of the decentering of psychic sovereignty both Benjamin and Walker invite.[77] The details on which I have focused seem, then, to offer little contact with dream-work or the dreamworld, displaced or misrecognized desire. Yet, for all the science informing Agassiz's aspirations, are not these forces, too, present in his terrible pictures?

Just as Agassiz never published the fifteen daguerreotypes he commissioned from Zealy, he never brought to the public any of the more than one hundred pictures he later took of dark, often naked bodies while investigating racial mixing and purity on an expedition to Brazil.[78] Perhaps something in all those other photos failed to suit his purposes, too—but we might then think further about what the purposes were. Start with one of the most striking things one cannot see in any of the pictures, a trace of any scientific apparatus or metric. As Suzanne Schneider notes, evidently no one involved in arranging the slave daguerreotypes attempted to present the kind of information crucial to the comparative assessments upon which an argument for polygenesis depended: "Agassiz, a man renowned for his standardization of scientific cataloguing techniques, appears to have neglected to request that any actual measurement be made of the subjects of his taxonomic inquiry," nor did he solicit similar (if, of necessity, more decorous) images of white bodies.[79] Agassiz held his own powers of visual discrimination in extraordinarily high regard, and may have believed that he needed no other materials, just an opportunity to pore over these pictures of bodies.[80] But when he gazed at the unadorned black body, what did he see?

We might consult a letter, often quoted in discussions of the photos, that Agassiz wrote to his mother from a Philadelphia hotel in 1846, shortly after first arriving in the United States. The black workers who served him meals unsettled him in ways he could "scarcely express," leaving him "feeling that they are not of the same blood as us." His panic palpable, he inventoried in grotesque detail the physical features that disturbed him and then concluded, "I could not take my eyes off their face in order to tell them to stay far away. And when they advanced that hideous hand toward my plate in order to serve me, I wished I were able to depart in order to eat a piece of bread elsewhere, rather than dine with such service. What unhappiness for the white race—to have tied their existence so closely with that of the Negroes in certain countries! God preserve us from such a contact."[81] The letter tends to be read as expressing the visceral aversion underpinning what would become Agassiz's intellectual case for polygenesis and against racial mixing.[82] And so, on some level, it was. Yet the element of fascination and compulsion—"I could not take my eyes off their face"—points, too, toward a more ambivalent response. Agassiz indeed kept looking for decades, in the fields of plantations, in Brazil, and often through the medium of photography. Perhaps the daguerreotypes have more to tell us about how and why he did so.

We can easily overlook how rare it was in 1850 to photograph either slaves or unclothed bodies. While the topless pictures of the women, Delia and Drana, offer much worth critical scrutiny, the most striking pictures may be those of Alfred and Jem, each of whom is shown naked from front, side, and rear.

Schneider points out that critics tend not to see or discuss "the machinations of desire" at work in the whole series, or to make much of the focus on black male bodies. One need neither accept her claim that Agassiz's embrace of polygenesis was nothing more than a scheme to deflect attention from a sexual scandal in which he was embroiled in Boston, nor see the photographic project as a displaced expression of Agassiz's "socially transgressive and class-crossing love for his male secretary," to recognize that scientific curiosity and the thirst for evidence were not the only kinds of fascination coursing through the photographs.[83] Science, one could say, provided a kind of fig leaf for the pleasure white men took in looking at black bodies, but it seems more helpful to think of the (fraught, ambivalent) scopic pleasures of racial science as entangling erotic and epistemological drives than to see the one as merely the other's calculated moral alibi. Nor, for all the stress I, like others, have placed on Agassiz, does it seem on this point helpful to focus too single-mindedly on him. That the photographs were, as Azoulay argues, produced though exchanges among several white men makes the sexual dynamic all the more interesting, not least because, even if the pictures languished in such obscurity that one would be hard-pressed to assign them a causal role, they anticipated what would become the conventions of colonial ethnography.

Does my stress on fascination and pleasure seem misplaced? Skeptical readers might view this picture of Jem (fig. 8.13) alongside a photo taken more than a century later (fig. 8.14). Robert Mapplethorpe's renderings of the black male body have drawn their own share of controversy, but no one doubts their aesthetic and erotic intent. I find it hard, however — despite the radical differences between the two photographic situations — to keep wholly separate the investments visible on the surface of each work. Is this just a matter of the inevitable but inconsequential similarities arising when picturing two naked bodies from behind? A misreading, abetted by my use of reproductions that narrow the gap between a small daguerreotype and a large gelatin silver print? Merely my own fantasy or erotic projection? How can one be sure? Yet I find obvious certain similarities between the two cameras' engagements with the naked body (head in each case tilted slightly forward) and the play of light on dark skin.[84] Both photographers have lit the scene so that the camera seems to give the skin something like a caress. Both pictures lead the eyes to the buttocks, though by contrary means (one by centering, the other by placing them at the picture's lower edge, cutting off the legs). Both are, on some level, offers to take possession — offers that underscore connections between looking and consuming, photographing and penetrating.

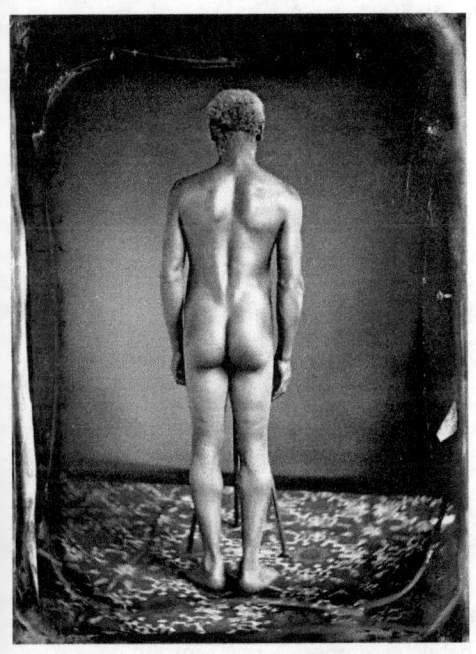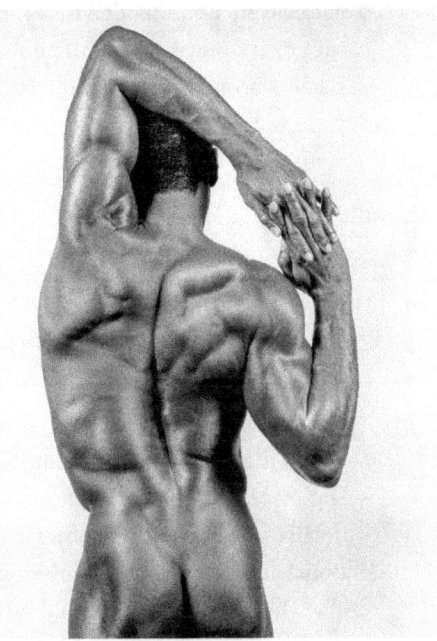

FIGURE 8.13 *left* J. T. Zealy, "Jem, Gullah, belonging to F.N. Green" (Gibbes's label), 3.25 × 4.25 inches. Courtesy of the Peabody Museum of Archaeology and Ethnology, Harvard University, PM#35-5-10/53045 (digital file # 101260009).

FIGURE 8.14 *right* Robert Mapplethorpe, *Derrick Cross*, 1983. 19 3/16 × 15 3/8 inches. Copyright Robert Mapplethorpe Foundation. Used by permission.

Of course there is nothing in the daguerreotype comparable to the way Derrick Cross's stagy pose frankly signals the photographer's artistic ambitions. Nor does the Mapplethorpe photo offer up the trappings of science. But, as we have seen, those trappings are not easy to locate in the daguerreotypes, either, and one can argue that Mapplethorpe's pictures of black men also have ethnographic or documentary aims, serving as insider records of a specific subcultural moment; one can even wonder, as Kobena Mercer has, whether such pictures seek to display "the return of the repressed in the ethnocentric imaginary."[85] However one understands Mapplethorpe's project, looking at the two photographs together makes it even harder, I think, to view the daguerreotypes as free of disavowed, cross-racial desire.

Perhaps, then, the Agassiz-Zealy photographs harbor dreamscapes like the silhouettes. But while Walker and Mapplethorpe's provocations are in important ways deliberate, the daguerreotypist's camera captured something we surely were not intended to see.[86] Engaging Walker's art after Benjamin helped me go on to elicit aspects of photographs taken long before either artist or theorist was born. What about photographs taken in their wake? One answer comes from watching Walker's work assume photographic form.

See You, Sugar

May 10, 2014, saw the opening of Walker's *A Subtlety*, a monumental installation in an immense, soon-to-be-demolished building that had, for nearly a century, served as part of the Domino Sugar Refinery in Brooklyn. Made of polystyrene blocks covered with 70,000 pounds of white sugar, a sphinx-like, female figure more than thirty-five feet tall and seventy-five feet long filled one end of the hall, wearing nothing but the handkerchief wrapped around her head (fig. 8.15). Her scale and countenance imposing, her eyes blank—so lacking in detail that one couldn't know if they were open or closed—she offered no emotional access, no sense of interior life, yet her bare body was shockingly available (fig. 8.16). Viewers could not approach her without walking past thirteen dark, smiling, subservient boys—sugar babies, I suppose—five-foot-tall enlargements of small figurines that Walker found on the Internet and had cast in resin and coated in a sugary mix (ten figures) or made from sugar alone (three more). During the show's two-month run, those made of sugar came apart, collapsing as they suddenly fractured, or slowly dissolving and melting onto the floor. Molasses trickled down the resin figures and oozed from the walls. When crowds were large and the exhibit at capacity, filling a space reeking of burned sugar, industrial by-products, and postindustrial rot, visitors stepped in the puddles or brushed against the ooze. The 130,000 people who passed through the installation found an art experience that was three-dimensional, multisensory, material, even sticky.[87] Despite all one might say about this complex, layered, allusive installation—and even as its scale, use of sculpture, and exquisite site specificity took Walker's work in a new direction, *A Subtlety* also revisited major preoccupations of her oeuvre. For that reason, I will not offer a critical reading of the exhibit's kinesthetics, aesthetics, or semantics. The topic at hand, after all, is photography.

Yet, adding a final turn to this discussion of the optical unconscious, *A Subtlety* created a kind of photographic situation, one many visitors found integral to their encounter with the work. In an era when museums seeking control over reproduction of the art they display often limit or prohibit the taking of photographs, Creative Time, the public arts organization that commissioned

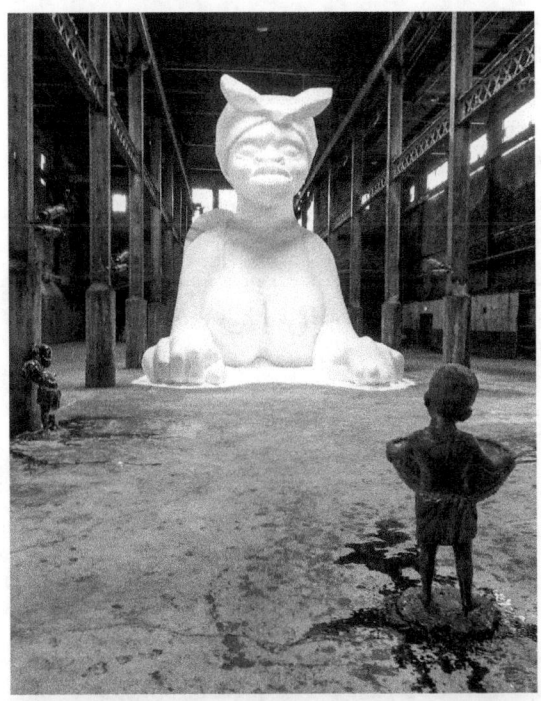

FIGURE 8.15 Kara Walker, *A Subtlety, or the Marvelous Sugar Baby, an Homage to the unpaid and overworked Artisans who have refined our Sweet tastes from the cane fields to the Kitchens of the New World on the Occasion of the Demolition of the Domino Sugar Refining Plant*, 2014. Photo: Mark Reinhardt.

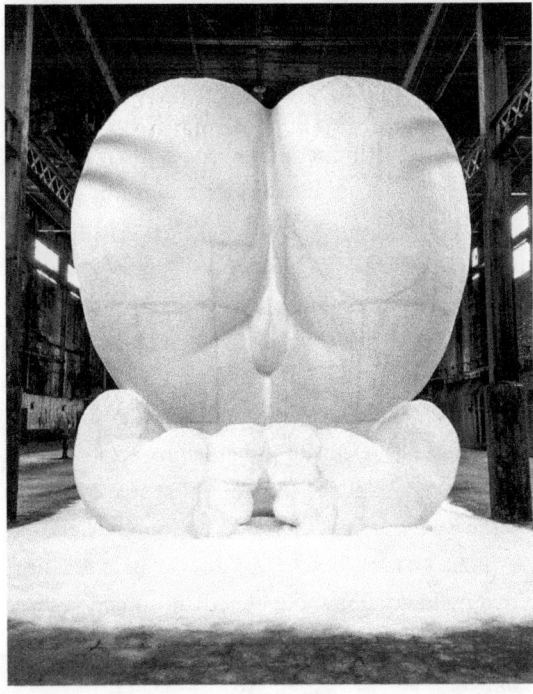

FIGURE 8.16 Kara Walker, *A Subtlety, or the Marvelous Sugar Baby, an Homage to the unpaid and overworked Artisans who have refined our Sweet tastes from the cane fields to the Kitchens of the New World on the Occasion of the Demolition of the Domino Sugar Refining Plant*, 2014. Photo: Mark Reinhardt.

the installation, did more than merely permit photography: upon entering, visitors were greeted by a sign reading, "Please do not touch the artwork, but do share pictures on social media with #KaraWalkerDomino."[88] Many visitors embraced the invitation, as I used my cell phone to take the pictures included as illustrations here. (*An Audience*, a twenty-seven-minute film Walker assembled from footage shot during the final hours *A Subtlety* was open to the public, reveals how thoroughly phones and cameras mediated visitors' experiences.)[89] Twitter, Instagram, and Facebook were awash with photos of people posing with the sugary sphinx. In some of the pictures, taking advantage of the camera's capacity to collapse depth and distort scale, the smiling or laughing (and usually white) spectator becomes an active participant, appearing to pinch the giant figure's nipples or lick her genitals. These kinds of responses provoked controversy in the blogosphere, the press, and the installation space itself. I do not reproduce any of those images here—I see no need to grant the subjects another fifteen minutes of fame—but you can find examples in an instant if you like: they are just a mouse click away. I do, however, want to conclude with a simple point about how the photographs inform the argument pursued so far.

At once sexual and withholding, subordinate and overpowering, the vast sculpture (towering, perhaps monstrous, like the *Leviathan* frontispiece's sovereign body politic) confronted viewers with a challenge or question about what it meant to look at her. A "subtlety," Walker explains, was a medieval term for an elaborate, edible, sugar paste or marzipan sculpture made especially for a royal banquet, so that in eating the confection one ingested both a "precious substance" and "the power of the King."[90] In medium, form, setting, and title, then, *A Subtlety* brought all of the desiring and devouring dimensions of looking to the fore, relating them to the problem of sovereignty.[91] But in subverting psychic sovereignty, Walker's art, I have tried to say, has always played with introjection and projection. Returning for a moment to her game of doubling, it is worth noting that all her silhouettes are doubles insofar as each is a kind of shadow, and a shadow a kind of double. Well over a decade ago, she made the connection explicit, more or less literalizing the metaphor, when she began mingling silhouettes with projected images, positioning the projectors so that viewers could not move the length or breadth of the exhibition space without casting their own shadows on the wall. But how do viewers respond when thus incorporated? No matter how nuanced in argument or powerful in expression, any criticism of artistic form that makes claims about effects and affects is shadowed by a skeptical question: "For whom—and how do you know?" The stakes of the question are particularly high for Walker's work, given the explosive material with which she engages. Well, one might say, looking at the visitors' photos and the responses they generated, we know now.

The posted photos confront us with a kind of optical unconscious. The jokey viewers act out the fantasies Walker's work—itself suffused with humor—has always engaged. The resulting pictures externalize the fantasies, making them visible. Of course, photos of this kind may not represent the dominant reaction, even from white viewers. Nor is the clowning captured by the cameras necessarily an unambiguous matter (merely a sign of, say, lighthearted dismissal), for laughter can be a response to powerful and complicated currents of discomfort. Though some of the photos are troubling, indeed infuriating, I do not claim they damn the art that generated them.[92] I merely suggest that one part of Walker's gambit has always been to engage certain aspects of the racial unconscious, to bring them into the open, and that photography here becomes another—and singular—means of doing the work. As Walker observed after the show was over, "Some people were moved to tears; some people felt nothing and nipple tweaked; some people felt nothing and nipple tweaked and then were castigated by somebody who was moved to tears. And in that moment, there's something of . . . the best possible thing I think that could happen in a work. I don't know that you change minds necessarily with art work, or behaviors, but sometimes you can change a moment."[93] The organized groups of black spectators who—angered by the photos, the disrespectful interactions observed in the exhibition space, and the whiteness of the show's initial audiences—arrived wearing stickers reading "We Are Here" and seeking to alter or comment on the way others responded to the exhibit thus intensified, complicated, and extended the encounter Walker had initiated.[94]

That seems, however, too safe and tidy to serve as an ending. My description's critical distance invites certain questions. The most important, perhaps, concern disavowal. Walker's work always prompts the question, but the query's edge sharpens when put by a sphinx. Though she is, as Walker remarks, a distinctively New World reworking of the famous Egyptian monument, this sphinx also calls to mind the mythical riddler who plagued Thebes. (In a preparatory sketch Walker drew while working on the project, her sphinx says, "Go ahead, ask.")[95] The puzzles confronting Oedipus were ultimately personal. He solved the sphinx's riddle, but imperfectly, because his answer was general, abstract; the plague returned because he had failed to see his own intimate implication in the riddle.[96] And mine? I announced my prim refusal to reproduce jokey pictures from *A Subtlety*, but what of the photographs included in my earlier discussion? I acknowledged above the possibility that the real subject of the story told by juxtaposing the pictures taken by Agassiz-Zealy and Mapplethorpe is my own desires and investments. When returning to such photographs — which, after all, have already been discussed many times — the issue of investments and desires ought to arise. Given the way each of the daguerreotypes performed a kind of violation, and the risks that, in displaying them yet again, one merely reenacts the original scene, why look again — why look now? Do whatever insights arise through critical analysis of the images provide a sufficient answer? Can one know?

The questions lead us back to Benjamin, for whom, as Eduardo Cadava observes, "what links the laws of photography to those of psychoanalysis is that both require a thinking of the way in which [the] passage between the unconscious and the conscious, the invisible and the visible, takes place."[97] Easy to repeat, harder to absorb and enact. How to follow the passages when encountering a photograph? If one views the optical unconscious as a subversion of psychic sovereignty, then one's own work as a critic must renounce certain claims to mastery: if the dynamite of the split second blows open a portal to the dreamworld, we can move through it only by leaving critical certainty behind.

Notes

Thanks to the enthusiasm and support of James Martel and Davide Panagia, a version of this essay originally appeared in *Theory and Event* 18, no. 4 (October 2015). The staff at the Chapin Library of Rare Books at Williams College, especially Wayne Hammond, proved invaluable as I conducted preliminary research for this chapter. Early drafts were presented at the Toronto Photography Seminar and the University of Virginia Political Theory Colloquium and benefited from the respective discussants for those events, Elspeth Brown and Colin Kielty. At UVA, Stephen White identified the key thread running through the essay at a time when it seemed in danger of being lost. For assorted comments and suggestions, I thank Ulie Baer, Lawrie Balfour, Mary Bergstein, Laura Ephraim, Jason Frank, Liza Johnson, Keith Moxey, Nimu Njoya, Chris Pye, Neil Roberts, Jen Rubenstein, Andrés Zervigón, and the readers for Duke University Press. On multiple drafts, George Shulman made suggestions that are now so woven through the essay that I could not cite each instance without an impassable thicket of footnotes. I hope it suffices to offer instead this blanket acknowledgment. Finally, I would not have written this piece at all, without an invitation and much nudging from Shawn Michelle Smith and Sharon Sliwinski. I think I thank them for that; I know I benefited from their insightful commentary on early versions.

1. One major exception is Miriam Bratu Hansen, whose *Cinema and Experience: Siegfried Kracauer, Walter Benjamin, and Theodor W. Adorno* (Berkeley: University of California Press, 2012) offers incisive accounts of the optical unconscious and its relation to

other key elements in Benjamin's writing. Though my account differs, I am indebted to her study. While Hansen investigates Benjamin's meaning, Shawn Michelle Smith uses the optical unconscious in engaging early American photography in *At the Edge of Sight: Photography and the Unseen* (Durham, NC: Duke University Press, 2013).

2. The relevance of the first two items needs, I trust, no argument. On contemporary border walls as spectacles and the psychic interests they serve, see Wendy Brown, *Walled States, Waning Sovereignty* (New York: Zone, 2010).

3. Susan Buck-Morss, "Visual Empire," *Diacritics* 37, no. 2/3 (2007): 172.

4. Buck-Morss, "Visual Empire."

5. Counting an abridged French translation of the second version, published in 1936, there were four versions. See Miriam Hansen's account of the publication history in *Cinema and Experience*, 307n28. My subsequent discussion of versions two and three excludes the French version in that numbering. In this I follow not only Hansen's critical discussions but also Howard Eiland and Michael Jennings in their four-volume edition of Benjamin's work.

6. Walter Benjamin, "The Work of Art in the Age of Its Technological Reproducibility: Third Version," in *Walter Benjamin: Selected Writings, vol. 4, 1938–1940,* ed. Howard Eiland and Michael W. Jennings (Cambridge, MA: Harvard University Press, 2006), 266. The passage differs slightly in what was for years the only English translation of the third version, in Walter Benjamin, *Illuminations,* ed. Hannah Arendt (New York: Schocken, 1969), 236–237.

7. Rosalind Krauss, *The Optical Unconscious* (Cambridge, MA: MIT Press, 1994), 178, 179.

8. Smith, *At the Edge of Sight,* 6. Margaret Iverson also reads Benjamin as offering a parallel, but finds the move "disappointing." See Margaret Iverson, *Beyond Pleasure: Freud, Lacan, Barthes* (University Park, PA: Penn State University Press, 2007), 117.

9. Eric Kandel, *The Age of Insight: The Quest to Understand the Unconscious in Art, Mind, and Brain* (New York: Random House, 2012), 234.

10. Thomas Hobbes, *Leviathan,* ed. Richard Tuck (New York: Cambridge University Press, 1996), 117, emphasis added. All subsequent citations refer to this edition.

11. Hobbes, *Leviathan,* 9, 120, emphasis in original.

12. Krauss, *The Optical Unconscious,* 6.

13. The best account of this dynamic is developed in George Shulman, "Metaphor and Modernization in the Political Thought of Thomas Hobbes," *Political Theory* 17, no. 3 (1989): 392–416.

14. Christopher Pye, "The Sovereign, the Theater, and the Kingdome of Darknesse: Hobbes and the Spectacle of Power," *Representations,* no. 8 (autumn 1984): 101. See also Pye's discussion at 89.

15. Pye, "The Sovereign, the Theater, and the Kingdome of Darknesse," 102, 103.

16. Pye, "The Sovereign, the Theater, and the Kingdome of Darknesse," 101–102.

17. At least I know of no case in which a scholar says otherwise. Among those con-

tributing to this consensus one finds even Horst Bredekamp, an acute art historian who has produced the most illuminating work on Hobbes's engagement with imagery. "The eyes of each one, regardless of position," Bredekamp writes in words that closely echo Pye's, "is [*sic*] directed toward the giant's head and returns through his eyes back to the viewer." Horst Bredekamp, "Thomas Hobbes's Visual Strategies," in *The Cambridge Companion to Hobbes's Leviathan*, ed. Patricia Springborg (New York: Cambridge University Press, 2007), 40. Other sources making variations on this point include Danielle Allen, *Talking to Strangers: Anxieties of Citizenship since Brown vs. Board of Education* (Chicago: University of Chicago Press, 2004), 82; Keith Brown, "The Artist of the *Leviathan* Title-Page," *British Library Journal* 3, no. 1 (spring 1977): 24–36; Margery Corbett and R. W. Lightbown, *The Comely Frontispiece: The Emblematic Title-Page in England, 1550–1660* (London: Routledge and Kegan Paul, 1979), 224; Magnus Kristiansson and Johan Tralau, "Hobbes's Hidden Monster," *European Journal of Political Theory* 13, no. 3 (2014): 303; Davide Panagia, "Delicate Discriminations: Thomas Hobbes's Science of Politics," *Polity* 36, no. 1 (2003): 108; Michael Rogin, *Ronald Reagan, the Movie: And Other Episodes in Political Demonology* (Berkeley: University of California Press, 1987), 300; Quentin Skinner, *Hobbes and Republican Liberty* (New York: Cambridge, 2008), 192; Richard Tuck, introduction to Hobbes, *Leviathan*, xii. Although his discussion of glances is so brief as to be ambiguous, Giorgio Agamben also seems to hold the same view in his commentary on the frontispiece. Giorgio Agamben, *Stasis: Civil War as a Political Paradigm* (Stanford, CA: Stanford University Press, 2015), 30.

18. The attribution to Bosse dates back to the seventeenth century and remains common. Though contested in some scholarship, it is defended compellingly by Horst Bredekamp. See his "Thomas Hobbes's Visual Strategies" and *Stratégies visuelles de Thomas Hobbes: Le Léviathan, archétype de l'État moderne. Illustrations des oeuvres et portraits*, trans. Denise Modigliani (Paris: Fondation Maison de sciences de l'homme, 2003).

19. On those paradoxes, see Bonnie Honig, *Emergency Politics: Paradox, Law, Sovereignty* (Princeton, NJ: Princeton University Press, 2011).

20. Noel Malcolm, "The Title Page of *Leviathan*, Seen in a Curious Perspective," in *Aspects of Hobbes* (New York: Oxford University Press, 2002), 200–233. See also Bredekamp, "Thomas Hobbes's Visual Strategies," on this question.

21. The original is in the collection of the British Library, whose permissions fee for reproducing a copy in this publication proved extortionate. It can be seen on their website, British Library, Images Online, accessed July 16, 2015, http://imagesonline.bl.uk/index.php?service=search&action=do_quick_search&language=en&q=%2337973.

22. On the rise and fall of the emblematic frontispiece, see Corbett and Lightbown, *The Comely Frontispiece*; for Hobbes's investment in frontispieces to his works, see especially Bredekamp, "Hobbes's Visual Strategies"; and Skinner, *Hobbes and Republican Liberty*.

23. Francesca Falk, "Hobbes' *Leviathan* und die aus dem Blick gefallenen Schnable-

masken," *Leviathan* 39 (2011): 247–266. As Falk notes, and I hope to pursue in a separate essay, this is highly suggestive for discussions about the relationship between sovereignty and biopolitics in *Leviathan*.

24. Kristiansson and Tralau, "Hobbes's Hidden Monster." There is a problem with holding simultaneously, as they do, that the Leviathan is rising out of the water (a claim in itself plausible) and that the circled items are part of the creature's tail—for those in the left two circles, at least, are clearly resting on land. For my purposes, however, the pertinent point is merely the link between engagements of this kind and the spread of digital reproduction.

25. See, e.g., Rogin, *Ronald Reagan*, or older versions of the Penguin Classics edition of *Leviathan*. I possessed each for decades without noticing the details in question.

26. Quoted words from Kristiansson and Tralau, "Hobbes's Hidden Monser," 303; the shaggy-haired man stares out at the reader on 308.

27. William Connolly, *Neuropolitics: Thinking, Culture, Speed* (Minneapolis: University of Minnesota Press, 2002), 15. My account borrows substantially from this moment in Connolly's discussion.

28. Connolly, *Neuropolitics*, 14.

29. Connolly, *Neuropolitics*, 36.

30. Walter Benjamin, "Surrealism," in *Selected Writings, vol. 2, part 1, 1927–1930*, 217–218.

31. Benjamin, "Surrealism," 217. James Martel develops a fascinating argument for previously unnoted affinities between Hobbes and Benjamin's thinking about images, in his "The Spectacle of the Leviathan: Thomas Hobbes, Guy Debord, and Walter Benjamin on Representation and Its Misuses," *Law, Culture and the Humanities* 2 (2006): 67–90; and James Martel, *Subverting the Leviathan: Reading Thomas Hobbes as a Radical Democrat* (New York: Columbia University Press, 2007), 211–220. On links between images and bodies, see also Hans Belting, "Image, Medium, Body: A New Approach to Iconology," *Critical Inquiry* 31, no. 2 (2005): 302–319.

32. Benjamin, "The Work of Art," *Selected Writings, vol. 3*, 120, and *vol. 4*, 268–269, emphasis in original. The third version develops these ideas differently, dropping the notion of innervation but expanding the treatment of other terms. Susan Buck-Morss develops a compelling reading of Benjamin on the historical tasks and turning points in "Aesthetics and Anaesthetics: Walter Benjamin's Artwork Essay," *October* 62 (autumn 1992): 3–41.

33. For a sustained analysis of Benjamin's borrowing and transformation of innervation, see Hansen, *Cinema and Experience*, 135–137.

34. Brian Massumi, "The Autonomy of Affect," *Cultural Critique* 31 (autumn 1995): 104.

35. The quoted words are from the discussion of subliminal perception in Siri Hustvedt, "Embodied Visions: What Does It Mean to Look at a Work of Art?," *Yale Review* 98 (October 2010): 24, but the surrounding points about the brain and the effects of

faces are drawn from Kandel, who explores the relevant experiments and findings in more detail. See Kandel, *The Age of Insight*, chapters 17–21, especially 302, 333, 360–361.

36. Eric Santner, *The Royal Remains: The People's Two Bodies and the Endgames of Sovereignty* (Chicago: University of Chicago Press, 2011), 60. Is *dissidence* quite the right word for those who look away? Is the swerve indifference or resistance? Should we view the former as tantamount to the latter? I am not sure, and have tried to vary my language to reflect the range of possibilities. What seems clear, though, is that the wayward glance escapes Hobbes's program.

37. Slavoj Žižek, "Philosophy, the 'Unknown Knowns,' and the Public Use of Reason," *Topoi* 25 (2006): 137.

38. I am here indebted to Colin Kielty for his response to an early draft of this chapter.

39. On the fantasies elicited by images and displays of sovereignty, see, again, Brown, *Walled States*, 115–123; and Rogin, *Ronald Reagan*, 297–300.

40. Hobbes, *Leviathan*, 9.

41. Hobbes, *Leviathan*, 270. On the pictorial need to substitute head for soul, see Skinner, *Hobbes and Republican Liberty*, 190.

42. Mary Bergstein suggests to me that one could read the man as a *festaiuolo*, a figure who mediates between audience and spectacle by pointing out what is going on. This would make him a reinforcement of the case for sovereignty. But neither the size nor the formal features of the figures turned our way seem conducive to that role. The eyes confront us; the hands point nothing out. On the *festaiuolo*, see Michael Baxandall, *Painting and Experience in Fifteenth Century Italy: A Primer in the Social History of a Pictorial Style* (New York: Oxford University Press, 1972), 71–77.

43. Walter Benjamin, "The Work of Art in the Age of Its Technological Reproducibility: Second Version," in *Selected Writings*, vol. 3, *1935–1938*, 117–118. See also Walter Benjamin, "The Work of Art in the Age of Its Technological Reproducibility [First Version]," trans. Michael Jennings, *Grey Room*, spring 2010, 30–31.

44. Benjamin, *Selected Writings*, vol. 3, 118.

45. In a late footnote, even the third version argues that the psychology and dynamics of crowds and mass movements can be grasped better by the camera than the eye, both for the perspectives lenses offer and the possibility of enlarging details. The second version contains the same note, while the first incorporates similar language into the body of the main text. Benjamin, "The Work of Art [First Version]," 34–35; Benjamin, "The Work of Art," *vol. 3*, 132–133n37; *vol. 4*, 282n47.

46. Hansen, *Cinema and Experience*, 179. Although my sentence closely follows Hansen, it does so in the service of introducing an argument different from (perhaps contrary to) hers.

47. Benjamin, *Selected Writings*, vol. 3, 102. The phrase is used in all three versions.

48. Glancing treatments of Mickey's derivation from Jolson and blackface have been available for some time. See Hugh Kenner, *Chuck Jones: A Flurry of Drawings* (Berkeley:

University of California Press, 1993), 24, 27–28; Christopher P. Lehman, *The Colored Cartoon: Black Representation in American Animated Short Films, 1907–1954* (Amherst: University of Massachusetts Press, 2007), 5, 16–18; Michael Rogin, *Blackface, White Noise: Jewish Immigrants in the Hollywood Melting Pot* (Berkeley: University of California Press, 1996), 29; Susan Willis, *A Primer for Daily Life* (New York: Routledge, 1991), 130–132. While the foregoing informed the writing of this chapter, shortly before my submission of the final copy, Nicholas Sammond published *Birth of an Industry: Blackface Minstrelsy and the Rise of American Animation* (Durham, NC: Duke University Press, 2015). Sammond does not so much refute the Jolson claim as broaden and deepen arguments about the intimate, constitutive relationship between early American animation and blackface. I am sure my own treatment would be richer had I more time to absorb this insightful book; even a selective and cursory reading has proved helpful, however, and I thank Davide Panagia for bringing it to my attention.

49. *Steamboat Willie* and *Mickey's Mellerdrammer* are available at, respectively, Walt Disney Animation Studios, *Steamboat Willie*, YouTube, August 27, 2009, http://www .youtube.com/watch?v=BBgghnQF6E4; and Toons Village, *Mickey's Mellerdrammer* (1930), YouTube, August 17, 2010, http://www.youtube.com/watch?v=Dwo6KodG1Zw. On the music in the former, see Willis, *A Primer for Daily Life*, 131–132; and Sammond, *Birth of an Industry*, 142, 223, 310.

50. Rogin, *Blackface, White Noise*, 73–120. I had intended to include here a still of this crux moment from *Mickey's Mellerdrammer*, but Disney Enterprises did not view my discussion as falling within their "brand integrity guidelines" and denied permission to reproduce the image. You can, however, find it here: Tumblr, accessed April 21, 2015, http://33.media.tumblr.com/98b3388e6b643206faa19b973f4e3dd1/tumblr_inline_ne 2wgx3eR41qzkia9.jpg.

51. Kobena Mercer, "Skin Head Sex Thing," in *Only Skin Deep: Changing Visions of the American Self*, ed. Coco Fusco and Brian Wallis (New York: Abrams, 2003), 251.

52. This paragraph largely paraphrases the argument of Rogin's remarkable *Blackface, White Noise*, which documents and theorizes the role of blackface in the making of individual and national identity. See especially p. 25.

53. Sammond, *Birth of an Industry*.

54. Sammond, *Birth of an Industry*, 3.

55. In a footnote to the second version, Benjamin writes that the Mickey Mouse cartoons in color reveal "how easily fascism takes over 'revolutionary' innovations in this field, too," and he wonders whether this retrospectively reveals a "cozy acceptance of bestiality and violence" already "latent" in the earlier, black-and-white films. Benjamin, *Selected Writings*, vol. 3, 130. But he does not touch on the racializing elements, even though they found an especially degrading echo in Nazi Germany where, Hansen notes, Mickey was ideologically conflated with jazz and caricatured "with protruding white teeth and Africanized features" in some instances and as "an inversion of blackface" in others. Hansen, *Cinema and Experience*, 167. But for all her insight, Hansen

never comes to terms with Mickey's American blackface origins or what follows from making such a figure the emblem of a kind of unconscious. Sammond, in contrast, is a learned student of those blackface origins, and notes in passing that Mickey appears when Benjamin treats the optical unconscious in the artwork essay, but Benjamin is of only peripheral interest in his study.

never comes to terms with Mickey's American blackface origins or what follows from making such a figure the emblem of a kind of unconscious. Sammond, in contrast, is a learned student of those blackface origins, and notes in passing that Mickey appears when Benjamin treats the optical unconscious in the artwork essay, but Benjamin is of only peripheral interest in his study.

56. "If [the optical unconscious] can be spoken of at all as externalized within the visual field," Krauss writes, "this is because a disparate group of artists have so constructed it there" (*Optical Unconscious*, 179). On my reading, Benjamin's own use of the concept would accommodate that approach, while including more. Krauss here seems unaware of the affinity, presumably because she relies only on the "Little History" and the third version. In a brief passage in a more recent work, she does underscore Benjamin's links between the optical unconscious and film's figures of fantasy; revealingly, she is discussing the artwork essay's earlier versions. Yet though she focuses on Mickey Mouse, Krauss again passes over the racial entailments. See Rosalind Krauss, *Perpetual Inventory* (Cambridge, MA: MIT Press, 2010), 83–85.

57. The figure is modeled closely on the central subject of Delacroix's *Liberty Leading the People*, whose Phrygian cap Walker has essentially replaced with a Mickey Mouse ears hat. I say "essentially" because viewed up close the cap and ears resolve as the woman's hair, but the silhouette clearly invites the equation even as the hair reveals the woman to read as socially black. Like Bartholdi, who based the Statue of Liberty (another obvious referent of *No Mere Words*) on Delacroix's figure, Walker Americanizes her—but to rather different effect. In transfiguring Delacroix, Walker is, of course, also engaging the legacy of history painting, a recurring aspect of her visual practice that I slight in this essay's limited discussion.

58. Mark Reinhardt, "The Art of Racial Profiling," in *Kara Walker: Narratives of a Negress*, ed. Ian Berry, Darby English, Vivian Patterson, and Mark Reinhardt (New York: Rizzoli, 2007), 108–129.

59. Only after the visual elements of *Presenting Negro Scenes* had prompted my pastiche of Du Bois did I realize, belatedly, that the artist had long ago invited the comparison by presenting herself as "K.E.B. Walker" in the work's title. See W. E. B. Du Bois, *The Souls of Black Folk* (New York: Bantam, 1989), 3; I also borrow my terms from Judith Butler, *The Psychic Life of Power: Theories in Subjection* (Stanford, CA: Stanford University Press, 1997).

60. I discuss the relationship of the Freudian uncanny to Walker's art at more length in "The Art of Racial Profiling."

61. Whether the sovereign's head is a portrait of a known and public personage is a different question: Cromwell, Charles II, Christ, William Cavendish, and even Hobbes himself have all been proposed, though the issue is hard to resolve. See, for instance, Bredekamp, *Stratégies visuelles de Thomas Hobbes*; Kristiansson and Tralau, "Hobbes's Hidden Monster"; and A. P. Martinich, *The Two Gods of Leviathan: Thomas Hobbes on Religion and Politics* (New York: Cambridge University Press, 2003).

62. Lisa Saltzman, *Making Memory Matter: Strategies of Remembrance in Contemporary Art* (Chicago: University of Chicago Press, 2006), 66–67. On Walker's works in relation to the history of silhouette, see also Anne Wagner, "Kara Walker: 'The Black-White Relation,'" in Berry et al., *Kara Walker*, 90–101; and Darby English, "This Is Not About the Past: Silhouettes in the Work of Kara Walker," in Berry et al., *Kara Walker*, 140–167.

63. Benjamin, *Selected Writings, vol. 3*, 117.

64. My narrative of the events behind the photos relies on the following sources: Elinor Reichlin, "Faces of Slavery," *American Heritage*, June 1977, 4–11; Brian Wallis, "Black Bodies, White Science: Louis Agassiz's Slave Daguerreotypes," *American Art 9*, no. 2 (summer 1995): 38–61; Lisa Gail Collins, *The Art of History: African American Women Artists Engage the Past* (New Brunswick, NJ: Rutgers University Press, 2002), 17–22; Molly Rogers, *Delia's Tears: Race, Science, and Photography in Nineteenth-Century America* (New Haven, CT: Yale University Press, 2010); Suzanne Schneider, "Louis Agassiz and the American School of Ethnoeroticism: Polygenesis, Pornography, and other 'Perfidious Influences,'" in *Pictures and Progress: Early Photography and the Making of African American Identity*, ed. Maurice O. Wallace and Shawn Michelle Smith (Durham, NC: Duke University Press, 2012), 211–243.

65. Deborah Willis and Barbara Krauthamer, *Envisioning Emancipation: Black Americans and the End of Slavery* (Philadelphia: Temple University Press, 2013), 4.

66. Although *Delia's Tears* explores the lives of all involved in the photos, Rogers can provide so little additional information about the seven enslaved men and women that she is reduced to fictionalizing their thoughts and actions.

67. Ariella Azoulay, *The Civil Contract of Photography*, trans. Reia Mazali and Ruvik Danielli (New York: Zone, 2008), 178.

68. Azoulay, *The Civil Contract of Photography*, 183.

69. Azoulay, *The Civil Contract of Photography*, 178.

70. Azoulay, *The Civil Contract of Photography*, 179, 182.

71. Azoulay, *The Civil Contract of Photography*, 179, 176.

72. Azoulay, *The Civil Contract of Photography*, 183.

73. Azoulay, *The Civil Contract of Photography*, 183, 184. Noting that white sitters in the studio were typically directed "to stare off into the distance" in order to suggest contemplation, Willis and Krauthamer argue that, even though it transgressed one of the most fundamental rules whites imposed on enslaved persons (as on black persons long after emancipation), the direct stare in the Agassiz-Zealy frontal photos was demanded in the attempt to demonstrate black inferiority. Willis and Krauthamer, *Envisioning Emancipation*, 7. Azoulay's account, however, would make the enforced directness part of how the photographs defeated the project they were designed to support.

74. More accurately, there are other readings, running the gamut from those who, like Azoulay, find glimmers of emancipation in the range of emotions shown to those who, like Brian Wallis, see the gazes as "detached, unemotional, workmanlike." Wallis, "Black Bodies," 40.

75. Wallis, "Black Bodies," 184.

76. Rogers discusses the meeting, which took place in members' homes; though her framework for approaching the pictures is quite different from Azoulay's, she also argues that the pictures failed as types due to the individuality of the men and women pictured. Rogers, *Delia's Tears*, 233–234, 248–249.

77. Ariella Azoulay, "What Is a Photograph? What Is Photography?," *Philosophy of Photography* 1, no. 1 (2010): 10. Azoulay's insightful and influential work is generally taken as a dismantling of notions of sovereignty in photography. In seeking to mobilize photography's democratic and anticolonial possibilities, her analyses clearly do uncouple photography from state control (perhaps even to a wishful extent), and her stress on multiple agencies aims to undercut the sovereignty of any one party to a photograph. But that does not, I am suggesting, go far enough. *Civil Contract* grounds much of its argument in the contractarian idiom and the subject that idiom presumes and constructs. Benjamin's optical unconscious shakes that subject to its core; Azoulay's attachment to contract makes psychic sovereignty persist in her work more than she avows. I say more about sovereignty in her work in my "Theorizing the Event of Photography—the Visual Politics of Violence and Terror in Azoulay's *Civil Imagination*, Linfield's *The Cruel Radiance*, and Mitchell's *Cloning Terror*," *Theory and Event* 16, no. 3 (2013).

78. Nancy Leys Stepan, *Picturing Tropical Nature* (Ithaca, NY: Cornell University Press, 2001), 100–112.

79. Schneider, "Louis Agassiz," 221.

80. Rogers points out that on his visits to South Carolina plantations, Agassiz, who had never been to Africa and had minimal experience with its peoples, was certain that his own visual inspection of enslaved men and women trumped their own reports as guides to their heritage. Rogers, *Delia's Tears*, 219–220. Stepan reports that William James, who accompanied him on his Brazil expedition, thought that Agassiz regularly misclassified people. Stepan, *Picturing Tropical Nature*, 105.

81. Cited in Rogers, *Delia's Tears*, 118.

82. See, for instance, Wallis, "Black Bodies," 42–44.

83. Schneider, "Louis Agassiz," 233, 230, 237. Schneider's argument turns on an interpretation of Agassiz's biography, especially archival evidence about the embarrassing, quasi-legal dispute that arose when Agassiz fired his secretary, Edward Desor. I find the documents she invokes more ambiguous than she indicates. I may be mistaken (and those wishing to go down this rabbit hole should begin with the bizarre verdict issued by the mediators Agassiz and Desor called in to adjudicate their dispute: Houghton Library, Harvard, Louis Agassiz Correspondence and Other Papers (MS Am 1419), 713, seq. 6 (http://pds.lib.harvard.edu/pds/view/12436302?n=6), but how, precisely, to read the materials seems to me not the main thing. Agassiz's investment in polygenesis was older and deeper than Schneider's account allows, and it is hard to see how his public articulation of the polygenesist case or his commissioning of the photographs could

have functioned as deflections from the Desor controversy. Still, Schneider stands out for her attention to the erotic questions raised by the photographs, and for that reason I am in her debt.

84. I may not be the only one. After I had circulated drafts that included this two-paragraph comparison between the two pictures, a colleague called to my attention Harvey Young's powerful meditation on the daguerreotypes. Although focusing on the pictures of Renty, Young makes the following observation in passing: "In one daguerreotype, the fully nude backside of Jem has been photographed. The camera's gaze, never challenged by Jem's direct address, lingers upon his body and invites comparisons to the more contemporary photographs of Robert Mapplethorpe, Thierry Le Goues, and Lyle Ashton Harris. In turn, it creates ambivalence in the spectator that resembles that experienced by the art critic Kobena Mercer upon encountering Mapplethorpe's photographs of black male nudes." Harvey Young, *Embodying Black Experience: Stillness, Critical Memory, and the Black Body* (Ann Arbor: University of Michigan Press, 2010), 38. Young's purposes and argument are different from mine. His interest is in how the performance of stillness by each of the black men pictured echoes performances from the Middle Passage. That we both independently made this association thus says something about the Agassiz-Zealy photos.

85. Mercer, "Skin Head Sex Thing," 248. Mercer quotes Mapplethorpe himself on his ambition to document a passing milieu, and credits the account (247–248).

86. That is not to say that Mapplethorpe and Walker, for all their aesthetic precision, are themselves—or think of themselves as—simply in control.

87. I toured the exhibit well into the melting of the figures, on a day when the space was not open to the public. I thank the curator, Nato Thompson, for arranging the visit, the staff of Creative Time for information about the use of the space by crowds at maximum capacity, and George Shulman for discussions during that visit.

88. The sign went on to note that the photos would become part of a crowd-sourced, digital sugar baby. The result (much less instructive than the photos on the Internet and the disputes they engendered) can be seen here: Creative Time Presents Kara Walker, http://creativetime.org/karawalker/digital-sugar-baby/.

89. Exhibited as part of *Afterword*, Walker's late 2014–early 2015 show at the Sikkema Jenkins Gallery in which she presented material related to *A Subtlety*, the film focuses almost exclusively on the responses of black spectators. (The whole film is not available online, but a five-minute trailer can be seen here: Kara Walker, "An Audience" [trailer], Sikkema Jenkins and Co., Vimeo, 2014, https://vimeo.com/112396045.) Walker says she wanted the film to explore the question, "What does it look like when you see a black audience looking and thinking?" The subject is, she notes, "kind of simple, but something you never see." Kara Walker, "Sweet Talk," lecture at the Radcliffe Institute for Advanced Study, December 8, 2014, https://www.radcliffe.harvard.edu/event/2014-kara-walker-lecture, at 43:33–43:40.

90. Walker speaking in http://creativetime.org/projects/karawalker/, at 0:47–1:07.

She elsewhere adds clergy and aristocrats to the list of those serving up subtleties, but she says that it was in learning the associations with sovereignty that she decided that her piece in Brooklyn had to be a sugar sculpture.

91. On these dimensions, see Otto Fenichel, "The Scopophilic Instinct and Identification," *International Journal of Psychoanalysis* 18 (1937): 6–34.

92. Some online commentators raised ethical and political questions about the exhibit, based on the worst responses. A thoughtful first-person reflection was posted by Nicholas Powers, who had, he reports, long wondered if "exposing the details of Black victimization was truly freeing." Visiting *A Subtlety* and observing a process in which "an artwork about how Black people's pain was transformed into money was a tourist attraction" for jocular white spectators, he gets into a verbal altercation with both other viewers and Creative Time staff. See Nicholas Powers, "Why I Yelled at the Kara Walker Exhibit," *The Indypendent*, June 30, 2014, http://indypendent.org/2014/06/30/why-i-yelled-kara-walker-exhibit#sthash.BuBznys4.dpuf. Walker's art has always generated this kind of debate. I skirt the issues here not because they are unimportant, but because they require more consideration than the end of this essay can provide. I take my own stab at defending Walker's practice from this line of criticism in Reinhardt, "The Art of Racial Profiling."

93. Walker, "Sweet Talk," at 45:15–45:39.

94. We Are Here was an event organized by four activists and publicized through social media as "a gathering for people of color at Kara Walker's art installation in the Domino Sugar factory" ("The Kara Walker Experience: We Are Here," Facebook, June 22, 2014, https://www.facebook.com/events/656753121061038/). Roughly one thousand people, responding to the call to "experience this space as the majority," attended on June 22. All had the opportunity to write responses to the show on a display outside the refinery's grounds. Some handed out pamphlets or confronted spectators inside. The group's mission statement, pictures from the event, and other materials can be found at We Are Here, Tumblr, http://weareherekwe.tumblr.com/. For reporting and commentary on the event, see "We Are Here: Black Women Claim Their Space at Kara Walker's Controversial Sugar Sphinx Show," *Ebony*, July 2, 2014, http://www.ebony.com/photos/entertainment-culture/kara-walker-domino-003#axzz3D7KIgVxP; Jamilah King, "Kara Walker's Sugar Sphinx Evokes Call from Black Women: 'We Are Here,'" *Colorlines*, June 23, 2014, http://colorlines.com/archives/2014/06/kara_walkers_sugar_sphinx_evokes_call_from_black_women_we_are_here.html; and Matthew Shen Goodman, "'We Are Here': People of Color Gather at Kara Walker Show," *Art in America*, June 20, 2014, http://www.artinamericamagazine.com/news-features/previews/we-are-here-people-of-color-gather-at-kara-walker-show-/.

95. See Creative Time, Kara Walker, http://creativetime.org/projects/karawalker/, at 0:28.

96. As Peter Euben puts it, "The answer 'man' required a kind of abstract knowledge available to Oedipus because he was ignorant of the concrete circumstances of

his birth. . . . Ignorant of what was closest and nearest, Oedipus did not know that he was the answer to the second riddle, Who killed Laius? and so the 'cause' of the plague." J. Peter Euben, *Corrupting Youth: Political Education, Democratic Culture, and Political Theory* (Princeton, NJ: Princeton University Press, 1997), 182–183. Also relevant to Walker's work is the parallel point the sphinx makes to Oedipus in Muriel Rukeyser's poem, "Myth": "'You didn't say anything about woman.' / 'When you say Man,' said Oedipus, 'you include women / too. Everyone knows that.' She said, 'That's what / you think.'" Muriel Rukeyser, *The Collected Poems of Muriel Rukeyser* (Pittsburgh: University of Pittsburgh Press, 2006), 480.

97. Eduardo Cadava, *Words of Light: Theses on the Photography of History* (Princeton, NJ: Princeton University Press 1998), 99.

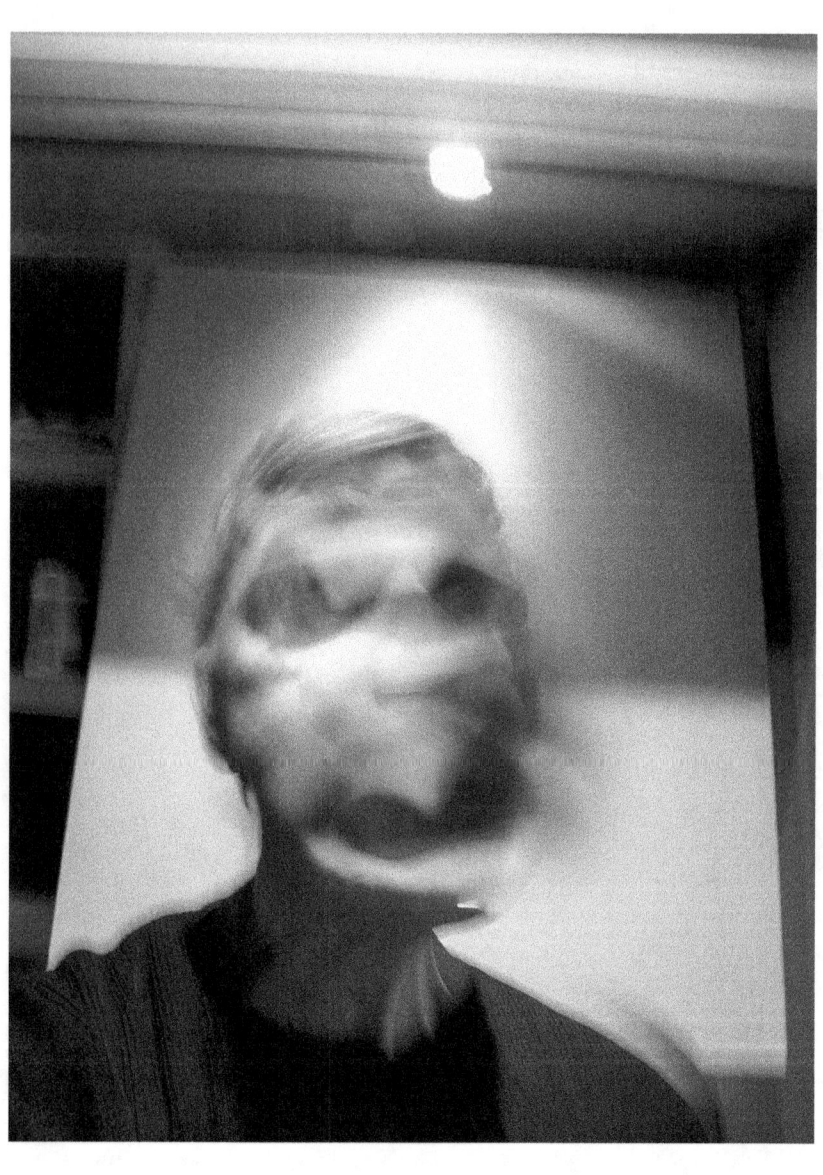

CHAPTER NINE

SLIGO HEADS

KRISTAN HORTON

> Over the course of an evening I am watching his face. He smiles, he re-
> laxes, and he shows disgust quickly then laughs. There are so many things
> to keep track of. The next day I attempt to recall and I do not, as I had
> wished, see amalgams but instead discreet moments. There appears to be
> no use for the amalgamated image in recall. Perhaps this is the reason I
> am making the amalgamated portrait. It is an image that does not exist
> for me internally.[1]

Sligo Heads is a series of photographic portraits where I continue experimentation with perception and material transformation and is named after the city
in Ireland where they were initially created (see plates 7–11).

Zero State

Nothing will come of nothing.
William Shakespeare, King Lear, Act 1.1

It was in that room previously occupied by Boris Groys, who was preparing
and thinking the contents of a book, that I noticed a spider motionless on a
wall. The very spider I had to assume had bitten me the previous evening as I
slept. I spent a long time staring at it, plotting some revenge perhaps, when the
thought occurred to me that it may have also bitten Groys and somewhere in
that beast our blood was intermingled, transforming this spider into art critic/
media theorist/philosopher/artist, though I saw no web or action as evidence
to support this.

In fact, I saw very little in this room. Nothing to inspire or place a hinge onto. Over the course of a month little changed in my perception of it. The only development was a deeper sense of the nothingness to the point of being palpable, which became an anchor. A quick shot with my camera trained at myself and held at arm's length recorded a moment that came simultaneously with the phrase "the zero state." The camera recorded me conjoined with a streak of light; a result familiar to anyone who has used a handheld digital camera. What I saw in the result was an opening up of a possibility to use my own image as a generator of color and form. More shots, more whiskey, more color, more form. The zero state had given way to a surplus that was the genesis of the *Sligo Heads*. I had forgotten any notion of a once impoverished room.

Reflecting on the well-publicized anecdote from the American artist Bruce Nauman:

> I had no support structure for my art then. . . . There was no chance to talk about my work. And a lot of things I was doing didn't make sense so I quit doing them. That left me alone in the studio: this in turn raised the fundamental question of what an artist does when left alone in the studio. My conclusion was that [if] I was an artist and I was in the studio, then whatever I was doing in the studio must be art. . . . At this point art became more of an activity and less of a product.[3]

Part of Nauman's activity at the time included his appropriation of neon advertising signage. *Window or Wall Sign* (1967) was installed in his ground-floor studio window, where a spiraling neon text reads, "The true artist helps the world by revealing mystic truths." The question of his activity in the studio simultaneous with his broadcasting of a conviction through the studio window to the outside in the mode of advertising makes a circuitous enterprise. A thing that circles back on itself.

Orbits

Predecessor to the *Sligo Heads* is the photographic series titled *Orbits* (2009). The *Orbits* and other previous series evolved from an intense studio practice where mundane materials at hand provided the basis for wholly constructed images. In this case, the materials were piles of debris cast off from ongoing activity in the studio.

The Orbits were actually piles of piles.

A stack of similar objects each directly on top of the last; a structure well prepared to do something. A pile of things thrown together so as to form an elevation; a provisional structure. A stack can become a pile just as a pile can become a stack.[3]

In the relative isolation of a Collingwood winter I saw great opportunity in rereading Ludwig Wittgenstein's *Tractatus Logico-Philosophicus*, something I had wanted to do for a long time. In those snow-covered, bleak, and remote conditions, I would delve deeply into a text whose center rested perhaps on:

4.01 A proposition is a picture of reality.[4]

A tandem yearning to more fully understand my studio piles and the *Tractatus* occurred day after day. A confused tandem because I ultimately took from that text an anxiety about getting things right, a feeling that the least error on my part in describing the world would be, somehow, disastrous. Since my world seemed to all but have collapsed onto these piles, they became a receptor like a family pet that takes on all the bad habits of its owners.

A proposition is a model of reality as we imagine it.[5]

Eventually I got up from where I had been sitting for so long and encircled the piles in a 360-degree arc; I documented them with a camera at approximate intervals, which I could later use to render a single image that would be superior in some way to, or at least a relief from, the single perspective that vexed me.

2.01 A state of affairs (a state of things) is a combination of objects (things).[6]

Assisted by a digital process and like an insidious game of three-dimensional chess, or if one prefers, the painstaking technique of onion-skinning in traditional cell animation, I focused on the relations between things. At first it was an unintelligible mess composing in this void until I had established arteries amid perspective moments among the photos I had taken.

I recognized an immediate sympathy to cubist painting—something I hadn't anticipated. I dubbed the coincidence as "arriving at an aesthetic," by which I mean inadvertently retracing steps in history.

> Collapsing time makes everything available for use.[7]

Portrait Propositions

I was viewing many portraits during a year of travel and suspect that I was building up a desire to produce my own. I'm moving around in a space in front of the paintings and photographs; far, close, from the right, from the left, dead center — what have I gained from this? I had heard of an art historian that encouraged students to assume the posture of the subjects they were looking at.

> 2. They are not self-portraits as much as the self used for portraits.
> 11. To what end; the self as raw material? . . . an account, an accumulation, an economy.
> 4. I'm following a pattern that evolves in practice. One thing leads to another. Am I defined by patterns laid down by practice? Am I redeemed by consistency? (The self as a consistent pattern.)[8]

At one point I thought about the *Sligo Heads* as portraits of the subject(s) that view the *Orbits*.

The results are constructed grotesques that otherwise reside in mundane self-documentation. With blurred and distorted features, the figures are chilling and remarkably painterly, recalling Francis Bacon's grotesquely expressive works.[9]

> I felt some kinship there not so much with the likeness of his visual/visceral distortions, but when he downplays the disturbing nature of his subject matter. Any notion of the monster for me gets eclipsed by my myopic process in building them. I lose touch with anything disturbing. Bacon once said: "Technique is always dissolving. The technique of recording

has to all the time be remade. It's like a continuous invention to record a fact." Which could mean any number of things, but it raises a filmic image for me . . . something like ravenous celluloid, or celluloid and triage, something about recording and moving on fast and the trauma along with that.[10]

In self-deprecating fashion the sixteenth-century French philosopher Michel de Montaigne described his essays as grotesques bolted together, himself the thread.

When I lately retired to my own house, with a resolution, as much as possibly I could, to avoid all manner of concern in affairs, and to spend in privacy and repose the little remainder of time I have to live, I fancied I could not more oblige my mind than to suffer it at full leisure to entertain and divert itself, which I now hoped it might henceforth do, as being by time become more settled and mature; but I find: —

"Leisure ever operates differently on minds."

—that, quite contrary, it is like a horse that has broke from his rider, who voluntarily runs into a much more violent career than any horseman would put him to, and creates me so many chimeras and fantastic monsters, one upon another, without order or design, that, the better at leisure to contemplate their strangeness and absurdity, I have begun to commit them to writing, hoping in time to make it ashamed of itself.[11]

I use only myself in all the *Sligo Heads* to generate the image — and have, elsewhere, a fascination for what I call the *false generator.*

10. More is less: Increasing aspects lead to a break in recognition.[12]

Notes

1. From artist notes taken throughout the production of the *Sligo Heads.*

2. Bruce Nauman, in Ian Wallace and Russell Keziere, "Bruce Nauman Interviewed," *Vanguard* (Canada) 8, no. 1 (1979): 18. Early in his career, Jasper Johns came to a similar realization: "Before, whenever anybody asked me what I did, I said I was going to be-

come an artist. Finally, I decided that I could be going to become an artist forever, all my life. I decided to stop becoming, and to be an artist." Michael Crichton, *Jasper Johns* (New York: Harry N. Abrams, 1977), 27.

3. From artist notes taken throughout the production of the *Orbits*, 4.

4. Ludwig Wittgenstein, *Tractatus Logico-Philosophicus*, trans. D. F. Pears and B. F. McGuinness (New York: Humanities Press, 1961).

5. Wittgenstein, *Tractatus Logico-Philosophicus*.

6. Wittgenstein, *Tractatus Logico-Philosophicus*.

7. Artist notes, 1 *Sligo Heads*.

8. Artist notes, 1 *Sligo Heads*.

9. Excerpt from exhibition text for *One for Yourself*, curated by Ryan Doherty, Southern Alberta Art Gallery, 2012.

10. Artist notes, 1 *Sligo Heads*.

11. Michel de Montaigne, "Of Idleness," in *Essays of Montaigne*, vol. 1, trans. Charles Cotton, rev. William Carew Hazlett (New York: Edwin C. Hill, 1910).

12. Artist notes, 1 *Sligo Heads*.

CHAPTER TEN

_____

DEVELOPING HISTORICAL NEGATIVES

The Colonial Photographic Archive
as Optical Unconscious

_____

GABRIELLE MOSER

The woman standing on the left-hand side of the photograph is the only human figure in the frame, yet she is not the subject of the image (fig. 10.1). At least, not according to the photographer's title, scrawled on the album page above it: a simple, declarative sentence that describes its focus to be the "Entrance to a village on the Rungeet River, in Sikkim—in front coolie woman carrying camera." Appended with a dash, the archival caption locates the woman as an afterthought in this scene. Its main subjects, it tells us, are several huts, elevated on stilts, at the edge of a river in the Himalayas. Yet everything about the photograph's composition directs our gaze toward the woman: the curved path that leads to her firmly planted feet and the sloping contours of the mountains in the background that conclude at the top of her head; the line of three tall, spindly trees that mimic her upright stance, casting long shadows across the foreground of the image. Her face is obscured by dark shadows, grainy and out of focus, but if you look closely, it is possible to make out the gesture of her hands as she adjusts the load on her back, and the layers of plain dark clothing that she wears against the late afternoon sun (fig. 10.2). She looks toward the viewer, stopped and posed for the camera rather than caught midstride on her way down the road.

In many ways, this photograph is a nonevent within the larger archive to which it belongs: the collection of more than 7,600 images made by Alfred Hugh Fisher for the Colonial Office Visual Instruction Committee (COVIC) between 1907 and 1910, documenting the land and peoples of every major dominion and colonial holding in the British Empire. An artist and newspaper

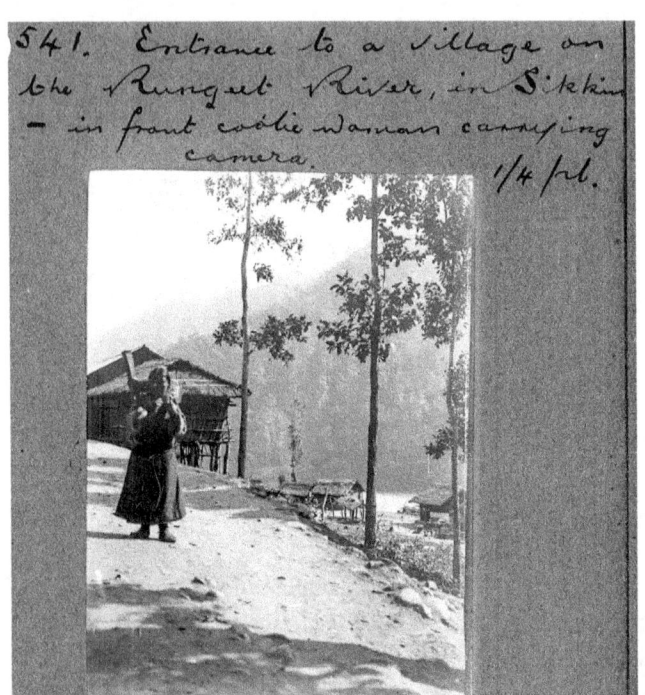
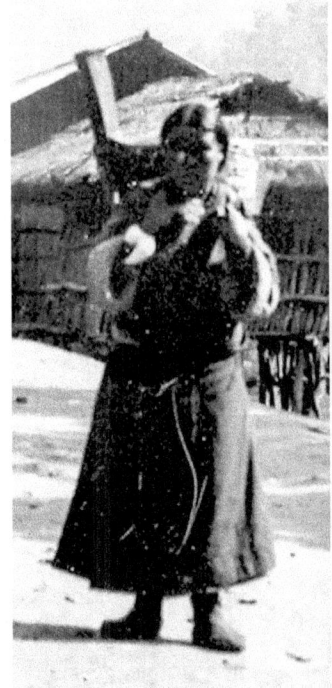

FIGURE 10.1 *left* Alfred Hugh Fisher, *Entrance to a Village on the Rungeet River, in Sikkim — in front coolie woman carrying camera*, India, 1908, quarter plate. From Fisher photographs, Royal Commonwealth Society (RCS), Album IV, no. 541. Reproduced by the kind permission of the Syndics of Cambridge University Library.

FIGURE 10.2 *right* Alfred Hugh Fisher, detail of *Entrance to a Village on the Rungeet River, in Sikkim — in front coolie woman carrying camera*, India, 1908, quarter plate. Reproduced by the kind permission of the Syndics of Cambridge University Library.

illustrator-turned-photographer (he had been provided with a six-week crash course in photography in London earlier that year), Fisher was on a three-year trip around the world under a contract with COVIC, a group of volunteers within the British government that met to design and implement a program of geography lectures, illustrated with photographic lantern slides, that would be shown throughout the empire.[1] Advertised as a set of geography lectures for colonial and English schoolchildren, the COVIC lectures used more than three thousand photographic lantern slides and seven textbooks to describe the British Empire to its student viewers in classrooms all over the world between 1907 and 1945. Designed to "illustrat[e] life in the different parts of the British Empire, as an educational means of strengthening the feeling of Imperial unity and citizenship," the COVIC project not only attempted to capture the empire and its people, but to build a photographic catalog of what it meant to look and feel like an imperial citizen.[2]

Though the COVIC project acknowledged, and often reinforced, racial and ethnic differences between the peoples of the British Empire, its main goal was to represent the behaviors and affects that permitted a subject to enter into the community of citizenry. The COVIC photographs therefore picture people from all over the empire in the midst of their daily activities: working, shopping, farming, traveling, raising children, and going to school (figs. 10.3 and 10.4). The COVIC textbooks, read aloud by the classroom teacher, directed students on how to understand the hundreds of images projected onto the screen by a magic lantern, stressing the differences between the peoples and cultures of England, India, Canada, Australia, Africa, the West Indies, and "the Sea Road to the East" (Malta, Gibraltar, Cyprus, Ceylon, Singapore, and Hong Kong) while also insisting on their membership in the invisible community of imperial citizenship. Notions of civic duty and responsibility were integral to the project's goals. As Michael E. Sadler, director of the Department of Special Inquiries and Reports at the Board of Education, wrote in his proposal for the COVIC project in 1902, "The object in view is to give *every citizen of the Empire* an opportunity of seeing what the different parts of the Empire are like . . . and of learning what duties its possession entails."[3] From its inception, the very premise of the COVIC project brought together the discourses of imperialism, education, and photographic representation as concomitant forces in the making of imperial citizens.

Structured as travelogues that were read aloud by the teacher, each of the COVIC lectures opened with images of a steamship departing from the viewer's home country and then journeyed through one of the empire's major holdings.[4] Halford J. Mackinder, a geographer and the former director of the London School of Economics, chaired the COVIC committee in its early years and authored many of its textbooks, and it was under his guidance that the lectures came to treat the study of geography as an imaginative and visual endeavor, encouraging students to project themselves into the photographed spaces projected onto the screen.[5] As he wrote in an introduction to schoolteachers in a 1908 textbook: though the study of the geography and history of the modern world is complex, "it is worth taking some trouble to make these things live in the minds and sympathies of future citizens of the British Empire."[6] Addressing his school-aged audience as "we," Mackinder's textbooks insisted that British subjects would be welcome in any part of the empire, where they would find themselves among equals and friends.

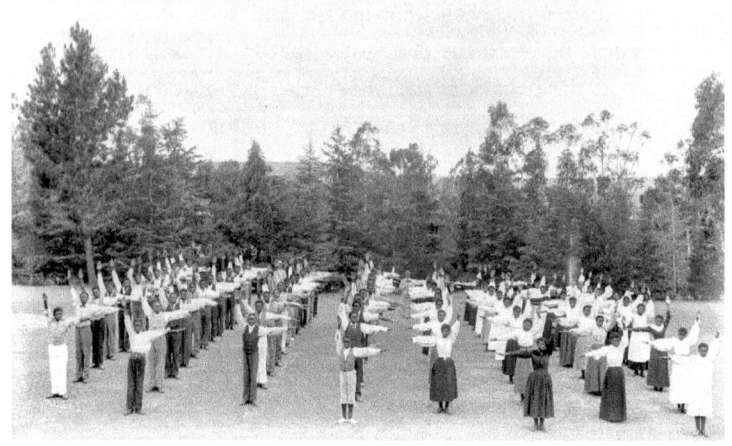

FIGURE 10.3 Photographer unknown, *Pupils at Drill*, Lovedale Missionary Institution, circa 1900–1910. From RCS photography collection, University of Cambridge Library, RCS Fisher Y305J no. 73. Reproduced by the kind permission of the Syndics of Cambridge University Library.

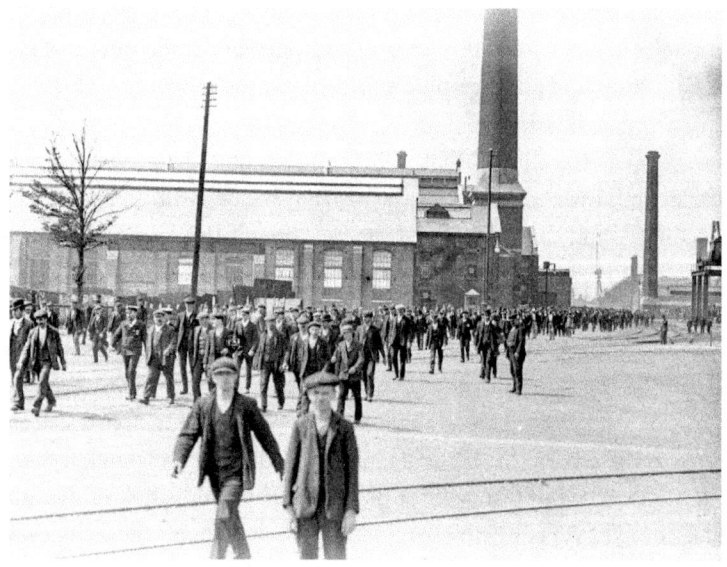

FIGURE 10.4 Alfred Hugh Fisher, *Men Leaving Portsmouth Dockyard for Saturday Half-Holiday*, 1909, Portsmouth, England, quarter plate. From RCS photography collection, University of Cambridge Library, RCS Fisher XXI, no. 5043. Reproduced by the kind permission of the Syndics of Cambridge University Library.

Despite the evocative language that Mackinder employed to describe the aims of the COVIC project, the images Fisher produced for the slide lectures are, for the most part, quite boring. As the British government's only peacetime exercise in imperial propaganda, the COVIC project had no devastating wars to capture, nor any symbolic victories to record.[7] In Edwardian-era England, the Colonial Office's main goals were colonial consolidation and imperial unity: to convince the general population, starting with its impressionable children, that the empire was still a worthwhile project despite increasingly vocal demands from the dominions and colonies for political self-determination.[8] The focus of the COVIC lectures is therefore on everyday life in the empire, drawing viewers' attention to the interconnectedness of economic, trade, and military systems between the colonial periphery and the imperial center.

In its attempt at producing imperial citizenship as a visible category, the COVIC lectures invoked a desire to see something that is unseeable, a quality that Kenneth Hayes proposes is characteristic of the optical unconscious. "The photographic image is specular and speculative," he writes; "it exposes all that is *imagined* to occur in events that are too sudden, too minute or too subtle to be directly observed."[9] Following Walter Benjamin's descriptions of the optical unconscious, Hayes puts emphasis on the psychoanalytic dimensions of the moment that a photograph is produced, relying on the camera's ability to capture fleeting or microscopic events. In Benjamin's earliest writing about the optical unconscious, in his 1931 essay "Little History of Photography," he underscores the importance of the camera's mechanical operations, using the snapshot, slow-motion film, and the microscopic photograph to argue for the medium's ability to reveal occurrences that would ordinarily pass unnoticed in human vision. This does not mean that photography allows human perception to gain mastery over the visible world, however; instead, Benjamin argues for the radical unruliness of the event of photography. Despite our efforts to control what it captures, photography does not conform to the will of the subject or operator, containing within it that "tiny spark of contingency" which draws us to its images.[10] For Benjamin, there is something beyond the physical, visible world that presents itself to the camera—sometimes accidentally—in these moments of encounter between subject and operator that can only be seen latently, once the photograph is developed and printed.

Processes of development and printing play a central role in Benjamin's conception of the optical unconscious, yet they have not received the same amount of analytic attention as the moment in which the shutter is released. References to enlargement, in particular, appear throughout Benjamin's writing on

FIGURE 10.5 Alfred Hugh Fisher, *My First Servant, John, a Madrassee Tamil in Rickshaw*, Colombo, Ceylon, 1907, quarter plate. From Fisher photographs, RCS, Album I, no. 31. Reproduced by the kind permission of the Syndics of Cambridge University Library.

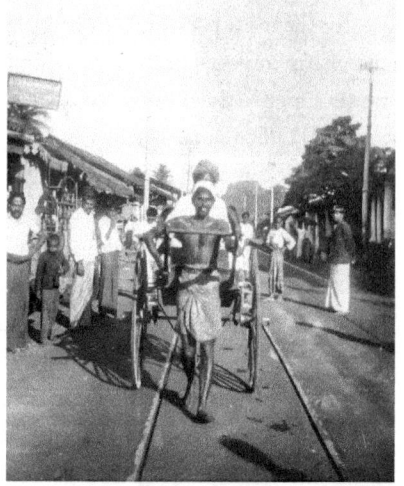

the optical unconscious, serving to reveal the physiognomy of the visual world and to blur the line between technology and magic.[11] In his 1936 essay, "The Work of Art in the Age of Mechanical Reproduction," he even goes so far as to argue that the practice of photographic enlargement is akin to the psychic processes of subject formation: "The enlargement of a snapshot does not simply render more precise what in any case was visible, though unclear: it reveals entirely new structural formations of the subject."[12] For Benjamin, it is not just the moment of production, but the subsequent moments of developing and looking at photographs, that reveal these new structural formations.

Though the kinds of enlargement that Benjamin discusses were not yet technically possible in the period in which the COVIC photographs were produced, I want to think about these strategies of cropping, developing, and enlarging metaphorically, to describe the kinds of looking that are possible in the space of the photographic archive. In particular, I want to look at the COVIC images with attention to the ways that the "coolie," or indentured laborer, comes in and out of focus as a member of the imperial community. As a type, the woman laborer in Sikkim is not unusual in COVIC's photographic catalog of imperial citizenship. Photographs of indentured laborers, referred to as "coolies" in the lecture texts, were common in the COVIC project, serving as signs of the empire's economic interdependence in five of the series' seven textbooks. In the lectures on India, South Africa, the Sea Road to the East, Australia, and the West Indies, these imported laborers appear as rickshaw drivers (fig. 10.5), as work for hire

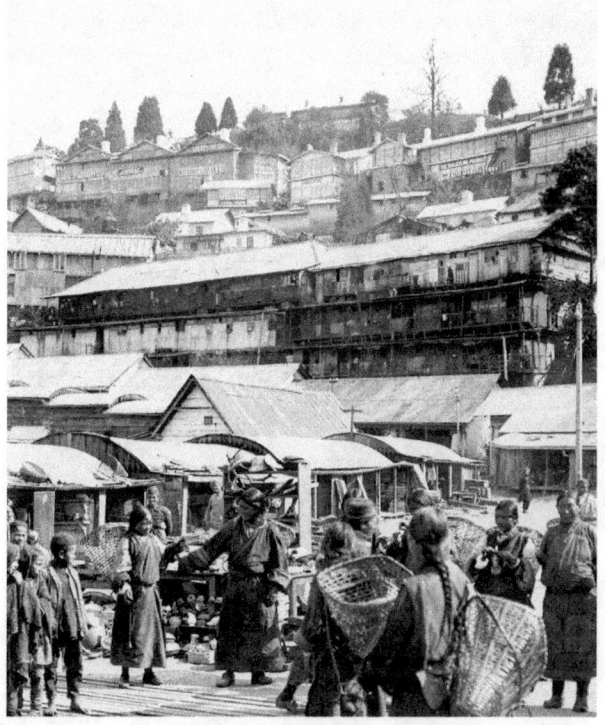

FIGURE 10.6 Alfred Hugh Fisher, *Tibetan Women Doing Coolie Work in the Bazaar*, Darjeeling, India, 1908, half plate. From Fisher photographs, RCS, Album IV, no. 516. Reproduced by the kind permission of the Syndics of Cambridge University Library.

in local markets (fig. 10.6), as rubber tappers (fig. 10.7), and as porters (fig. 10.8), as well as manual laborers who break stones, construct roads, and perform other physically taxing work in the service of building and maintaining colonial infrastructure. The frequency with which the figure of the indentured laborer appears in the COVIC series perhaps signals the "everydayness" of this form of transnational labor in the British Empire at the beginning of the twentieth century. Although the term "coolie" originally referred to (East) Indian laborers brought to other dominions and colonies to work, by the early 1900s, the category had expanded to include all emigrant workers originating in Asia, making it a term that obscured and confused racial boundaries.[13] As a recurring motif, the "coolie" reads as a type within imperial citizenship, one that can reliably be found in any corner of the empire alongside her counterparts, the naval officer and the colonial bureaucrat.

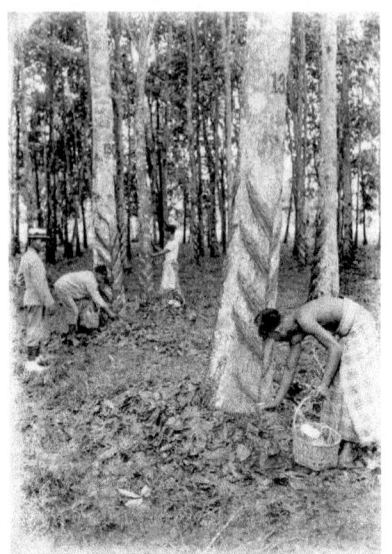 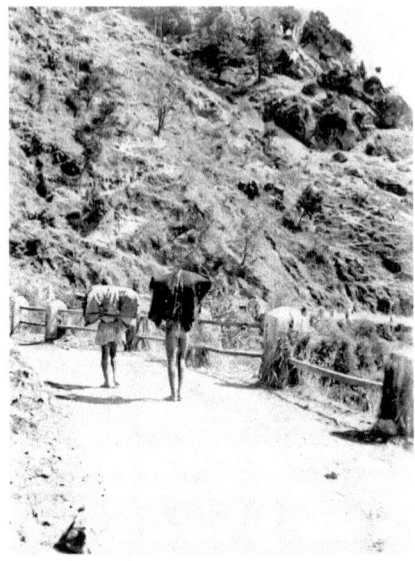

FIGURE 10.7 *left* Alfred Hugh Fisher, *Collecting Latex*, Singapore, 1908, half plate. From Fisher photographs, RCS, Album XVIII, no. 4209. Reproduced by the kind permission of the Syndics of Cambridge University Library.

FIGURE 10.8 *right* Alfred Hugh Fisher, *The Road Down from Mussoorie, Coolies Carrying My Baggage*, India, 1908, quarter plate. From Fisher photographs, RCS, Album V, no. 788. Reproduced by the kind permission of the Syndics of Cambridge University Library.

But the lectures' textual descriptions of these figures undermine their seemingly status quo presence in the empire. The COVIC lecture texts obsess over how to categorize these imperial subjects that do not neatly conform to existing racial and class categories, and worry about how this ambiguous status might cause problems for the functioning of the empire in the future. These anxieties about how the indentured laborer's ambiguous racial status might undermine notions of imperial belonging were exacerbated when the subjects that Fisher photographed crossed multiple categories of difference. Women indentured laborers—who were not native to the country in which they worked, but also not British; who were neither working class nor part of the middle-class colonial bureaucracy; who provided not just physical but also reproductive and affective labor as mothers of and caregivers to the children of the empire— put particular stress on COVIC's catalog of imperial citizenship. The woman "coolie" reappears throughout the COVIC archive as a figure that is not immediately threatening, but that might one day, through her ability to literally and figuratively create colonial subjects, disrupt the spirit of cooperation and imperial unity espoused by the project. To fixate on the figure of the indentured laborer in the COVIC photographs is to enlarge her psychic presence within the narrative of imperial citizenship. To make her the focus of my gaze—rather than the subjects that the captions describe—is a political gesture, motivated by a desire to see her as an active, agentic citizen; to acknowledge her specific position in the empire rather than relegating her to a type; and to take seriously the trouble she caused for colonial bureaucrats. This focus engages what Ariella Azoulay has termed a "civil imagination," the ability "to imagine the non-citizen or second-class citizen as citizen."[14]

By attending to the conditional, latent force of the representation of the woman indentured laborer in the COVIC archive, I follow historian and anthropologist Ann Laura Stoler's advice to read "along the archival grain," foregrounding the epistemic uncertainties that structure the archive's organizational logic.[15] Rather than trying to identify omissions, biases, and blind spots in the archive's master narrative, Stoler suggests we look for the nonevents contained within the archive's materials: the conditional, projected, and prefigured encounters that the archive tries to anticipate and manage, often without success.[16] Such nonevents might include memoranda about an imagined and impending political crisis (such as a "Second Mutiny" in India), educational policies for managing a yet-to-be-constituted population (such as mixed-race children), or exhaustive reworkings of immigration laws—usually in response to catastrophes in neighboring countries—to preempt a "foreign flood" of immigrants into the empire. In Stoler's estimation, the fact that these events do not come to pass does not detract from their significance in the archive. Their affective textures— the panics they signal, the uncertainties of colonial knowledge production they reveal—are not anomalies in the archive, but constitute its logic.

Interestingly, Stoler employs a photographic metaphor to describe the archival researcher's work in uncovering these prefigured, planned-for, but never realized events, describing it as a strategy of "developing historical negatives."[17] For Stoler, the archive's negatives are expressed in the "subjunctive mood of official imaginings," in the concrete responses that colonial officials planned for crises that might not ever materialize.[18] In psychoanalytic terms, they are fantasies—often negative ones—that may never be fulfilled, but which are acted out and repeated, registered through symptoms: in this case through the creation of massive volumes of colonial paperwork and enormous photographic archives.

While for Stoler the photographic process is a metaphor for how the archive anticipates events before they happen—with the double meaning of the word *negative* also connoting the worst-case-scenario thinking that characterizes colonial bureaucratic rhetoric—this essay aims to elaborate the psychoanalytic implications of Stoler's approach to photographic archives. It takes Stoler's analogy seriously, exploring the developing process as a metaphor for the work that the scholar can perform by adopting a disobedient gaze within the colonial photographic archive. By looking for representations of the indentured laborer across the COVIC lectures, and particularly in those on Australia, South Africa, and the West Indies, I stress the photographic archive's role as a negative of empire: the possibility that the very images used to constitute imperial citizenship might also register a latent critique of that form of belonging. Following Stoler, and drawing on Sarah Kofman's work on the photographic apparatus as a model for psychic phenomena, my interest is in considering how the notion of latent development might offer a way to think about the political work that is done by colonial photographs that are produced but not (immediately) seen.[19] The idea of the archive as a repository of latent images is especially useful when analyzing the COVIC archive, where more than half of the photographs taken by Fisher did not circulate publicly, but were seen by only a small group of colonial officials who decided which images would be "developed" into lantern slides and which would remain prints in the semi-private archive.[20] Though these images went unseen by the lectures' immediate audience, they nonetheless registered COVIC's priorities, goals, and imagined spectators: impressions that could be developed by later viewers to perform a critique of imperial citizenship's partialities and double standards.

It is not just the uncirculated and unseen COVIC photographs that offer an undeveloped and latent critique of the empire. Those photographs that were developed by the committee and included in the final lectures also offer photographic evidence that is suppressed by the lecture texts. Fisher's image of the indentured female laborer in front of the village in Sikkim is included in the final lectures on India, for instance, but under the simple title *Village in Sikkim: A Woman Carrying Baggage*. Any reference to the presence of camera equipment has been removed, perhaps because it too obviously called attention to the means of the lectures' production and the role of the photographer as author: cues that might impair viewers' ability to imaginatively project themselves into the photograph.[21] But Fisher's original caption for the image—"Entrance to a village on the Rungeet River, in Sikkim—in front coolie woman carrying camera"—is equally deceptive. It does not just displace the woman as the main subject of the photograph; it also functions to obscure the work she is performing. The photographer's caption describes the contents of the load on the woman's back as a camera, when Fisher's only camera is, of course, not in the bag, but in his hands, being used to take this photograph. What the "coolie" woman carries instead is the supporting apparatus for the camera—the tripod sticking out at an awkward angle behind her head—as well as the portable darkroom and developing agents that the photographer hauled around the world with him.[22] This double slip between what the photograph shows and what the caption tries to pin down as its subject suggests a kind of optical repression on Fisher's part: a refusal to acknowledge the signs of the means of production (the woman's labor) and reproduction (the photographic developing equipment) that sustained the British Empire.

These repressed subjects—the woman, the darkroom equipment, and the figure of the indentured laborer—are not hidden by the archive or by the final lectures presented to students, but their presence does not immediately register on the first viewing of the photograph. It is only through careful, repeated looking—a kind of looking that disobeys the direct, pedagogical message communicated by COVIC, and that imagines other meanings for the photograph—that inconsistencies between the image's photographic evidence and the meaning inscribed upon it by its captions begin to emerge. To dwell on these contradictions, hidden in plain sight, is to draw attention to the ways the COVIC photographs "embodied and exposed hypocrisies that stretched beyond the native population—that only some [British subjects] had rights, that rights and race were not always aligned, and that . . . those inconsistencies were evident to, and expressed among, empire's practitioners themselves."[23] This kind of looking argues for the critical and imaginative capacity of the spectator, past and present, who is savvy enough to see past the committee's directives, and to develop oppositional meanings from the COVIC photographs. It also insists that photographic accidents, much like psychoanalytic symptoms, are invested with meaning. A photograph is never sovereign: it registers unimportant details and unseen phenomena just as clearly as its intended subject matter. This correlation between photography and unconscious phenomena is perhaps why Benjamin became so fixated on the medium's political and psychoanalytic potential, the capacity for these photographic accidents to reveal the optical unconscious. How might photography, with its ability to initiate relations between producers, subjects, and viewers that its operators cannot anticipate or control, allow the anxieties of colonial rule to come into view? And how might the photographic archive, when read with an attention to these repressed meanings, operate as the optical unconscious of colonial projects like COVIC?

To put the focus on the latent critique registered by the indentured laborer's presence in the colonial photographic archive is to see COVIC not as an apparatus for reproducing colonial rule, but instead as a repository of attempts at managing the committee's fantasies about imperial belonging: a repository in which alternative visions of the future (for the equal rights promised by imperial citizenship) could be developed from the same historical negatives.

If these potential meanings sit dormant in the colonial photographic archive, waiting to be activated, our role as researchers is to act as their developing agents, working to make their latent critique visible. To look at the archive in this way is to allow our gaze to wander, to focus on details that the captions tell us are unimportant, and to pay attention to how clearly certain figures register, while others remain grainy and out of focus. Far from being aporetic breaks in the archive's dominant message, these negative impressions lend the photographic archive its affective force, demonstrating the remarkable flexibility of the colonial archive in accommodating and subsuming difference. In the COVIC archive in particular, the potential, latent meanings of the photographs Fisher produced are just as important as their immanent and immediate meanings. The rhetoric of imperial citizenship, which promised a form of equal belonging only to subjects who demonstrated their capacity to be ruled as model citizens, was articulated in the future tense: as a status that was always yet to come, especially for those non-European subjects of the British Empire who were consistently found to be not quite ready for self-sovereignty.[24]

While the childhood viewers of the COVIC lectures had a limited view of the project, one directed by the textbooks and their teachers' pedagogical methods, I can look through the COVIC archive at a different tempo, one that allows me to watch the subjects of the photographs as they move through, across, and between photographic frames, and to return to figures who reappear throughout the albums, haunting the COVIC project.[25] It is in this slowed-down space of looking that the affective textures of the COVIC photographs can be felt: literally touched through the glossy surfaces of the photo albums where they are stored in the University of Cambridge library, but also through a more ephemeral kind of contact between the viewer and the archive.[26] Much as a film negative must make physical contact with the photographic paper to produce a positive print, the colonial photographic archive is a site of physical and psychic transference, where the potential meanings of an image can be imprinted upon and relayed by the researcher. This space of touching feeling, as queer theorist Eve Sedgwick has put it, collapses the distinctions between reading and seeing, tactility and affect.[27] It allows the unsaid, implicit meanings of the photographs to emerge, both those that hit the viewer immediately and those that only register latently, after repeated viewings, prolonged contact, and extensive looking.

Though these affective meanings reside in and on the skin of the fixed photographic image, there are also unconscious affective resonances, below and beneath the surface of the image, that the archival researcher-viewer can draw out. These meanings may register not as explicit representations, but through a dialogue between images and texts, where meanings and associations brush up against one another. In this way, the viewer mimics the work of an analysand, working through her associations with the image to draw out its potential meanings. These latent meanings—what I think of as the optical unconscious of the colonial photographic archive—are fluid and shifting. Each time they are developed by the viewer, a different aspect comes into view: some figures become clearer, sharper, and more in focus. As they enter our field of sight, they pose challenges to the coherence of the archive, allowing viewers to contest or undermine the dominant message imposed on photographs by the state. In the context of the COVIC archive, these latent meanings often push at the limits of imperial citizenship as a category of belonging, provoking a critique of the COVIC project's strategic inclusions and exclusions, and drawing attention to the inequities at the heart of its constitution. The figure of the indentured laborer, as a type that is nearly constant within the COVIC archive but who appears in a wide array of specific interactions, locations, and roles, can be understood as a reverse, negative image of the imperial citizen. Like a repeated nightmare, the indentured laborer visits the COVIC archive with the force of a repressed memory, insisting that her position in the empire be reckoned with.

Projecting Imperial Citizenship

Work and the production of goods are recurring tropes in the COVIC lectures. Used to demonstrate each colony and dominion's specific resources and their subjects' way of life, and to assert the empire's financial successes, photographs of factories, farms, and markets dominate the lectures. Representing work as a common, panimperial activity was also an important way to assert one of COVIC's most forceful fantasies about the empire, a delusion about it as an organized, cooperative system where each citizen's work contributed to the well-being of the greater imagined community. This worldview of the empire is embedded in the premise of the COVIC project, which sent a single photographer out "to travel steadily through the Empire with first-rate apparatus at his command" at a time when the British Empire encompassed more than a quarter of the world's population.[28] From the outset, the practicalities of implementing this plan demonstrated just how fantastical this vision of the empire was. Fisher's three-year journey aboard the empire's mail ships followed a circuitous route that had little bearing on geographical proximity, influenced instead by the committee's priorities about which colonies would most benefit from seeing the lectures first: a list that repeatedly placed the "more developed" colonies of India and Canada at the top of the list, and the "less developed" (and significantly less white) at the bottom, with South Africa and the West Indies consistently coming last.[29] But, plagued by a dwindling budget and the limitations of the steamship mail routes he was traveling on, Fisher ended up missing several destinations on his itinerary—including the whole of Africa—and was instructed to purchase views of those locations from professional photographers along his journey.[30]

The desire for imperial unity was not just evident in the paperwork that organized the production of the COVIC photographs; it also structured the textbooks' address to viewers. At the close of the Age of Empire, the COVIC textbooks attempted to respond to major transformations in the economic and social conditions of the empire; transformations that included the growing internationalization of human affairs, the relative decline of Britain's finances in the world economy, and the increasingly vocal demands for political recognition by overseas colonial subjects and, closer to home, by women and the working class.[31] These transformations were a source of anxiety for the members of COVIC, and particularly for Mackinder. Drawing on romantic conceptions of the empire as a living entity that had grown naturally, Mackinder argued that modernization, rapid industrialization, and unfettered transnational capitalism had damaged the social body of the imperial community.[32] The COVIC lectures therefore sought to bring the community of the empire back into a natural state of equilibrium by encouraging an affiliative relationship between its distant subjects. As the preface to each textbook asserted, "The component parts of the British Empire are so remote and so different from one another, that it is evident the Empire can only be held together by sympathy and understanding . . . imparted to the coming generation . . . [and] taught in the Schools of the Empire."[33]

To bring cohesion back to the empire, the COVIC lectures borrowed from the rhetoric of imperial citizenship that circulated in popular discourse in this period. As Sukanya Banerjee observes, although the category of the citizen was not formally codified in British law until after World War II, "the idea of a common but equal status across the empire gained . . . currency toward the end of the nineteenth century" as a rhetorical compromise: a way for Britain to appease the settler colonies' demands for autonomy without losing authority over the dominions.[34] A shifting, nonlegal category of belonging that simultaneously displayed and suppressed markers of racial difference, imperial citizenship recognized the specific nationality of each British subject (based on where she was born), but promised her equal rights under the policies and regulations of the empire. Imperial citizenship was, in other words, invisible: a virtual, transnational community sustained by rhetoric and public discourse rather than law. As a category based on a process of identification that was until this point invisible, it needed to be taught, through photographs, in the schools of the empire.

Visualizing imperial citizenship proved difficult for the COVIC committee, even with Fisher's 7,600 images at their disposal, because it relied on performative cues, such as dress, comportment, and the expression of emotions, as criteria for membership, rather than the more fixed visual cues that were usually used to secure racial categories. Service, duty, and industriousness — qualities associated with work — were integral in shaping representations of the ideal imperial citizen who, alongside the colonial bureaucrat and the military serviceman, directed their behavior toward the maintenance of the empire.[35] In the COVIC lectures on South Africa, for instance, authored by economist Arthur John Sargent and published in 1914, representations of the ideal imperial laborer tended to blur racial distinctions between subjects. Here, imperial labor is centered on the production of food: "exotic" fruit and vegetables that will circulate back to England, literally and metaphorically feeding the imperial center. Describing a tour of a fruit farm just outside of Cape Town, Sargent's lecture text notes the "native workers who are a very necessary element in the agricultural population of South Africa."[36] In the photograph that accompanies his description, titled *Native Workers on a Farm*, eleven workers, both men and women, are seen standing over several wooden crates of peaches (fig. 10.9). The work that is being shown on the farm is not that of planting or harvesting, but rather the sorting of fruit into containers. Though it is not an assembly line that is pictured, the workers' position in rows on each side of the crates denotes a systematic method of labor, while the way the materials are laid out on the table — a tall stack of crates in the background, two boxes piled high with peaches at the far end, a container of packing straw in the center, and a beautifully organized crate of lined-up fruit at the end of the table — illustrate a controlled process of inventory management.

What is not immediately clear in the lectures, or photographs, is that this is not just any rural farm, but a site of social and agricultural experimenta-

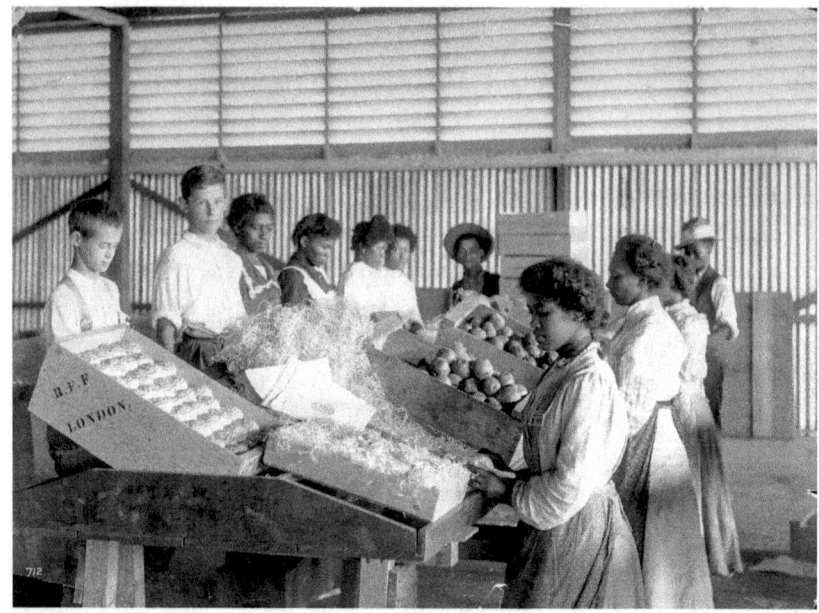

FIGURE 10.9 Photographer unknown, Groot Drakenstein, *Native Workers on a Farm*, packing fruit for export (London and continental markets), South Africa, circa 1900–1910, medium unknown. Courtesy the Cape Government Railways. From Fisher photographs, RCS, Y305J9. Reproduced by the kind permission of the Syndics of Cambridge University Library.

tion that typified British colonialism in South Africa. Commissioned by the Cape Government Railways and lent to COVIC for reproduction in the lectures, the photograph was taken at one of the Rhodes Fruit Farms, a series of more than twenty model farms throughout South Africa that were established by Cecil John Rhodes in the early 1900s. A politician, mining magnate (Rhodes was one owner of the De Beers diamond company), railway developer, and proponent of British colonial policy, Rhodes aimed to rehabilitate farming in the region by transforming old vineyards (which had been afflicted by an insect epidemic in the 1880s and 1890s) into fruit farms. Between 1897 and 1902, more than 200,000 pear, apricot, plum, and peach trees were planted across Rhodes's properties, and the farms became the largest source of employment in the region.[37] The success of the farms was meant, in part, to form a pedagogical model, demonstrating how British colonialism could benefit, and benefit from, intervention in South Africa. Though Rhodes died in 1902, the farms continued to operate until 1969, when the properties were converted back into vineyards. The photograph of the workers at the fruit farm therefore draws together the key activities that constituted British colonialism in South Africa: resource extraction, railways, and the harvesting of luxury foods for European consumption. The COVIC textbook does not explicitly note Rhodes's involvement in the farm, but the lectures do make a typical connection between the colonies as networked sites of production and England as a centralized hub of consumption. As Sargent tells his student audience, "From this district hundreds of thousands of boxes of fresh fruit are shipped annually to England and sold at Covent Garden."[38] The photograph underscores this network of trade, literally spelling out the fruit's destination in the text printed on the side of the crate in the foreground of the image: "R.F.F. London."

Curiously, though Sargent describes this as a photograph of native labor, two of the boys in the image are clearly of European descent, while the other nine workers appear to be native South Africans. This blurring of who constitutes the native population of South Africa—the settler colonialists, or the dominion's indigenous peoples—seems intentional in this instance, designed to prove that cooperation across the so-called imperial races was not only possible but vital to a successful colonial enterprise. In the image of the Rhodes fruit farm, this cooperation takes on a haptic dimension, with the workers standing so closely to one another that their shoulders nearly touch. Although the workers are supposedly in the midst of organizing the peaches into containers, their hands are noticeably inactive, removed from the fruit and placed at the edge of the worktable. These gestures of untouching, of inaction, may be the result of directions from the photographer in an effort to reduce blur in the final image, but they also suggest a tension. If the peaches are too fragile to be sorted by machinery and must be carefully placed in crates, nested in straw for protection, then surely human hands are vital in preparing them for shipment. This visual repression of the act of touching seems forced, as though the owner or producer of the image hoped to obscure the fruit's function as an object of transference, where traces of the hands of the native workers will eventually make contact with the hands of British consumers. But such a repression also invites a desire for contact on the part of the viewer: an impulse to reach out and touch the fruit that has been so elegantly displayed. It is in moments like this—where the photographs both depict and elicit contact between imperial subjects—that the fixity of race seems to slip in the COVIC lectures, loosened by the images' appeal to the viewer, and by the constantly shifting definitions of imperial citizenship.

Maintaining racial distinctions became more complicated, and more dire, in representations of indentured labor, where it was not the native population that was seen to be cooperating in the success of the empire's economy, but a foreign, displaced group whose working conditions rarely resembled the modern efficiency of Indian textile factories (pictured in earlier lectures) or the sociable atmosphere of the Rhodes Fruit Farms. Picturing indentured labor required a great deal of textual explication, forcing the COVIC lectures to make tentative distinctions between subjects that were not always visually evident in the photographs. In the section on Singapore included in the lectures on the Sea Road to the East, for instance, viewers are introduced to photographs of laborers on a rubber plantation (figs. 10.7 and 10.10) where, "if we pay the planter a visit we see coolies tapping the trees by slicing the bark—the planter is English, perhaps from Ceylon, while the coolies are Tamils from India since the Malay are not interested in the steady work of cultivation."[39] Distinguishing between the ongoing and logical form of labor being organized by the English plantation owner and the seasonal (and implicitly irregular) work practiced by the indigenous population, the lectures suggest that the "artificial cultivation of rubber" is one of the "super-added characteristics due to British rule" that the COVIC project hoped to picture for its viewers. But while the lecture texts make it sound as though the ethnic and racial distinctions that separate the planter-owner from his workers (and both of these groups from the native population) would be obvious to the casual visitor, in Fisher's photographs these categories are less clear. Three figures, all in sarongs, tap rubber from an orderly line of trees while a fourth, wearing a boater hat, stands a short distance away, watching them work. Their stances and clothing demarcate their roles within the plantation, but it is unclear if the man in the boater hat is the English planter the caption refers to, or another Tamil laborer acting as a supervisor. His white hat and shoes form a striking tonal contrast to his skin that make it impossible to read him as a white European, and yet the lecture texts give the viewer few other categorical options with which to understand him.

Like the photograph of the fruit farm workers in South Africa, this depiction of the cooperative project of resource extraction insists on a form of photographic identification between colonizing and colonized workers, and between viewers and subjects: forms of affective identification that confuse the taxonomies of race established by anthropological photographs from the same era. Photography historian Tina Campt has argued that institutionally produced group portraits like these, which stress affiliation while still acknowledging differences of race, class, and ethnicity, "challenge our ability to pinpoint exactly how and where we 'see race,' and whether that perception is ever . . . solely or

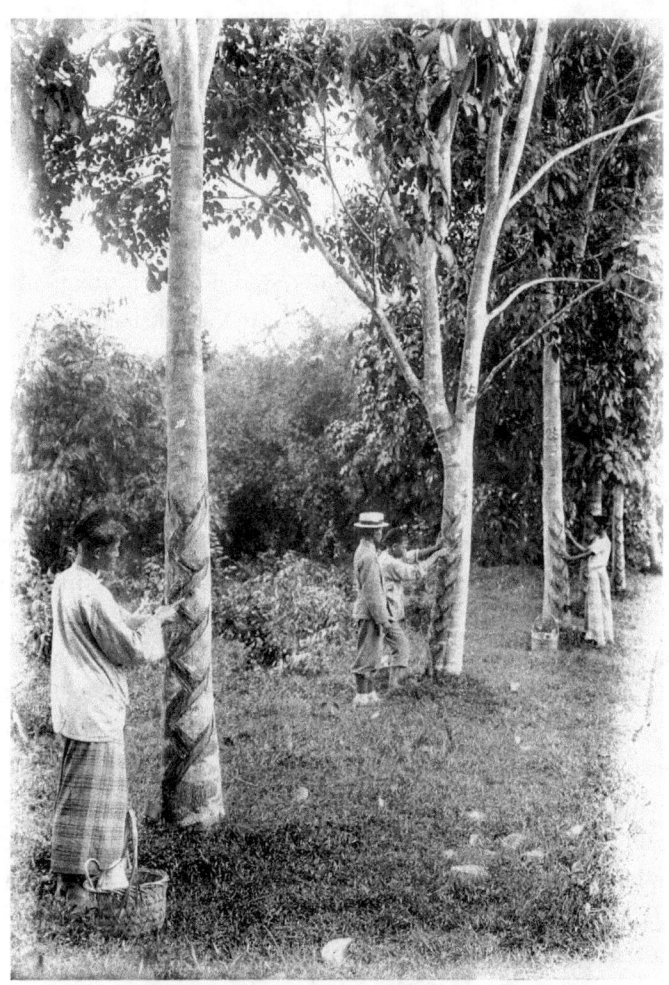

FIGURE 10.10 Alfred Hugh Fisher, *Tapping Rubber*: Chain-Gamma
system invented by Mr. C. Bolden Kloss, and considered to get best
flow of latex, Singapore, 1908, half plate. From Fisher photographs,
RCS, Album XVIII, no. 4210. Reproduced by the kind permission
of the Syndics of Cambridge University Library.

primarily about vision or visibility at all."[40] In the COVIC photographs of indentured laborers, race becomes a sign that is as difficult to recognize and to guarantee as that of imperial citizenship. But, unlike the image of the Rhodes fruit farm, which attested (however indirectly) to the ways the farm benefited the local population by providing employment, in Singapore the empire's intervention into the local economy is wholesale, replacing the local workforce with imported labor. Here, it is more difficult to see how Singaporean subjects qualify as imperial citizens, since they are "uninterested" in participating in the kinds of organized, orderly work that will contribute to the sustenance of the empire. The lectures' presentation of Fisher's image seems to suggest that imperial citizenship is a category that subjects can enter into, by agreeing to participate in necessary forms of indentured labor—and fall out of, by remaining uninterested in it or by refusing to participate in it.

That COVIC's representation of indentured labor in Singapore focuses on rubber extraction is also significant for the ways in which it echoes contemporary discourses about labor and violence in the colonies. Fisher's images of latex cultivation performed by indentured laborers in the British Empire operate psychoanalytically as the "good object" of colonial labor to the "bad object" of photographs of rubber extraction in the Belgian Congo. For many British viewers, Fisher's photographs of rubber tapping in Singapore must have brought to mind the Congo Reform Association's (CRA's) use of photographs to denounce the atrocities committed by King Leopold and the Belgian government as part of the rubber industry in the Congo Free State. Presented in government reports and published in newspapers between 1904 and 1913—the same period in which the COVIC lectures were published—the CRA used photographs of Congolese workers with amputated limbs, sometimes picturing severed hands and body parts, to try to incite the British public to intervene in the atrocities taking place there.[41] In much the same way that COVIC tried to visualize and constitute a virtual community of imperial citizens in their lectures, the CRA appealed to a yet-to-be-formed community of humanity. As Sharon Sliwinski has shown, the CRA's use of the term "crimes against humanity" to critique Leopold "call[ed] into being a form of political community that exceeds the typical boundaries of nation and citizenship. Indeed these crimes presuppose a human subject who belongs to a citizenry of humanity."[42]

The CRA's work was significant as one of "the earliest critics of empire and advocates of a secular human rights ideology," so much so that its depictions of forced colonial labor cast a dark shadow over projects like COVIC.[43] In the public discourse about the Congo, the premodern forms of native slavery that colonial expansion was meant to correct through its civilizing mission had gone horribly awry, replaced with a twentieth-century version that was so appalling it required further intervention. Implicit in these critiques was the notion that the Belgian version of colonial intervention in Africa was the negative kind of colonialism, one that needed correcting through the positive system being practiced in the British Empire. Indentured labor was central to this positive form of colonialism. Both a literal and rhetorical solution to the abolition of slavery in the British Empire, indentured labor was officially introduced in 1833 as a way for colonial officials to continue to provide cheap labor and meet international demands for resource extraction. But the idea of creating a system of indentured Chinese labor in the British Empire emerged even earlier than abolition laws, dating back to a secret memorandum sent from the Colonial Office to the East India Office in 1803: a date that importantly also marks the Haitian revolution, an unprecedented historical moment in which the local population — the product of the transatlantic slave trade — overthrew the French colonial government.[44] The British system of indentured labor was therefore a practical solution to the end of a highly profitable form of work, and a blueprint for preventing a black revolution like the one that had occurred in Haiti. As Banerjee argues, indentureship's historical genesis means that representations of indentured labor were always charged with the specter of slavery, necessitating extensive paperwork to distinguish it from the system it supposedly replaced: "The compulsive nature of this documentation, a compulsiveness evident in the sheer voluminousness of the archive on indentured labour, may have been occasioned by the fact that the system of indentured labour was often not very different from the one it was designed to supersede, both in its recruitment and treatment of the workers."[45] At the center of the indentured labor system was the legal contract between the worker and the imperial government, which "legitimated itself on the premise that [laborers] were rights-bearing subjects . . . that 'they too were citizens of empire.' . . . In what seems a strange paradox, then, the discourses of imperial citizenship and indentured labour became mutually constitutive, with the result that the relation between labour and citizenship took on an added edge in imperial debates."[46] COVIC's obsession with managing representations of indentured labor in the empire — by securing the indentured laborer's non-English racial identity while also assuring the viewer of his or her political autonomy — can be seen as a form of overcompensation for these anxieties about indentured labor appearing as an inversion of slavery: a way of planning for a critique of colonial labor practices, or a demand for equal treatment by laborers, that may one day materialize.

While the lectures appear to be able to accommodate indentured laborers within the catalog of imperial citizenship, a closer inspection of the COVIC photographs of women indentured laborers reveals slippages between what the images show and what the texts assert. These accidents and omissions signal that photographing indentured labor, and women laborers in particular, risked exposing the double standards of imperial citizenship and troubled the ideals of agency, civility, and presentability that were so vital in constituting that form of belonging. The female indentured laborer was also a figure whose political significance was marked by latency. She posed a potential, belated problem for the unity of the empire, one that needed to be developed by colonial officials, COVIC viewers, and now by contemporary archival researchers to be fully reckoned with. It is here that I think Benjamin's ideas about how the optical unconscious makes itself known through processes of photographic development are useful in understanding both the political and symbolic force of the female indentured laborer for viewers. My interest here is in putting analytic pressure on the layered meanings of latent development in the COVIC project, as a concept that structures the photographic process, the dismantling of slavery in the British Empire, the beginnings of modern conceptions of citizenship, and the claims made by imperial citizens through their encounters with photographs. In each of these cases, the critical force of the laborer, the photograph, and the archive arrives too late to be immediately useful.

It seems strange that so little critical focus has been put on the function of the developing process in Benjamin's theories of the optical unconscious, and on development in our theories of photography more generally; especially since the invention of the medium is marked not by the creation of the first camera (which came in the Renaissance), but by the invention of the first successful development process to fix the impressions made by the camera obscura. Henry Fox Talbot and Louis Daguerre were in many ways developers just as much as they were photographers. This oversight may have its own psychoanalytic causes, as Jeff Wall has suggested in his essay on photography's "liquid intelligence."[47] Writing in 1989, at a historical moment that saw artists increasingly turning to digital photography, Wall speculated that the developing bath had been suppressed in most theories of photography because its reliance on liquids undermined our fantasies about the medium as dry, optical, and rational. For Wall, the liquidity of photography had been excised from photography theory because it represents that which is excessive, alchemical, and primal about the medium. Liquid seeps into places it should not be, often changing their very structure. But the liquid intelligence of photography is also one of the medium's strengths. In Wall's estimation, photography is self-reflexive because, while the "dry intelligence" of optics and camera mechanics capture an image, it is the "liquid intelligence" of the developing process that "achieves a historical self-reflection, a memory of the path it has traversed."[48]

In the context of the COVIC lectures, the developing process was literally a moment of self-reflection for Fisher, the photographer, who would often convert his hotel bathrooms into darkrooms to process and print his images at the end of each day of shooting. These evenings were also spent writing captions for the images, designing diagrams and instructions about the coloring of each scene for the lantern slide company, and writing in his journals (sent back to the Colonial Office in London in regular dispatches) about what he had seen during his travels. To encounter the remnants of this process one hundred years after the production of the COVIC images presents another opportunity for reflection, one where another narrative about citizenship and labor can be developed. Instead of examining the official narratives told by the printed and circulated photographs, Stoler's approach to developing the archive's historical negatives looks for the "pliable coordinates of what constituted colonial common sense," paying attention to how knowledge was written and rewritten as the committee's fantasies about imperial unity were refuted and the British government's preparations for future calamities went unrealized.[49]

While for Stoler photographic negatives are convenient, and not always consistent, metaphors for the anxieties that structure the colonial project, novelist and theorist Sarah Kofman made the link between psychoanalysis and photographic negatives explicit.[50] Elucidating Sigmund Freud's use of the photographic apparatus in his writing on the unconscious, Kofman argued that it was actually the movement of the negative impressions registered on film to the positive photographic print that interested the psychoanalyst: "Freud's use of the model of the photographic apparatus is intended to show that all psychic phenomena necessarily pass first through an unconscious phase, through darkness and the negative, before acceding to consciousness, before developing within the clarity of the positive."[51] But, as Kofman is careful to point out, this development from the unconscious to consciousness is neither natural nor inevitable. Freud "adds other metaphors, making it clearly understood that, between the negative and positive phases, there intervene forces which enact a selection from among the negatives. The metaphor here is that of the watchman, the censor, present at the entrance to the dark antechamber, forbidding certain drives from entering into the clear room of consciousness."[52] In Freud's model of the unconscious as a photographic developing process, these censoring forces can prevent the negative from developing through to the level of consciousness. The passage to light, when it happens, does not take place through a theoretical procedure, but a practical one: through the analytic cure.

If we try to adapt Kofman's (and Freud's) thinking to the context of British colonialism, seeing the patient not as a single human subject but as colonial common sense itself, then these undeveloped negatives become a repository of the unrepresentable anxieties that structured imperial rule. Our work then, as researchers in the colonial photographic archive, is not to imagine that we can find missing pieces of the archive that would undo the ideological work it performs. Rather, as in dream analysis, the work lies in narrativizing the slips and accidents already present in the archive, to articulate those moments when photography's "tiny spark of contingency" reveals a possibility for seeing the archive differently.

More importantly, I want to suggest that foregrounding development as a mode of analytic inquiry not only allows for a more nuanced understanding of the workings of British colonialism, but also allows for a critique of the blind spots—the watchmen and censors—in modern political thought about photography and subjectivity: areas to which Benjamin has contributed so forcefully. The language of development united the discourses on childhood education, imperial management, and colonial photography in Britain at the beginning of the twentieth century: while education policy advocated that schools provide an environment for the development of children into imperial citizens, colonial bureaucrats worried about the unevenness of colonial development, all while photographers—literally and figuratively—developed images of the empire. But development, of course, is not a racially neutral term. It was mobilized in colonial paperwork to distinguish between the more settled (white) colonies and the more remote (nonwhite) periphery and was imbricated in pseudo-scientific theories of evolution that positioned white Europeans as more evolved than the peoples of the Global South.

While these discourses do not appear explicitly in Benjamin's writing about photography, the notion of development underpins many of his ideas about shifts in human perception and reappears in his writing about the optical unconscious, as I have shown. As he writes in "The Work of Art in the Age of Its Technological Reproducibility," "Just as the entire mode of existence of human collectives changes over long historical periods, so too does their mode of perception."[53] The development of technological reproducibility that Benjamin narrates in his writing about the optical unconscious, which he thought would free spectators from their auratic relationship to the work of art, assumes a universal spectator who is capable of developing, or evolving, in response to new technologies. This universal spectator, like the universal subject of much modern political philosophy, is of course implicitly white and implicitly holds the agency to participate in these transformations of perception through technology. Race and imperialism are blind spots—side perceptions, or latent images—in Benjamin's thinking about the modern spectatorial subject (as Mark Reinhardt so deftly demonstrates, in chapter 8, this volume).

Focusing on the presence and disappearance of the indentured laborer in histories of modernity helps illuminate this unconscious aspect of Benjamin's work and of histories of modernity more generally. As Lisa Lowe demonstrates, the figure of the transatlantic "coolie" has been absent from most Western histories of modernity, a critical repression that has worked to obscure "the global *intimacies* out of which emerged not only modern humanism but a modern racialized division of labour."[54] The indentured laborer was not hidden from public view, nor was she absent from government paperwork and photographic representation. While the British government ferried more than one million indentured laborers to more than a dozen colonies across the globe, producing a rich record of photographic postcards of "coolie belles" in their wake, politicians, government officials, and even anticolonial critics wrote about the freedoms afforded by imperial citizenship.[55] This is not merely a contradiction or oversight. The intimacies wrought by indentured labor made the idea of the free and agentic modern subject possible. As Lowe writes, "Colonial labour relations on the plantations in the Americas were the conditions of possibility for European philosophy to think the universality of human freedom, however much freedom for colonized peoples was precisely foreclosed within that philosophy."[56] Benjamin's theories of modernity, and his notion of the optical unconscious, emerge out of the same conditions that produced indentured labor. To make the indentured laborer central to our study of modernity is to foreground both the interconnectedness of empires around the world—an intimacy developed through a shared division of labor along racial lines and the forcible movement of bodies from Africa and Asia to the colonies—and the proximity of modern ideas of agency and citizenship to the conditions of exploitation and forced migration that sustain modern liberal capitalism.

"Framed with an Eye to Coolies": COVIC's Historical Negatives

I want to return to the figure of the indentured female laborer as she appears and disappears from the COVIC lectures, haunting the archive as a negative image of the imperial citizen. Women, in general, appear infrequently in the COVIC lectures, perhaps in part because the settings that Fisher was encouraged to tour—factories, naval yards, and schools—were spaces dominated by men. The relative absence of women might also be the result of Fisher's shyness around female subjects: when images of women do appear in the archive, they are often taken covertly, showing the backs of figures as they recede into the horizon (fig. 10.11) or at such great distances that it is almost impossible to make out the subject of the image. What is even more surprising is the way that motherhood is almost completely obscured in the COVIC lectures. Despite the project's stated aim of stirring the sympathies and sentiments of its child viewers, references to love and family are rare. When family units are depicted, they are firmly located in the white settler colonies of Canada and Australia, under the direction of a paternal figurehead. Representations of motherhood are always charged, but in the COVIC project they took on added significance. Educational projects such as COVIC were attempts at managing the sentiments of students and future citizens, lessons motivated by fantastical fears on the part of colonial officials that children of mixed parentage, or those who were raised by native caregivers, would always remain "natives in disguise, fictive Europeans . . . affectively bound to the sentiments and cultural affiliations of their native mothers."[57] Sympathies and attachments, when encouraged in the children who viewed the COVIC lectures, were directed toward one's fellow citizens, rather than toward the intimate space of the family or domestic sphere. To represent mothers, biological or surrogate, was to risk confusing the intended object of these identifications.

Images of motherhood seep into the final COVIC lectures nonetheless. In Fisher's photograph *Tibetan Women Doing Coolie Work* in a Darjeeling market (fig. 10.6), for instance, a group of adult women carrying baskets on their backs is meant to draw our gaze as the main subject of the image. But the COVIC lectures' school-aged audience must have surely also noticed the group of children, clustered together at the edge of the frame, who look back toward the women, and the scene at the center of the image: a young girl, carrying a basket like the "coolie" women, who reaches out to take a hand offered by an older woman, moving away from her peers and toward the group of laborers in the market. Though it is impossible to know if it is in fact her mother that reaches

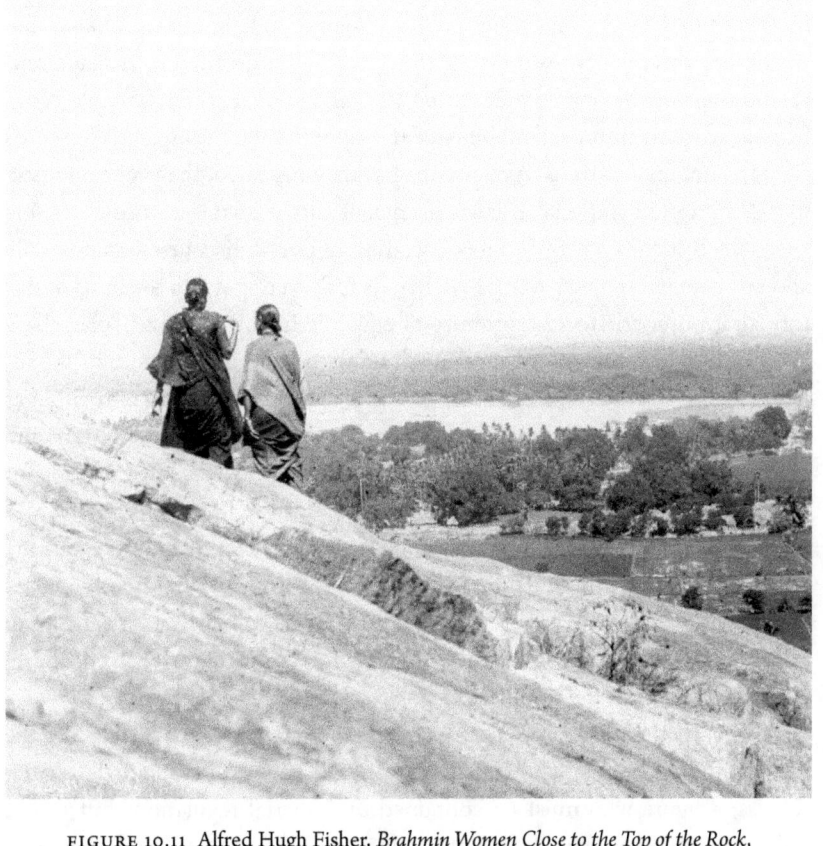

FIGURE 10.11 Alfred Hugh Fisher, *Brahmin Women Close to the Top of the Rock*,
Trichinopoly, looking northward toward Surangam. Women's dress red and
saffron, India, 1907, quarter plate. From Fisher photographs, RCS, Album II, no. 218.
Reproduced by the kind permission of the Syndics of Cambridge University Library.

for her hand, the photograph's staging and composition read as an allegory of the journey from childhood to the adulthood of indentured labor, one that is shepherded by a maternal figure. Unlike the British viewers of the COVIC lectures, who in this period were legislated to stay in school until the age of twelve, these Tibetan children are receiving a different kind of sentimental education, one about the limits and partialities of the rights promised by imperial citizenship.

As the COVIC lectures continued to circulate in classrooms and beyond, as late as 1945, the photographic meanings that viewers constructed from these images shifted, taking on greater political urgency in light of the colonies' demands for sovereignty. And just as the COVIC lectures tried to manage representations of the female indentured laborer, colonial critics were also confronted with the unrepresentability of this figure in their campaigns for equal rights as imperial citizens. As Banerjee has demonstrated, the vague and flexible definition of imperial citizenship meant that it guaranteed few tangible rights for British subjects, but its circulation in public discourse paradoxically allowed colonial subjects to make demands for sovereignty on the basis of this formal, if purely rhetorical, promise of equality. In India, in particular, these claims often drew on the psychic investments tied up in the figure of the indentured laborer, but this time cast him as a male worker, using him either as victim of the uneven application of the law across the empire's dominions and colonies, or as limit case for those colonial subjects who were not yet ready for self-determination. In a series of memoranda addressed to the Imperial Conference of 1911, held just one year after COVIC published its first lectures, the contradictory roles the indentured laborer was forced to play are obvious as groups from across the empire employ the rhetoric of imperial citizenship to point to the ways in which colonial policy was inconsistent with itself, and to make demands that the promises of imperial citizenship be upheld.

In one, written by representatives of the India Office and addressed to the Colonial Office, the "coolie" appears as a sign of insubordination and ungratefulness; a figure who must be contained by imperial regulations but whose inferior moral character should not reflect poorly on India's model imperial citizens. Appealing to the Colonial Office to change immigration laws that prevented the movement of Indian subjects through and across the empire, the letter is hyperbolic in its comparison of the indentured laborer with other, more loyal imperial citizens: "If the question were not so grave, it would be seen to be ludicrous that regulations framed with an eye to coolies should affect ruling princes who are in subordinate alliance with His Majesty . . . , members of the

Privy Council of the Empire, or gentlemen who have the honour to be His Majesty's own Aides-de-Camp."[58] In this case, the male indentured laborer is cast as a weak imperial citizen who is not capable of achieving full equality with ruling princes or gentlemen, because of his class status and the lowly work he performs for the empire. Such a reading of the indentured laborer makes him an "other" to the "other" of the Indian imperial citizen, nearly erasing him from political claims to self-sovereignty.

Similarly, Banerjee traces the way in which British suffragettes used the figure of the Indian woman laborer to counter critics' claims that they did not deserve the vote because they were unfit to govern the British Empire. In a strange logic of hierarchized affective labor, the suffragettes argued that Indian women "needed the kind of political and social work that only British women, in their capacity as imperial citizens, could undertake on their behalf."[59] In other words, by invoking the Indian woman as an inferior, weakened citizen, British suffragettes articulated their demands for sovereignty as necessary to — and not a corrective of — British colonialism.

By contrast, a letter from the Hindu Friend Society in Victoria, British Columbia, employs the indentured laborer as its central protagonist. Using the transnational logic of imperial citizenship against itself, the letter petitions the Colonial Office to ensure that the families of indentured laborers who have decided to settle in Canada at the end of their contract are "allowed to enter this country on the same terms as the Japanese, Chinese, or even Negroes."[60] The memo closes with a demand not only that the equality of the indentured laborer be recognized through written policies, but that it also be seen by distant imperial spectators: "Does imperialism mean Canada for the Empire, Australia for the Empire, India for the Empire, or can there be two definitions for subjects of one and the same Empire? If there is but one recognized definition under the flag over which the sun is supposed to never set, then it is for us to see that *no injustice shall minimise the rights or privileges of that citizenship, whether that holder is black or white*."[61] This emphasis on the visual dimension of imperial citizenship, either through the regulations invented "with an eye to coolies" or in the demand for rights to not just be legally encoded but also seen, underscores the political potential of photographic representations, both developed and undeveloped, in the colonial context.[62]

Whether the indentured laborer was invoked as the victim of the imperial system or its scapegoat, the qualities of masculinity, efficiency, and rationality were employed as the currency for these claims, inevitably rendering the female indentured laborer invisible. As Banerjee notes, "Indian claims of citizenship [in the colonies] were modeled on particular idioms of character, credit, and cleanliness in ways that rendered indentured labourers both indispensable to—and unrepresentable within—the rhetoric of imperial citizenship."[63] Even in anticolonial critiques, the negative of the female indentured laborer that lies dormant in the COVIC archive has yet to be fully developed. Here, too, she is repressed into the optical unconscious of the campaign for citizen rights. Though her absent presence suggests imperial citizens were sometimes—perhaps unconsciously—complicit in the uneven distribution of the promise of rights if it allowed them to make strategic political claims, the latent force of her image also suggests the colonial archive's representation of imperial citizenship is not yet finished, open to edits, enlargements, and recroppings by the very subjects it was designed to control.

Coda: An Unworlding Inquiry into Photographic Citizenship

Though this essay has been an experiment in thinking of the photographic archive as the latent negative, or optical unconscious, of the COVIC project, and of the critical potential of the researcher in developing its historical negatives, I do not mean to imply that the photographic archive is fully knowable. The optical unconscious, much like the psychic unconscious, can never be fully "developed." It will always remain outside of representation and conscious capture, registering instead through what Freud described as symptoms: slips of the tongue, mistaken memories, repetitive gestures, and dreams, which at first seem random or accidental but which, when put through analysis, are discovered to be spurred on by psychic processes occurring at the level of the unconscious. While these symptoms can be analyzed, allowing us to consider some of their possible meanings, we can never have complete access to the unconscious itself. The force of repressed thoughts and experiences mean they are not just unspeakable, but also unthinkable. So while I want to suggest the possibility that I, and others, can work as agents to "develop" the critique latent in the colonial photographic archive, I want to do so cautiously. There are undoubtedly limits—both practical and theoretical, both conscious and unconscious—to how far I can develop the shadow figures of imperial citizenship. There are surely some figures of un-belonging in the COVIC archive that cannot be fully seen (yet), and those who might pose too great a threat to my sense of self as a viewer to be consciously acknowledged.

To keep these limitations in mind, to conjure what might be unrepresentable in the archive, is to insist on the ongoing potency of this photographic archive: its use to future viewers who might be able to more fully develop its critical potential. It is also to refuse an imperializing gaze that assumes the world and its inhabitants can be visually captured and contained, to adopt, as the art historian Louis Kaplan has suggested, a mode of "unworldly thinking and unworlding inquiry [that] would expose photography and community to a reading that dares to lose track of the shape of the world."[64] To let the world of the COVIC photographs lose its coherent shape, to immerse oneself in its fluid meanings, its contradictory affects, and its glossy surfaces is a frightening prospect, in part because it threatens to unsettle the already shaky terrain of defining and picturing citizenship. For, despite its problematic origins in the colonial context and the residue of noncitizens it produces in its wake, citizenship continues to be a powerful and affective model for understanding our relationship to one another, as spectators and subjects who often see one another photographically, across great physical distances. But it is only by courting this incoherence, by allowing our gaze to wander, that we can begin to grapple with both the promises and failures of photographic citizenship.

Notes

1. James R. Ryan, *Picturing Empire: Photography and the Visualization of the British Empire* (Chicago: University of Chicago Press, 1998), 190.

2. Michael E. Sadler, "Misc. No. 150: Lantern Lectures on the British Empire, December 1902," CO 885/8/8, Colonial Office archives, National Archives, London, 1.

3. Sadler, "Misc. No. 150," 2, emphasis added.

4. COVIC's records show that the slides were often exhibited to parents as well as schoolchildren, and that several sets were purchased by the Department of the Interior in Canada and Australia, expanding the project's audience beyond the classroom. Copies of individual photographs were also printed and mailed to Fisher's subjects by the COVIC secretary whenever they were requested. See Miscellaneous Correspondence (April 4, 1905–November 16, 1907) Relating to Visual Instruction, Colonial Office archives, National Archives, London.

5. James R. Ryan, "Visualizing Imperial Geography: Halford Mackinder and the Colonial Office Visual Instruction Committee, 1902–11," *Ecumene* 1, no. 2 (1994): 169. Mackinder reflected on the COVIC project's aims and successes in a paper presented at the Board of Education's Imperial Education Conference in 1911, tellingly titled "The Teaching of Geography from an Imperial Point of View, and the Use Which Could and Should Be Made of Visual Instruction."

6. H. J. Mackinder, *Lands beyond the Channel: An Elementary Study in Geography* (London: George Philip & Son, 1908), vi.

7. John M. MacKenzie, *Propaganda and Empire: The Manipulation of British Public Opinion, 1880–1960* (Manchester: Manchester University Press, 1984), 165.

8. Gearóid Ó Tuathail, "Putting Mackinder in His Place: Material Transformations and Myth," *Political Geography* 11, no. 1 (January 1992): 100–118.

9. Kenneth Hayes, *Milk and Melancholy* (Toronto: Prefix, 2008), 115.

10. Walter Benjamin, "Little History of Photography," in *Selected Writings, vol. 2, part 2, 1931–1934*, trans. Rodney Livingstone et al., ed. Michael W. Jennings, Howard Eiland, and Gary Smith (Cambridge, MA: Belknap, 1999), 507–530, 510.

11. Benjamin, "Little History of Photography," 512.

12. Walter Benjamin, "The Work of Art in the Age of Mechanical Reproduction," in *Illuminations*, trans. Harry Zohn, ed. Hannah Arendt (New York: Schocken, 1969), 217–251, 236. Translations of this passage from "The Work of Art" vary widely. Here I draw on the translation provided by Harry Zohn (via Hannah Arendt) because of the ways it foregrounds both the materiality of photography (through the reference to the snapshot) and of psychoanalytic process (through subject formation). In the Belknap translation, the passage reads, "And just as enlargement not merely clarifies what we see indistinctly 'in any case,' but brings to light entirely new structures of matter, slow motion not only reveals familiar aspects of movements, but discloses quite unknown aspects within them." Walter Benjamin, "The Work of Art in the Age of Its Technological Reproducibility, Second Version" (1936), in *Selected Writings, vol. 3, 1935–1938*, trans. Edmund Jephcott, Howard Eiland, et al., ed. Howard Eiland and Michael W. Jennings (Cambridge, MA: Belknap, 2002), 101–133, 117.

13. Gaiutra Bahadur, *Coolie Woman: The Odyssey of Indenture* (London: Hurst, 2013), xx.

14. Ariella Azoulay, *Civil Imagination: A Political Ontology of Photography* (New York: Verso, 2012), 9.

15. Ann Laura Stoler, *Along the Archival Grain: Epistemic Anxieties and Colonial Common Sense* (Princeton, NJ: Princeton University Press, 2009), 21.

16. Stoler, *Along the Archival Grain*, 21.

17. Stoler, *Along the Archival Grain*, 22.

18. Stoler, *Along the Archival Grain*, 106.

19. Sarah Kofman, *Camera Obscura: Of Ideology*, trans. Will Straw (Ithaca, NY: Cornell University Press, 1998).

20. Factually, it is incorrect to say that certain negatives were "developed" into lantern slides, which is why I use quotation marks here. Technically speaking, the images would have only been reproduced as lantern slides, but I use the word "develop" to gesture to Ann Stoler's thinking from *Along the Archival Grain* in my analysis of these images.

Many of Fisher's photographs that were not selected to be reproduced as lantern slides circulated afterward, sent as prints to the subjects of the photographs, and reproduced as illustrations in classrooms around the empire. See William E. Noall to Education Officer, London City Council, February 12, 1912 (CO 885/22/3), Further Correspondence (1912–1913) Relating to Visual Instruction, Colonial Office archives, National Archives, London.

21. Indeed, it is one of the only times the photographic archive represents Fisher's role as author: the other appears in two self-portraits, taken in Canada while the artist was — rather heroically, the images imply — scaling a glacier to get a better perspective on a scene. See Fisher photographs, RCS, Album X, nos. 2212–2213: photographer unknown, *A.H.F. on the Illecilliwait [i.e. Illecillewaet] Glacier.* Standing on side of a crevasse: view looking up towards the Serac on the top, Alberta, 1908, quarter plates.

22. Fisher was supplied with one camera by the Colonial Office and provided with a budget of £100 to purchase "film, plates, printing papers and chemicals" to take with him on his journey. His journals record that he spent many evenings creating makeshift darkrooms in his hotel rooms, where he would develop the film that he shot each day, make contact prints of the images, and mail them back to the committee in London. See Halford Mackinder to Sir Charles Lucas, September 6, 1907, CO 885/17/8, Miscellaneous Correspondence Relating to Visual Instruction, Colonial Office archives, National Archives, London.

23. Stoler, *Along the Archival Grain*, 6.

24. For a nuanced discussion of how the idea of the model citizen, much like the imperial citizen, was used by Asian diasporic subjects to make claims to rights in the United States, see Thy Phu, *Picturing Model Citizens: Civility in Asian American Visual Culture* (Philadelphia: Temple University Press, 2012).

25. Here I draw on Ariella Azoulay's directive that viewers "watch," rather than "look at," photographs of citizens and noncitizens, attentive to how the subject's political status shifts from one image to the next. See Ariella Azoulay, *The Civil Contract of Photography* (New York: Zone, 2008), 14.

26. For a thoughtful analysis of how the glossy or shiny surface of the photograph both elicits contact from the viewer and insists on the limits of the surface or skin of both the image and the subject, see Elizabeth Abel, "Skin, Flesh, and the Affective Wrinkles of Civil Rights Photography," *Qui Parle: Critical Humanities and Social Sciences* 20, no. 2 (spring/summer 2012): 35–69.

27. Eve Sedgwick, *Touching Feeling: Affect, Pedagogy, Performativity* (Durham, NC: Duke University Press, 2003).

28. Halford Mackinder, "Memo for the Consideration of the Colonial Office Committee on Visual Instruction," November 28, 1906, Miscellaneous Correspondence (April 4, 1905–November 16, 1907) Relating to Visual Instruction, Colonial Office archives, National Archives, London.

29. See, for instance, "Miscellaneous No. 158: Minutes of Meeting by Subcommittee at Colonial Office, 29 July 1907," Miscellaneous Correspondence (April 4, 1905–November 16, 1907) Relating to Visual Instruction, Colonial Office archives, National Archives, London.

30. In 1909, after projecting a deficit of £360 in their annual budget for the coming year, the committee sent a telegram to Fisher, alerting him that the project had run out of money and advising him to cut the last leg of his trip short, skipping his visit to

Papua New Guinea, postponing his trip to Australia (but purchasing photographs of the colony if he could), and concentrating the remainder of his time on capturing Fiji and New Zealand ("Minutes from Meeting," December 3, 1909, CO 885/19/8, Miscellaneous 218: Further Correspondence Related to Visual Instruction [1908–1909], Colonial Office archives, National Archives, London). Fisher's final route saw him visit Ceylon, India, Burma, Aden, Somaliland, and Cyprus between October 1907 and June 1908; Canada's east coast, Newfoundland, Weihaiwei, Hong Kong, Borneo, and Singapore with a return trip through Canada to photograph winter scenes between July 1908 and May 1909; and Gibraltar, Malta, Australia, New Zealand, and Fiji between October 1909 and August 1910. This means that Africa is another latent and undeveloped subject within the COVIC archive.

31. MacKenzie, *Propaganda and Empire*, 165.

32. Ó Tuathail, "Putting Mackinder in His Place," 109.

33. H. J. Mackinder, "The Visual Instruction Committee of the Colonial Office," in *Eight Lectures on India* (London: Visual Instruction Committee/Waterlow and Sons, 1910), v.

34. The first citizenship laws in the British Empire were passed in 1947, in Canada. See Sukanya Banerjee, *Becoming Imperial Citizens: Indians in the Late-Victorian Empire* (Durham, NC: Duke University Press, 2010), 23.

35. Sukanya Banerjee notes that service and duty increasingly became the ethos of imperial citizenship as part of a growing civic sensibility in England and abroad. Banerjee, *Becoming Imperial Citizens*, 118.

36. A. J. Sargent, *South Africa: Seven Lectures* (London: George Philip and Son, 1914), 11.

37. Chris Aucamp, "Rhodes Fruit Farms: A Small Beginning in the Paarl Valley 1897–1910," *Contree* 31 (1992): 11–16.

38. Sargent, *South Africa*, 11.

39. A. J. Sargent, *The Sea Road to the East: Gibraltar to Wei-hai-wei* (London: George Philip and Son, 1912), 85–86.

40. Tina M. Campt, *Image Matters: Archive, Photography and the African Diaspora in Europe* (Durham, NC: Duke University Press, 2012), 59.

41. Sharon Sliwinski, "The Kodak on the Congo," in *Human Rights in Camera* (Chicago: University of Chicago Press, 2011), 57–81.

42. Sliwinski, "The Kodak on the Congo," 69.

43. Sliwinski, "The Kodak on the Congo," 58.

44. Lisa Lowe, "The Intimacy of Four Continents," in *Haunted by Empire: Geographies of Intimacy in North American History*, ed. Ann Laura Stoler (Durham, NC: Duke University Press, 2006), 191–212, 193. Susan Buck-Morss has also carefully illuminated the historical conjunction of post-Enlightenment liberal discourses of freedom and autonomy and the height of the slave trade in the Caribbean, arguing that Hegel's essay on the master-slave dialectic emerges as a direct response to the Haitian revolution

of 1803. See Susan Buck-Morss, "Hegel and Haiti," *Critical Inquiry* 26, no. 4 (summer 2000): 821–865.

45. Banerjee, *Becoming Imperial Citizens*, 77.

46. Banerjee, *Becoming Imperial Citizens*, 77. Though I do not have the time or space to address it here, the function of the contract in indentured labor raises provocative questions about how Azoulay's concept of the civil contract of photography operates in the context of British imperialism: a system that employed the same two central concepts — citizenship and the contract — to justify colonial consolidation.

47. Jeff Wall, "Photography and Liquid Intelligence" (1989), in *Jeff Wall: The Complete Edition*, ed. Thierry de Duve et al. (New York: Phaidon, 2010), 209–210.

48. Wall, "Photography and Liquid Intelligence," 209.

49. Stoler, *Along the Archival Grain*, 3.

50. Stoler often mixes her photographic metaphors, conflating the decisions made in the taking of photographs (such as adjusting the aperture, framing, or shutter speed) with steps in development and printing (cropping, enlarging, distortion).

51. Kofman, *Camera Obscura: Of Ideology*, 22.

52. Kofman, *Camera Obscura: Of Ideology*, 22.

53. Benjamin, "The Work of Art in the Age of Its Technological Reproducibility," 104.

54. Lowe, "The Intimacy of Four Continents," 192.

55. Bahadur, *Coolie Woman*, xx.

56. Lowe, "The Intimacy of Four Continents," 193.

57. Ann Laura Stoler, *Carnal Knowledge and Imperial Power: Race and the Intimate in Colonial Rule* (Berkeley: University of California Press, 2002), 114.

58. "'Memorandum by the India Office, to the Colonial Office: Position of British Indians in the Dominions, No. 1, June 1911,' *Imperial Conference, 1911. Papers Laid Before the Conference*. London: His Majesty's Stationery Office, 1911. In *Parliamentary Papers*, IOR V/4/Session 1911, Vol. 54," 272–279.

59. Banerjee, *Becoming Imperial Citizens*, 21.

60. "Memorandum from Hindu Friend Society of Victoria, British Columbia, to Colonial Office, April 28, 1911," in *Papers before the Conference*, 279–281, 279.

61. "Memorandum from Hindu Friend Society of Victoria," 281, emphasis in original.

62. Ariella Azoulay, "Photography: The Ontological Question," *Mafte'akh* 2 (2011): 65–80.

63. Banerjee, *Becoming Imperial Citizens*, 76.

64. Louis Kaplan, *American Exposures: Photography and Community in the Twentieth Century* (Minneapolis: University of Minnesota Press, 2005), 79.

———

CHAPTER ELEVEN

THE PURLOINED IMAGE

———

LAURA WEXLER

"Perhaps the mystery is a little too plain," said Dupin.
Edgar Allan Poe, "The Purloined Letter"

Renowned for his ideas about photography, and for the intimacy with which he imbued the images he shared, the Roland Barthes of *Camera Lucida* is also famous for an image he withheld: the Winter Garden Photograph of his mother as a five-year old child.[1] As we learn in *Mourning Diary*, posthumously published but composed as a precursor to *Camera Lucida*, this photograph is the animating principle of the entire volume.[2] It provides the occasion for the meditation in the first place, and the second half of the book revolves around its discovery. Yet the reader never sees it. The reason Barthes gives for withholding it from our view is that the Winter Garden Photograph could never mean the same thing to the reader as it does to the writer, for whom it is literally an emanation of his mother, an assertion that seems defensible and that has been widely accepted.

Yet it is at the same time unsatisfying because it is, at least in part, a sleight of hand. Like the stolen letter that is left in plain view in Poe's short story "The Purloined Letter," its supposed absence is a decoy, for that photograph is everywhere present in *Camera Lucida*. The entire text is fixated upon that image. It is invisible in a literal sense, while cunning substitutions for it are distributed throughout. By the very same stroke, what is most proximate to the mother in that image, the image of his mother's brother, Philippe Binger, is made to disappear.

To the list of Barthes's contributions to the theory of photography, therefore, I would add what the late Barthes's study of photography teaches us about the optical unconscious. Read in this light, *Camera Lucida* is an astounding exhumation of what we may call the Barthes effect, that is to say, the workings of the Troxler effect in the visual field, an illusion that disappears colonialism. In 1804, Swiss physician and philosopher Ignaz Paul Vital Troxler wrote an article on peripheral fading titled "On the Disappearance of Given Objects from Our Visual Field." In the article he noted that a certain given kind of stimulus that does not change over time will eventually be ignored by the neurons that receive the stimulus, a phenomenon that was eventually named the Troxler effect. If one keeps a fixation point steadily under one's gaze without moving it or oneself, eventually an unchanging stimulus close by it will fade and disappear from sight, due to neural adaption in the retina and in the brain. In the case of Barthes, it is his mother's brother Philippe, the Binger name, and the Binger history that he intends to fade from view.

In *Camera Lucida*, Barthes describes his discovery of the Winter Garden Photograph as follows:

> There I was, alone in the apartment where she had died, looking at these pictures of my mother, one by one, under the lamp, gradually moving back in time with her, looking for the truth of the face I had loved. And I found it.
>
> The photograph was very old. The corners were blunted from having been pasted into an album, the sepia print had faded, and the picture just managed to show two children standing together at the end of a little wooden bridge in a glassed-in conservatory, what was called a Winter Garden in those days. My mother was five at the time (1898), her brother seven. He was leaning against the bridge railing, along which he had extended one arm; she, shorter than he, was standing a little back, facing the camera; you could tell that the photographer had said, "Step forward a little so we can see you"; she was holding one finger in the other hand, as children often do, in an awkward gesture. The brother and sister, united, as I knew, by the discord of their parents, who were soon to divorce, had posed side by side, alone, under the palms of the Winter Garden (it was the house where my mother was born, in Chennevieres-sur-Marne).[3]

In *Mourning Diary*, the moment of his discovery is recorded thus:

JUNE 13, 1978

[M's fit of anger yesterday evening. R's complaints.]
  This morning, painfully returning to the photographs, overwhelmed by

one in which *maman*, a gentle, discreet little girl beside Philippe Binger (the Winter Garden of Chennevières, 1898).

I weep.

Not even the desire to commit suicide.[4]

Henceforth, all of the writing about this photograph that Barthes commits to paper will be about his relationship with the little girl in the picture: he himself will feel alive only in retrieving her expression amid the desolation of her loss. His "Ariadne" appears in this (re)appearance of his mother, at the center of the "Labyrinth": "Something like an essence of the Photograph floated in this particular picture. I therefore decided to 'derive' all Photography (its 'nature') from the only photography which assuredly existed for me, and to take it somehow as a guide for my last investigation."[5]

Certainly he is correct that for his readers, no such thing is incarnate in this picture. For us, as he says, "(I cannot reproduce the Winter Garden Photograph. It exists only for me. For you, it would be nothing but an indifferent picture, one of the thousand manifestations of the 'ordinary'; it cannot in any way constitute the visible object of a science; it cannot establish an objectivity, in the positive sense of the term; at most it would interest your *studium*: period, clothes, photogeny; but in it, for you, no wound.)."[6]

But indeed, Barthes has reproduced the photograph. Back in Paris, working on the observations that will eventually become *Mourning Diary*, as well as *Camera Lucida*, he is looking not at the original photograph, but its reproduction. He writes:

DECEMBER 29, 1978

Having received yesterday the photo I've had reproduced of *maman* as a little girl in the Winter Garden of Chennevières, I try to keep it in front of me, on my work table. But it's too much — intolerable — too painful. This image enters into conflict with all the ignoble little combats of my life. The image is really a measure, a judge (I understand now how a photo can be sanctified, how it can guide → it's not the *identity* that is recalled, it's, within that identity, a rare *expression*, a "virtue").[7]

Furthermore, he consented at least one other time to the Winter Garden Photograph being reproduced. In the portfolio of images included in *Mourning Diary*, Nathalie Léger, who "established and annotated" the text, has published a photograph of Barthes in his Paris study, taken by the famous portraitist François Lagarde. Under it is this caption: "Roland Barthes at his desk in

Paris, April 25, 1979. On the wall, three frames: the house in Urt (left, reproduced in this edition); a picture of camels (right); and the picture of Barthes's
mother at age five in the Winter Garden (center). This last photograph is discussed in *Camera Lucida* (© François Lagard)." Apparently, sometime between
the end of April and the end of December 1979, while he was composing *Camera Lucida*, Barthes moved the reproduction he had made of the Winter Garden
Photograph from his desk, as described above, to the wall, where it is shown in
the Lagarde photograph. There, it is still in his range of vision but is perhaps a
bit less painful to encounter than it was while it was sitting in front of him on
his work table. In the sightlines of this triangulation, the object remains visible
to the writer's peripheral vision while at the same time he is inscribing, or writing, its image language. It rests "at the edge of sight."[8] He does not have to confront it directly, but neither does he have to lose sight of it. These are the viewing relations produced by the camera lucida, the device after which Barthes
named his book:

> It is a mistake to associate Photography, by reason of its technical origins,
> with the notion of a dark passage (*camera obscura*). It is *camera lucida* that
> we should say (such was the name of that apparatus anterior to Photog-
> raphy, which permitted drawing an object through a prism, one eye on the
> model, the other on the paper); for, from the eye's viewpoint, "the essence
> of the image is to be altogether outside, without intimacy, and yet more
> inaccessible and mysterious than the thought of the innermost being;
> without signification, yet summoning up the depth of any possible mean-
> ing; unrevealed yet manifest, having that absence-as-presence which con-
> stitutes the lure and the fascination of the Sirens" (Blanchot).[9]

Notably, this is not a photographic relation. The camera obscura of photography's customary genealogy is a dark room, a black box, ultimately a coffin for
Barthes ("From now on I could do no more than await my total, undialectical
death. That is what I read in the Winter Garden Photograph"). Situating himself within the constellation of the camera lucida shifts his relation to the lost
object by keeping an image of it in plain view—where it can also be seen by
others. As Barthes explains in the same passage:

> I must therefore submit to this law: I cannot penetrate, cannot reach into
> the Photograph. I can only sweep it with my glance, like a smooth surface.
> The Photograph is *flat*, platitudinous in the true sense of the word, that is
> what I must acknowledge. . . .
> If the Photograph cannot be penetrated, it is because of its evidential

power. In the image, as Sartre says, the object yields itself wholly, and our vision of it is *certain*—contrary to the text or to other perceptions which give me the object in a vague, arguable manner, and therefore incite me to suspicions as to what I think I am seeing. This certitude is sovereign because I have the leisure to observe the photograph with intensity; but also, however long I extend this observation it teaches me nothing. It is precisely in this *arrest* of interpretation that the Photograph's certainty resides: I exhaust myself realizing that *this-has-been*; for anyone who holds a photograph in his hand, here is a fundamental belief, an "ur-doxa" nothing can undo, unless you prove to me that this image *is not* a photograph. But also, unfortunately, it is in proportion to its certainty that I can say nothing about this photograph.[10]

Apparently for this reason Barthes withholds the image. He does not want other people to have the leisure to stare at the photograph while learning nothing. It is intolerable for him to stare directly at it. "In proportion to its certainty," he has nothing to say. He prefers to encounter it in the periphery of lucida where an animating glance can sweep over it, rather than the fixed frontal stare of the camera, which arrests interpretation and exhausts him. But this, he cannot ensure that strangers will do. Rather they will stop and stare, turning the beloved mother/child into Medusa's ugly kin.

The publication of Lagarde's portrait of Barthes, in which the Winter Garden Photograph appears *mis-en-abyme* in a copy of its copy, settles certain controversies. For one thing, as Kathrin Yacavone reports in *Benjamin, Barthes and the Singularity of Photography*, disbelief has arisen that there ever was such a photograph in the first place. She observes, "Predominant views among Anglo-American Barthes scholars [presume] that the Winter Garden photograph of the mother is likely a fiction and/or that it simply does not matter whether it exists."[11] If, as Barthes asserts, the photograph exists solely for him and not for us, in the way he has defined, why must we believe that it even materially existed at all? It could have been a product of Barthes's own imagination. Diana Knight first published such an argument in *Barthes and Utopia*.[12] In "Touching Photographs," Barthes scholar Margaret Olin makes an even tighter case that Barthes has "mis-remembered" the existence of the image, mentally compositing it out of several others, including: *La souche*, a portrait of Kafka as a child, the Van Der Zee portrait of an African American family, a portrait of Aunt Alice, and a portrait of Barthes himself as a child.[13] "But most likely," she writes, "there was no Winter Garden Photograph to reproduce, or perhaps only the one of Franz Kafka at the age of six, described, with its palm trees and

Kafka's soulful eyes, as well as an oversized hat, by Walter Benjamin in his essay, 'A Short History of Photography.'"[14]

Lagarde's photograph, as published by Léger, puts an end to the literal aspects of this Anglo-American hermeneutic. This-has-been, the sensation of what Barthes calls the essence (*noeme*) of photography, is so. In a sense it reproduces the Winter Garden image as our own lost object, like the mother, now found, like Barthes's discovery of the meaning of her being in the image. Olin's analysis retains its resonance, if not its factual detail. Our perception of any object is clearly an amalgamation of the meaning of other images in a semiotic chain that establishes meaning through sameness and difference. As Olin traces this chain, the Winter Garden Photograph is a hybrid of superficially similar photographs of the stock that Barthes does reproduce — the childhood portrait of Franz Kafka that Benjamin discusses in "Little History of Photography," and a childhood portrait of Barthes himself, exhibiting the characteristic gesture with his hands that he observes his mother also does. Olin has the added credibility of having shown that Barthes misremembers other photographs, notably mistaking one necklace for another in his reading of a James Van Der Zee portrait. Olin's reading is another brilliant demonstration of the optical unconscious. Nonetheless, there was an actual Winter Garden Photograph about which Barthes wrote; it was not a misremembered other.

Interestingly, Yacavone further asserts that in "a French-speaking context, in contrast, the prevalent assumption is that the photograph did or does exist, and — rightly I would argue — that the photograph's actual existence gives genuine meaning to its absence from the text."[15] Why would its existence seem evident to the French and not to the Anglo-Americans? Kris Belden-Adams asks, in an excellent review of Yacavone, *"what is at stake here for French scholars but not for English-speaking ones?"* Belden-Adams believes that it matters for Yacavone because for her, "the 'existential confrontation between the self and the other' prompted by portrait photographs 'can only be triggered by an actual photograph, felt and perceived as external to oneself, as opposed to an only imaginary one which is by nature never outside of the self.'"[16] This is what Yacavone calls "the singularity" of the photographic image. But like Olin, Belden-Adams believes that its materiality actually does not matter for Barthes. For him, she writes, "the narration of the photograph by Barthes is still *about Barthes*, as Olin suggests."[17] Quoting Olin's deconstruction of Barthes's description of the Winter Garden Photograph, Belden-Adams reminds us that "in the *Winter Garden* Photograph, Roland Barthes discovered not his mother, or not only his mother, but also himself, himself as a child, specifically as a

child known from photographs. A chain of photographs leads Barthes, searching from image to image, to the unexpected discovery of himself as his own
mother, just as he had been his mother's mother while he cared for her during
her last illness."[18] And, continuing in Belden-Adams's words,

> Even without the photograph's material existence . . . Barthes's story for
> the *Winter Garden* image is really an encounter with the "otherness" of *his
> own* childhood, which Barthes knew partially from photographs and oral
> histories. Barthes's mother might not even have remembered herself at
> that age, either, and may have similarly constructed her notion of "child-
> hood" from images such as the *Winter Garden* photograph. What results,
> in part, from Barthes's discussion is a preponderance of the modern/post-
> modern phenomenon of *knowing oneself and others through photographs.*[19]

This would be fine except for one thing: Roland Barthes is French. If it is so,
as Yacavone asserts, that in France the French tend to believe that the Winter
Garden Photograph does exist, or did exist, that may be because it has, in fact,
a direct and public relation to the actual, lived history of the French people, and
not solely to the interior life of a single little boy and his mother. The imaginary
of the Winter Garden Photograph is abstract for Anglo-Americans but manifest for the French. Its optical relations are—as Barthes declares—that of the
camera lucida rather than the camera obscura. In this geometry the mother
remains visible in her relationship to the real world. She and her family are in
plain view. She is not an ideological inversion, as Sarah Kofman traced the significance of the metaphor of the camera obscura of Marx, in *Camera Obscura:
Of Ideology.* She is not an unconscious imprint to be developed later, as Kofman shows Freud's uses of the photographic metaphor to be. Nor is she necessarily Nietzsche's mechanism "for forgetting," another of the metaphors of
photography illuminated by Kofman.[20] She is, and she has been. What is it that
is almost too much in his face while looking at her, as Barthes himself admits
when it is "too painful" to keep the photograph on his desk? From what is he
so assiduously protecting himself as well as her?

I believe it is her connection to her father's name through the presence of
her brother, *le nom du pere*, in straightforward fact as well as Lacanian terms.
That name is Binger. It is Philippe Binger's patronym, and Henriette Barthes's
maiden name. It is also the name of the father under whose sign both brother
and sister are united for their photograph. "The brother and sister, united, as I
knew, by the discord of their parents, who were soon to divorce, had posed side
by side, alone, under the palms of the Winter Garden (it was the house where

my mother was born in Chennevières-sur-Marne)."[21] Moreover, the term that Yacavone in fact uses is not "French," but "French-speaking," which opens out to the image repertoire of the colonies as well as that of the motherland. Those with French as their mother tongue might well have already formed an image of the meaning of this name. French imperial history has inscribed an image of her into the text. In Europe, Africa, and the Caribbean, French-speaking children may well have learned about Binger at school. In this sense, the mother in the Winter Garden Photograph would be hypervisible and not absent at all. Sitting for a camera lucida portrait, rather than a photograph, she is exposed to other interpretations while her image is being made. His delineation also is visible, not hidden away in a dark box. Thus the knowledge that Barthes wants to produce and protect is not only, as he professes, his intimate knowledge of her character. It is also his intimate knowledge of her relation to a public family history, which he fears cannot sustain the truth of what he sees against the error of the public gaze.

Thus Barthes's reasoning for protecting the Winter Garden Photograph from his readers' view is not fully accounted for in the rationale that he is at such pains to keep before us. Of course we may believe him when he says he fears that others will impose meanings that are foreign to his knowledge of mother, and not see what was there. "In this little girl's image I saw the kindness which had formed her being immediately and forever, without her having inherited it from anyone; how could this kindness have proceeded from the imperfect parents who had loved her so badly—in short: from a family?"[22] Because we cannot know the pain of this meeting of kindness and imperfection as he does, the Winter Garden Photograph would be meaningless to us and so he hides it while writing incessantly about it, a game of *fort-da* quite up to the high symbolic standards of Freud. But is there a further plot to the purloined picture? In focusing so continually upon the absence of his mother and making it so present—is she there, is she not—we are adeptly deflected from the presence that can be seen. Focusing on his mother makes the brother disappear.

Louis-Gustave Binger, the father of both Henriette and Philippe, was a famous French military officer and explorer of Senegal, Sudan, and Cote d'Ivoire in West Africa, who claimed Cote d'Ivoire for France. Later, Captain Binger was the colonial governor of Cote d'Ivoire, and then Directeur des Affaires de l'Afrique. The town of Bingerville is named after him. He wrote a number of books and treatises on the enlightened imperialism of his day, including *Esclavage, islamisme, et christianisme* (Paris, 1891); *Du Niger au golfe de Guinée par le pays de Kong et le Mossi, 1887–1889* (2 volumes, Paris, 1892; fig. 11.1); "La Cote-

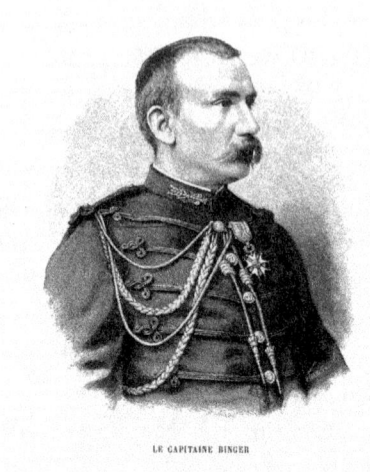

DU NIGER

AU

GOLFE DE GUINÉE

PAR LE PAYS DE KONG ET LE MOSSI

PAR

LE CAPITAINE BINGER

(1887–1889)

OUVRAGE CONTENANT

UNE CARTE D'ENSEMBLE, DE NOMBREUX CROQUIS DE DÉTAIL
ET CENT SOIXANTE-SEIZE GRAVURES SUR BOIS

D'APRÈS LES DESSINS DE RIOU

TOME PREMIER

PARIS

LIBRAIRIE HACHETTE ET C⁽ⁱᵉ⁾

79, BOULEVARD SAINT-GERMAIN, 79

1892

LE CAPITAINE BINGER

FIGURE 11.1 *Le Capitaine Binger,* from *Du Niger au golfe de Guinée par le pays de Kong et le Mossi,* 1887–1889. Portrait of Binger also reproduced in *Roland Barthes by Roland Barthes.*

d'Ivoire: Son passé, son present, son avenir" (*Marseille* 19 [1895]: 380–399); and *Le Peril de L'islam* (Paris, 1906). In these works he advocated pacification of local tribal wars and encouraged French alliances with Islamic rulers in order to make the country safe for economic development, meaning, of course, safe for French capitalist colonial enterprises to exploit the timber, minerals, and other natural resources of the region. Henri Brunschwig, one of his biographers, writes, "The native policy put forward by Binger reflects notions current at the time. In his work *Esclavage, islamisme, et christianisme* (1891) and later in *Le Peril de l'Islam* (1906), Binger, relying on Faidherbe's authority, rebuked those who believed that black Islam was hostile to Christianity; he stressed the humane nature of slavery as practiced in African societies and preached tolerance. There was nothing original in these views. They had all been put forward by Verdier in his *35 Annees de lutte aux colonies* (1896). Most contemporary explorers shared them."[23]

Binger had a long career, and became rich, famous, and honored in France, dying at age eighty, in 1936, when his grandson Roland Barthes was twenty. A

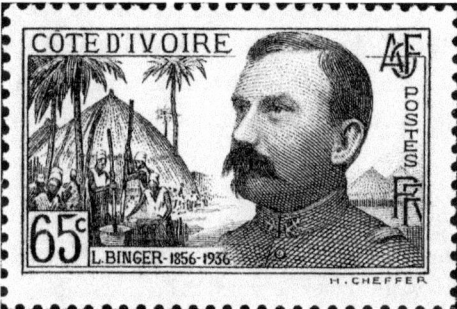

French postage stamp was issued in his honor (fig. 11.2). He cut a dashing figure in the mode of the time.

According to Barthes's timing of the Winter Garden Photograph, the first two of these books would have been published while Philippe and Henriette were very small children, and Binger was back for a time in France due to problems with his health as well as ambitions beyond Africa. In 1890 he had married Noemie Lepret, of a wealthy Paris family. Her father owned an iron foundry and she brought tens of thousands of francs to him as her dowry, with the expectation of inheriting hundreds of thousands more. This was the family situation into which Henriette and Philippe were born. It rapidly deteriorated. The last book, *Le Peril de L'islam*, was published soon after their parents divorced.

The image of Louis-Gustave Binger does not appear in *Camera Lucida*, but it does appear in *Roland Barthes by Roland Barthes*. Barthes captioned it, "In old age he grew bored. Always coming early to table (though the dinner hour was constantly moved up), he lived further and further ahead of time, more and more bored. He had no part in language."[24] One gets the sense of a petty, if brilliant, tyrant. This boredom Barthes claims for himself as well, while admitting to sharing nothing else belonging to his grandfather Binger. In *Roland Barthes by Roland Barthes* he writes, "As a child, I was often and intensely bored. This evidently began very early, it has continued my whole life, in gusts (increasingly rare, it is true, thanks to work and to friends), and it has always been noticeable to others. A panic boredom, to the point of distress: like the kind I feel in panel discussions, lectures, parties among strangers, group amusements: wherever boredom can be seen. Might boredom be my form of hysteria?"[25] But an image of Pietro Paolo Savorgnan di Brazza (1852–1905), a famous Italian explorer and adventurer who later became a Frenchman, does appear in *Camera Lucida*. It is a striking picture of a striking man. He was Barthes's grandfather's contemporary, and someone whom Binger greatly admired as a role model. Known for his reputedly easy manner and physical charm, the capital of the Republic of the Congo was named Brazzaville after him and the name was retained by the post-colonial rulers. Like Brazza, Binger too has a town named after him: Brazzaville in the Congo, Bingerville in Cote d'Ivoire. Musing on the *punctum* in that photograph, Barthes says,

> The *studium* is ultimately always coded, the *punctum* is not (I trust I am not using these words abusively). Nadar, in his time (1882), photographed Savorgnan de Brazza between two young blacks dressed as French sailors; one of the two boys, oddly, has rested his hand on Brazza's thigh; this incongruous gesture is bound to arrest my gaze, to constitute a *punctum*. And yet it is not one, for I immediately code the posture, whether I want to or not, as "aberrant" (for me, the *punctum* is the other boy's crossed arms).

Barthes cannot say what it is about that boy's crossed arms that affects him. His reaction reminds him of Mapplethorpe's photograph of Robert Wilson and Philip Glass. But "the effect is certain but unlocatable, it does not find its sign, its name; it is sharp and yet lands in a vague zone of myself; it is acute yet muffled, it cries out in silence. Odd contradiction: a floating flash."[26] That "acute yet muffled" cry of the punctum is also what defines the Winter Garden Photograph. Perhaps it comes too near to the "zone of myself."

The letter that drives the plot in Edgar Allan Poe's short story "The Purloined Letter" is several times hidden before the very noses of its protagonists. First, the queen who has received it hides it on a tabletop in her chambers, so that the king will not notice it in her hand. Next the minister, who steals it from the queen, hides it in a decorative basket hanging from the fireplace mantle in his apartments, because the police will not think to look for it in such a place. Finally, it is hidden from the sergeant for months in the library of the private detective because despite the fact that the private detective has already retrieved it from the minister's hiding place, his actions do not become intelligible to the sergeant until the private detective demands ransom money for it. In the first two instances, the letter is quite visible to those who know where to look or how to see; and in the third it is produced immediately when the sergeant finally becomes aware enough to demand it. In all cases, what to some is apparent to others is unseen. Seeing is possible. The king is simply unaware that there is anything to look at. The police are diverted because their strategy is wrong. They think the minister will secrete the letter when in fact he displays it openly. And the sergeant is fooled ideologically: his framing of the situation simply does not encapsulate the possibility that the private detective could be hiding the letter from him. He must be shocked into widening his grasp on the real.

Two justly famous disquisitions on this story, Jacques Lacan's "Seminar on the Purloined Letter," and Jacques Derrida's "The Purveyor of Truth," brilliantly display the productivity of Poe for French philosophy (as well as for internecine disagreements). Lacan's psychoanalytic approach traces the movement of the letter through a chain of repetitious situations (fort-da), to demonstrate that each subject position expresses a shifting relation to the signifier. One is or is not potentially a criminal with regard to whether or not one is caught with the letter in hand. For Derrida, nothing is conclusive but continual difference (deferral) in the language that describes the letter and its circulation, as Poe never reveals its contents to the reader. Rather, the reader's knowledge of the meaning of the letter must be made up fully of a series of intimations that lack confirmations. Both of these interpretations highlight French post-structuralism's fascination with the use of language as an explanatory template. Yet their focus is wholly on the behavior of linguistic signs. The fact that "The Purloined Letter" is a story about seeing, or not seeing, letters hardly rates analysis.[27]

This oversight is particularly curious given that both Lacan and Derrida were normally very attentive to the visual—Lacan in his diagrams and Derrida in his thematic preoccupations. But while they understood "The Purloined Letter" to be at the origin of the detective story as invented by Poe, they did not see that it also peopled a theater of the optical unconscious as newly described by Walter Benjamin. Dupin, the private detective who solves the mystery, does so while insisting on sitting in a small dark room, a literal camera obscura. Given that what is stolen is letters—language—it is significant that a proto-photographic practice enables recuperation. Yet neither Lacan nor Derrida, wrapped up in the meaning of words, is attentive to this fact. Among the French post-structuralists, it was Roland Barthes, their less disciplined colleague, who first put the photographic image in his books and at the center of his thoughts. Indeed, it is as if he was himself using Poe for that very purpose.

Normally, as Barthes writes, the photograph is deictic. It is a pointer, the jab of a finger, an exclamation, the upbeat of a baton. "A photograph cannot be transformed (spoken) philosophically, it is wholly ballasted by the contingency of which it is the weightless, transparent envelope. Show your photographs to someone—he will immediately show you his . . . 'Look,' 'See,' 'Here it is'; it points a finger at certain vis-à-vis, and cannot escape this pure deictic language. This is why, insofar as it is licit to speak of a photograph, it seemed to me just as improbable to speak of *the* Photograph."[28] If a photographic image is "glued," "like the condemned man and the corpse in certain tortures," this Winter Garden Photograph cannot be peeled from the deceased it designates.[29] The rest of us can follow the pointing finger, but unattached to the memory of her, for us the image will be without meaning and cannot be seen.

Barthes's initial observation agrees with that of his slightly younger and still living contemporary John Berger, also a magnificent theorist of photography. In "Understanding a Photograph," Berger observes:

> Photographs bear witness to a human choice being exercised in a given situation. A photograph is a result of the photographer's decision that it is worth recording that this particular event or this particular object has been seen. If everything there existed were continually being photographed, every photograph would become meaningless. A photograph celebrates neither the event itself nor the faculty of sight in itself. A photograph is already a message about the event it records. The urgency of this message is not entirely dependent on the urgency of the event but neither can it be entirely independent from it. At its simplest the message, decoded, means: *I have decided that seeing this is worth recording.*[30]

Photography, for Berger, is "the process of rendering observation self-conscious." A photograph qua photograph presents itself both as image and act; the image exists because someone thought it should. That is its raison d'être. The act of the image is to make the optical unconscious appear.

In the passage from the unconscious to the self-conscious of which Berger speaks, the photographer's decision to extract a photograph from time at a particular moment—to point to a cut—also includes reference to the moments and meanings that are not shown. Indeed, the photograph depends upon this linkage with the invisible for its legibility and for the self-knowledge it confers. By making a selection of part from whole, Berger's photographer exposes— precipitates—the ideological world as it is experienced by the photographer and can then be objectified and shared with the spectator. In showing a piece, the photographer opens access to the whole. The photograph is powerful

> when the chosen moment contains a quantum of truth which is generally applicable, which is as revealing about what is absent from the photograph as about what is present in it. The nature of this quantum of truth, and the ways in which it can be discerned, vary greatly. It may be found in an expression, an action, a juxtaposition, a visual ambiguity, a configuration. Nor can this truth ever be independent of the spectator.

For the man with a Polyfoto of his girl in his pocket, the quantum of truth in an "impersonal" photograph must still depend upon the general categories already in the spectator's mind.[31]

In this way, Berger demonstrates, all photography is ideological: "Every photograph is in fact a means of testing, confirming and constructing a total view of reality. Hence the crucial role of photography in ideological struggle. Hence the necessity of our understanding a weapon which we can use and which can be used against us."[32]

For Barthes as well, the meaning of any photograph is a small personal slice of a larger whole. "So I decided to take myself as mediator for all Photography. Starting from a few personal impulses, I would try to formulate the fundamental feature, the universal without which there would be no Photography."[33] In fact, Berger's scattered locations of connective meaning—"an expression, an action, a juxtaposition, a visual ambiguity, a configuration"—sound a good deal like the Barthean punctum, the detail that unpredictably though not randomly descends in an "odd contradiction: a floating flash." But why is it contradictory for a flash to float? The optical self-consciousness that Barthes will claim from these photographs differs greatly from the conclusions of Berger. Whereas for Berger, threading the part back into the whole is "a weapon which we can use," Barthes renounces this kind of action of the photograph in the world. For him, as he makes abundantly clear in his exegesis of the image of his mother, meaning is radically subjective. Others are forbidden to use his photograph of his mother to replace the missing part back into the whole. He desires the whole to remain eternally divided. He is worried when the flash draws near. His "process of rendering observation self-conscious" refers instead to an uneasy and uncomfortable hyperawareness of self, to which he refers incessantly and that is impossible for him to overcome.

And yet, in the very doubleness of that meaning of self-consciousness—an attribute, according to Freud, of all primal terms—another knowledge arises out of *Camera Lucida* and takes us mostly by surprise. Far from resisting the psychoanalytic unconscious, or shifting the burden of the real to the ideological, as does Berger, or limiting it to the purely neurotic, as Barthes himself often seems to prefer, Barthes's self-consciousness here also demonstrates a powerful grasp of another kind of "*significance*" that derives from his contemplation of historical images of that which decisively "has been." That this additional perspective in *Camera Lucida* has been essentially invisible for so long—despite his putting so many images of his struggle with it right before our eyes—attests to the power of the Barthes effect, inviting us to stare at the point of his mother while her brother, still named Binger, disappears. It is due, as well, to his readers' ambivalence vis-à-vis the optically visible but as yet unclaimed colonial past that silences, still, the evidence in front of our eyes.

Notes

1. Roland Barthes, *Camera Lucida: Reflections on Photography*, trans. Richard Howard (New York: Hill and Wang, 2010).

2. Roland Barthes, *Mourning Diary: October 26, 1977–September 15, 1979*, trans. Nathalie Léger and Richard Howard (New York: Hill and Wang, 2010).

3. Barthes, *Camera Lucida*, 67.

4. Barthes, *Mourning Diary*, 143.

5. Barthes, *Camera Lucida*, 73.

6. Barthes, *Camera Lucida*, 73.

7. Barthes, *Mourning Diary*, 220.

8. Shawn Michelle Smith, *At the Edge of Sight: Photography and the Unseen* (Durham, NC: Duke University Press, 2013).

9. Barthes, *Camera Lucida*, 106.

10. Barthes, *Camera Lucida*, 106–107.

11. Kathrin Yacavone, *Benjamin, Barthes and the Singularity of Photography* (New York: Continuum, 2012), 164.

12. Diana Knight, *Barthes and Utopia: Space, Travel, Writing* (Oxford: Clarendon, 1997).

13. Margaret Olin, "Touching Photographs: Roland Barthes's 'Mistaken' Identification," *Representations* 80, no. 1 (fall 2002): 99–118.

14. Olin, "Touching Photographs," 108.

15. Yacavone, *Benjamin, Barthes and the Singularity of Photography*, 164.

16. Kris Belden-Adams, review of Kathrin Yacavone, *Benjamin, Barthes and the Singularity of Photography*, H-France Review 14, no. 105 (July 2014): 1–5, 3. Emphasis in original.

17. Belden-Adams, review, 4.

18. Belden-Adams, review, 4.

19. Belden-Adams, review, 4. Emphasis in original.

20. Sarah Kofman, *Camera Obscura: Of Ideology* (1973), trans. Will Straw (Ithaca, NY: Cornell University Press, 1999).

21. Barthes, *Camera Lucida*, 69.

22. Barthes, *Camera Lucida*, 69.

23. Henri Brunschwig, "Louis-Gustave Binger (1856–1936)," in *African Proconsuls: European Governors in Africa*, ed. L. H. Gann and Peter Duignan (New York: Free Press, 1978), http://www.webafriqa.net/library/african_proconsuls/binger.html.

24. Roland Barthes, *Roland Barthes by Roland Barthes* (1975), trans. Richard Howard (Berkeley: University of California Press, 1994), n.p.

25. Barthes, *Roland Barthes by Roland Barthes.*

26. Barthes, *Camera Lucida*, 51–53.

27. Jacques Lacan, "Seminar on 'The Purloined Letter,'" trans. Jeffrey Mehlman, *Yale French Studies* 48 (1972): 39–72; Jacques Derrida, "The Purveyor of Truth," trans. Willis Domingo, James Hulbert, Moshe Ron, and M.-R. L., *Yale French Studies* 52 (1975): 31–113.

28. Barthes, *Camera Lucida*, 5.

29. Barthes, *Camera Lucida*, 6.

30. John Berger, "Understanding a Photograph," in *Understanding a Photograph*, ed. and intro. Geoff Dyer (New York: Aperture, 2013).

31. Berger, "Understanding a Photograph."

32. Berger, "Understanding a Photograph."

33. Barthes, *Camera Lucida*, 8–9.

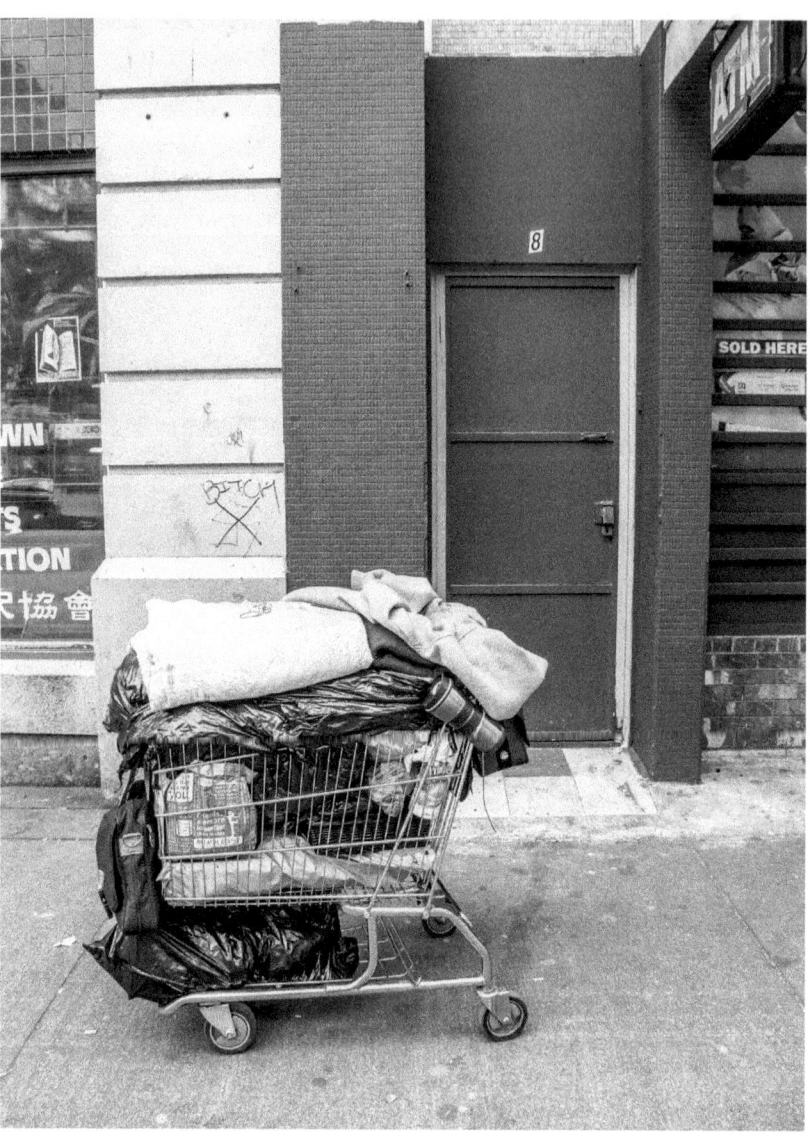

——

CHAPTER TWELVE

THE VANCOUVER CARTS

A Brief Mémoire

——

KELLY WOOD

I began to photograph this series of (repurposed) shopping carts in Vancouver in 2004–2005 (see plates 12 to 16). Vancouver was my home then, and I had been living there since 1981. I had long witnessed the rising flow of transpacific capital and investment that turned Vancouver into a global real estate market beyond the reach of most locals—certainly beyond the reach of most of the artists and writers I knew. By the time the millennium came around, it was getting difficult to be an emerging artist in a city that had been steadily gentrifying since Expo '86. By 2005, I was in a bad way, which wasn't unusual as far as artists' lives go. I began to see that I might not be able to ride out changes that would continue to unfold exponentially, as I had done in the past. It was then that I got a job offer from Western University. It was an offer, it has to be said, too good to refuse. And so I opted for a change in location, and life, in order to survive as an artist and hauled my business east. Leaving behind Vancouver, and those photographs, was a personal tragedy. It was, and will remain, more of a crisis than I can describe here. Though it might appear that because I lost my home, homelessness became my cause, in fact these images foretold the future, and preceded my exile by at least a year. And that fact now remains the strangest thing about those difficult days. It seems appropriate, given this book's title, to say, in retrospect, that an optical unconscious structured this work from within, and from without, at once. For in them, I seem to have produced my exile as an art premonition that dreamed itself into being. Thus, I was never more invested in these photos than when my exile began and when my ability to produce the imagery was not taken away, but certainly diminished. I had to content myself with summer returns to continue to photograph the series, and so I took up the work again in fits and starts over the next several years. The project became attenuated, but this allowed a long-term study of the visible changes that came with the era of "people without homes" and "homes without people" that was so much a feature of Vancouver's urban evolution at the fin de siècle. (I was motivated to photograph this cart culture as much as other photographers were motivated to photograph oil refineries in the era of oil.)

Documenting at least some of this cart culture over a long period of time revealed an interesting feature of the carts themselves. Early on in the project, I noticed that many of the carts I was seeing were filled with personal possessions—blankets, tarps, coffee mugs, clothes, Tupperware . . . even little items of personal pleasure and totems like plush toys. Later images, however, show more of a cart kit; the poles, diggers, boxes, and bags needed for scavenging, and not a home wagon per se. The personal items were not as present. Had the homeless who had constructed the earlier carts been flushed out, slowly but assuredly, replaced by individual gleaners supplementing their income in the invisible economy with daily bottle collecting and street vending of "last ditch use before the landfill" items? On occasion I encountered some of the cart owners on my photo walks, but at least half the time I only saw the cart. In fact, it was an isolated, abandoned cart full of stuff that first caught my attention and began the whole series. It surprised me that it was just there, for hours, on its own. And suddenly I began finding them stashed here and there, half-hidden, or half-protected in the open street where people know what's what. These carts were territories within worlds—wheels within wheels—and I had to know and remain aware of that obscurity.

I walked the city nearly every day on my summer photo shoots. Vancouver has the kind of climate that facilitates photography. It is no coincidence, I think, that photography developed in Vancouver. The weather is mild and rarely drops below freezing, and so, unlike in other parts of Canada, snow is not an aesthetic (or allegorical) problem at certain times of the year. The sky is generally gray and overcast—perfect for diffuse and shadowless light—you can photograph in similar conditions almost all year round. The nearly nine-month rainy season only helps to saturate the city with gloss and depth. Though no discussion of the so-called Vancouver School has ever made this point, I want to stress how wonderful it is to photograph in this city. It has also been said that Vancouver possesses a generic, "nowhere yet anywhere" quality that epitomizes an internationalism useful for the related art of the film industry, but this is something I never experienced in practice. Vancouver is distinctive and idiosyncratic if you allow it to be. It has a light and surface quality that is inherently translucent and brooding. The dimness of a West Coast rain forest is like nothing else.

The same mildness that makes the city a photographer's paradise also allows for the cart culture I came to document. These singularities of climate and gentrification are emphatically linked. No other Canadian city has such a developed cart (some would say homeless) culture. Colder climates dissuade the street spillage of what Agamben has called "bare life," but there in Vancouver it is out in the open — citizenship rights and civic space become two opposing dialogues about common ground but without a certain legal common ground. I was intensely focused on this as a political issue, visual conundrum, and challenge, because politics, so fugitive and invisible, have to be seen to be believed. The combination of force and consent that makes homeless people visible and at the same time denies their existence is both hard to prove and hard to picture.

In the summer of 2011, there occurred what was categorized in the press as "a micro-house demolition." Photographic evidence emerged of members of the City Engineering Department throwing a homeless cart into a dumpster.[1] This was just one example of many such incidents that had peaked perhaps in 2009 in the lead-up to the Winter Olympics in 2010, and launched a political controversy about ownership and property. Vancouver prohibits the demolition of a homeless person's property under the Abandoned Property Policy, but police officers and others regularly violate the rule.[2] At the same time, Vancouver's Revitalization Strategy (primarily for the Downtown East Side where homelessness is rampant) saw the criminalization of poverty and sweeping evictions from single-room-occupancy apartments and hotels. These actions cannot be considered in isolation. Interesting dilemmas emerge. Can you only have property if you already have property (that is, a home)? There was some public sympathy for those who sought property rights for belongings left on the street, especially if the street was, in fact, their home. Homelessness became a focal point in a city that was rapidly gentrifying, and the carts of the homeless became lightning rods for all that had gone wrong in certain parts of town. This is why I photographed them; they were profoundly emblematic.

I never moved or arranged anyone's cart or property — that is the ethic that structured my work and photographs. I photographed the carts where I found them, in situ. Most of the people I encountered while doing so were not homeless, as one might expect. Rather, most were supplementing their social assistance income, or making a go of it on their own in the underground economy.

These people worked. A fellow told me he could make about $40 a day for four hours work. He worked when he wanted, how he wanted, and he did it by choice. I paused. I had to think about that. After taxes and such, that was almost the return I was making, and by contrast I felt trapped by an indefinable system.

The carts, then, are symbolic stand-ins for some of these politics. They are icons of labor, economies, mobility, commodity relations, citizenship, property value, ethics, and, yes, homelessness. They stand as conduits of property, even as their impermanence and mobility suggest that they aren't property—this is one of the ways their value is occluded in the realpolitik of the civic space. They are impossible figurations—the homes of the homeless. To see and to photograph these manifestations is to give some permanence to their being in the world and to begin to address the unconscious hold they have on the forces of gentrification—the ways in which their very presence signals the inequities of the gentrification deal. The carts are not merely emblems of an underground economy—a subconscious figuration of some lack of inclusivity—they are a moving force and symptom of the organic entanglement of city life.

Artists, likewise, participate in this entanglement, as a force and a symptom of underground, low-end economic pursuits and trouble. Often, in my Vancouver, we occupied the same spaces as those without permanent addresses—if I can put it this way. The single room occupancy hotels and the galleries were often in the same older neighborhoods. Like every other major city, Vancouver had some shabby, neglected zones that made space for low-overhead art activities. For us, though, these places were glamorous and dripping with a distorted and fraught history—the last remnant of a city fabric from a time before globalization—and I . . . we artists . . . reveled in them. You see, we were the avant-garde of art there; but also the avant-garde of gentrification. We were the problem and we had no solutions to offer ourselves, or anyone else, despite what creative culture boosters may say.

In addressing the theme of the optical unconscious in these photographs, I want to do much more than suggest these carts are overlooked in society. These photographs, whether as a type of concerned documentary or as works of art in themselves, have thus far been dismissed in the gallery systems and public venues. I met with one Vancouver curator who plainly said that they could not be shown in that gallery. While these phenomena can occur right outside the doors of Vancouver's artistic venues, it seems the thought of giving conscious acknowledgment to the phenomena of gentrification, in which art galleries play a major role, is too much. It suggests that there is a deeply buried unconscious in the galleries and artists' communities themselves that cannot acknowledge the displacement role that art plays in the gentrification cycle. It is no coincidence, either, that the biggest art patrons in Vancouver are real estate developers — almost every gallery and institution now carries a developer's name. Thus, to me, these links were ever more the reason to make this work during this time. They are evidence of a very conscious and purposeful effort to challenge and record — through a motif — an era when homes became the means by which to disenfranchise ordinary people of their citizenship. The optical unconscious is, in these images, made explicit in ways that make for uncomfortable viewing. I have been pleased to discover that photography still has this force; yet equally disappointed to also discover that there are some things in the world that are yet too socially and politically loaded to record and optically analyze — to really commit to seeing.

Notes

1. Tristan Markle, "Shopping-Cart Demolitions," *Mainlander*, July 3, 2011.
2. Maria Wallstam, "VPD Continues Illegal Shopping-Cart Demolitions in Downtown Eastside," *Mainlander*, September 7, 2012.

———

CHAPTER THIRTEEN

VIETNAMESE PHOTOGRAPHY AND THE LOOK OF REVOLUTION

———

THY PHU

In 1972, Đoàn Công Tính, a photographer for the communist Vietnam News Agency (VNA), gathered his modest supplies and headed toward the citadel in Quảng Trị, the northernmost city in what was then South Vietnam. He had heard that a great battle would take place there, between the National Liberation Front and its opponents, the U.S.-backed Army of the Republic of Vietnam.[1] He was keen to capture the action, but getting to the citadel was arduous and involved hitching a ride with a fisherman for part of the way and swimming the remaining distance, all the while keeping lens, film, and camera body dry. Once inside, he had to contend with the limitations of poor equipment. Đoàn's photographs offer a glimpse of imperfection, the result of shaky hands and blurry eyes, of equipment that reveals not the extension of vision—the camera's reputed technical advantage—but instead the obscuring of vision (fig. 13.1). When it comes to representing revolution, photography's view may be flawed rather than flawless. What accounts for the quality of this way of looking, and how might it enrich our understanding of the relationship between photography and revolution?

Writers reflecting on the significance of photography in the nineteenth century were preoccupied with a less overtly political matter: the revolutionary nature of the camera. Many focused on explaining how photography might influence the arts; some pondered how it might alter faculties of perception; few considered how it might transform the structure of social relations. It was not until the 1930s, during the Nazi Party's tumultuous rise to power, that Walter Benjamin helped bring into focus a more urgent issue: photography's relation to revolution. While seemingly slight, this shift in approach was crucial, for it emphasized photography's transformative political potential.

Nowhere are the political stakes of photography more apparent than in

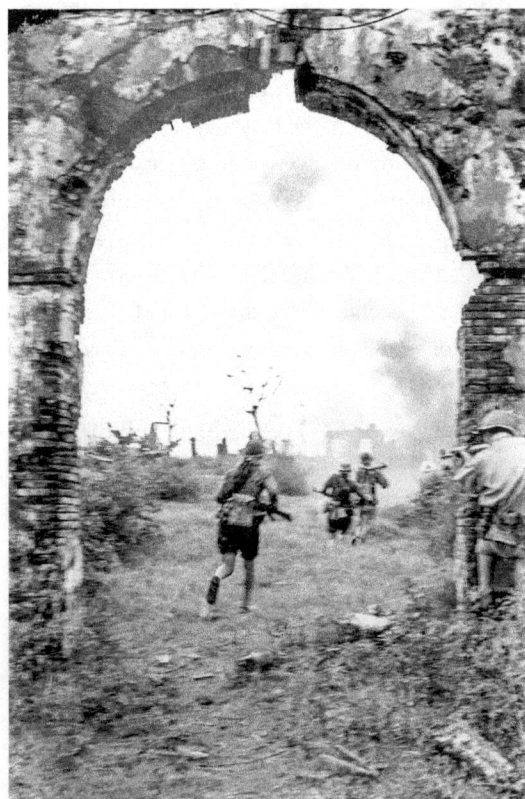

FIGURE 13.1

Đoàn Công Tính,
Untitled.

Benjamin's landmark essay, "The Work of Art in the Age of Its Technological Reproducibility." While characteristically unclear about the precise nature of this political transformation, Benjamin introduced interesting possibilities through his concept of an "optical unconscious," first outlined in his earlier "Little History of Photography" and elaborated in "The Work of Art" essay.[2] According to Benjamin, an optical unconscious carries not only a psychoanalytic resonance (the term establishes an analogy between the operation of the camera and that of psychic drives) but also a technical one (it underscores the camera's capacity for visual enhancement). In their introduction to this volume, Shawn Michelle Smith and Sharon Sliwinski extend the insights of Christopher Bollas to highlight the signal importance of the "unthought known," that which the camera sees but which the mind has yet to grasp. In so doing, they align the political stakes of Benjamin's argument with the psychic registers of the optical unconscious. However, Benjamin also tethered his political stakes to its technical dimensions.

Like his contemporaries, Benjamin marveled at the image worlds revealed by the camera. For Benjamin, photography could be drawn on as a potent political weapon for revolutionary struggle against fascism precisely because of the camera's wondrous capacity to capture images that "escape natural vision." He insisted that the camera conferred agency to the masses because its capacity to reproduce images diminished the auratic power of an original image. Accordingly, Benjamin deployed military tropes to stress photography's forcefulness; in the skilled, unerring hands of Dadaists, still photos were "an instrument of ballistics," which "hit the spectator like a bullet," and motion pictures "burst this prison-world [of familiar objects] by the dynamite of a tenth of a second." Viewed thus, the concept of an unconscious optics offers a visual parallel to the literary theory of the political unconscious that Marxist scholar Fredric Jameson would develop many decades after Benjamin's untimely death in 1941.[3] Photography activates its political potential when it enables the masses to penetrate and thereby battle ideology with unprecedented acuity and accelerated speed. Benjamin's essay introduces unspoken assumptions about technical capacity, which would prove pivotal to, even as it remained unremarked in, subsequent Marxist debates on the relationship between photography and revolution.

Although limited space prevents me from summarizing familiar chapters in the history of photography, a brief outline reveals a telling pattern in debates. From the mid-twentieth century to the present, stark lines of allegiance emerge in response, whether directly or indirectly, to the Cold War. Positioned in one camp, we find modernists such as John Szarkowski and Edward Steichen, who disseminated their interest in aesthetics in reviews, books, and exhibitions. Notably, Steichen's 1955 *Family of Man* circulated within and contributed its immensely popular vision of humanism to the cultural politics of the Cold War.[4]

While the Cold War context broadly shaped photo-criticism, it was specifically the war in Vietnam — an event remarkable for receiving unprecedented visual coverage — that intensified viewers' suspicions of photography.[5] Indeed, this coverage of Vietnam prompted a generation of theorists to reconsider their views on photography and revolution, even moving some to advocate against looking at photography altogether. For example, in her 1968 *Trip to Hanoi*, Susan Sontag reflects on the contradiction between the Vietnam she sees and the version represented in press photos that circulated widely in the United States and in Europe.[6] Only through direct observation and experience of the nation and its people could she correct the Vietnam in her mind. Although she occasionally alludes to Vietnamese photographs of the war in her journals, curiously, neither her notes nor the two published editions of her book contain any photographs. Sontag's trip to Hanoi drove her to look beyond photographs, to reject them as decadent phantasms and falsities, conduits to, rather than means of exposing, capitalism's dreamworlds. So marked is Sontag's rejection of photography, Franny Nudelman argues, that this trip influenced the writer's invective against the camera in *On Photography*, a book that, significantly, was published several years after a second visit to Hanoi.[7] In 1967, Guy Debord summed up a general judgment of visual repudiation when he inveighed against the "society of the spectacle" and its reduction of images to commodities.[8] Of the pronounced disdain that is the prevailing mood of twentieth- and even twenty-first-century photography criticism, Susie Linfield remarks, "The postmodern and poststructuralist children of Sontag, Berger, and Barthes transformed their predecessors' skepticism about the photograph into outright venom."[9]

Yet despite evincing a suspicion of images so acute as to amount to a kind of Marxist iconophobia, these critics stopped short of developing a sustained socialist analysis of photography. Instead of reflecting on unconscious optics — the dimensions of the camera that were, for Benjamin, amenable to revolution — these critics focused on exposing photography's false consciousness: although it purports to tell a universal truth, the camera lies. Scholars struggled with increasingly capitalist image worlds at the same time as they grappled with the long shadow of Benjamin's Marxist legacy. Yet many luminaries — Roland Barthes, Susan Sontag, Allan Sekula, John Tagg, to name just a few — found that, rather than unveiling ideology, photography instead masked it.[10]

By grouping luminaries in the development of twentieth-century photography criticism in this way, my intent is neither to simplify nor unify complex and often contentious arguments.[11] Rather, I bring them together to pause on a revealing pattern: some of the most outspoken critics did not just distrust the camera, but they also expressed their distrust in the course of advancing a Marxist analysis of photography. Moreover, these critics continued to affirm the discourse of enablement; for them, the camera could see all too well rather than not enough. None challenged the discourse of enablement; instead they increasingly doubted the political value of the camera's technical advantage of visual enhancement. Rather than quickening revolutionary hope, the camera's superhuman capacity to see threatened to surveil, control, and dehumanize.

It is within this climate of a reactive Marxist iconophobia that I turn to the work of Vietnamese socialist photographers to explore an emerging practice of revolutionary looking. I turn here because, as numerous media theorists have observed, the war in Vietnam transformed the visual representation of conflict, so that widely circulated spectacles of violence brought scenes of far-away suffering home to distant spectators in the United States.[12] Moreover, the irony, that images from the war in Vietnam moved American and French visual theorists to reject photography, is compounded by the fact that most of them looked at images taken by the Western press but few took account of images by Vietnamese photographers.[13] The Marxists' resounding rejection of photography is at odds with the practice of socialist photographers in Vietnam: Sontag may have turned away from photographs after her trip to Hanoi as a gesture of political solidarity with the left's antiwar stance, but Vietnamese patriots turned to the camera for political purposes. By exploring the practice of socialist photographers, we are better able to assess the revolutionary promise of the optical unconscious.

Focusing on select works by Vietnamese socialist photographers, this chapter examines revolutionary forms of looking. Without claiming that socialist photographers responded to or were even aware of Benjamin's theories, I consider how their approaches, in effect, affirm the discourse of enablement that lies at the core of the concept of unconscious optics, while at intriguing times also complicating this discourse. A close look at the work of patriotic Vietnamese photographers shows how the camera could be enlisted for the purposes of promoting revolution. By examining oral histories and archival documents, I provide a critical description of revolutionary looking and consider the ways that it entails overcoming conditions of deprivation and violence—the result of asymmetrical warfare—in order to produce photographs; exhibiting images where least expected; and disarming opposing views by unsettling entrenched assumptions about what revolutionary photography is and the ideologies that it by turns obscures and reveals.

The work of socialist photographers also provides glimpses of the limits of vision. In contrast to their counterparts in the Western press who benefited from access to ample technical and financial resources, socialist photographers made do with what they had, and strove to bring to view that which often remains outside the scope of vision, whether due to physical constraints, such as physiological impairment, or material constraints, such as defective or limited supplies. Whether blurry, scratched, torn, or patched together, the perceptible imperfections that characterize such photographs are signatures of a practice of revolutionary looking. This practice even attempts to account for an issue that Marxist discussions seldom broach, namely disability. In select works by Vietnamese photographers, the issue of disability surfaces literally and symbolically, that is, through the figure of injured bodies and the flawed quality of images. Although I would not go so far as to suggest that these representations amount to a fully developed theory of disability, they are important to consider for their potential, albeit ultimately unrealized, to unsettle the dominant discourse of enablement.

Yet, when we consider recent postwar displays of these photographs, an intriguing pattern of reversal reveals itself: socialist images tend to be scrubbed so clean as to remove traces of the material conditions of their making. When revised versions of revolutionary events are considered alongside older prints, the pairings do not necessarily constitute a dialectical image, that process of critical re-visioning which, according to Shawn Michelle Smith and Sharon Sliwinski, is necessary for perceptual analysis of contingency. Indeed, as Andrés Mario Zervigón reminds us in chapter 1, contingency is the crucial political foundation of the optical unconscious. By altering the look of revolution—by making it sharper, brighter, better—these recent displays of socialist photographs offer a corrective re-visioning that obviates contingency, instead of the critical re-visioning called for by Smith and Sliwinski in their discussion of the dialectical image.

Contemporary official histories of the American war in Vietnam deploy socialist photographs to bolster state-sanctioned metanarratives of national reunification and the policy of economic renovation, launched in 1986, known as Đổi Mới. The state's projection of a postwar vision of seamless renewal glosses over the imperfections that are the hallmarks of revolutionary Vietnamese photography. In so doing, the Đổi Mới gaze entrenches the familiar discourse of enablement, while disavowing the flawed qualities that had brought a complex picture of socialism into focus in the first place. Efforts to retouch the visual records mark a conceptual shift in relation to the optical unconscious; instead of constituting a dialectical image, the retouched re-presentations transform the political stakes of socialist photography.

Imperfect Conditions, Revolutionary Visions

Mai Nam's living room is typical of homes in Vietnam because it features an ancestral shrine, where he and his wife pour tea, offer sweets, and burn incense as a filial rite, which was once shunned by the state as bourgeois tradition, but is now embraced as part of the new Vietnam.[14] What sets the room apart is its brightest corner, where the ceiling extends to the rooftop instead of dropping as it does in the receiving area. Mounted on the highest wall of this corner is a shrine that honors photography and not the customary ancestors. At the top of weathered plaster spotted with mildew ascends Mai Nam's portrait (fig. 13.2),

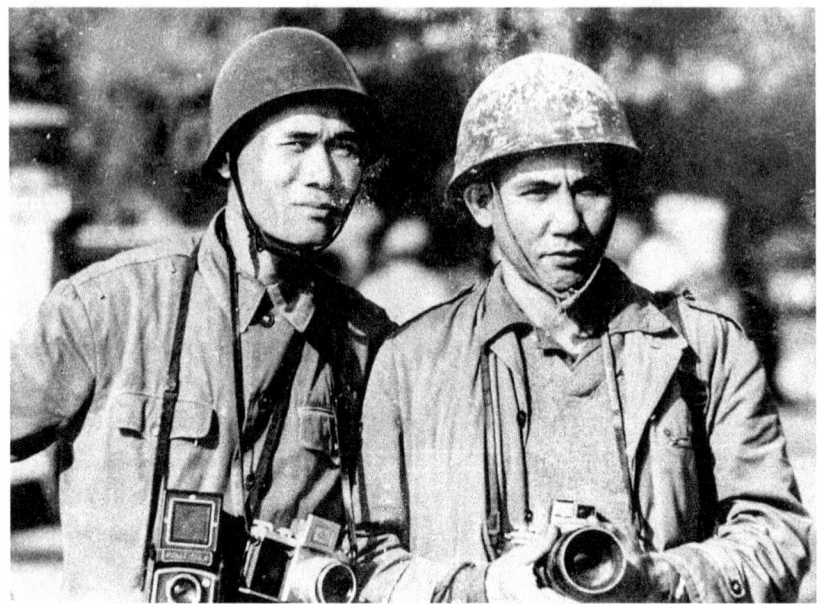

FIGURE 13.2 Châu Đoàn, Portrait of Mai Nam (pictured on right).

taken in the 1960s when he was a handsome photographer for the Young Pio
neers, who documented the efforts of the communist youth organization to
build roads and cultivate crops in northern Vietnam: in it he poses with another
photographer who, like him, wears a uniform and helmet. Squinting into the
camera, he poses with his own camera dangling, like a prized jewel, from a strap
around his neck.

When I ask whether the artifacts hanging on the wall along with this picture
are from the war, Mai Nam's face brightens when he sees that I am pointing to
his greatest treasures, a rifle and camera, which hang just below his self-portrait.
"That's a Praktika I bought in a vintage shop in the 1980s—like the camera I'm
holding in my photo but not the same one," he explains.[15] The original German
model, which replaced the Russian Kiev that Mai Nam first used, was not well
made, and had likely been discarded after it could no longer be repaired. When
Mai Nam and his colleagues occasionally met with foreign photojournalists,
who would travel to Hanoi to cover press conferences about prisoners of war,
they coveted the sophisticated Nikons and Minoltas that their counterparts
carried, well aware that their own equipment was inferior. And yet, acquiring
this equipment, especially during the leanest early years of the conflict, was difficult. "It wasn't easy to have a camera at that time," Mai Nam recalls.[16] He did

not own the one he used; it was loaned to him by the Young Pioneers, which likely acquired it when its delegation traveled covertly, by way of the northern mountains of Vietnam and China, to Berlin for a youth conference.

Vietnamese photographers who covered the American war relied on equipment made and supplied by communist allies. These included cameras and lenses that were made in East Germany and the USSR, which were delivered to Vietnam via Hong Kong or over the northern mountains, presumably along the same routes traveled by Soviet-made weapons. Images produced by Vietnamese photographers were then wired outside the country. During the conflict, two main groups would have seen a selection of these images: antiwar and peace organizations that subscribed to *Vietnam Pictorial*, where many of these photos were included; and audiences within communist bloc countries, which featured them in exhibitions.

In the 1960s and early 1970s, cameras, accessories, and film were in such short supply that they were not issued to individual photographers, but rather were stored at the headquarters of organizations such as the Young Pioneers, the VNA, and the army's photographic department, which sparingly doled them out to photographers, who had to account for and return this equipment once they came home from their assignments at the front. Who received what depended on experience and renown. Fancy lenses such as telephotos were in even shorter supply than camera bodies and standard lenses. For this reason, they were seldom issued. One photographer lucky enough to receive this special lens was Văn Bảo, renowned for capturing on film the downing of an American plane. Đoàn Công Tính marvels at the time he found a Minolta in a helicopter that had crashed. "They were so well made, they survived the wreckage," he recalls, and regretted having to turn the camera over to the VNA for safekeeping.[17]

Although Mai Nam's photos are now some of those most celebrated by the state, during the war he was treated no differently than his colleagues. A self-trained photographer who learned the craft by reading a French manual purchased in a secondhand bookstore in the late 1950s, Mai Nam had access to only one camera and a single lens. When he went out on assignment, he received at most ten rolls of film, though in some cases even fewer were issued. (Legend has it that one photographer somehow managed to cover the war with only one roll of film.) Most of the VNA photographers, however, were selected from among Hanoi's university elite. Plucked from their programs, these students were enrolled in eighteen-month training courses in journalism, followed by another six-month program on photojournalism, which was led by veteran

Vietnamese photographers, some of whom were trained in Germany and Russia. Kim Đảng remarks that knowledge of both journalism and photojournalism was a benefit: "I think that if I were just a writer then I would be quite ordinary. I have to use a camera. If I were to see an interesting and good visual story then I would record that story by photos. But if I cannot shoot or I cannot shoot very well, then I would use my writing, my pen."[18]

Although mostly men enrolled in these courses, I was told by the director of the VNA that as many as four women completed them. One of them, Thu Hoài, is an active photographer today, who credits her training in 1973 for introducing her to the craft. Despite this, the profession is still dominated by men and, to my knowledge, women were seldom sent to the front as photographers, apparently to spare them the hardship and danger of covering the war. When it comes to honoring contributions to the war effort, women are praised as mothers of revolutionaries, seldom as revolutionaries themselves.[19] However, doubt about this explanation of their absence from the task of photographing the war surely arises when we consider that women actively fought in the war, particularly in the south, not to mention the fact that the figure of women at war—whom Hồ Chí Minh is reputed to have described as "long-haired warriors"—was a favorite subject of many communist photographers (fig. 13.3).[20] Though the important story of women at war lies outside the scope of this chapter, the veteran photographers' speculations suggest that the practice of revolutionary looking is profoundly gendered.

While men and a few women were trained in journalism and photography, it was predominantly men who were then sent out into the field and onto the front, most of them carrying, as Mai Nam did, a camera, a standard lens, and no more than ten rolls of film. In such conditions of scarcity, photographers did not have the luxury afforded to today's digital generation; instead they were forced by these conditions to shoot sparingly, and indeed to compose and even stage their images prior to shooting instead of indulging in the now-common practice of rapid-fire snapping.

The arduous travel required to complete assignments resulted in numerous delays, which frequently meant that the photos that made their way back to VNA head offices accompanied stories that were no longer news. Whereas photojournalists working for the West hitched rides on U.S. Air Force helicopters that brought them to the action and immediately back out, socialist photographers traveled by bicycle, most often the same Czech-made bikes that volunteers used to clear the Hồ Chí Minh Trail. In addition to documenting stories about socialist struggles, the photographers did double duty, assisting

FIGURE 13.3
Mai Nam,
Untitled.

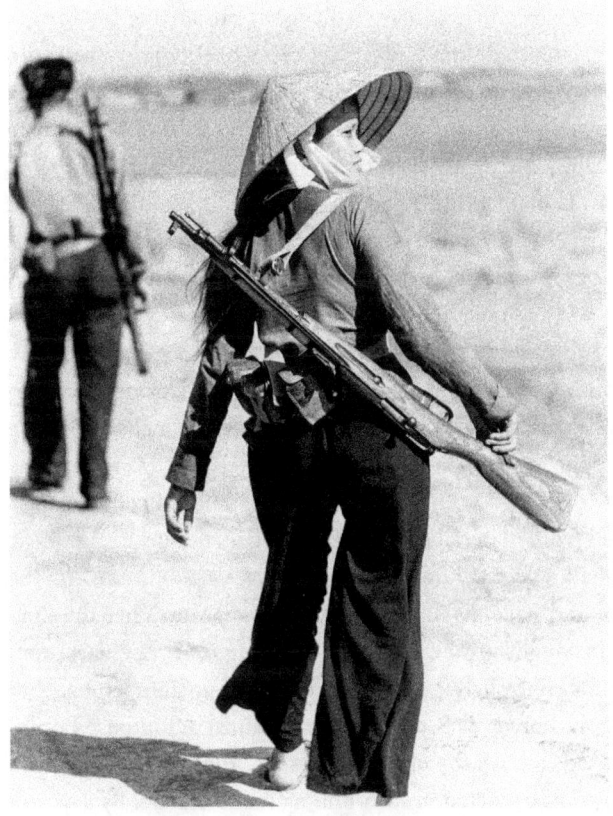

in the tasks of transporting food and conveying communications. Because in the early years of the war the trail was more of a clearing, photographers had to carry their bicycles over otherwise impassable areas and sometimes arrived at their destination only after months of arduous travel.

Văn Sắc recalls one such adventure: "There was one bridge that was disguised. During the day it was only two tracks. From the air, it looked unimportant, but at night the militiamen placed wooden planks across the tracks so they could move equipment and supplies quickly."[21] He came upon the tracks during the day and, despite the risk of being discovered, resolved to cross quickly, reasoning that the story would not wait for him. Spreading his legs wide across the thin rails, he inched forward with his bicycle awkwardly balanced in his hands and his camera slung on his back. Halfway across, however, he paused:

a plane had started circling overhead. With a racing heart and shaking legs, he waited for shooting to start and bombs to drop, but after a few breaths the plane drifted away. "I was lucky," he said.[22]

Getting to the story was only the first challenge. Transporting the images back to headquarters was also difficult. Although messengers were tasked with carrying rolls of film to VNA offices, their unreliability prompted some photographers to take matters in their own hands. To ensure his rolls of film arrived at their destination, Định Quảng Thành took on the responsibility of acting as courier himself. Đoàn Công Tính traveled on the Hồ Chí Minh Trail after it was wide enough to let trucks rumble along rocky, uneven roads. Sometimes he carried paperwork that authorized him to hitch along, but when he did not, he would sneak on board and hope that the vehicle would convey him to headquarters before he was detected.

For Kim Đảng, who was an army photographer, it was not necessary to move images to distant viewers. His photos were meant for inclusion in the army newspaper; his viewers were the soldiers themselves. For this reason, the darkroom he used was located within the very encampment itself, dug into the earth and adapted from material extracted from the natural surroundings. Fashioned out of a shallow bunker described by the VNA's publication as "the darkest place in the world" (*một buồng tối tối nhất thế giới*), much like the shelters in which soldiers sought protection from bombing raids, the darkroom had a small opening for controlled light exposure.[23] Although hidden beneath the earth, the darkroom-bunker was too shallow to withstand intense bombing. The water Kim used to wash the film was scooped from nearby rivers and streams, or from the pools collected in surrounding bomb craters. By day, volunteer youth groups labored to fill these craters, so that vehicles could pass along wrecked roads more easily; by night the water gathered there was used to relieve thirst and wash film. Organic elements thus inspired creative solutions to material problems and served as inspiration for revolutionary photographers.

The jungle offered an array of resources: cover for the transport of supplies, shelter for soldiers' camps, amenities for the construction of darkrooms, and a venue for photo exhibitions. Pieced together out of the physical environment, indeed carved from nature itself, these camouflaged darkrooms were portable rather than fixed, and as such attest to tactics of mobility and adaptability. Often associated with guerrilla warfare, such tactics were also deployed in practices of photography in response to conditions that necessitated rendering material deprivation into resources for the making of images, whether through the conversion of spaces into darkrooms or of ready-made materials into camera parts. Moreover, the stunning landscape itself often was an important backdrop to, if not the very subject of, revolutionary photography (fig. 13.4). In this way, as I explain below, socialist photographers could reconcile their revolutionary objectives with the decadent aesthetic sensibility associated with corrupt French colonial tastes.

In addition to illustrating stories published in the army newspaper, which were meant to boost the morale of soldiers, Kim Đảng's photos were displayed in makeshift jungle exhibitions assembled from humble materials, such as a line of string tied to several trees, on which photos would hang on clips. Võ An Khánh displayed photos in jungle exhibitions in the south, where surrounding villagers would gather to view images he captured as well as those smuggled from the north. He describes these events as crowded with curious villagers, who flocked to exhibitions with excitement "because in the countryside, there wasn't TV and the exhibitions were a kind of entertainment."[24] Besides offering a pleasant distraction from the tedium of daily life, such photos were important in illustrating the progress of war in the north, information that he says was censored by the Government of the Republic of Vietnam, which was based in the southern capital of Saigon. They served an additional purpose of recruiting local peasants.

Võ An Khánh had extensive experience in promoting socialism in the south. His contributions began, not with photography, but rather with the production of propaganda posters, which were also displayed in these jungle exhibitions. His turn to photography was an extension of this earlier practice, and he embraced it with the enthusiasm and resourcefulness of the soldiers that his work celebrated. Like the rebels who crafted pongee traps of bamboo spikes hidden deep in the earth or who improvised long-range weapons by exerting the force of their bodies, Võ An Khánh approached photography as a weapon that could strengthen allies and wound enemies. While he stops short of invoking an explicit link between the practices of asymmetrical warfare and the shooting of pictures with scarce supplies and inferior equipment, his approach nevertheless implies an analogy. Like other photographers, he stored his camera and film in sturdy U.S. ammunition containers, packed with bags of roasted rice, which acted as a desiccant, necessary in a humid climate where mold compromised technical equipment. During the day, the likeliest time for bombing raids, he buried these containers in the ground for safekeeping, and dug them up at night.

Unlike Võ An Khánh, Mai Nam is not shy about establishing an analogy be-

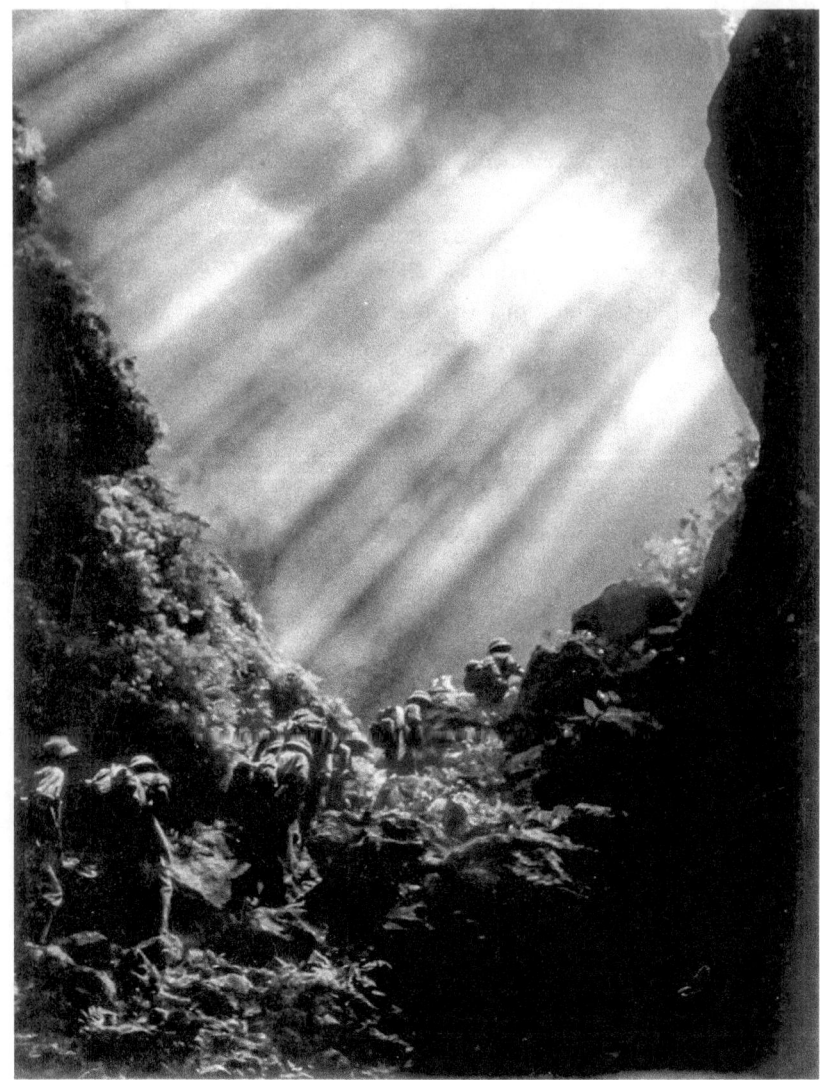

FIGURE 13.4 Lê Minh Trường, *Truong Son Road* (East Truong Son), 1966.

tween asymmetrical warfare and photography. After all, beneath his self-portrait hangs a camera—and a rifle. When I ask him about this weapon, he laughs. "I was a photographer; we shot the war, not soldiers."[25] However, he goes on to explain that he made the hunting rifle himself, out of material he gathered and repurposed. This approach of making do is the hardscrabble survival response of the disadvantaged, of which the refashioning of discarded enemy equipment

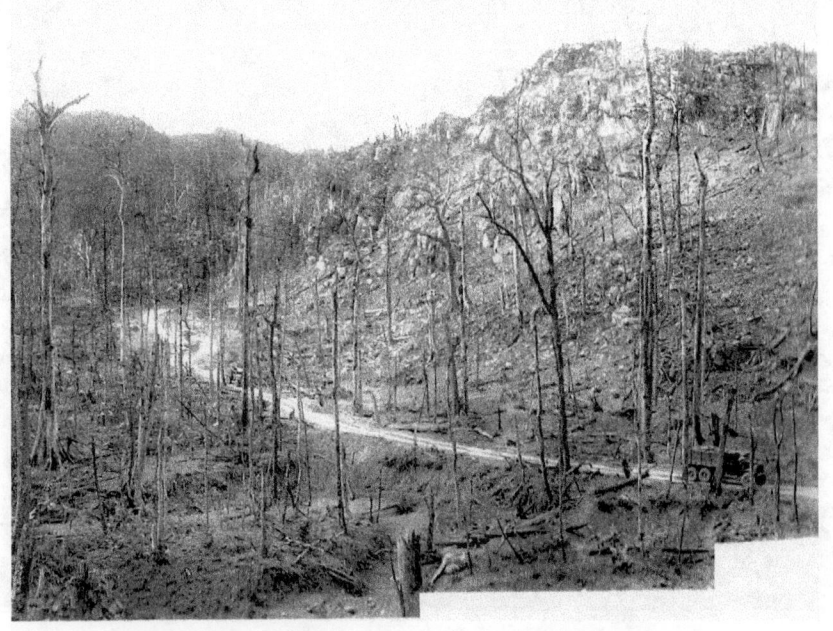

FIGURE 13.5 Photographer unknown. Courtesy Vietnam News Agency.

to protect film and camera (as Võ An Khánh and others did) is only one of many techniques. The art of making do is one passed on from one generation to the next, each familiar with conditions of scarcity that fueled innovation.

Further innovations arose in the wake of rationed equipment. For example, the piecing together of multiple shots (*ghép*) is a technique designed to create a panoramic view without the benefit of a wide-angle lens (fig. 13.5). Editors would later suture these shots together, with the seams and repetition of foreground figures as telling indicators of a flawed style of expedience.

Another innovation became a trick shared by so many photographers that it generates almost a subgenre of photos: rockets firing against a dark sky (fig. 13.6). Photographers would sit back with steady hands on the camera's switch, waiting for the right moment when the weapons of war would double as accessories to cameras that lacked the flash necessary for nighttime shooting. Waiting required patience and luck as much as skill. In such photos, flares are improvised flashes that illuminate the shadows of soldiers cast against a deadly sky.

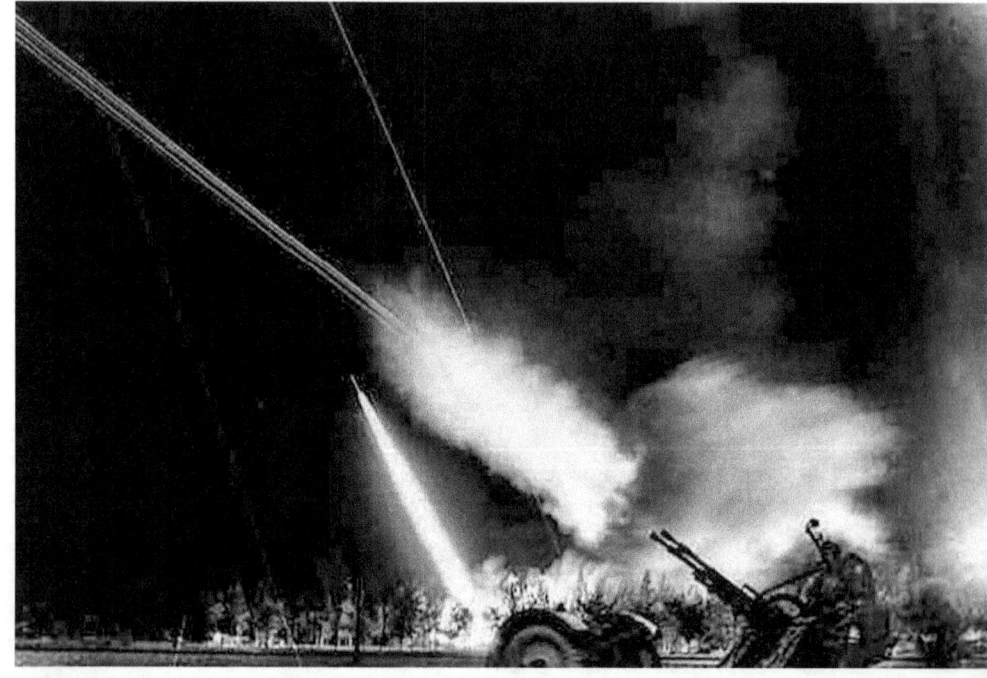

FIGURE 13.6 Photographer unknown. Courtesy Vietnam News Agency.

Though the night sky was challenging, it was still possible to photograph. Beneath the earth, where soldiers and villagers retreated for shelter during bombing raids, it was even harder for photographers to operate. If above-ground rockets lit the way, bullets provided a solution to less than ideal light-ing conditions in underground tunnels. Having memorized chemistry lessons from his French photography textbook, Mai Nam reasoned that gunpowder offered a viable substitute for the magnesium powder used for flash photog-raphy. First, he composed the scene, then whittled apart a bullet and tapped out the gunpowder. When it was ignited, he was able to capture a vision of life in the notorious tunnels.[26]

Antiwar activists who participated in what Judy Tzu-Chun Wu calls "radi-cal tourism" by visiting Hanoi admired these ingenious improvisations.[27] Akin to the bricolage that cultural anthropologist Claude Lévi-Strauss and others have theorized as a creative method of the impoverished, the primary aim of this response to material deprivation was to make use of the seemingly un-usable. While such a practice is hardly unique to socialist photographers, this recycling ethos is nevertheless singled out as a signature style of the revolutionaries. Susan Sontag, in particular, praised this enterprising spirit in her 1968 travel memoir *Trip to Hanoi*. Out of the scraps of downed warplanes, recyclers were able to salvage metal that was then repurposed as fences, flowerpots, and even combs and knives, which were given as gifts to radical tourists. Many of these tourists marveled at how little was wasted, in contrast to the habits of mindless consumption with which they were familiar and against which Debord cautioned. For the state, the recycling ethos served other purposes besides this understandably pragmatic one. As the admiration of antiwar tourists suggests, the ethos promotes an ideological position that contrasted tactical intelligence against superior U.S. military forces and maintained that, despite overwhelming odds, the former upset the latter.

Not surprisingly, the recycled objects were war trophies, everyday reminders of the triumph of cunning and unified effort. Later, these recycled objects became more than just everyday reminders; they are monuments of tenacity and perseverance. Exhibitions at the Army Museum (now called the Military History Museum) in Hanoi perhaps best exemplify this spirit of grim triumph. Among intact fighter jets, tanks, and helicopters is the wreckage of one of the greatest wartime prizes, a B-52 bomber. Pieces of the bomber's rusted shell are massed together and crowned with its broken nose. Firmly buried on the cement grounds devoted to the story of socialist success, the upward thrust of the nose exposes the hubris of American military ambition (fig. 13.7).[28]

However, sculpture tells only part of the story of the ideological roots of the recycling ethos. Photography is also an integral component of this display. Beside the twisted metal is an image blown up to an exaggerated scale proportionate to the massive sculpture itself. This famous photo, taken by an unknown photographer of an unnamed woman salvaging wreckage, is not just an illustration of the process of reconstruction. Rather, it feminizes and aestheticizes the recycling ethos. More than the subject of the photo, salvage is here revealed to be a defining feature of Vietnamese photography, forming the material of, and lending inspiration for, an aesthetically pleasing vision of revolution.

Yet another technique is a reversal of the discourse of enablement: if the notion of a prosthetic lens assumes that the camera extends the limits of the body, for some VNA photographers, embodied photographic practices suggest the limits of the camera's vision. One such limit can be discerned in the static and posed quality of their images. When they are action shots, as is the case with the photograph of the battle for Quảng Trị that introduces this chapter, blurred vision results when the eye must divide its focus between the unfolding battle and imminent dangers (fig. 13.1). The documentary qualities of veri-

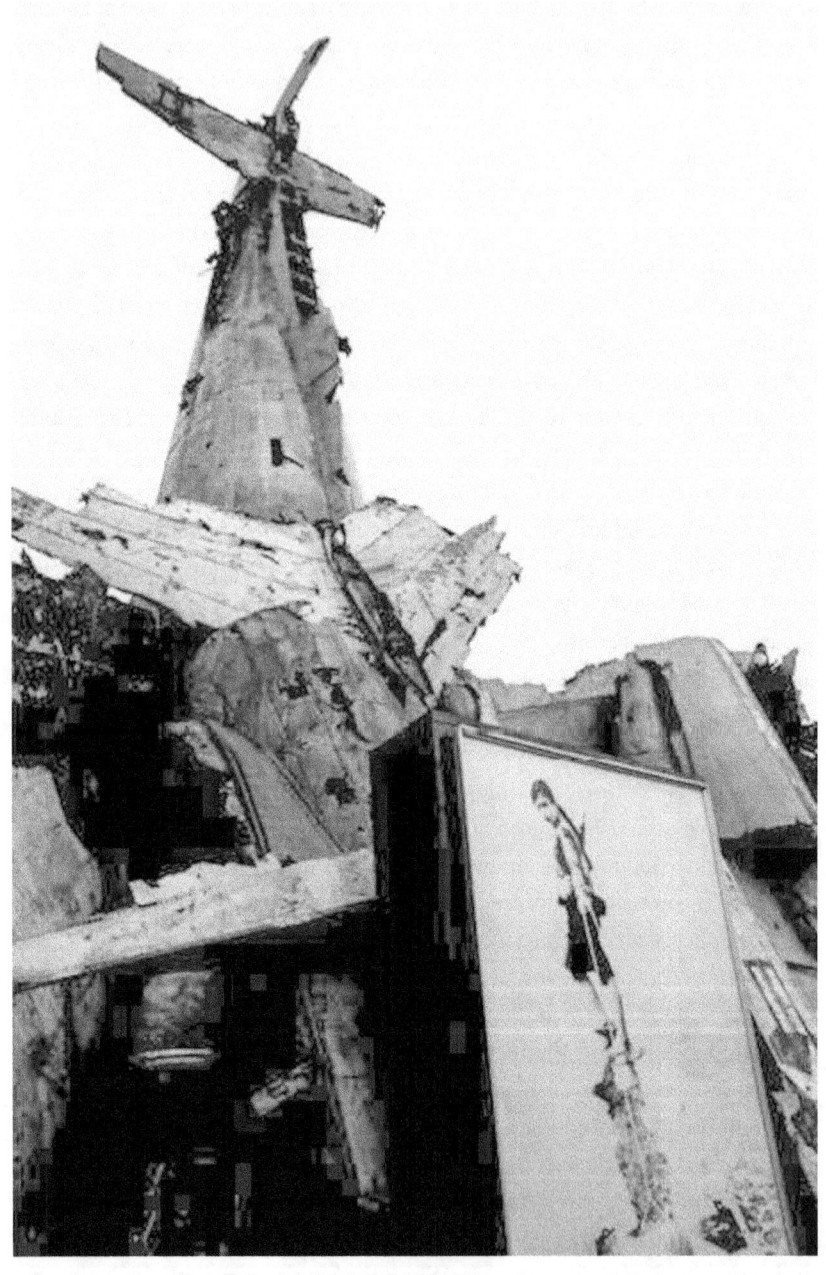

FIGURE 13.7 Michael Tang, Military History Museum.

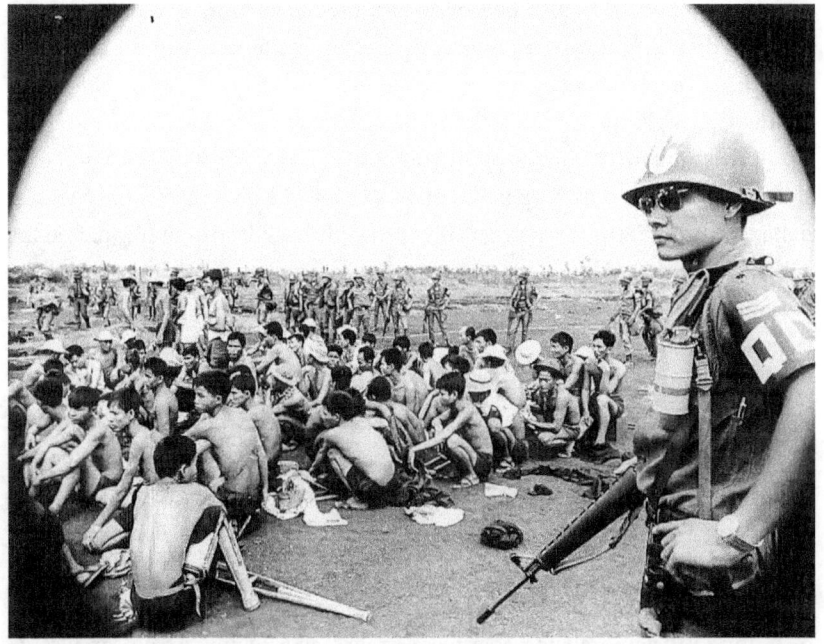

FIGURE 13.8 Lâm Tấn Tài, *Lộc Ninh*, 1973. Courtesy Vietnam News Agency.

similitude and immediacy in such photographs attest to material constraints and exigencies, which contribute to an imperfect overall picture of revolution.

The limits of vision are poignantly displayed in the work of Lâm Tấn Tài, whose camera reveals blindness. Though Lâm was blinded in one eye while covering the 1968 Tet Offensive, he continued to photograph. In 1973, he was in Lộc Ninh, on the border of Vietnam and Cambodia, to report on an exchange of prisoners. Given the glare of the midday sun, he must have squinted across the baking tarmac where the men awaited their freedom. To correct for the harsh light, he attached a shade to his lens, but it was the wrong one. The resulting photo is framed by inky curved edges (fig. 13.8).

More than just a mistake, these black edges are the imprint of the unseeable, transforming Lâm's photograph into a paradoxical display of imperfect vision: this is what it looks like when a blind eye sees. Yet so solid is the blackness of the framed edges, which attest to technical imperfection, that impress of compromised peripheral vision so seldom seen and so rarely reproduced, that it is easy to miss what is squarely captured in the center: most of the prisoners awaiting exchange are themselves injured. They sit on the tarmac cradling their amputated limbs with their crutches and prostheses close by. This is not just a photograph by a disabled photographer; the image hints at the ways that a vision of disability, however partial, might offer an alternative to the dominant discourse of enablement.

Additional glimpses of this alternative perspective can be found in one of Võ An Khánh's most famous photographs from 1970, which portrays a makeshift surgical operation deep in the midst of the U Minh jungle in the Mekong delta (fig. 13.9). Set as it is against an improbable backdrop of unhygienic slime and sticky heat, it is little wonder that many viewers question its authenticity, reasoning that a scene so surreal as to come with a gauzy scrim must have been staged.

These photographs are also unsettling because they stand out as some of the few revolutionary representations of injured bodies, a subject that was at odds with the decidedly positive objectives of uplifting spirits and promoting struggle. Yet injury appears to enter the picture obliquely, enveloped in a misty and incongruously artful setting, as in Võ An Khánh's photographs, which focus on repair of injury, or as in Lâm Tấn Tài's photograph, hidden in the plain sight of blind vision. Because injured and dead bodies were considered dispiriting and demoralizing, they were rarely seen, and pulled from circulation if not censored outright as unsuitable for revolution, perhaps even as counter-revolutionary.

This is not to say, however, that socialist photography should be dismissed as mere propaganda (tuyên truyền). As Sabine Kriebel points out, labeling images as propaganda is often an unsatisfactory method of visual analysis: it forecloses rather than provokes critical inquiry.[29] In its fixation on, and derision of, obvious techniques of persuasion, the pejorative judgment of propaganda risks missing other, no less important, parts of the story. Although Kriebel's discussion of the aesthetics of information and politics of persuasion focuses on Weimar-era photography, her call to take propaganda seriously promises to offer a more nuanced approach to seemingly simplistic images.[30] How did propanda seek to disable the enemy's resolve and to shift the terms in which war would be represented? To what extent is there a style to propaganda? In what contexts does propaganda eschew style and, for that matter, the category of aesthetics altogether? Conversely, how might aesthetics be amenable to the imperatives of propaganda?

According to Pham Tiên Dũng, the now retired photo editor at the VNA, while aesthetics mattered, other elements of photography took precedence. During my meeting with him, he explained that the "basic nature of news photography" includes the following: (1) ideology, (2) truthfulness, (3) news cur-

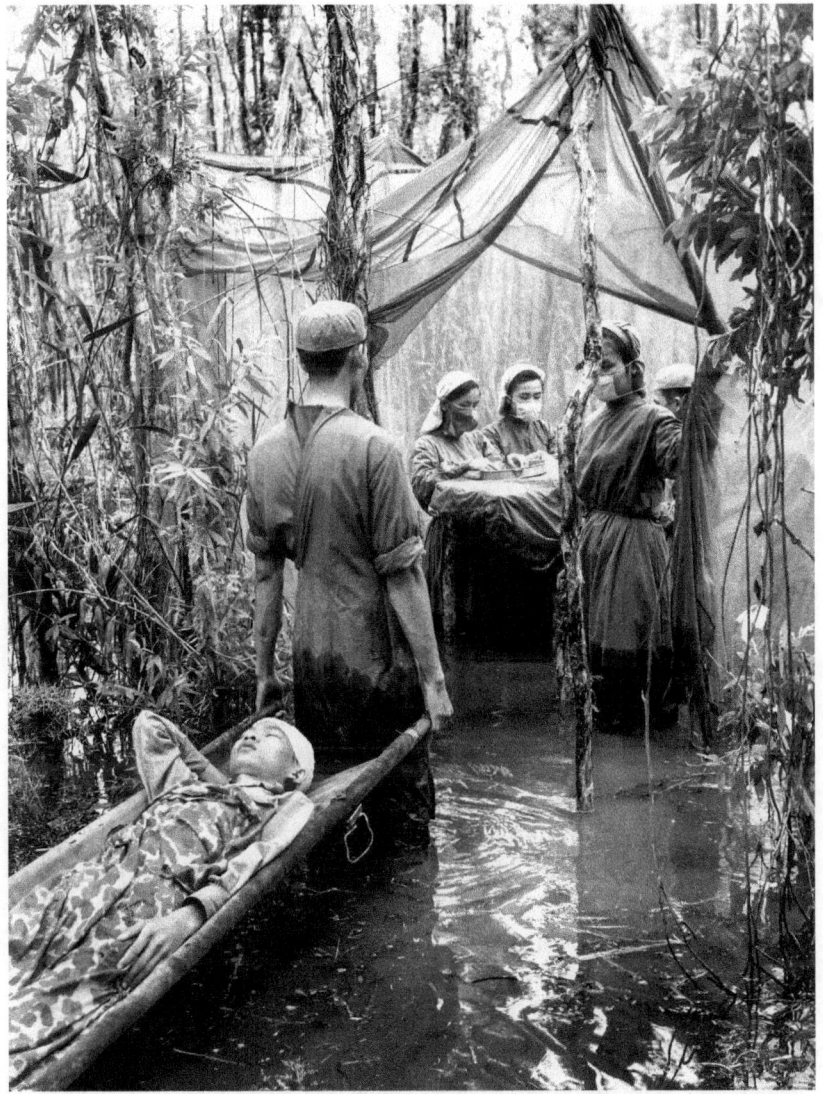

FIGURE 13.9 Võ An Khánh, Untitled.

rency, (4) mass appeal, and (5) aesthetics, named last. The VNA's history of photography outlines an additional five key themes that emerged in the post-1954 era, when the north broke the yoke of French colonial rule, and the first photographers' organization assembled a number of exhibitions meant to lay claim to photography, the very instrument that their oppressors had introduced. Specifically, these exhibitions stressed the themes of socialist values, expression of clarity, praise of national unity, honoring of country and people, and building of friendship and world peace.[31] Accordingly, there were two quintessentially revolutionary subjects that were to be represented in photography: the sacrifice of heroic fighters and the toil of laborers in fields and factories; in short, total war, the unified effort on and off the battlefield. Taken together, these themes constitute the ideological basis of revolutionary photography. Ideology informed the subject matter of these photographs and guided practitioners into what to look at, how to represent it, and how to instruct spectators to look in a revolutionary way.

While these primary components of ideology and aesthetics seem balanced (the latter followed from the former), members of this first photography organization acknowledged the difficulty of achieving such a balance. In short, a problem arose when "the pictures that conveyed ideology were dry and lifeless, but beautiful pictures lacked the breath of the new life [of communism]."[32] While the VNA's explanation of its principles does not account for how the problem of balancing ideology and aesthetics was resolved, a hint is offered in a 1969 conference of patriotic photographers. At this event, the participants urged photographers to abandon aesthetics in favor of more urgent, political subjects: "There are those who have yet to renounce old habits, and fool themselves by looking through distorted lenses in pursuit of beautiful subjects. . . . Saigon, through our clear [communist] lenses, we will produce a new day."[33] In short, socialist photography had to eschew aesthetics so it might adhere faithfully to ideological principles.

Yet, if we look closely, we can discern how beauty slips back into the socialist picture. The works of Lâm Tấn Tài and Võ An Khánh, in effect, reverse directives about the primacy of appropriate subject matter over aesthetics by presenting otherwise inappropriate (and thus unrepresentable) subject matter in accord with revolutionary objectives. Specifically, Lâm Tấn Tài hides blindness and injury in plain sight, in a photograph that speaks explicitly about the theme of liberation. Similarly, Võ An Khánh's jungle MASH unit appears as a consoling dream of healing so that the injured body may enter the field of view. Women, otherwise missing from the battlefield as photographers, also entered the visual field, to the extent that feminine beauty served to enliven the otherwise "dry and lifeless" substance of revolutionary ideology (fig. 13.10). Similarly, photographs taken of roadwork and military operations along the Ho Chi Minh Trail, on the formidable Trường Sơn mountain chain, highlight the spectacular and sublime landscape as the source and symbol of revolutionary resolve, endurance, and triumph (fig. 13.4). In these varied ways, revolutionary photography

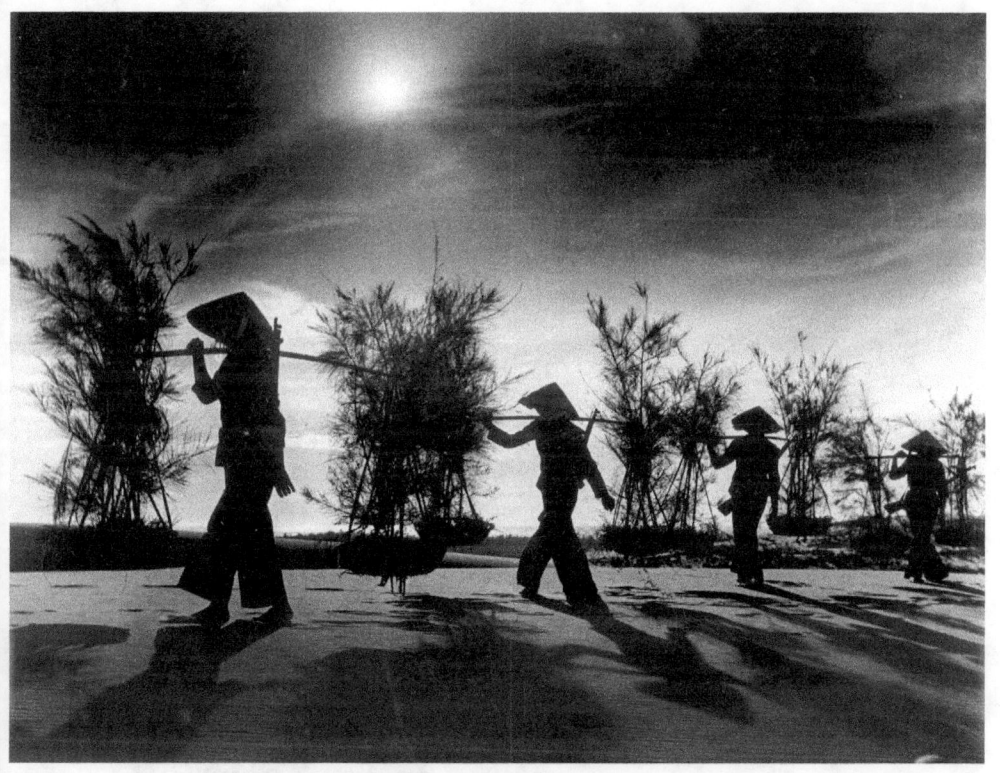

FIGURE 13.10 Lê Minh Trường, *Getting Ready for Battle*
(female members of Quynh Thang agricultural cooperatives), 1966.

sought to correct the ideological distortions of a decadent bourgeois aesthetics and, in so doing, represent unrepresentable subjects deemed antithetical to the building of a new society. By beautifying the message of socialist uplift, photographers thus resolved the problem of aesthetics. The visual record of revolution in Vietnam is marked by contradictions, most notably, the uneasy reconciliation of beauty and ideology, and the material constraints that produce glimpses of imperfection despite the overriding message of socialist uplift.

Corrective Re-visioning in the Đổi Mới Era
of Economic Renovation

In the postwar period, the concern with beautification has intensified to produce an intriguing tension. On the one hand, as we have seen, there are the imperfections that characterize revolutionary forms of looking. On the other

FIGURE 13.11
Đoàn Công Tính,
Untitled.

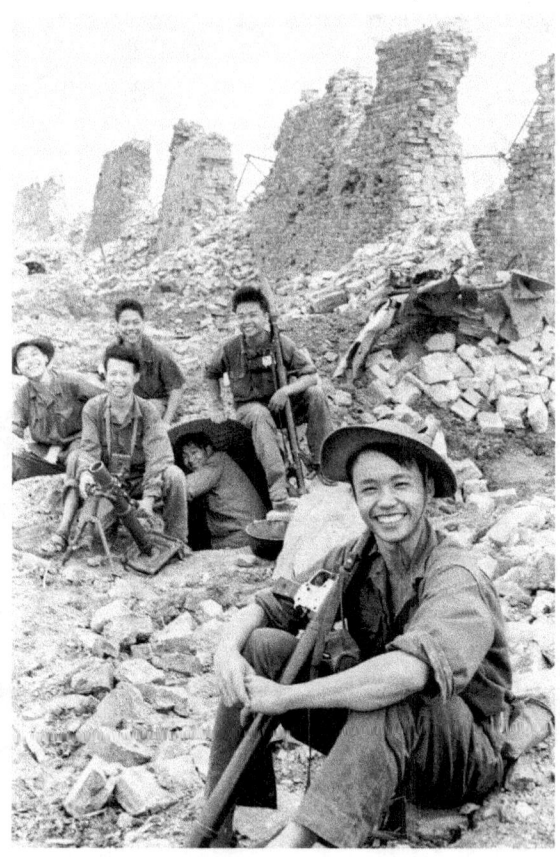

hand, the state projects a flawless picture of reunification. As I learned in the course of research in Hanoi, recent versions of the national narrative emphasize triumph over adversity, and discount if not altogether disavow the flawed quality of the revolutionary visual record.

In the nation's capital of Hanoi and in Hồ Chí Minh City, the southern hub of commerce that everyone still calls by the old name of Saigon, museums memorialize the spirit of revolution by displaying photographs of proud peasants, defiant workers, and smiling soldiers. Đoàn Công Tính's portrayal of the third group, posed during a lull in the fight for Quảng Trị, exemplifies this preference for positive images (fig. 13.11). Against the backdrop of the ruined citadel, the young men's wide grins celebrate a victory that was not yet certain at the time the photograph was taken. Đoàn explains how he produced this photo op: "I coaxed them from their bunkers and asked them to show me how they felt about the battle so far." He points to the shadowed background.

"Look, this one stayed underground. After the rockets started falling, the rest scrambled back to their shelters. I don't know what happened to them after the battle ended."[34]

These strong features and able bodies, hallmarks of an optimistic vision of enablement, are in stark contrast to the broken figures featured in images of atrocity that were the staple offerings of the Western press, of which icons such as the Pulitzer prize-winning trinity of Malcolm Browne's self-immolating monk (1963), Eddie Adams's public execution (1968), and Nick Ut's napalm girl (1972) are the most recognizable but hardly unusual. More often than not, the Western view of the war emphasizes Vietnamese victimhood. While I am told that similar dispiriting images of mangled, dead bodies exist and are held in a folder at the VNA archives, they were not among the volumes that I reviewed during this trip. Indeed, I am told they have long been strictly censored, and the veteran photographers whom I interviewed admit they were ordered to refrain from taking such morbid photos.[35] When it comes to representing the American war, the state promotes uplifting images and frowns on, even though it no longer officially censors, dispiriting ones.

And yet sometimes photographers recount a different story that dampens this mood of uplift, of what happened after their cameras captured workers and fighters, men and women with the tools of their craft. Kim Đằng expresses gratitude to a soldier who led him to a high mountaintop perch for an unobstructed view of the Hồ Chí Minh Trail. "I found out he died the next week," he recalls, his voice trailing off.[36]

On a similar stretch of road, Đình Quảng Thành came across a group of a dozen women working, as the sun set, to fill an enormous bomb crater. The light plays tricks in this photo, so that the women's bodies cast an eerily doubled reflection, with shadows on the ground and rippling in the water (fig. 13.12). There is the illusion, then, of three rows of women, each blending into each other, each becoming less distinct. This blending of bodies is at the same time fracturing, lending to the photo a premonitory ambiguity—of the dozen Thanh saw that day, ten were killed when a bomb exploded.

Despite the occasional premonition, the overall emphasis was on the production of a whole vision of nationhood. Given the latter, it is all the more fitting that Hồ Chí Minh's brief experience with photography was as a retoucher. While Hồ Chí Minh himself deliberately hid much of his past, biographers list this job as one of many he took on for nearly three years, from July 1921 to March 1923, during his sojourn in Paris. (He was also credited for authorizing the 1954 launch of the photo magazine *Vietnam Pictorial*.) Although Hồ

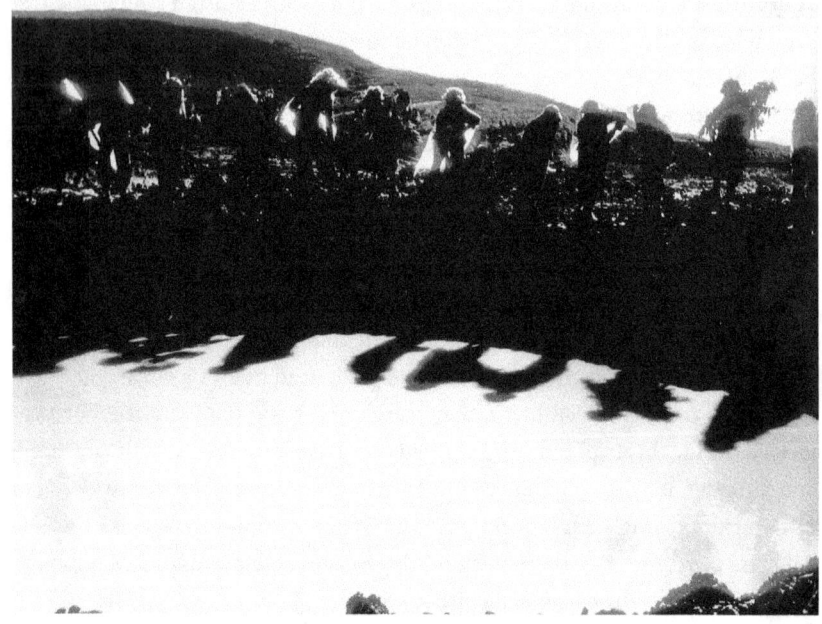

FIGURE 13.12 Đình Quảng Thành. Courtesy Vietnam News Agency.

Chí Minh was only paid modest wages, biographers emphasize that photo retouching was crucial for his revolutionary activities, for this work funded the
publication of tracts attacking the brutality of the French colonial regime in
Indochina.[37]

Retouching is also significant because it is a job that requires covering up
blemishes, removing imperfections, and producing beauty. Nina Hien observes
that the opening of markets in the Đổi Mới era also introduced a new tolerance
for photographic self-representation that the state had once shunned as bourgeois decadence. According to Hien, although this commercialized "beauty
regime" enables subjects to express individual identities in contrast to, even in
resistance of, the state's collective ideology, at times this beauty regime aligns
with the state's own political priorities. That is, the beauty regime offers a style
that complements Đổi Mới renovation.[38] Hien's insight can be extended further: the state has cultivated a beauty regime to tackle the dual tasks of reckoning with the past and heralding a prosperous future. Drawing on sentimental
aesthetic conventions that favor the soothing over the disturbing, the state's approach to renovation entails producing pleasing, instead of wounding, images.

Against this backdrop, the previous section's focus on the imperfect qualities

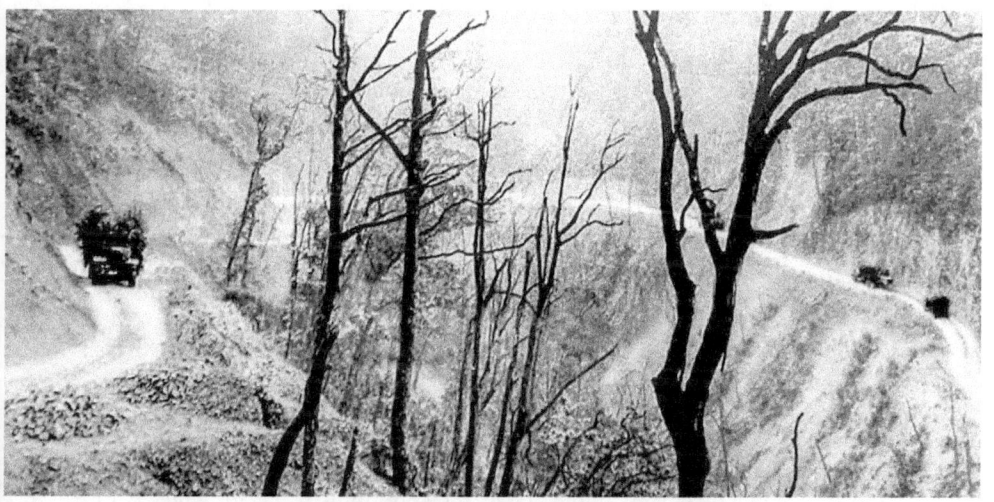

FIGURE 13.13 Photographer unknown. Courtesy Vietnam News Agency.

of revolutionary practices of looking during this extended conflict contradicts the state's own memorialization practices. In the era of market reform, of national renovation that Đổi Mới promotes, today's displays of socialist photography emphasize the camera's enabling capacities. Contemporary rites of remembrance repudiate the imperfect conditions from which this visual record was made, substituting a revisionist nationalist narrative of ability and wholeness, altogether overlooking occasional glimpses of disability, not to mention the haphazard, imperfect qualities that defined the production of socialist photography. The visual history of Vietnam unfolds amid the ideological clash between positive and negative images.

I encountered this beautifying approach to the past in the archival offices of the VNA's photographic division, where for this project I requested a copy of a panoramic view made by Văn Sắc, among many other images. As mentioned above, these panoramas were created from several developed images joined together and, during the war, this piecemeal approach to photographic production betrayed its imperfect methods: uneven lengths of paper and repetitive motifs. No longer. When I received my digital print, I found that the VNA employed digital techniques to stitch together shots (fig. 13.13). It could have been a misunderstanding. Still, I had tried to ask for one image made out of three that showed signs of suture, but either they misheard, or possibly they found my preference for the imperfect composition odd given that the alternative—a seamless whole—was now possible. Digital enhancement offered a means for this official archive to represent, stylistically, the nation's moderniz-ing aspirations.

Only Nguyễn Minh Lộc, a veteran VNA photographer, at first appears to depart from this fondness for the beautiful. Although his fellow photographers scoffed when I asked about him in Hanoi—"He doesn't have many photos, and none are interesting," they said—I resolved to meet him after coming across the set depicting a cave MASH unit at the archives. He lived in Hồ Chí Minh City, on the top floor of an alley house, where I met with him to discuss his work during the war.

Minh Lộc was responsible for covering the coal industry near Hanoi toward the tail end of the war. Studies in contrast, his images set stalwart workers against the striking backdrop of yawning pits and massive factories. I had set aside a few for reproduction and kept returning to one image, of explosion and smoke in a quarry. As noted above, the communist VNA, for which Minh Lộc worked, emphasized two central subjects in war photography: the heroic struggle of soldiers and the toil of workers. In its simultaneous depiction of these two subjects, an attack at a worker's factory, Minh Lộc's photographs were fascinating and unusual, for they clearly took up the core elements of communist war photography.

There was a problem, however. When I looked closely, it was obvious that the explosions that spread across a number of images turned out to be the same one (fig. 13.14). Whether this attack had even occurred under Minh Lộc's watch was debatable, since the United States' Vietnamization policy meant that bombing had ceased by the time the Paris Peace Agreement was signed in 1973, before he started photographing. But when I asked him why he pasted explo-sions into the photos, he did not reply, insisting that his images looked good. He seemed indifferent about the fact that digital enhancement undermined the historical importance of his photographs.

Perhaps, I reflected, he wished to imply that he was witness to military action and not just industrial labor. Although both military and industrial efforts were considered valuable subjects, today it is the spectacles of war, such as the down-ing of American airplanes and the victories on the battlefield, that are most celebrated. My puzzlement over the second issue, of why he altered the photos, initially obscured the significance of the first (that doing so obscured, even fal-sified, historical events), and I was not satisfied by the photographer's evasive replies. Yet there was no question that Minh Lộc's altered images were arrest-ing, for they challenged the divisions, outlined above, between beauty and de-struction, wholeness and injury. Although he denies altering his images, the evi-

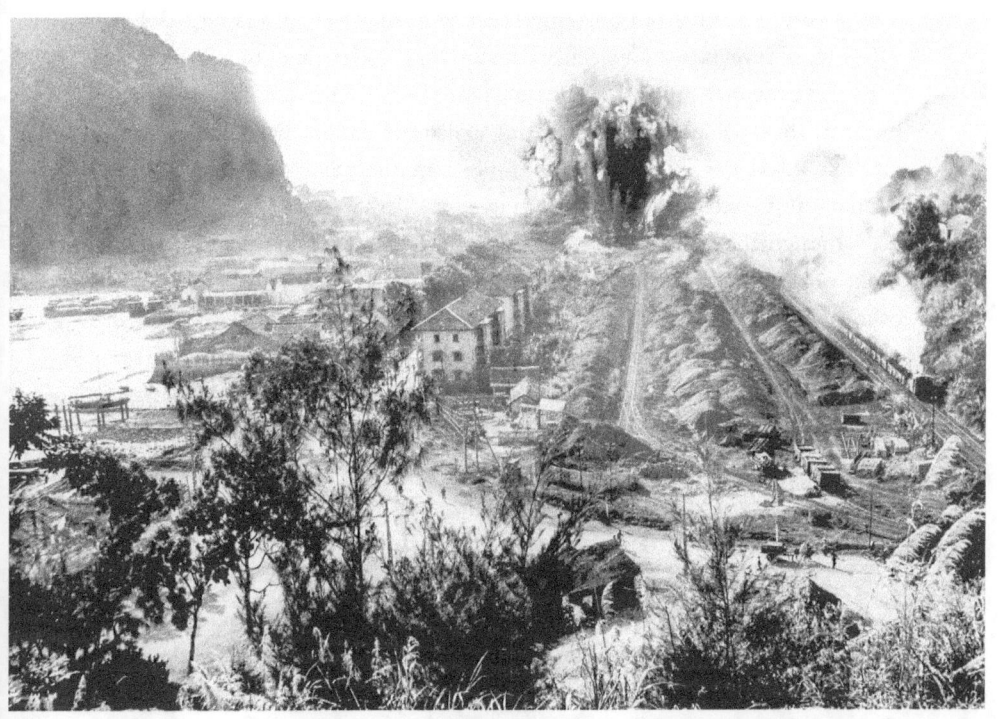

FIGURE 13.14 Photograph by Minh Lộc, Untitled.

dence is clear: rather than shying away from destruction, Minh Lộc produced it even when none was to be found.

This fondness for Photoshop at once exemplifies and revises Hien's concept of the beauty regime, in which retouching offers a modern technique that creates the look, to complement the policy, of renovation. On the one hand, such a practice keeps pace with that of contemporary photographers who, as Hien documents, heal scarred bodies, lighten dark skin, and unify families with disappeared members. On the other hand, Minh Lộc's idea of perfection brushes up against the wholeness of these idealistic illusions; he conjures picturesque destruction where there was none. When Đoàn Công Tính posed his smiling soldiers against a crumbling citadel, it was to celebrate strength and perseverance, not to revel in ruin. The flawed condition and imperfect quality of socialist Vietnamese war photography cannot be categorized as ruin porn, the style so popular in contemporary depictions of postindustrial and postsocialist cityscapes.

Unsurprisingly, his peers among VNA veteran photographers dismiss Minh

Lộc's work. But far from breaking ranks with the VNA in this regard, Minh Lộc's work reveals just how central aesthetics is today (and, to a different extent, was even in the 1970s), as the state grapples with the task of memorializing the war. Thus, while it may be tempting to dismiss retouching as a rare element of Vietnamese war photography, it is more commonly employed than most veteran photographers are willing to admit.

Although the issue of retouching is an open secret, it blew open in the wake of explosive revelations that one of the most iconic photographs of the war, by none other than Đoàn Công Tính, had been manipulated. The untitled photograph from 1970 features soldiers climbing a rope against the spectacular backdrop of a waterfall (fig. 13.15). This photograph was displayed in 2014, alongside other well-known works by North Vietnamese photographers, at France's International Photojournalism Festival of Perpignan (Visa Pour L'Image Perpignan). Exhibition co-organizer Patrick Chauvel, a respected and award-winning photographer who had covered the war for France, timed the event to coincide with the publication of his new book on the subject, *Ceux du Nord* (Those in the North).[39] The *New York Times'* Lens blog selected Đoàn Công Tính's spectacular waterfall to illustrate its positive coverage of the event. Chauvel followed up on this successful launch with an exhibition at the Institut Français in Hanoi, as a companion to the Perpignan show. *Reporters du Guerre* (War reporters) opened during the fortieth anniversary of the end of the war, in April 2015, where once again Đoàn Công Tính's photograph was singled out as the image to grace the poster for the event.

But a scandal was brewing. Photojournalist Jørn Stjerneklar points out on his blog that this iconic image was doctored.[40] The extent of manipulation is obvious when we compare the two versions, the recent print that appears in the exhibitions on the right, and the original on the left, which was published in Đoàn Công Tính's 2001 book *Khoảng Khách* (Moments; fig. 13.15). The very details that make the photograph iconic—the intricate path of the rushing water, the addition of figures and foliage, and the sharpness of the soldiers' silhouettes, among others—are precisely the ones that have been altered. In a follow-up article on his blog, Stjerneklar credits a keen-eyed reader for pointing out that even the original had been Photoshopped, as is evident by the repeating pattern of the water, and was likely a composite of another VNA photograph, which is displayed at the War Remnants Museum in Hồ Chí Minh City. Stjerneklar's story was picked up worldwide and Chauvel as well as Perpignan Festival founder and director Jean François Leroy went on the defensive, accusing the photo-blogger of "spoil[ing] a beautiful event."[41] The two only

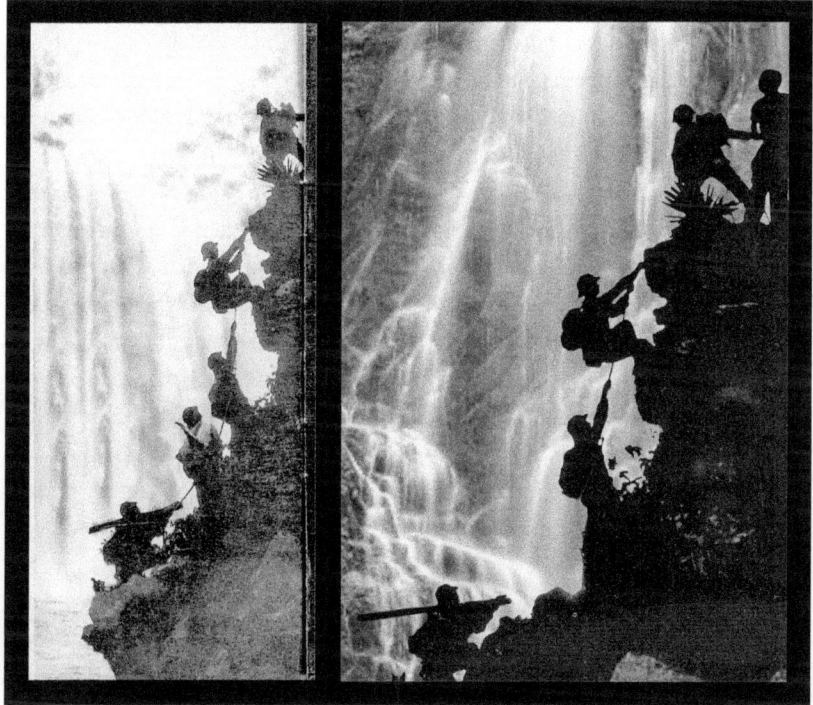

FIGURE 13.15 Đoàn Công Tính, Untitled. Courtesy Jørn Stjerneklar.

backed down in the face of overwhelming condemnation. As for Đoàn Công
Tính, he initially denied knowledge of the manipulation, and, when pressed,
speculated that someone else had altered the photograph after the negative had
been damaged.

In quick order, the reputations of all three—Leroy, Chauvel, and Đoàn
Công Tính—were irrevocably tarnished. Critics slammed the festival for its
hypocrisy: how could it claim to champion the integrity of documentary photography when the exhibition had so flagrantly relaxed its own standards? Although Đoàn Công Tính denied Photoshopping the waterfall photograph, he
was held to account for compromising journalistic ethics.[42] Indeed, many who
weighed in on the scandal conflated ideological manipulativeness with technical manipulation, by dismissing communist photography outright for its pro-
pagandistic zeal.

Given the widely accepted belief in the necessity of accurate reporting, these
responses are understandable. However, the outpouring of moral outrage focuses only on the compelling question raised by the photographer who broke

the story on his blog: "Aber Warum?" In response to the incredulous "but why," the resounding judgment is the admonishing "don't manipulate," a throwback, of sorts, to the foreclosing judgment of propaganda. Few pause to consider the different, but no less important, question: what such manipulation might mean for the historical record and for the politics of memory?

When we look at these two images, the original (on the left) and its further Photoshopped revision (on the right), there is no doubt that these are manipulated visions of war. Taken together, the pairing in effect undoes the dialectical image, which Walter Benjamin imbued with political weight in his reflections on the optical unconscious. This is not to say that manipulated images do not perform their own political work. Rather, considering them together enables us to perceive how the paired images exemplify, while also undermining, the state's recent approach to photography and official account of the camera's function during and after the American war. That this impossibly perfect counterrevolutionary picture of socialist struggle has proved seductive, at least for Patrick Chauvel and the organizers of the French festival, suggests that the process of re-visioning history is not only a state initiative but at times enjoys, if it does not actively solicit, collaborative oversight. This contradiction shakes the very foundations of revolutionary looking, a practice that, as the earlier section of this chapter showed, attends to the importance of repurposing salvaged material, making do with the resources available in one's environment, and alternately acknowledging and disavowing injury.

I close by juxtaposing this latest scandal alongside Minh Lộc's spectacle of ruin because together they are an illuminating fantasy of the past, reimagined as beautiful and sublime. Recent displays of war photography draw on the visual record of revolution as a resource for uplift, beautification, and national unification. This repurposing projects a renewed vision of revolution, one that draws on and strives to improve the visual tropes of socialism. Yet such repurposing is at odds with the spirit of socialist struggle, and at times even amounts to a counterrevolutionary fantasy of the war in Vietnam. In the Đổi Mới era, a politics of visual renovation rewrites the key components of revolutionary looking for the ends of ideological renovation.[43]

Notes

1. His instincts, it turns out, were spot on: the communist victory at Quảng Trị citadel was pivotal in putting pressure on Americans at the Paris Peace Talks in 1973.

2. Walter Benjamin, "Little History of Photography," in *Walter Benjamin: Selected*

Writings, vol. 2, 1927–1934, ed. Michael W. Jennings, Howard Eiland, and Gary Smith, trans. Rodney Livingstone et al. (Cambridge, MA: Belknap, 2005), 507–530, and "The Work of Art in the Age of Its Technological Reproducibility," Second Version (1936), in *Walter Benjamin: Selected Writings, vol. 3, 1931–1938*, ed. Howard Eiland and Michael W. Jennings, trans. Edmund Jephcott, Howard Eiland, et al. (Cambridge, MA: Belknap, 2002).

3. Fredric Jameson, *The Political Unconscious: Narrative as a Socially Symbolic Act* (Ithaca, NY: Cornell University Press, 1981).

4. By famously closing the exhibition with a photograph of the sublime mushroom cloud, the *Family of Man* resolved a problem that vexed Cold War ideologues, how to make visible and manageable invisible phenomena such as the emotions. Photographs conferred color and form to the most chilling of Cold War fears, nuclear annihilation. According to Joseph Masco, visual culture not only produced but also discursively salved these fears. See Joseph Masco, *The Theater of Operations: National Security Affect from the Cold War to the War on Terror* (Durham, NC: Duke University Press, 2014).

5. For more on Cold War visuality, see the special issue edited by Sarah Bassnett, Andrea Noble, and Thy Phu, "Cold War Visual Alliances," *Visual Studies* 30, no. 2 (2015).

6. Susan Sontag, *Trip to Hanoi* (New York: Farrar, Straus and Giroux, 1968).

7. Franny Nudelman, "Against Photography: Susan Sontag's Vietnam," *Photography and Culture* 7, no. 1 (2014): 7–20.

8. Guy Debord, *The Society of the Spectacle* (1967; reprint, New York: Zone, 1995).

9. Susie Linfield, *The Cruel Radiance: Photography and Political Violence* (Chicago: University of Chicago Press, 2010), 7.

10. Robin Kelsey, "Making Photography into Public Memory," paper presented at symposium, The "Public Life" of Photographs, Ryerson Image Centre, Toronto, Canada, May 10, 2013.

11. See Roland Barthes, *Image, Music, Text*, trans. Stephen Heath (New York: Hill and Wang, 1977); and Roland Barthes, *Mythologies*, trans. Annette Lavers (New York: Hill and Wang, 1972). See also Susan Sontag, *On Photography* (New York: Farrar, Straus and Giroux, 1977); John Tagg, *The Burden of Representation* (Amherst: University of Massachusetts Press, 1988); Allan Sekula, *Photography against the Grain: Essays and Photo Works, 1973–1983* (Halifax: Press of the Nova Scotia College of Art and Design, 1984).

12. See, for example, Michael J. Arlen, *Living-Room War* (New York: Viking, 1968); Liam Kennedy, "Securing Vision: Photography and US Foreign Policy," *Media, Culture, Society* 20 (2008); and Melvin Small, *Covering Dissent: The Media and the Anti–Vietnam War Movement* (New Brunswick, NJ: Rutgers University Press, 1994).

13. Although Vietnam might have been on the minds of many of these visual theorists, critics writing outside Hanoi and Saigon likely did not see the work of these revolutionary photographers and probably responded to more familiar images produced by the Western press (Sontag seems to have been a rare exception). Even today, few outside Vietnam view Vietnamese photography of this war. The rare exceptions include

Timothy Page and Horst Faas, eds., *Requiem: By the Photographers Who Died in Vietnam and Indochina* (New York: Random House, 1997); Timothy Page and Douglas Niven, *Another Vietnam: Pictures of the War from the Other Side* (New York: National Geographic Society, 2002); and Patrick Chauvel, *Ceux du Nord* (Paris: Arènes, 2014). For a compelling analysis of the ways that the Vietnamese state draws on revolutionary photography for postwar memorialization practices, see Christina Schwenkel, *The American War in Contemporary Vietnam: Transnational Memory and Representation* (Bloomington: Indiana University Press, 2009); and Christina Schwenkel, "Exhibiting War, Reconciling Pasts: Photographic Representation and Transnational Commemoration in Contemporary Vietnam," *Journal of Vietnamese Studies* 3, no. 1 (2008): 36–77. This closing of distance moved many to antiwar activism in order to end this suffering, and prompted others to reject such images as themselves dehumanizing. Even the Vietnamese insist on the enduring influence of the war in establishing a visual vocabulary for coverage of subsequent conflicts.

14. Heonik Kwon, *The Other Cold War* (New York: Columbia University Press, 2009). See also Heonik Kwon, "Cold War in a Vietnamese Community," in *Four Decades On*, ed. Scott Laderman and Edwin A. Martin (Durham, NC: Duke University Press, 2013), 84–102.

15. Interview with Mai Nam, Hanoi, May 14, 2013.

16. Interview with Mai Nam, Hanoi, May 14, 2013.

17. Interview with Đoàn Công Tính, Ho Chi Minh City, May 16, 2013.

18. Interview with Kim Đằng, Hanoi, May 12, 2013.

19. Although books and exhibitions refer to several female photojournalists who were an exception to this overwhelming rule, such as Nguyễn Thị Thế, Lê Thị Nang, and Ngộc Hương, they do not provide extensive information. See *Requiem: By the Photographers Who Died in Vietnam and Indochina*, ed. Horst Faas and Tim Page (New York and London: Jonathan Cape, 1997), and Nguyễn Đức Chính, *Văn Hóa Nhiếp Ảnh* (Hanoi: Nhà Xuất Bản Thông Tấn, 2008).

20. The term "long-haired warriors," which describes militiawomen, is often attributed to Hồ Chí Minh, who insisted that women's liberation was integral to socialist revolution. However, historians also attribute it to South Vietnamese president Ngô Đình Diem. Sandra C. Taylor asserts that the term applied mainly to the female fighters of the National Liberation Front. See Sandra C. Taylor, *Vietnamese Women at War* (Kansas: University of Kansas Press, 1999).

21. Interview with Văn Sắc, Hanoi, May 10, 2013.

22. Interview with Văn Sắc, Hanoi, May 10, 2013.

23. Nguyễn, *Văn Hóa Nhiếp Ảnh*, 58.

24. Interview with Võ An Khánh, Bạc Liêu, May 20, 2013.

25. Interview with Mai Nam, Hanoi, May 14, 2013.

26. A reenactment of this clever technique can be seen in Robert Guenette, dir., *Vietnam's Unseen War: Photographs from the Other Side* (National Geographic video, 2002).

27. Judy Tzu-Chun Wu, *Radicals on the Road: Internationalism, Orientalism, and Feminism during the Vietnam Era* (Ithaca, NY: Cornell University Press, 2013).

28. Karen Gottschang Turner adds that the planting of the broken frame on the firmness of the soil reorients viewers' perspectives on war, from the abstract heights of aerial supremacy to the ground where innocent civilians are targeted. This museum thus offers a grounded perspective on the war. See Karen Gottschang Turner, *Even the Women Must Fight: Memories of War from North Vietnam* (New York: Wiley, 1998).

29. Sabine Kriebel, "Photomontage in the Year 1932: John Heartfield and the National Socialists," *Oxford Art Journal* 31, no. 1 (2008): 92–127.

30. Indeed, to observe that Vietnamese revolutionary photography was produced as propaganda is news to no one. Photography lay under the purview of the Ministry of Information, not the Minstry of Art and Culture; training courses were explicitly designed to educate practitioners in methods of producing propaganda; and a directive of ten points distributed by the National Liberation Front photography division listed, as its primary and most important point, photography as a "sharp weapon" of information and propaganda (nhiếp ảnh là võ khí thông tin, tuyên truyền sắc bén). Nguyễn, *Văn Hóa Nhiếp Ảnh*, 55.

31. Nguyễn, *Văn Hóa Nhiếp Ảnh*, 55.

32. Nguyễn, *Văn Hóa Nhiếp Ảnh*, 56.

33. Nguyễn, *Văn Hóa Nhiếp Ảnh*, 65.

34. Interview with Đoàn Công Tính, Hô Chí Minh City, May 16, 2013.

35. However, recent publications are starting to feature disabled bodies that previously had been censored.

36. Interview with Kim Đảng, Hanoi, May 12, 2013.

37. Nguyễn, *Văn Hóa Nhiếp Ảnh*.

38. See Nina Hien, "Ho Chi Minh City's Beauty Regime: Haptic Technologies of the Self in the New Millenium," *positions: east asia critique* 20, no. 2 (2012): 473–493. See also Nina Hien, "The Good, the Bad, and the Not Beautiful: In the Street and on the Ground in Vietnam," *Trans Asia Photography Review* 3, no. 2 (2013); and "Photo Resurrections Before and After Images: An Ancestor Story," *Trans Asia Photography Review* 1, no. 1 (2010).

39. Chauvel, *Ceux du Nord*.

40. Jørn Stjerneklar, "Aber Warum," *Mayday Press*, June 2, 2015, http://www.mayday press.com/blog/files/Opinions%20from%20Africa.html. A follow-up article argues that even the original image appears to have been Photoshopped. See Helle Maj and Jørn Stjerneklar, "Excuse My French!," *Mayday Press*, June 10, 2015, http://www.may daypress.com/blog/files/2ce9a7cd940027138ec550756d76716b-25.html.

41. Pierre Haski, "Une 'affaire Photoshop' dans le temple photojournalisme," *Rue 89*, June 9, 2015, http://rue89.nouvelobs.com/rue89-culture/2015/06/09/affaire-photo shop-temple-photojournalisme-259652.

42. David Campbell has written extensively, on behalf of the World Press Photo As-

sociation, on the topic of manipulation and journalistic ethics. See, for example, David Campbell, "Photo Manipulation and Verification," accessed August 13, 2015, https://www.david-campbell.org/topics/photo-manipulation-verification/.

43. For a fascinating account of memorialization practices in Vietnam, see Christina Schwenkel, *The American War in Contemporary Vietnam: Transnational Remembrance and Representation* (Bloomington: Indiana University Press, 2009).

—

CHAPTER FOURTEEN

SHOOTING IN THE DARK

A Note on the Photographic Imagination

SHARON SLIWINSKI

—

Photographs can be used for both ordering
and disordering the world.
Zoe Leonard, "The Politics of Contemplation"

I do feel we photographers are impacted in ways that we
don't yet know fully. . . . I am preoccupied by the question:
can we become haunted by images we haven't seen —
or that we haven't made?
Susan Meiselas, "Body on a Hillside"

In his book of essays titled *Writing in the Dark,* the Israeli writer David Grossman describes the ways that living in a state of prolonged political conflict can make the world grow smaller. He speaks of a void that slowly opens between the individual and the chaotic political situation that encompasses almost all aspects of life. This void does not remain empty but is quickly filled up with apathy, cynicism, and above all despair. According to Grossman, this is the price of living in a protracted state of conflict: "the shrinking of our soul's surface area — those parts of us that touch the violent, menacing world outside — and a diminished ability and willingness to empathize at all with other people in pain."[1]

Grossman's discussion is a variation of Bertolt Brecht's well-known account of "dark times," which appears in his poem "An die Nachgeborenen" ("To Posterity" or, more literally, "To Those Born After").[2] Written around 1939, while Brecht was in exile, the narrator of the poem articulates the cruel transformation that happens in such climates, when citizens are sustained on despair rather than hope, when simply maintaining daily routines can begin to feel inhumane. Something also happens to our speech in dark times. In these unyielding climates, language is no longer used to disclose and expose, but to obfuscate and hide what is. A kind of perverse language emerges that seeks to limit knowledge and prolong the distorted situation. As Grossman evocatively puts it, the speech available to citizens living through prolonged political turmoil "becomes flatter and flatter as the conflict goes on, gradually evolving into a series of clichés and slogans."[3] When death becomes the way of life, language seems to be divested of its power to sustain and enrich human imagination.

While reading Grossman's book I found myself wondering if something similar happens to our visual forms of language. Does photography, for instance, become divested of its power to illuminate in dark times? What would it mean for photography to grow "flatter and flatter" in periods of prolonged political conflict?

In a way, this is not a particularly new idea. In the short essays that make up *Mythologies*, for instance, Roland Barthes took great delight in describing occasions when our political theater abandons itself to spectacle. Of such spectacles, he wrote, "What the public wants is the image of passion, not passion itself."[4] What is demanded is a representation of the moral situation that is emptied of all interiority. Spectacle is a visual landscape that has been permeated with a kind of barrenness, Barthes suggests, crafted for "the benefit of its exterior signs." Like Grossman, Barthes suspects that our imagination atrophies in dark times. To cast this in visual terms, one could say that prolonged political conflict withers the spectator's powers of judgment and regard for the other. Instead of leading to recognition, our tools of communication promote misrecognition, invoking a fascinated gaze that looks but does not see.[5]

The target of Barthes's criticism was primarily the public, which is to say, he took aim at the spectators of the spectacle. But what about those who make and those who manage the images that populate our visual landscapes? Where do our imagined communities first begin to lock their gates?

As a kind of thought experiment, this chapter considers a small slice of the photographic landscape of South Africa at the end of apartheid. I should admit that I have no particular expertise in this area. I am not an Africanist, although I espouse a version of Toni Morrison's definition of this term, which is to say, I follow her idea that what appears to be subjective devastation—language growing "flatter and flatter"—is inextricably aligned with a socially governed relationship to race.[6] Morrison's query involves the literary imagination, and primarily the ways that the image of blackness appears in the literary imagination of white writers in the early history of the United States. In an analogous, although not exactly parallel, way, I am interested in what we might call the photographic imagination and, in particular, the ways that the image of blackness appears in the work of white photographers in South Africa at the end of apartheid. The central idea here—adapted from a handful of thinkers who have spent time studying the particular warp and weft of dark times—is that prolonged political violence will produce a disturbance in the visual field.[7]

To be clear, I do not mean to suggest that there was a lack of pictures during the apartheid years. In fact, quite the opposite was true, as the rich field of scholarship on South African photography shows.[8] What is of interest to me here, however, is how the social imaginary can become leveled by political violence, how it can become flatter and flatter, to use Grossman's terms. My exemplar is the Bang-Bang Club, a label that was assigned to a group of four white photojournalists whose collective body of work greatly contributed to (if not quite dominated) the visual horizon at the end of apartheid: Kevin Carter, Greg Marinovich, Ken Oosterbroek, and João Silva. Because these photographers worked primarily in the genre of photojournalism, their images tend to be treated as documentary, which is to say, their work is granted a privileged status as objective evidence of reality. Theorists have rightly put pressure on this view, however, arguing that what gets called documentary should be understood as a particular strategy of encoding meaning that can work both to construct and constrain the field of the social imaginary. John Tagg, for instance, has gone to some lengths to show how documentary realism lends itself to conservative uses. The genre's ability to secure a regime of truth is relied upon to forestall crises in the field of meaning and the field of the subject, because "after all, the real is the real, and no one can argue with that."[9]

The story of the so-called Bang-Bang Club—a club that was never a club— provides an apt site to consider this vexed contest of meaning.[10] In this chapter, I use the exemplar to raise two modest points: first, while most of these photographers understood themselves to be sympathetic to (and in some cases active agents for) the anti-apartheid struggle, their work became absorbed into a larger journalistic apparatus that sought to shape the reception of information about the transition of power in South Africa. Put more simply, some of their photographs were co-opted in ways that disordered our capacity to see the world clearly—used as tools to flatten the social imaginary. In this respect, the example offers a potent reminder that what gets called photography is, in fact, a complex situation that involves a wide range of actors and actions. Photography may produce pictures, but it is also a way of seeing—a process that involves a series of social relationships. And as Ariella Azoulay has emphasized, the encounter between these various actors is never entirely in anyone's control: "no one is the sole signatory of the event of photography."[11] Photography, as such, will always exceed the range of human intentionality.

It bears pointing out, in this respect, that the surviving photographers, Greg Marinovich and João Silva, have subsequently gone to lengths to reclaim and reenrich the imaginary realm in the time of afterward. Their reflections, recorded in a coauthored memoir titled *The Bang-Bang Club: Snapshots from a Hidden War*, offer crucial insights into the ways the photographic imagination is both constituted and constrained by political conflict. The text is especially important because it encourages readers to rotate their critical gaze: to shift attention from the photographed subject to the photographer, indeed, from the real world that is purportedly represented in photographs to the dynamic imagination that animates it.

The example confirms a familiar story about the violence of photographic meaning, which is to say, it provides another instance of the ways that the evidential force granted to certain images has a history that is inextricably bound up with relations of power. But there is something else here, too, and this is my second point: photography affects us in ways that are not fully knowable. As the renowned photojournalist Susan Meiselas suggests in the epigraph above, this is not only a concern for spectators; photographers, too, are impacted in ways that they do not fully understand. Walter Benjamin has provided one avenue to think about this dimension of the medium: "Clearly it is another nature that speaks to the camera as compared to the eye," he writes, "'Other' above all in the sense that a space informed by human consciousness gives way to a space informed by the unconscious."[12] The story of the Bang-Bang Club offers a glimpse of this "other discourse" that speaks to the camera, which in turn opens new questions about how photography might affect the social imaginary and, in particular, about photography as a medium of unconscious communication.

Apartheid is an elaborate political apparatus for a devastating racial oppression. It is exceedingly difficult to try to grasp how photography played a role in the transformation of this worldview in South Africa. But when this worldview is taken seriously as an agency, the images produced within it offer an opportunity to comprehend both the inadequacy and the force of the imaginative act.[13]

Shrinking Surface Area

South Africa's dark times seemed like they had finally come to an end on February 2, 1990. On this day, after more than four decades of legalized racial segregation, President F. W. de Klerk delivered a speech at the opening of parliament that formally began the process of abolishing the apartheid state. The president summarily lifted the ban on the African National Congress (ANC), the Communist Party, and scores of other political organizations that had opposed the regime. He freed Nelson Mandela, along with thousands of other political prisoners, and opened the door for negotiations for a new democratic constitution, an independent judiciary, and universal franchise. This hopeful act of rapprochement should have brought with it a more variegated visual landscape. But this high-water mark in the country's achingly slow transition to democracy was almost immediately marred by violence. The emotional void opened by decades of political conflict was not to be eradicated so easily. The surface area of the soul is not as elastic as one might hope.

While the public negotiations for the transition of power were just getting underway, an internecine conflict erupted in several black townships around Johannesburg.[14] In one incident on September 13, 1990, twenty-six people were murdered and another one hundred were injured in an attack on a commuter train running between Johannesburg and Soweto, a black township that lies at the southwest edge of the city. According to some estimates, as many as fourteen thousand people were killed during the period of transition between 1990 and April 1994, when the first fully democratic elections took place.[15] The violence itself had a spectacular character: apart from the terrorist-style attacks on commuter trains and massacres in the hostels and the streets in between, victims were sometimes killed by "necklacing," a slow, painful death that involved being collared with a rubber tire that was then set on fire.

The explanation that circulated in the mainstream media at the time was that this outbreak of violence had to do with a bloody rivalry between Nelson Mandela's ANC party and Chief Mangosuthu Buthelezi's Inkatha Freedom Party, which is to say, the violence was explained away as an old ethnic rivalry between the Xhosa-dominated ANC and the Zulu-dominated Inkatha party.[16] Local and international press seemed transfixed by the so-called black-on-black violence—a descriptor that was used over and over by authorities as a way to obfuscate the political nature of the conflict. As Derek Hook has argued, the social imaginary of postapartheid South Africa was fixated on images of black bodily destruction: one of the staples of apartheid news during the transition of power was the "schema of the abject black body."[17] Archbishop Desmond Tutu himself recalls that nearly everyone was making dire predictions about where South Africa was headed: "They believed that that beautiful land would be overwhelmed by the most awful bloodbath, that as sure as anything, a catastrophic race war would devastate that country."[18] During the period of transition, in other words, the imagined community of South Africa was bound together by a particularly anxious and gory image of itself.

Less often reported was the fact that a Third Force—directly linked to the apartheid government's security forces—was responsible for fomenting much of the violence: by supplying weapons, by importing mercenaries from neighboring countries, and, in some cases, by committing the murders themselves.[19] Apartheid stalwarts and their supporters sought to manufacture evidence that the "kaffirs" were not yet ready for democracy. The Goldstone Commission, tasked with investigating the violence during the transition of power, later confirmed that this Third Force was the explicit design of certain members of the National Party and was directly responsible for fueling the internecine conflict.[20]

Although the government's efforts to promote civil violence were deemed "the least well-kept secret in South Africa" at the time, the complexity of the situation proved difficult to capture photographically.[21] Local and international newspapers were nevertheless eager for images of the mounting carnage. In September 1990, just seven months after Mandela's release, they got their wish. Greg Marinovich, who was on assignment for the Associated Press (AP), produced a series of photographs depicting the mob murder of a man who was mistakenly identified as an Inkatha supporter. Early in the morning on September 15, 1990, Marinovich traveled into Soweto with Tom Cohen, another AP journalist who had been posted to Johannesburg just days prior. In his memoir, Marinovich readily admits that "like most people," he had not initially understood the roots of this conflict and "was confused by the seemingly indiscriminate acts of violence."[22] Around dawn, Cohen and Marinovich pulled up to Inhlazane train station where an unwitting commuter was swarmed by a crowd of comtsotsis (a local name for the thugs who masqueraded as militant liberation activists). The unsuspecting victim, who was on his way home from work, was punched, stoned, stabbed, and eventually dosed with gasoline and set on fire.

As Marinovich reports in his memoir, his attempt to intervene on the murder failed, but he did manage to capture the brutal scene on film. When he brought his pictures to the AP office in Johannesburg, the local editors were uncertain whether to send them over the agency's wire service. There was an unspoken rule that overly graphic pictures should not run on the wire (the

United States, in particular, had a lower tolerance for violent images than the rest of the world). After seeing the first few photographs, the AP's chief photo editor, Horst Faas, sent a brief reply back to Johannesburg directing them to "send all pictures." The entire series went out across the agency's wire service, and the photographs appeared in many newspapers around the world the next day, some accompanied by a textual account of the murder written by Cohen.

In South Africa, the publication of the photographs had an explosive effect. The government seized upon them as "a perfect opportunity to portray the ANC as killers who could never be entrusted with leading a country."[23] In other words, Marinovich had unintentionally furnished the authorities with evidence that the violence was driven by a vicious ethnic rivalry. A few months later, he was awarded the Pulitzer Prize for Spot News Photography. The images took on a kind of iconic status, becoming emblems of the so-called black-on-black violence that afflicted the country during the transition of power.

The photographs of the murder are undoubtedly harrowing, but they are devoid of information that could aid in the larger project of understanding the complex political situation. As Susan Sontag warned, "All photographs wait to be explained by their captions."[24] The original AP caption that was appended to the most dramatic of Marinovich's photographs identified the figures with the most basic of signs, like algebra that aims to make the relationship between a cause and its representational effect transparent (fig. 14.1):

(JOH-106) SOWETO, SOUTH AFRICA, SEPT. 15 [1990] — HUMAN TORCH — A small boy runs past as a youth clubs the burning body of a man identified as a Zulu Inkatha supporter and set alight by rival African National Congress supporters, Soweto, South Africa, Saturday morning. (AP ColourPhoto) (mon71224/str. SEB BALIC) 1990 EDS. NOTE: COLOUR CONTENT: ORANGE/RED FLAMES — PERSONS IN SILHOUETTE, VERY LITTLE DETAIL.[25]

The world spectator is given a terse account of the interaction between protagonists. There is little need to labor over meaning. One of the unwritten rules of spectacular journalism is that no suffering can appear without a readily intelligible cause. Or as Walter Benjamin put it, "Nowadays no event comes to us without already being shot through with explanation."[26] The explanation in this case is provided by keywords, tags that are still appended to the series in the AP archives: "Violence, Aggression, Revenge, Human, Blood, Murder."

But this particular event — and indeed the larger conflict that it embodied — did call for an extended explanation, eventually prompting Marinovich and

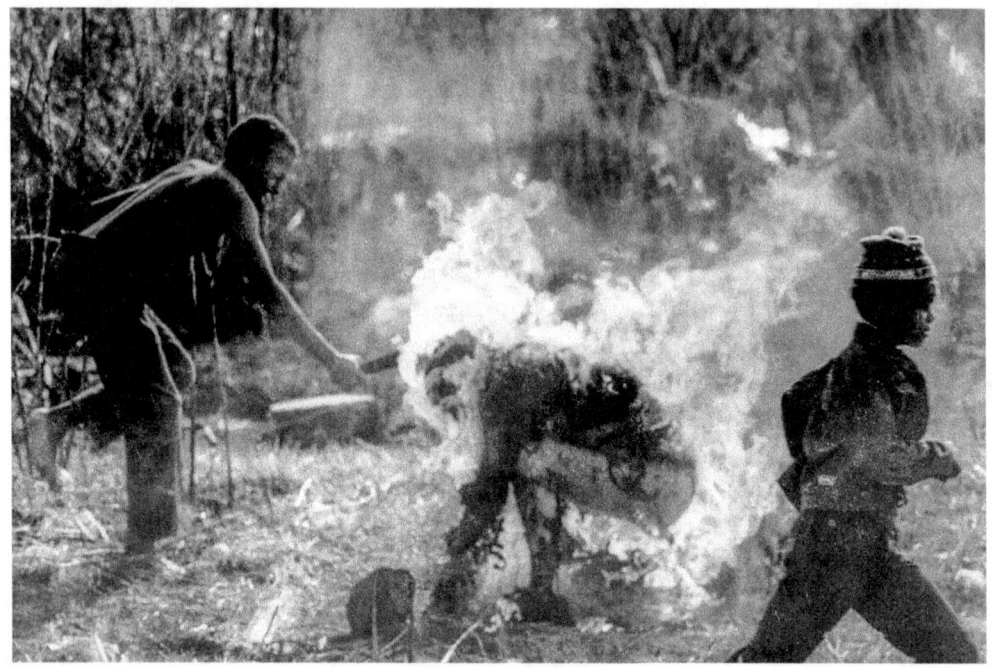
FIGURE 14.1 Gregory Marinovich, untitled photograph, September 15, 1990.
Courtesy of Gregory Marinovich.

Silva to write a memoir about their experience photographing the "hidden war" that gripped South Africa at the end of apartheid. The book contains a detailed account of this particular murder. Readers learn the victim's name — Lindsaye Tshabalala — and the ways the authorities sought to use the photographs for their own ends. The book provides a narrative frame through which readers might be better able to apprehend the victim as a knowable human person and therefore regard his death as a tragedy, an important condition of recognition that Judith Butler has termed "grievability."[27] At the same time, the narrative gives a first-hand account of the photographers' disillusionment with the idea that capturing images of political violence will somehow ameliorate the suffering. The gesture is significant: the memoir is a seething, sweaty fight for meaning and responsibility, an earnest inquiry into the nature of the frames that structure and limit both the photographer and the world spectator's capacity for recognition and response. In so doing, the book testifies to the fickleness of photographic meaning. This apparatus is just as willing to serve those wearing the jackboots as those who find themselves under the heel.

Photography—File Under: Unconscious Communication

So we shall have buried Apartheid—
how shall we look at each other then . . . ?

Mongane Wally Serote, A Tough Tale

As the photographs of the political conflict became more and more dramatic, the visual horizon of South Africa seemed to grow more and more shallow. Decades of apartheid rule seemed to transform the country into a two-dimensional and relentlessly frontal environment. One of the ways this flatness manifested was through a congealing of the forms of relationality. Somewhat akin to the way that language devolves into a series of slogans and clichés in dark times, it seems the gaze, too, can become frozen—fixed into a static relationship to the other.

One can glean a sense of this stifled mode of relating in some of the Bang-Bang Club photographs. It is perhaps most obvious in Kevin Carter's infamous 1993 image of a vulture lurking behind a starving child in Southern Sudan (an image that also won a Pulitzer prize). The photograph's narrow depth of field lends a sense of ominous proximity between the vulture and the crumpled toddler, while simultaneously keeping the spectator suspended. The compression in the visual plane makes it difficult for the spectator to know where she or he stands in relation to the scene. Perhaps not surprisingly, the image inspired an enormous commentary—both from spectators in the days immediately after its publication in the *New York Times* and subsequently by a wide variety of artists and scholars.[28] But this disconcerting sense of propinquity is evident elsewhere in the Bang-Bang Club photographers' work. Spectators are afforded little way to develop a sense of rapport with Ken Oosterbroek's 1993 *Resistance Fighter in Military Uniform*, for instance, despite the camera's proximity to its subject (fig. 14.2). The photograph works a bit like a pane of glass: a transparent barrier that is initially unnoticeable, but which quietly and firmly separates subjects on one side or the other.

How does political turmoil pass through the psyche to leave its mark on the aesthetic field? Can these visual disturbances, as I am calling them here, be read as symptomatic of the effects of apartheid, indicators of the subtle ways in which the de jure becomes the de facto? Put differently, I am interested in shifting the terms of critique from ideological exposé to an inquiry into the ways that photography can help us understand how society's laws become unconsciously internalized, how the social imaginary itself is structured and partitioned in a delicate dialogue with material conditions.

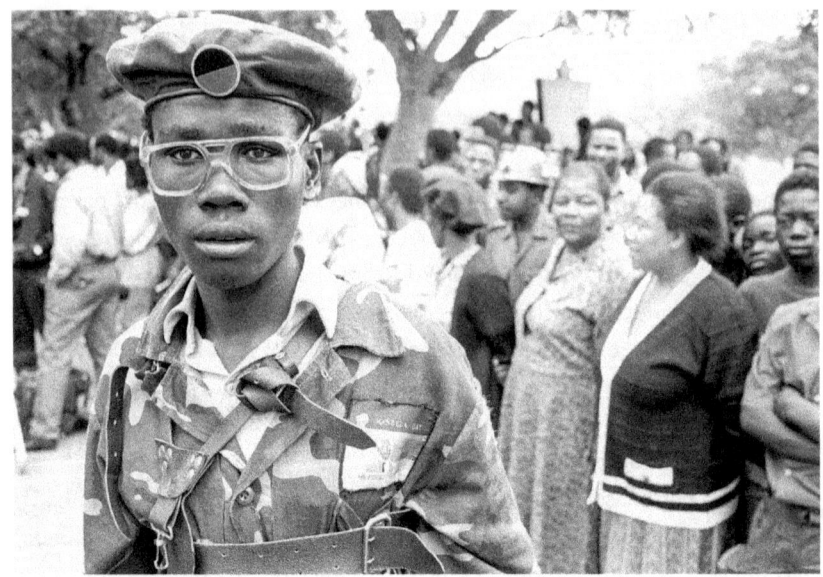

FIGURE 14.2 Ken Oosterbroek, *Resistance Fighter in Military Uniform*, 1993.
Courtesy of Ken Oosterbroek and PictureNET Africa, Ltd.

Apartheid literally means "separateness," of course, and among the National Party's most draconian laws was the Group Areas Act of 1950, which divided urban areas into racially segregated zones. The physical organization of the material world makes its way into psychic life via a process that Sigmund Freud called "introjection" or, alternatively, "incorporation."[29] Although he used the terms interchangeably, the latter emphasizes the corporeal qualities of the imaginary world: the way subjects take in, or indeed ingest, aspects of the outside world as structuring components of their own interior architecture. Humans consciously and unconsciously borrow external objects to delimit the boundaries of their bodies and sense of space. Growing up, or simply residing in a place, means that one is partly constituted by the environment. Indeed, by taking the world around us into ourselves, subjects actually become part of the preexistent fabric in all the profound ways that verb implies.

According to Jacques Lacan, verbal language is the most significant means by which subjects unconsciously incorporate the world they live in. This is one way to understand his famous claim that the unconscious is structured like a language. If we follow Walter Benjamin, however, photography also serves as an important *dispositif* in this process: "It is another nature that speaks to the camera rather than to the eye," he first wrote in his 1931 "Little History of Photography" and then repeated in his "Work of Art" essay: "'Other' above all in the sense that a space informed by human consciousness gives way to a space informed by the unconscious."[30] I take Benjamin to mean that photography is a medium that lends itself to unconscious communication. Or as Freud might have put it, photography provides an ideal vehicle through which "the unconscious of one human being can react upon that of another, without passing through consciousness."[31]

Every photograph contains a complex tapestry of meaning, much of which remains latent. The public (and private) circulation of photographic images is one means by which citizens carry on this unconscious conversation with each other, both projecting and introjecting social relations, populating and furnishing their imagined communities. But how does this conversation change in periods of prolonged political violence, or through the process of transitional justice, when old certainties have crumbled and new authorities must take root? How might the effects of these turbulent periods emerge as a problem of seeing?

Freud taught us that the relationship between spectator and image is always one of fracture, partial identification, desire, and mistrust—an insight that Lacan placed at the center of his work. The question remains, however, how the kinds of visual disturbances that have long preoccupied psychoanalysis might be used as prototypes to grasp the unconscious psychic processes involved in dramatic political transformations such as the period of transition in South Africa. Such an approach would go beyond the issue of content (scrutinizing images for the reproduction of stereotypes, for instance) to take in broader parameters of form: apart from the question of what is given to sight, there is the question of how subjects see. Here the photographic situation becomes something more than a field of recognition (or nonrecognition), something more than a visual arena that is constituted by a politics exerted from the outside.

Unfinished Pictures

I have been trying to make inroads into the ways that photography might be understood as a medium of unconscious communication, which is to say, a means by which human relationships are constituted in ways that exceed conscious intentionality. By way of a conclusion, I want to return to the photographer's position in this scene, to consider once more how this medium might affect subjects in ways that are not fully knowable.

At the peak of the bloody conflict that marked the transitional period in South Africa, two of the Bang-Bang Club photographers—Greg Marinovich and Kevin Carter—found themselves running through a shantytown district of Soweto called Chicken Farm. The photographers were chasing after policemen who, in turn, were chasing after armed suspects. The chase wove through a row of dilapidated shacks and the photographers plunged downhill along rough tracks that were muddy with sewage. At a clearing near a stream, they were confronted with a woman wailing in grief, her hands clutching her head. In front of her was a middle-aged man, lying on his back, his arms stretched out along a thick wooden beam. To Marinovich, the scene resembled an eerie crucifixion. The man's earlobes, pierced and enlarged in the Zulu fashion, were filled with blood from several head wounds. The photographer reports that "a professional thrill" ran through him: here was a scene that could serve as an icon of the conflict: "Kevin and I descended on the corpse, but once we started to photograph, I found myself struggling and failing to capture the image of the crucifixion properly. I was unnerved, jittery, my hands were shaking involuntarily. Perhaps it was because of the woman wailing or memories of childhood religion, of Christ on the cross. I looked at Kevin; he looked stunned. Suddenly the corpse groaned and rolled onto its side. We leapt back in terror—we had been so certain he was dead."[32] The incident could be chalked up to a moment of professional failure: the photographers didn't get their picture. But the event did not go entirely unrecorded. Although the emotional force of the event was not captured on film, it nevertheless left an imprint—indeed, the scene continued to produce images, albeit in a different medium.

Shortly after the incident at Chicken Farm, Kevin Carter began to be plagued by a recurring nightmare. He started compulsively reporting this dream to his colleagues, calling them in a panic at all hours of the night:

> In the dream, [Kevin] was near death, lying on the ground, crucified to a wooden beam, unable to move. A television camera with a massive lens zoomed closer and closer in on his face, until Kevin would wake up screaming. Kevin thought that the dream meant it might be time to leave photography. . . . He described the feelings of helplessness, the anger, the fear he lived through in that dream. It was all that he imagined our subjects must feel towards us in their last moments as we documented their deaths. The dream had variations: sometimes Kevin was the photographer, not the victim, and in that version, the "dead" man would roll over and grab him by the ankle, holding him captive with bloody hands.[33]

Like many traumatic dreams that are tethered to material conflicts and conditions, the nightmare seems to involve a compulsive return to an unmastered incident from the dreamer's lived experience. There are strong elements of the uncanny: a difficulty distinguishing the living from the dead, a sense of displacement, an emotional tone dominated by helplessness and guilt. The central action turns on a spectacular substitution: Carter exchanges positions with the gravely wounded man from Chicken Farm.

There is so much to be said about this remarkable event—about the experience from which the nightmare arose, but also about the ways that images of the scene continued to circulate. Since it could not be captured within the frame of a photograph, the event seemed to require representation elsewhere. One might say this image *inhabited* the photographer, demanding another venue of reproduction, in this case in the form of a compulsive dream, a psychic event that was so profound it even managed to outlive the death of the dreamer. Carter committed suicide in July 1994, but the image continued to circulate in textual form in Marinovich and Silva's memoir and, indeed, again in the text you are holding in your hands.

How far does the photographic situation stretch? Can we understand Carter's nightmare as a continuation of his work as a witness to history, as a kind of insistent and persistent laboring over an unfinished picture? How does a nightmare serve in the larger, ongoing effort to symbolize the violence that gripped South Africa at the turn of the millennium? If past events can repeat themselves in this way—appearing within the frame of our mind—it is because the event has never been lived in the fullness of its meaning, its presence not yet digested.[34]

There is precedent to add dream life to our catalog of image-work. Freud himself was fond of using photography as a metaphor for the psyche, including in his *Interpretation of Dreams*, but it was Walter Benjamin who first grasped the acute political significance of this connection. In one of the more speculative moments of his "Work of Art" essay, Benjamin argued that what shows itself to the camera is less like the normal perceptions given to human sight and more like the hallucinatory images that populate our dream life. The comparison was meant to help illustrate the "vast and unsuspected field of action" that speaks to the camera rather than to the eye.[35] The study of unconscious life is a project that we associate with Freud's announcement of the formation of psychoanalysis but, as Benjamin argued, this project need not stop with the limits of the individual self. Indeed, dream-life and photography might be the ideal venues to capture a glimpse of this "other" scene, those "diverse aspects of reality" not given directly to sight. If nothing else, the harrowing story of Carter's nightmare testifies to the devastating psychological cost exerted by dark times — the ways in which prolonged political violence can level our imaginary landscapes.

Gauging the effects of sovereign violence on the human imagination demands that we take into account all the ways that subjects are inhabited by an otherness. This otherness both is and is not a property of each subject; it marks the way the human is freighted with a form of social knowledge that exceeds its conscious grasp. Photography can provide one location to interrogate this otherness that each of us bears, although I suspect there is much yet for us to learn about all the ways this medium animates the unconscious.

Notes

A version of this chapter was presented at the Photographic Imagination conference, which took place at Tel Aviv University on May 26–28, 2014, in collaboration with the Shpilman Institute for Photography, Yale University, and the Bucerius Institute for Research of Contemporary German History and Society at the University of Haifa. I thank the organizers and participants of that conference for their thoughtful responses, in particular Margaret Olin, Amos Morris-Reich, and Vered Maimon. I would also like to extend my thanks to Greg Marinovich for his invaluable insights. This research was supported by the Social Sciences and Humanities Research Council of Canada.

1. David Grossman, *Writing in the Dark: Essays on Literature and Politics*, trans. Jessica Cohen (New York: Picador, 2009), 60.

2. Scott Horton has offered his translation of Brecht's poem. See his translation and discussion of the poem in "Brecht, 'To Those Who Follow in Our Wake,'" *Browsings, Harper's Magazine*, January 15, 2008, http://harpers.org/blog/2008/01/brecht-to -those-who-follow-in-our-wake/.

3. Grossman, *Writing in the Dark*, 61.

4. Roland Barthes, "The World of Wrestling," in *Mythologies*, trans. Annette Lavers (New York: Hill and Wang, 1972), 18.

5. Dora Apel offers an account of "looking without seeing" in "Lynching Photographs and the Politics of Public Shaming," in *Lynching Photographs*, by Dora Apel and Shawn Michelle Smith (Berkeley: University of California Press, 2007). I actually quarreled with Apel's phrasing in my review of that book (*RACAR* 33, no. 1–2 [2008]: 154– 156). There I insisted on calling the phenomenon "looking without knowing," which is to say, the problem is not a failure of vision, per se, but of moral judgment and imagination. I've returned to Apel's original phrasing here.

6. Toni Morrison, *Playing in the Dark: Whiteness and the Literary Imagination* (Cambridge, MA: Harvard University Press, 1992), 6.

7. Apart from Grossman and Morrison, I am also borrowing from Hannah Arendt's introduction to *Men in Dark Times* (San Diego: Harcourt Brace, 1968). My approach is

also deeply indebted to Jacqueline Rose's classic essay, "Sexuality in the Field of Vision," and in particular her insight that "a confusion at the level of sexuality brings with it a disturbance in the visual field." See Jacqueline Rose, *Sexuality in the Field of Vision* (London: Verso, 1986), 226.

8. The scholarship on South African photography is extensive. Drew Thompson provides a good review in: "(Re)exposing Old 'Negatives': New Discourses and Methodologies in Photographic Studies on Africa," *African Studies Association*, no. 3 (December 2014): 175–185. In relation to the apartheid years, in particular, Okwui Enwezor has suggested that at least two competing photographic practices emerged during the last decade of the regime. On one side was social documentary, which explicitly took up a position against inequality, an ethos that animated the Afrapix collective, whose photographers provided many of the iconic images in the alternative and independent media. On the other side was photojournalism, which embodied a more disinterested, frontline approach. Enwezor suggests the Bang-Bang Club belongs to the latter category. See Okwui Enwezor, "Rise and Fall of Apartheid: Photography and the Bureaucracy of Everyday Life," in *Rise and Fall of Apartheid: Photography and the Bureaucracy of Everyday Life*, ed. Okwui Enwezor and Rory Bester (New York: International Center of Photography/DelMonico Books, 2013), 31. See also Darren Newbury, *Defiant Images: Photography and Apartheid South Africa* (Pretoria: UNISA Press, 2009); Patricia Hayes, "Santu Mofokeng, Photographs: 'The Violence Is in the Knowing,'" *History and Theory* 48, no. 4 (2009): 34–51; Heidi M. Saayman Hattingh, "Photographer Autonomy and Images of Resistance: The Case of South Africa during the 1980s," *Visual Communication* 10, no. 4 (November 2011): 499–525; Bronwyn Law-Viljoen, "'Bang-Bang Has Been Good to Us': Photography and Violence in South Africa," *Theory, Culture and Society* 27, no. 708 (2010): 214–238.

9. John Tagg, *The Disciplinary Frame: Photographic Truths and the Capture of Meaning* (Minneapolis: University of Minnesota Press, 2009), 57.

10. The name "The Bang-Bang Club" originated in an article published in the South African magazine *Living* written by Chris Marais. Originally termed "The Bang-Bang Paparazzi," the moniker was changed to "Club" because some of the photographers felt the word paparazzi misrepresented their work. Marinovich and Silva make clear that such a club never existed, and that, in fact, dozens of journalists covered the violence during the period. See Greg Marinovich and João Silva, *The Bang-Bang Club: Snapshots from a Hidden War* (New York: Basic Books, 2000), 53 and xiv.

11. Ariella Azoulay, *Civil Imagination: A Political Ontology of Photography* (London: Verso, 2012), 17.

12. Walter Benjamin, "The Work of Art in the Age of Its Technological Reproducibility" (1936), in *Selected Writings, vol. 3, 1935–1938*, ed. Howard Eiland and Michael W. Jennings, , trans. Rodney Livingstone (Cambridge, MA: Belknap, 2002), 117.

13. I have deliberately not included a concrete definition of the imagination here, choosing instead to move fluidly between various uses of this term. At times, I am

working with Sigmund Freud's sense of the imagination as a field of fantasy, that is, as a series of imaginary scenes structured by anxiety and desire. Other times, I am thinking of Jacques Lacan's concept of the imaginary, which characterizes the way the ego is constituted on the basis of an image. Immanuel Kant understood this faculty as the mind's ability to make present what is absent, and his thinking was significant for Hannah Arendt's sense of the public realm. The chapter is also influenced by more recent scholars who have tried to show how the imaginary field intersects with the social realm: Benedict Anderson, *Imagined Communities: Reflections on the Origin and Spread of Nationalism* (New York: Verso, 1991); Cornelius Castoriadis, *The Imaginary Institution of Society* (Cambridge: Polity, 1987); and Arjun Appadurai, *Modernity at Large: Cultural Dimensions of Globalization* (Minneapolis: University of Minnesota Press, 1996).

14. The transition to democracy was a long, involved process. Secret meetings between the National Intelligence Service and Nelson Mandela had been taking place since the 1980s, and negotiations continued upon his release. A National Peace Accord was signed in September 1991 that paved the way for the CODESA talks (Convention for a Democratic South Africa). The first fully democratic election took place on April 27, 1994. See Allister Sparks, *Tomorrow Is Another Country: The Inside Story of South Africa's Road to Change* (Chicago: University of Chicago Press, 1990).

15. Okwui Enwezor and Rory Bester, eds., *Rise and Fall of Apartheid: Photography and the Bureaucracy of Everyday Life* (New York: International Center of Photography/ DelMonico Books, 2013), 468.

16. Christopher Wren's coverage in the *New York Times* is representative of how the conflict was covered internationally. See, for instance, Christopher Wren, "Zulu and Mandela Groups Begin Talks," *New York Times*, September 21, 1990.

17. Derek Hook, "The Racist Bodily Imaginary: The Image of the Body-in-Pieces in (Post)apartheid Culture," *Subjectivity* 6, no. 3 (2013): 255, 256.

18. Desmond Tutu, foreword to Marinovich and Silva, *The Bang-Bang Club*, ix.

19. Allister Sparks openly reported that witnesses to many of the attacks "have reported seeing whites with blackened faces, or faces covered with face masks" among the attackers. See Allister Sparks, "South Africans Massacred aboard Train," *Washington Post*, September 14, 1990. Human Rights Watch also released a report in January 1991, which presented compelling evidence that the national security force was behind much of the violence. The report also proposes that "ethnic differences have been overemphasized by both the government and press reports." See Human Rights Watch, "The Killings in South Africa: The Role of the Security Forces and the Response of the State," January 8, 1991, www.hrw.org/reports/1991/southafrica1/index.htm.

20. The Goldstone Commission, chaired by Richard Goldstone and formally known as the Commission of Inquiry Regarding the Prevention of Public Violence and Intimidation, was appointed by President de Klerk to investigate the violence that occurred between 1991 and 1994. The Commission sat for three years and produced dozens of reports. Stephen Ellis has offered a detailed account of the way in which the Third Force

was long integrated with the policies of the National Party, as well as the way the consequences of its tactics continue to haunt South African politics and society. See Stephen Ellis, "The Historical Significance of South Africa's Third Force," *Journal of Southern African Studies* 24, no. 2 (1998): 261–299.

21. Gail M. Gerhart, "Review of 'The Killings in South Africa: The Role of the Security Forces and the Response of the State'; South Africa: My Vision of the Future," *Foreign Affairs*, September 1, 1991.

22. Marinovich and Silva, *The Bang-Bang Club*, 11.

23. Marinovich and Silva, *The Bang-Bang Club*, 31.

24. Susan Sontag, *Regarding the Pain of Others* (New York: Picador, 2003), 10.

25. Marinovich and Silva, *The Bang-Bang Club*, 19.

26. Walter Benjamin, "The Storyteller: Observations on the Works of Nikolai Leskov," in *Selected Writings*, vol. 3, 147–148.

27. Judith Butler, *Frames of War: When Is Life Grievable?* (London: Verso, 2009).

28. The Chilean artist Alfredo Jaar created an installation called *The Sound of Silence* in 2006 in which Kevin Carter's image from the Sudan figures prominently; Dan Krauss produced a documentary in 2004 called *The Death of Kevin Carter: Casualty of the Bang-Bang Club*; the Chinese artist Xu Zhen created *The Starving of Sudan* in 2008, which featured a live African toddler menacingly eyed by a mechanical vulture in the middle of a brightly lit, hot desert scene; and the British artist Mat Collishaw produced a haunting 3D animated installation of Carter's image called *Prize Crop* for his 2013 solo show. The photograph has also inspired much scholarly debate. A partial list includes Arthur Kleinman and Joan Kleinman, "The Appeal of Experience; the Dismay of Images: Cultural Appropriations of Suffering in Our Times," *Daedalus* 125, no. 1 (1996): 1–23; David Perlmutter, *Photojournalism and Foreign Policy: Icons of Outrage in International Crises* (Westport, CT: Praeger, 1998); Griselda Pollock, "Picturing Atrocity: Becoming Iconic?," in *Picturing Atrocity: Photography in Crisis*, ed. Geoffrey Batchen et al. (London: Reaktion, 2012), 65–78; Yung Soo Kim and James D. Kelly, "Photojournalist on the Edge: Reactions to Kevin Carter's Sudan Famine Photo," *Visual Communication Quarterly* 20, no. 4 (2013): 205–219; Merlijn Geurts, "The Atrocity of Representing Atrocity: Watching Kevin Carter's 'Struggling Girl,'" *Aesthetic Investigations* 1, no. 1 (2015): 1–13.

29. Sigmund Freud, "Mourning and Melancholia" (1917), in *Standard Edition of the Complete Psychological Works of Sigmund Freud*, vol. 14, ed. and trans. James Strachey (London: Hogarth, 1955). See also Sandor Ferenczi, "The Meaning of Incorporation," in *Further Contributions to the Theory and Technique of Psychoanalysis* (New York: Fordham University Press, 2007).

30. Walter Benjamin, "Little History of Photography" (1931), in *Walter Benjamin: Selected Writings, vol. 2, part 2, 1931–1934*, trans. Rodney Livingstone et al., ed. Michael W. Jennings, Howard Eiland, and Gary Smith (Cambridge, MA: Belknap, 1999), 510. See also Benjamin, "The Work of Art," 117.

31. Sigmund Freud, "The Unconscious" (1915), in *The Standard Edition of the Com-

plete Psychological Works of Sigmund Freud, vol. 14, ed. and trans. James Strachey (London: Hogarth, 1953), 194.

32. Marinovich and Silva, *The Bang-Bang Club*, 55–56.

33. Marinovich and Silva, *The Bang-Bang Club*, 55.

34. See Sarah Kofman, *Camera Obscura: Of Ideology*, trans. Will Straw (Ithaca, NY: Cornell University Press, 1998), 24, and reproduced in this volume (page 77). Kofman, too, notes the connection between photography and dreams.

35. Benjamin, "The Work of Art," 117.

———

CHAPTER FIFTEEN

SLOW

———

TERRI KAPSALIS

March 13, 2014. An audience of more than eight hundred people fills the Rubloff Auditorium at the Art Institute of Chicago. Guitarist Thurston Moore is on stage facing the audience with his electric guitar and amp, his back to the seventy-two-foot-wide screen. The lights dim. James Nares's 2011 film *Street* begins. What am I seeing? A rich color image of a New York street. Are those models or actors on the sidewalk? The image is still. A photograph. No, it is not. There is movement. A pedestrian's eyelid. The pinks and reds of neon shop signs pulse up and down the street, beating like a vast circulatory system. We spectators float down the street by way of a tracking shot. *Street* is something between a photograph and a moving image, unlike anything I have ever seen. As my eyes and mind acclimate, I perceive more of the pedestrians' glacial movement. One man's finger unfurls into a point. A woman in a T-shirt, both palms facing out at chest level, flaps her fingers like a slow bird. This cannot be staged. It is found. I thought I knew what a person walking down the street looked like. Had I been misled by that second meaning of the term *pedestrian*—tedious, dull, monotonous? That definition must have been created by somebody who wasn't looking carefully.

Moore's guitar is dense and driving. His decision to turn his back to the screen infuses his improvisations with an element of chance. Surprising punctuations and unanticipated emotional tones arise through the indeterminate relationship between image and sound. The film scrolls from one tableau to another. The Times Square naked cowboy is a cutout midstrum, a visual counterpart to Moore's guitar sounds. Television monitors in a storefront window blink like square eyes. So many mouths caught open. A woman's arm crawling upward on the way to hailing a cab—a slow salute or a gesture to the heavens? A man, palm to the sky, pulls three fingers toward him. A woman stands at the corner, earbuds in place, her face in a serene trance with eyes closed; her arms

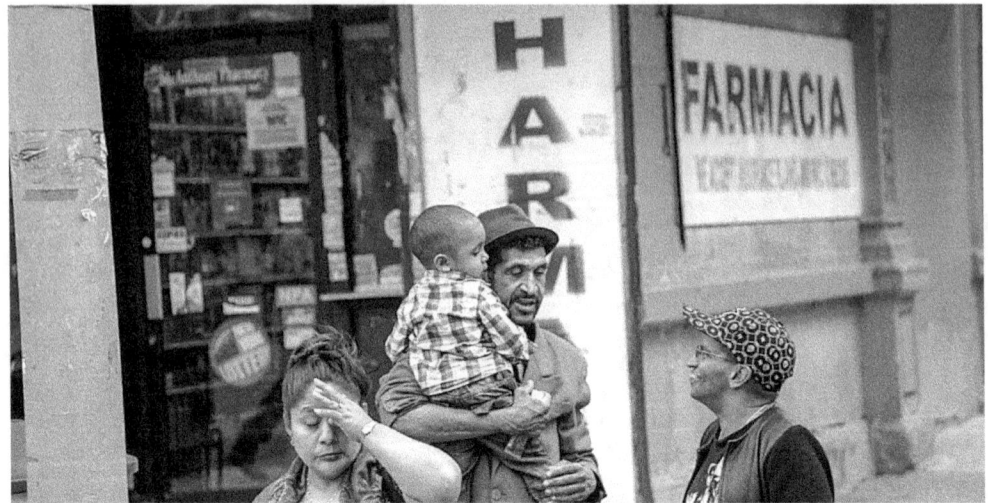

hover as if conducting a cloud of spirits. Two cops lean against metal rails like reliefs in reflective yellow vests. A baby's fat legs in pink tights float forward from her father's belly as if walking into air.

Nares made *Street* with a Phantom Flex high-speed camera, shooting 780–800 frames per second from the window of a car, while being driven around the streets of Manhattan. The street serves as a track, with the car providing the motion for the tracking shot. Nares could only shoot six seconds at a time because, if he wanted to keep the shot, he would need to transfer the files from the camera, which took a good ten minutes. Over the course of a week he shot a total of forty minutes in six-second increments. Forty minutes of real-time footage transformed into sixteen hours of slow-motion footage, which then was edited into an hour-long film with a soundtrack comprised of Thurston Moore twelve-string guitar improvisations (see plates 17–20). For the Art Institute performance, the film's recorded soundtrack was silenced and Moore created an improvised soundtrack on the spot.

A month or so following the screening I run into Margaret, a friend who had also been a member of the large audience that night at the Art Institute. She says she can't stop thinking about *Street*. I tell her I am haunted by it. We discuss favorite moments. The two young sisters who spy the camera in the car and transform from smiles to impish vixens with blazing hand signs. The sparrows that lift off to the liquor store awning like four beams of light. And the fly, the inimitable fly like a small hovering helicopter with wings that are nearly visible. We discuss two or three seconds of real time as though they are complex narratives.

In 1933, film theorist Rudolf Arnheim wrote, "[Slow motion] has hitherto been used almost exclusively in educational films in order to show the individual phases of rapid movements. In this way the technique of a boxer or of a violinist, the explosion of a bomb, the jump of a dog, can be analyzed closely. Slow motion has hardly been applied at all yet to artistic purposes, although it should be very useful. It might, for instance, serve to slow down natural movements grotesquely; but it can also create new movements, which do not appear as the retarding of natural movements but have a curious gliding, floating character of their own."[1]

Vision Research makes Phantom Camera Products for the entertainment, scientific, military, aerospace, and automotive industries. One camera is orbiting the earth on the International Space Station, where it will "provide high-speed image capture for ground breaking zero gravity experiments."[2] Phantom high-speed cameras catch things in fast motion: airbags inflating, dogs drinking water, spray bottles spraying, basketball players jumping, a rocket launching, sharks hunting, a crash dummy during impact, a table saw, a missile path, New York pedestrians.

Walter Benjamin wrote, "Even if one has a general knowledge of the way people walk, one knows nothing of a person's posture during the fractional second of a stride."[3]

A subject's quick tempo makes for more surprising slow motion. Muybridge shot a galloping horse, not a tortoise. Nares shot New York City streets. According to research conducted in the 1990s by social psychologist Robert Levine, New York City has the sixth fastest walking speed in the world. He was surprised by the results, expecting New York City to clock in faster, but after retesting, he found that clock speed does not account for the manner in which New York pedestrians maneuver streets — dodging cars and other pedestrians. There is a "skill and assertiveness on the streets of New York that doesn't necessarily show up on the stopwatch."[4]

Street could be seen as following in the slow-motion educational film tradition that Arnheim mentions. Take a fast-moving organism, like a running horse, and slow it down to see if all four feet are suspended at one time. Is there any reason to shoot with a Phantom camera on the Greek island of Ikaria where a large population of centenarians avoid watches and live with broken clocks?

Levine observed that pedestrian tempo in a city correlated with other characteristics of that city. The more robust the economy, the faster people walked. The more industrialized the country, the faster people walked. The bigger the population, the faster people walked. The cooler the climate, the faster people walked. And then there is this characteristic: "Individualistic cultures move faster than those that emphasize collectivism." In individualistic cultures, Levine surmises, more emphasis is placed on achievement than on social relationships, which "usually leads to a time-is-money mindset."[5]

A few months before the Art Institute of Chicago's screening of *Street*, cultural critic Anne Elizabeth Moore and I talk with students at the School of the Art Institute of Chicago. We have been invited to address issues of diversity and the critique process. Toward the end of the event, Anne talks about the idea of "radical noticing," that to actually notice the people near you seems like a radical act. I add that radical noticing requires time. How can we actually notice or see the person standing there if we do not slow down? How can we listen and take note of what they are saying or not saying? So, yes, noticing is radical, but what about slowness? Isn't that perhaps one of the most rebellious ways to be these days? Hands shoot up. Students want to discuss this slowness. There is a craving in the room.

As the discussion unfolds, I list as many slow movements as I can remember (food, museum experiences, television). In 2013, *Sakte-TV* or Slow TV was named "word of the year" in Norway. Half the country's population tuned in for a 134-hour live broadcast of a ship's voyage from Bergen to Kirkenes. Then there was a twelve-hour-long broadcast titled *National Firewood Night* that included eight hours of a live fireplace.[6] Soon after reading about Norwegian slow television, I saw an advertisement for an American Animal Planet special called *Meet the Sloths*.

I hadn't yet learned about Lorenz Potthast, a German artist, who designed the Decelerator helmet when he was a first-year art student. "The helmet is simply a shiny metal dome that records the view from a front camera and processes it through a small computer to a screen in front of the wearer's eyes. The slow-motion is controlled by a handheld remote. 'The first three minutes are just confusing, but then you get a feel for it and you become the director of your own perception,' he says. 'It's alienating, because you're experiencing time at a different speed to your own surroundings so you can't really interact, but it's also somehow fascinating. People often don't want to take it off again.'"[7]

Potthast did not intend to market his helmet, but he has been contacted regularly by interested parties. In March 2014, Potthast was contacted by the director of a physical rehabilitation clinic in Italy. "After numerous studies with volunteer patients at the clinic, Potthast and the Italian doctors eventually found an intriguing possible use for the helmet. One patient, who had suffered a stroke and could no longer fully open his hands, was motivated to overcome this physical barrier after wearing the helmet during his exercises and seeing his fingers unfold in slow motion."

I wonder aloud if slow might be an antidote for this fast world. If slow might be an important first step toward understanding and respecting how we are different from each other.

One student at the back of the room raises his hand. "But how can I explain this slowness thing to my mother, who works two jobs to pay for my education?" He is sincere with pen and notebook out, ready to take notes.

I answer that slowness doesn't necessarily mean that less gets done. I talk about days of quickly doing many things at once and then, at the end, wondering what actually happened. And then there is the slow, plodding person that always seems to have another project completed. Remember the tortoise and the hare?

Am I convinced by my own answer? Partly. Is slowness a privilege? Is slowness a luxury? And conversely, slowness is not always a matter of choice. "Slow" can be used as an admonition, even an accusation. So slowness must be considered in the context of a culture where expendable laborers are judged on the speed of their production. Where the health of an economy is measured by the quick rate of consumption.

Is slowness a possible form of resistance? As much as I question the prevalent emphasis on achievement over social relationships, I, too, feel the pressures of speedy production. I do not say to the students that there are times I feel deep shame for my slow working process and have excused myself with an apologetic tone: "I write slowly. Very very slow. So slow. Like a painter setting out on a wall-sized canvas with a single-hair brush."

I do not tell the students that, at times, I catch myself waiting to speak in lieu of listening to what someone is saying. That I find myself walking quickly from one place to another with a sole focus on arrival. Putting slow into action is not easy.

"Participants are invited to run a race with the aim of losing," writes Brazilian theater innovator Augusto Boal. Boal designed exercises to "undo the muscular structure of the participants" so they can understand how their labor and life shapes their bodies. Included within these disjunctive exercises is the slow-motion race: "The last one is the winner. Moving in slow motion, the body will find its center of gravity dislocated at each successive moment and so must find again a new muscular structure which will maintain its balance. The participants must never interrupt the motion or stand still; also they must take the longest step they can and their feet must rise above knee level. In this exercise, a 10 meter run can be more tiring than a conventional 500-meter run, for the effort needed to keep one's balance in each new position is intense."[8]

Rabbi Jonathan Sacks: "There is a wonderful story about an 18th-century rabbi, Levi Yitzchak of Berdichev, who is looking at people rushing to and fro in the town square. And he wonders why they're all running so frenetically. He stops one and he says, 'Why are you running?' And the man says, 'I'm running to make a living.' And the rabbi says to him, 'How come you're so sure that the living is in front of you and you have to run to catch up? Maybe it's behind you and you got to stop and let it catch up with you.'"[9]

It's there in the thesaurus. How did "slowness" become a synonym for "laziness," "idleness," and "sluggishness"? How did "slowness" become the antonym of "activity"? A sloth is not lazy. A sloth is just being a sloth.

A few words here. A sentence there. If lucky, a paragraph appears. When sitting at a keyboard or with paper and pen, is stillness the same as inactivity? Oftentimes, through stillness something happens. How to tell the stillness of activity from that of inactivity when they look the same?

Perhaps this is why *Street* is so comforting. Nares takes us deep into what might be considered unproductive time, the time of the movement between here and there. Hidden within these unremarkable pedestrian moments are exceptional micro-performances. A person does not appear to move distractedly from point A to point B. There is something at play that is much more complex, like a single word unfolding itself into a book-length poem.

Street sticks. Walking in downtown Chicago, I try to picture what I cannot see, the tiny dramas locked into the expressions and gestures of pedestrians who pass by. An older woman walks toward me, her eyes focused on a building in front of her. Her right hand rubs her left. If I could see her with *Street* vision, how might she appear? Joyful? Ecstatic? Forlorn?

I am not one to make sounds while watching a film, but while watching *Street* I find myself making utterances as though I am watching a spectacular display. Nares shows me the magnificence in the mundane — a billowing shirt or a pigeon's lift-off.

Might this slow vision be the superpower we need for these times? Take "faster than a speeding bullet" and flip it on its head? Slower than a sprouting seed! *Street* has changed the way I see.

How has *Street* changed the way Nares sees? I ask him about this in a phone interview. Nares's speech is slow and deliberate, which makes his words a dream to transcribe. He answers the question before it is asked.

JAMES NARES: . . . A big part of *Street* is how the viewer acclimates. You begin to understand what's going on and you're able to see more things happening within the moment. Myself, after watching it again and again, I've developed an ability to see live in the street. I can see things happen. I can take a little snapshot in my mind and see it as though it were in the film. Life is pretty rich when you look at it that way. There's so much going on.

TERRI KAPSALIS: I planned to ask if making *Street* has changed the way you see.

JN: It's changed . . . my ability to look. It's changed . . . yes, it's changed the way I see. It's changed how I see and what I see. And I appreciate the choice we have in what we see. The eye is nonjudgmental and absorbs everything coming at it. It's the mind that isolates and then does things with the things it isolates. Psychology and culture take their toll on what we see. That's why I love the way babies look. They just look. It's nonjudgmental and that's why they look so wise. . . .[10]

Urban theorist Jane Jacobs observed her stretch of Hudson Street in New York City. In her 1961 book *Life and Death of American Cities*, she notes how the daily rituals of inhabitants can be seen as a "sidewalk ballet": "Under the seeming disorder of the old city, wherever the old city is working successfully, is a marvelous order for maintaining the safety of the streets and the freedom of the city. It is a complex order. Its essence is intricacy of sidewalk use, bringing with it a constant succession of eyes. This order is all composed of movement and change, and although it is life, not art, we may fancifully call it the art form of the city and liken it to the dance . . . to an intricate ballet in which the individual dancers and ensembles all have distinctive parts which miraculously reinforce each other and compose an orderly whole. The ballet of the good city sidewalk never repeats itself from place to place, and in any one place is always replete with improvisations."

She offers a detailed description of the sidewalk ballet in her neighborhood that includes the following: "Mr. Lacey, the locksmith, shuts up his shop for a while and goes to exchange the time of day with Mr. Slube at the cigar store. Mr. Koochagian, the tailor, waters the luxuriant jungle of plants in his window, gives them a critical look from the outside, accepts a compliment on them from two passers-by, fingers the leaves on the plane tree with a thoughtful gardener's appraisal, and crosses the street for a bite at the Ideal where he can keep an eye on customers and wigwag across the message that he is coming."

She surmises, "I have made the daily ballet of Hudson Street sound more frenetic than it is, because writing telescopes it. In real life, it is not that way. In real life, to be sure, something is always going on, the ballet is never at a halt, but the general effect is peaceful and the general tenor even leisurely. People who know well such animated city streets will know how it is. I am afraid people who do not will always have it a little wrong in their heads—like the old prints of rhinoceroses from travelers' descriptions of rhinoceroses."[11]

When filming *Street*, Nares and his vehicle stayed on streets that allowed for a consistent speed of around thirty miles per hour. Perhaps that is why we don't see many of the kind of leisurely, neighborhood interactions that Jacobs describes. Or perhaps it is the fact that in the fifty-plus years since Jacobs wrote these words, cities have experienced unprecedented acceleration of growth as well as an increased speed associated with the growing consumption of digital media and technology. The sidewalk ballet has shifted to a quicker tempo, which, according to Levine, coincides with a pull to individualism.

Theoretical physicist Geoffrey West explains how this quicker tempo is actually counterintuitive when considering the growing city as a sprawling organism: "Every other creature gets slower as it gets bigger. That's why the elephant plods along. But in cities, the opposite happens. As cities get bigger, everything starts accelerating. There is no equivalent for this in nature. It would be like finding an elephant that's proportionally faster than a mouse."[12]

Nares slows the city organism and its frenetic streets and presents this elephantine organism in a pace proportional to its size. We can witness the city as a massive creature, pedestrians like cells on sidewalk pathways, neon lights that pulse and circulate. Beneath the city's slow streets, out of view, are unhurried sewer systems and electrical currents. In the tradition of early slow-motion education films, *Street* encourages us to consider the mystery of the organism and the way its many parts move and interact. Whereas in real time, pedestrians might appear as isolated, discrete units, in *Street* at times they appear to be reaching out to each other, as if to grasp one another's arms or to shake hands in the peaceful and leisurely manner of Jacobs's improvisational sidewalk ballet.

TK: Is there a particular moment when the idea for *Street* came to you? Something you saw or shot?

JN: I think it was just a slow meeting of a few areas of my interest and of different parts of my mind. One of which was super-slow-motion cinematography/videography. I guess my first slow-motion stuff started in 1975 with a Super 8 camera and continued in 1998 with a 16 mm high-speed camera. And I've always loved the *actualité* films, the films where they just stuck a camera on a cable car around the turn of the twentieth century, how they would drive it through the streets of London or New York.[13] And the camera wouldn't move — it would just look straight ahead in those films. It was a straight document and there was no interfering with what happened in front of the camera. There was just an absorption of what was happening on the street, in the world, and those films would usually show the streets of New York in Chicago and would show San Francisco in New York. You'd get to travel without actually having been there before travel became so easy. I think the most famous of those kinds of films was San Francisco before and after the earthquake. It was called "A Trip down Market Street." And the guy just happened to film it a couple of days before the earthquake, so he went back right after the earthquake and shot the same film. It's pretty great. There are other ones of going through the lower east side, Orchard Street, things like that. I've always loved those films and I've always loved Andy Warhol films, like the screen tests, and I love things where he just turned the camera on and let it run and really, no one did that. I guess people figured out how to use film, how to manipulate reality to tell a story, to piece it together to change what was happening. Even with things that were supposedly documentary, people learned how to tell or to show their bias through the documentary. And really, nobody just turned the camera on and let it run until Andy Warhol came along and revived the idea, but it was seeded with the very first motion pictures. The very first motion pictures are of somebody blowing a bubble or somebody smoking a cigarette or a bird flying through the air, events that are unmanipulated in a way. They may be set up, like when Thomas Edison electrocuted an elephant to show the magic of his new invention, but still I always responded to the idea of just turning the camera on. In *Street*, I just wanted to show what was out there in the world and try and allow people to see it a little differently. . . .

TK: *Street* shows me that some pedestrian movements, some gestures, are almost spiritual. They are not of this world.

JN: I saw my friend John Ahern the sculptor last night. He used that word last night, *spiritual*. And other people have used it. I am so happy that my plan worked. I was just looking at the very first footage I shot from a little Casio camera that had an ability to shoot at a high frame rate, very low resolution. But I was driving in the city with one hand on the wheel and one hand pointing out the window with the camera. When I started looking at the footage and putting it together, I realized there was something there. I saw what I had found. And it was immediately apparent to me that there were these beautiful moments that could encapsulate something that we could each identify with and to elevate the simplest things into a spiritual realm. I wrote a proposal for the film about three years before I actually shot it, and one of the things I said was something like, I will be filming in the city, looking for ordinary moments, not looking for moments of dramatic interest, but moments that could reveal the drama in the brief moments of our lives, the small dramas that are happening all the time. I feel I succeeded in doing that. . . . It has given me great pleasure to discover how people across the board seem to like this film — from kids to old people, people who know about film and art, people who don't. That's more than I could have hoped for.

TK: I wonder if part of that is due to the times we're living in with regard to speed.

JN: Yes, to see people slowing down and realizing that even though this thing is glacial in its movement through time, the fact that it's moving slowly doesn't mean that your mind has to move slowly too. You realize you become a very active participant in looking. It gives you time to look, and your eye can flit around the screen and see things and pick them out. . . . Particularly, it gives me pleasure when young people get hooked into it because the times we live in are so quick and multitasking with so many things happening simultaneously. There's such a sensory overload in the world, and it's nice to be able to do something that is completely opposite to that but to keep it interesting.

In 1923, spiritualist and writer Alexandra David-Neel saw a "moving black spot" on the horizon that, with the help of her field glasses, proved to be a man. She and her caravan were traversing the Tibetan countryside and had not seen another human being for ten days. The black spot approached quickly, and one of David-Neel's company proposed that this man was a *lung-gom-pa* lama. David-Neel was warned not to stop him or speak to him, for breaking his meditation would certainly kill him. She wrote in her book *Magic and Mystery in Tibet*: "By that time he had nearly reached us; I could clearly see his perfectly calm impassive face and wide-open eyes with their gaze fixed on some invisible far-distant object situated somewhere high up in space. The man did not run. He seemed to lift himself from the ground, proceeding by leaps. It looked as if he had been endowed with the elasticity of a ball and rebounded each time his feet touched the ground. His steps had the regularity of a pendulum. . . . He went his way apparently unaware of our presence." After seeing the lung-gom-pa lama, David-

Neel spoke with various people she met along the way and calculated that the lama had been running at that swift speed for a minimum of twenty-four hours straight. She then describes the spiritual purpose of the lung-gom-pa lamas' runs and their training, which included intensive breathing exercises, practices to lighten the body in order to make a form of levitation possible, and a three-year sitting meditation in darkness and seclusion. "It is difficult to understand that a training which compels a man to remain motionless for years can result in the acquisition of peculiar swiftness."[14]

At the same time that David-Neel was observing the lung-gom-pa lama, Frank and Lillian Gilbreth, efficiency engineers in the scientific management movement, were conducting time and motion studies in the United States. They filmed a worker's every movement and, using slow motion, identified any "waste" motions. They also developed the "standard time" needed for each job down to the thousandth of a minute. A wide assortment of laborers was analyzed, including typists, bricklayers, and handkerchief folders. A number of critics, including union organizers, were suspicious of the Gilbreths' time and motion studies and saw them as yet another way to speed and exhaust workers. So the Gilbreths pitched their work as beneficial to employees, leading to in-creased efficiency and higher pay.[15] Frank Gilbreth wrote, "There is no waste of any kind in the world that equals the waste from needless, ill-directed, and ineffective motions, and their resulting unnecessary fatigue."[16]

I write four words. I eliminate two of them and replace them with two others. In the previous sentence I remove three and swap in four different words. Then while writing the most recent sentence I delete three letters that start a word I decide I do not want and replace it with another. Now I read these three sentences. In the third sentence, I delete four words and replace them with a single word. Some people cannot compose on the keyboard, but I am com-forted by the disappearance of the edits. I am left with some words that appear to be exactly how they were intended to be from the beginning. I will reread this paragraph.

In an interview, William Burroughs said, "Most people don't see what's going on around them. That's my principal message to writers: for Godsake, keep your *eyes* open. Notice what's going on around you. I mean, I walk down the street with friends. I ask, 'Did you see him, that person who just walked by?' No, they didn't notice him."[17]

Writer friends claim they write slowly too. But if we were to conduct time and motion studies side by side, they would be astounded. A morning might reveal a single sentence, like one short take in a film. Then day after day, others appear. It is slowly additive, with intensive editing all along leading to innumerable drafts. Once a critical mass of paragraphs has accumulated with ideas adequately harvested, scissors are taken to the pages and discrete units are cut apart. They are then sorted and rearranged, not unlike the physical splicing of tape or film.

According to Burroughs and Brion Gysin, "All writing is in fact cut-ups." Gysin's early experiments with the "cut-up" involved short texts from newspapers and letters. He found that when he took scissors to a page and rearranged the four quadrants, new messages were revealed. "Word-locks" were cracked open and, at times, as Burroughs said, "The future leaked out." They claimed the cut-up as a "new optic" with a history that went back to Dada. Gysin wrote in 1978, "The cut-up method brings to writers the collage, which has been used by painters for fifty years. And used by the moving and still camera. In fact all street shots from movie or still cameras are by the unpredictable factors of passerby and juxtaposition cut-ups."[18]

. . . Hailing a taxi becomes pinks and reds floating behind her. Slow down children. Pale nails with no hint of impatience. A cold cigarette caught midexpression above the sidewalk. As if in prayer, a man and his cane keep moving.

A ghost in the form of a man that dresses like a little girl.

Little girl, alone on the sidewalk, holds an image of his church. . . .

Flaubert spent a full month writing a single sentence of *Madame Bovary*. Do people now complain, "That Flaubert. What a waste of time. How idiotic to spend a month on a single sentence of *Madame Bovary*!"?

Am I writing a confession or a manifesto?

JN: Another thing that became very clear to me in making *Street* and in the editing process was — it's something that still photographers know but I, in a way, discovered it because it was so obvious to me — the importance of what we bring to what we're looking at, the importance of how we see it. The example I've used time and again — but it's a good one — is . . . there was one shot I had, it didn't make it into the film but it was a shot of a guy walking down the street in Chinatown, and he's looking down at the ground. His head is bowed like he's lost everything. It's the end of his world. His wife has left him. Who knows what. He just looks really dejected. You get to see that very clearly and in great depth. But when you see it in regular speed as I did because we were scrubbing through, the guy is just glancing at his shoelaces to see if they're tied. To the same extent that the high-speed camera reveals things which we cannot experience or which we cannot see with the natural eye, it also obscures and creates things that don't exist. It obfuscates the world. . . . It's so obvious in a way. It made it very clear to me how our individual realities are a dance between one and the other. . . .

TK: In *Street*, I felt I could often see people think. The internal landscape has been slowed down as well.

JN: Yes, definitely. You can see thoughts forming. You can see people's minds moving from one thought to another. It seems to make thoughts visible in a way that is different from a still photograph. The relationship with still photography is strong, particularly with history. There's such a history of street photography. I think about that a lot. The film showed at the National Gallery in Washington at the same time as the Garry Winogrand show. Fantastic! So there was Garry Winogrand, his life's work there, and then *Street* playing a couple of doors down between Winogrand and nineteenth-century American furniture or something like that. And it made me realize — it didn't make me realize because I knew it already — that I could see the same things in moments that stood still. I like that about my film. It resides somewhere between motion picture and still photography. These things pass by with very little movement happening. They are like still photographs, but you see what happened just before and just after. You get just a little more information.

Scientists studied the rate at which various species perceive flashes of flickering light. They found that "the smaller an animal and the faster its metabolic rate, the slower time passes for it."[19] That is why the fly is so adept at avoiding the swatter. The fly perceives the world in the equivalent of slow motion and therefore has a greater ability to make quick decisions.

Neuroscientists David Eagleman and Chess Stetson found that during frightening experiences such as accidents or trauma, "the brain may lay down memories in a way that makes them 'stick' better."[20] Through recall, the exceptional density of memories offers the perception that time slows down during the actual event.

Athletes have recounted the experience of slowed time or what we might call "fly consciousness." Michael Jordan described his experience of key plays, of making decisions, seeing openings, reaching, jumping, and shooting as if the clock were suspended along with his body. As though the photographs and slow-motion replays of Jordan, hanging in midair, are evidence of his memories.

A similar phenomenon affects a child's perception of the passage of time. What Nares describes as "the way babies look," seeing things without judgment, is related to the idea that children perceive a vast array of new and therefore noteworthy sensory experience. Eagleman explains, "When you are a child, and everything is novel, the richness of the memory gives the impression of increased time passage — for example, when looking back at the end of a childhood summer."

In *Street*, a young girl runs down the sidewalk. Her arms and shoulders extend fully. There is a curve at her wrists. Her neck rocks. Later in the film, having spied the camera, a boy with an expansive smile runs alongside the car, nearly keeping pace. Legs and arms push with a slowed abandon. *Street* teaches us to notice the fully animated gestures and expressions of these energized creatures who are smaller and speedier than their adult counterparts.

Guido van de Werve is not walking on a street. In his video *Nummer Acht (#8) Everything Is Going to Be Alright* (2007), van de Werve is a small dot on a cold, white landscape. He walks at a steady, relaxed pace across the hard ice surface of the Gulf of Bothnia in Finland toward the stationary camera. Precariously close behind him, a giant ice-breaking ship crushes its way through the surface. As van de Werve and the ice breaker move closer to the camera, we can hear the crunch of his footsteps along with the roar of the mammoth ice breaker that crashes through the thick ice that van de Werve has stepped on just seconds before. How I would like to be reassured by the piece's title.

Nares says that *Street* moves at a glacial pace. But even glaciers don't perform that way anymore. No matter how quickly we move, the earth's decline nips at our heels like a giant ice breaker.

Part of the pleasure of *Street* is a kind of magical thinking. If New York City streets can be slowed, then why can't other speedy things be reversed? Is there a way to slow the earth's destruction to 1/25th of the expected rate of collapse? Is it a coincidence that there are slow enthusiasts at a time when there is an acceleration of decline?

If we can see thoughts form, might that enable us to make better decisions? Would fly consciousness allow us to avert the swatter?

Australian Buddhist nun Robina Courtin is a tornado of teachings. She hurries into the hall, a blur of saffron robes. She speaks at a tremendous clip in full essays, without distraction. Eight hours each day, for nine days, teaching without referring to a single written note. She says something like, it's not about being all slow and holy. You can think fast, you can act fast, you can speak fast, but what are you thinking, what are you doing, what are you saying? Another day, she exclaims, all this talk of mindfulness. A thief is mindful! A murderer is mindful! What do you *do* mindfully? Check up!

The Search Inside Yourself Institute was founded in 2012. From the website: "Developed at Google and based on the latest in neuroscience research, the Search Inside Yourself (SIY) programs offer attention and mindfulness training that build the core emotional intelligence skills needed for peak performance and effective leadership. We help professionals at all levels adapt, management teams evolve and leaders optimize their impact and influence."

If efficiency engineers Frank and Lillian Gilbreth were still alive, would they have paid thousands of dollars for tickets to the 2014 Google-sponsored Wisdom 2.0 conference in San Francisco? During a session on three steps to corporate mindfulness, a local activist group called Heart of the City surprised the presenters by taking center stage and hoisting a banner that read "Eviction Free San Francisco." With the help of a bullhorn, they asserted the connection between escalating rents and housing problems and the influx of high-paid Silicon Valley employees. As a guard played tug-of-war with a protester and her banner, one of the three seated workshop presenters diverted attention away from the fair housing intervention and, in a voice both slow and holy, asked the auditorium filled with participants to "check in with your body and see what's happening and what it's like to be around conflict and people with heartfelt ideas."[21]

On one full lane of Chicago's Michigan Avenue, a large and diverse group of bicyclists ride by at a leisurely pace. Some call out "Slow Roll" as they pass, and many of the riders wear "Slow Roll" T-shirts. Slow Roll Detroit has come to join Slow Roll Chicago on this ride. They have just biked from Pullman, where they visited the only black labor history museum in the nation and learned about the Brotherhood of Sleeping Car Porters. "'We ride slow because it's more about the journey than it is the destination,' says Olatunji Oboi Reed, 40, one of the co-founders of the initiative. . . . 'I really think that with Slow Roll we can change the narrative and participate in various forms of economic development,' says Jamal Julien, 40, a childhood friend of Reed's and a co-founder of the Chicago group.'"[22] Slow Roll has focused its rides on struggling communities on the West and South sides of Chicago. "'We ride because we believe the more people that ride in our community, the better we stand an opportunity of our communities being improved,' Reed said."[23]

TK: I wanted to ask you something about Thurston's soundtrack but now I realize that my question also relates to what you were saying in terms of Warhol and early cinema and turning on the camera and seeing what happens. Do you think there is a particular relationship between improvisation and slow motion?

JN: I guess I do. I never really thought of it as a relationship between the two, but I was very aware that I wanted Thurston to improvise his soundtrack because I wanted it to be one person's interior, one person's mind wandering. I wanted it to wander in the same way that we wandered around the city. Our improvisation while we were shooting. Let's try Fifth Avenue, let's go across on Fifty-Seventh and see. I guess wandering and improvising are similar, and then improvising also has rules and limits, boundaries of some sort. And our boundaries were dictated by light and speed and accessibility and one-way streets and that kind of thing. So we were improvising while shooting the film and Thurston was improvising while he did the music. I'm not really a purist because we took Thurston's music and chopped it up and made a soundtrack out of it. In the same way that I took what I had filmed and chopped it up and made a film out of it.

I had also originally thought of *Street* as having a soundtrack that revealed things about what you hear in the same way that slowing down what you see reveals things you can't normally see, but I realized that sound is just a different thing. I tried slowing down some street sounds and it just made the film drag. It felt like you were walking through mud in big boots or something. . . .

It seemed very important to me that Thurston should continue to do other improvisations at screenings, and it's been different each time he's done it. I still feel he has eyes in the back of his head. Which is kind of what happens when you can feel something happening. You know when you do that exquisite corpse game? When you draw the head and you turn it over and you draw the body and then do the legs and pass it around each time? When you play that game, after a while everybody gets on the same page and there are amazing coincidences. And I think there's something of that in there. It allows connections to happen that are unplanned and unexpected.

TK: And then you have this third coefficient, which is the energy of an audience. So you have an audience reacting to an image track, and a sensitive performer can feel the energy of the audience.

JN: You're absolutely right. It goes round and round in a circle. . . .

JN: I did a guitar thing the other night with Thurston at the Printed Matter book fair opening at MoMA PS 1. And that was really fun. The first time we ever played together. And it was loud.

TK: I wish I could have been there. I had the opportunity to play with Thurston in the late 1990s. We improvised together at the No Music festival in London, Ontario.

JN: What did you play?

TK: Improvised violin. I was trained classically from a young age. Later, I had a car accident which caused damage to my left hand, so I realized I would never play classically again. The intonation was impossible—there were just things that weren't going to happen. Not long after that I met John [Corbett] and started improvising with him. I realized there was a way to use the instrument differently. Work with what you've got.

JN: Did you have a head injury as well?

TK: No, just the hand.

JN: I ask because I had a head injury in 2001. It wasn't an injury, it was a stroke, an aneurysm in my brain. I was very lucky to survive. Half of the people who that happens to don't survive and of the half that do, I think only half of those have their faculties intact. I'm very lucky, but there have been consequences of that that I still live with. And it changed my way of seeing things and I think that it actually has something to do with *Street*, although I've never talked about this, but I do think . . . I'm easily overstimulated and I do have a need to see things slowly and quietly. [The phone goes quiet. Nares stops speaking suddenly, begins again, startled.] Hello?

TK: Can you hear me?

JN: Yes, I can. That was just a funny sound.

TK: Oh.

JN: And I do have a need to see and hear . . . [again, startled] hello?

TK: I don't know what's happening.

JN: Are you hearing it too?

TK: No. I heard just an echo of a noise this time but not the last time.

JN: It was like a loud beep.

TK: Oh, I'm sorry, just as you're talking about the need for quiet.

JN: Yes, right, exactly [laughter].

TK: If it keeps going, I can call you back without the recording app.

JN: It seems to have gone away. . . . I was just going to say, it's not something I talk about as a rule but the truth is that it does have something to do with how I see the world. When I first came out of hospital I was very disorientated.

I would be somewhere and I would know where I was but not recognize any-thing, or I would recognize things but not know where I was, and it was like everything was upside down and I saw the world in the same way as a baby, like the way I was talking earlier. It was like I had slightly lost the ability to distin-guish between things. As we go through life, the mind forms a way of seeing, and it sees the thing that interests it and it sees the things it wants to see, to some extent. And I lost that ability and then slowly reconstructed it. It's funny actually, because now I'm much more aware of those choices, in a way, or the decisions that create them.

Quite soon after coming out, I did a video piece called *My Cacophony*, which is . . . you know when you walk into a guitar shop and there are all these people standing around at different amps playing different instruments and it all hap-pens at the same time? I did a five-screen guitar installation video, which I've never shown, where I'm just improvising on the guitar and the idea is that they would be shown all together in a room where they would create that kind of confusion and cacophony, so I was alert to different ways of seeing since then and I think to some extent the film *Street* came out of my reconstructed reality that I've had to create for my own survival.

Is slow motion another form of cut-up? A portal that allows us to witness what is there all along locked into our daily speed? What would Burroughs and Gysin have thought about the super-slow motion that high-speed technology allows? Time stretched like the pliable material that it is, but somewhere in there, a breaking open, the unhinging of movement into near stillness. A new optics. Would they have seen the potential of the Phantom camera as yet another layer of cut-up through which to discover "the enigmatic at first but ultimately ex-plicit and often premonitory" narratives buried within the text of the already cut-up street? Yet another method for training us to keep our eyes open. See it slow enough and something is revealed. A devastated man in Chinatown caught looking at his laces.

. . . The fly was off. We could hear the thought in three inches. We see a picture of our-selves together in hair gone skyward.

Does slow motion know what they should be? A few seconds of smile. A turn of ela-tion, not to be repeated. Head cocked, midsentence. A bird's heart . . .

TK: Have you ever read the film theorist Rudolf Arnheim on slow motion?

JN: No.

TK: In "Work of Art in the Age of Mechanical Reproduction," Walter Benjamin quotes Arnheim when he writes about slow motion. I wrote down a quote to read to you.

JN: What does he say?

TK: First, he talks about slow motion as mainly being used for educational films.

JN: Or scientific films. Like Edgerton. When I did the show here at the Met—which was such a gas, I had such fun doing it—we had all kinds of work from the collections, paintings and drawings and objects and like a Roman foot and an Egyptian head and I also had a few things on TV monitors. One of them was Étienne-Jules Marey's cinematic experiments and they're so fantastic. Muybridge gets all the credit for that stuff but Marey's my man, all the way. Inventive. Like that gun that he made that makes photographs. Wow. Talk about shooting a film. He really did it. The other guy I had on a little monitor was Edgerton. Hummingbirds flying and that kind of thing. That shows what Arnheim is talking about.

TK: Arnheim came to mind when you were talking about your recovery. I'm thinking about the reeducation of the mind after something like an aneurysm. In a way, you've created your own educational film in *Street*.

JN: I like that. Reeducating myself.

TK: So in 1933, Arnheim writes, "Slow motion has hardly been applied at all yet to artistic purposes, although it should be very useful. It might, for instance, serve to slow down natural movements grotesquely; but it can also create new movements, which do not appear as the retarding of natural movement but have a curious gliding, floating character of their own [Nares laughs]. Slow motion should be a wonderful medium for showing visions and ghosts."[24]

JN: That's beautiful. Visions and ghosts.

TK: At first, I thought he was being metaphysical as in spirit photography, but then I realized he was talking about slow motion's use in narrative film.

JN: Visions and ghosts.

The Phantom camera reveals human vulnerability in the faces of *Street* pedestrians. Strangers are familiar. Release a few seconds from the burden of real time and feeling states are shed, past distraction or indifference or aggression to a certain tender openness that can be difficult to detect with the naked eye. Is speed a kind of armor?

Consider the maned three-toed sloth. Slow is his adaptive strategy, not the cause of his endangered status.

Street is an educational film showing visions and ghosts.

. . . Light and smoke and eyes aimed skyward. We see a picture of ourselves together without hesitation. Baby's fat legs in pink tights forward a rhythm with the shop window's neon sign. Hummingbirds hail cabs. Her father walks the wind, both hands upward as four sparrows lift off. . . .

Notes

1. Rudolf Arnheim, *Film as Art* (Berkeley: University of California Press, 1957), 116–117.

2. "Blasting Off with the Phantom v.7.3," November 13, 2014, https://www.phantom highspeed.com/Blog/category/aerospace.

3. Walter Benjamin, "The Work of Art in the Age of Mechanical Reproduction," in *Illuminations*, ed. Hannah Arendt, trans. Harry Zohn (New York: Schocken, 1969), 237.

4. Robert Levine, *A Geography of Time: On Tempo, Culture, and the Pace of Life* (New York: HarperCollins, 1997), 135.

5. Levine, *A Geography of Time*, 135.

6. Nathan Heller, "Slow TV Is Here," *New Yorker*, September 30, 2014.

7. Kit Buchan, "Decelerator Helmet: Viewing the World in Slow Motion," *The Guardian*, July 10, 2014, https://www.theguardian.com/technology/2014/jul/10/decelerator-helmet-lorenz-potthast-slow-motion.

8. Augusto Boal, *Theatre of the Oppressed*, trans. Charles A. and Maria-Odilia Leal McBride (New York: Theatre Communications Group, 1985), 128.

9. Jonathan Sacks, "His Holiness the 14th Dalai Lama of Tibet, Jonathan Sacks, Katherine Jefferts Schori, and Seyyed Hossein Nasr — Pursuing Happiness," *On Being*, September 25, 2014, http://www.onbeing.org/program/pursuing-happiness-dalai-lama /147.

10. James Nares, interview with author, September 2014.

11. Jane Jacobs, *The Death and Life of Great American Cities* (New York: Random House, 1961), 50–54.

12. Jonah Lehrer, "A Physicist Solves the City," *New York Times*, December 17, 2010, http://www.nytimes.com/2010/12/19/magazine/19Urban_West-t.html.

13. "Phantom ride" was a term used for a similar genre of film popular in the late nineteenth century. For these films, cameramen were often tied to the front of a moving train in order to shoot a film that offered the viewer the sensation of floating, ghostly movement through space. See Kolar, "Phantom Ride and Early Train Films," Mubi, accessed January 14, 2015, https://mubi.com/lists/phantom-ride-early-train-films.

14. Alexandra David-Neel, *Magic and Mystery in Tibet* (New York: Claude Kendall, 1932), 202–203, 209.

15. Brian Price, "Frank and Lillian Gilbreth and the Manufacture and Marketing of Motion Study, 1908–1924," *Business and Economic History*, Second Series, 18 (1989).

16. Frank Bunker Gilbreth and Lillian Moler Gilbreth, *Applied Motion Study: A Collection of Papers on the Efficient Method to Industrial Preparedness* (New York: Macmillan, 1919), 2.

17. William S. Burroughs and Brion Gysin, *The Third Mind* (New York: Viking, 1978).

18. Burroughs and Gysin, *The Third Mind*, n.p.

19. Rosa Silverman, "Flies See the World in Slow Motion, Say Scientists," *The Telegraph*, September 16, 2013, http://www.telegraph.co.uk/news/science/science-news /10311821/Flies-see-the-world-in-slow-motion-say-scientists.html.

20. Chess Stetson, Matthew P. Fiesta, and David M. Eagleman, "Does Time Really Slow Down during a Frightening Event?" *PLoS ONE*, December 12, 2007, http://journals .plos.org/plosone/article?id=10.1371/journal.pone.0001295.

21. Alex Caring-Lobel, "Protesters Crash Google Talk on Corporate Mindfulness at Wisdom 2.0 Conference," *Tricycle*, February 2014, http://tricycle.org/trikedaily /protesters-crash-google-talk-corporate-mindfulness-wisdom-20-conference/.

22. Tony Briscoe, "'Slow Roll' Cyclists Aim to Revive Neighborhoods," *Chicago Tribune*, September 19, 2014, http://www.chicagotribune.com/news/ct-slow-roll-chicago -met-20140919-story.html.

23. Adrienne Samuels Gibbs, "Bike for Good," *Chicago Sun Times*, October 17, 2014.

24. Rudolf Arnheim, *Film as Art*, 116–117.

CONTRIBUTORS

MARY BERGSTEIN has been a professor at the Rhode Island School of Design since 1990. Her books include *Mirrors of Memory: Freud, Photography, and the History of Art* (2010) and *In Looking Back One Learns to See: Marcel Proust and Photography* (2014). The author of scores of articles on art and visual culture, her new work has taken a more subjective turn: "Hotel Michelangelo" in *Afterimage* (2016) and "Palmyra and Palmyra," in *Arion: A Journal of Humanities and the Classics* (2016).

JONATHAN FARDY is a professor of Art History at the Savannah College of Art and Design in Hong Kong. His research focuses on photography, political theory, and subjectivity. He has published on nineteenth-century photography as well as on the work of numerous theorists, including Walter Benjamin, Félix Guattari, Jean Baudrillard, Peter Sloterdijk, and Carl Schmitt.

KRISTAN HORTON is a Canadian artist who has been widely recognized for his conceptual photographic practice. He has shown his work internationally in solo exhibitions at Work (London, 2016), White Columns (New York, 2008), and the Contemporary Art Gallery (Vancouver, 2007), among others, and in a range of group exhibitions at the Art Gallery of Ontario, Toronto; the National Gallery of Canada, Ottawa; Bard College's Center for Curatorial Studies, Annandale-on-Hudson; the Albright-Knox Gallery, Buffalo; and the Power Plant, Toronto. He is the 2010 winner of the Aimia Photography Prize from the Art Gallery of Ontario.

TERRI KAPSALIS teaches in Visual and Critical Studies at the School of the Art Institute of Chicago. She is the author of *Jane Addams' Travel Medicine Kit*, *The Hysterical Alphabet*, and *Public Privates: Performing Gynecology from Both Ends of the Speculum*. Along with John Corbett and Anthony Elms, she coedited *Traveling the Spaceways: Sun Ra, the Astro Black, and Other Solar Myths* and *Pathways to Unknown Worlds: Sun Ra, El Saturn, and Chicago's Afro-futurist Underground* and co-curated the touring exhibition *Pathways to Unknown Worlds*. She is a founding member of Theater Oobleck.

SARAH KOFMAN held the Chair of Philosophy at the University of Paris I. Among her numerous books are *The Enigma of Woman: Woman in Freud's Writings, Camera Obscura: Of Ideology*, and the autobiography *Rue Ordener, Rue Labat*.

ELISABETH LEBOVICI is a French art historian and critic. She served as arts and culture editor for the daily newspaper *Libération* (1991–2006). She regularly blogs at http://le-beau-vice.blogspot.fr. She co-organizes the seminar "Something You Should Know: Artists and Producers" at the School for Advanced Studies in the Social Sciences (EHESS) in Paris and is part of the research group "Travelling Féministe" working with the archives of the Centre audiovisuel Simone de Beauvoir in Paris.

ZOE LEONARD is an American artist who works primarily with photography and sculpture. She has exhibited extensively since the late 1980s in institutions around the world, and has been included in some of the most important exhibitions of recent decades, including Documenta IX and Documenta XII, as well as several Whitney Biennials. She received the Bucksbaum Award for the work she presented in the 2014 Whitney Biennial.

GABRIELLE MOSER is a Social Sciences and Humanities Research Council of Canada postdoctoral fellow in Art History at the University of British Columbia and a Fulbright Visiting Scholar in the Department of Modern Culture and Media at Brown University. Her writing appears in venues including Artforum. com, *Art in America, Fillip, Journal of Visual Culture, Photography & Culture*, and *Prefix Photo*. Moser has held fellowships at the Paul Mellon Centre for the Study of British Art, the Ryerson Image Centre, and the Huntington Library. She is an adjunct professor in art history at OCAD University.

MIGNON NIXON is Professor of Modern and Contemporary Art at University College London and an editor of the journal *October*. She is the author of *Fantastic Reality: Louise Bourgeois and a Story of Modern Art* (2006) and the editor of the *Eva Hesse October File* (2002) and the *Mary Kelly October File* (2016). She publishes widely on contemporary art, feminism, and psychoanalysis. Her next book, *Sperm Bomb: Art, Feminism, and the American War in Vietnam*, is forthcoming.

THY PHU is Associate Professor at Western University in Canada. She is the author of *Picturing Model Citizens: Civility in Asian American Visual Culture* and coeditor, with Elspeth Brown, of *Feeling Photography*, a book that develops affect as an analytic for exploring photography. She is currently completing *Warring Visions*, a book that offers a new visual history of the war in Vietnam by focusing on the works of Vietnamese photographers, and is developing the Family Camera Network, a collaborative project that considers how family photographs shape our ideas of family.

MARK REINHARDT is Class of 1956 Professor of American Civilization at Williams College where he teaches political theory and American Studies. He is working on a book titled *Visual Politics: Theories and Spectacles*, which includes many of the materials and concepts he engages here while moving from Plato to contemporary imaging technologies. He is coeditor of *Kara Walker: Narratives of a Negress* (2003) and *Beautiful Suffering: Photography and the Traffic in Pain* (2007).

SHARON SLIWINSKI is Associate Professor in the Faculty of Information & Media Studies and a core member of the Centre for the Study of Theory & Criticism at Western University in Canada. She is the author of *Human Rights in Camera* (2011), and *Dreaming in Dark Times: Six Exercises in Political Thought* (2017). She is currently working on a collaborative project called *The Museum of Dreams*.

SHAWN MICHELLE SMITH is Professor of Visual and Critical Studies at the School of the Art Institute of Chicago. She is the author of *American Archives: Gender, Race, and Class in Visual Culture* (1999), *Photography on the Color Line: W. E. B. Du Bois, Race, and Visual Culture* (2004), and *At the Edge of Sight: Photography and the Unseen* (2013), which won the 2014 Lawrence W. Levine Award for best book in American cultural history from the Organization of American Historians and the 2014 Jean Goldman Book Prize from the School of the Art Institute of Chicago. She is co-author with Dora Apel of *Lynching Photographs* (2007), and co-editor with Maurice O. Wallace of *Pictures and Progress: Early Photography and the Making of African American Identity* (2012).

LAURA WEXLER is Professor of Women's, Gender, and Sexuality Studies at Yale University, Co-chair of Public Humanities, and Founder and Director of The Photographic Memory Workshop. She is the author of many books and essays about photography, feminism and visual culture, including *Tender Vio-*

lence: Domestic Images in an Age of U.S. Imperialism and *Pregnant Pictures*. She serves on the editorial board of the *Trans-Asia Photography Review*. Since 2011 she has been Principal Investigator of the NEH and ACLS-supported *Photogrammar Project*, mapping the FSA/OWI archives (photogrammar.yale.edu). Since 2015 she has been collaborating with *Magnum* photographers Donovan Wylie and Jim Goldberg on a book about New Haven.

KELLY WOOD is Associate Professor in the Visual Arts Department at Western University in London, Ontario. She is a photographer and practicing artist whose research focuses on subjects that relate to the environmental impact of waste accumulation, waste economies, and all forms of visible and invisible pollution. She is currently involved in the collective project *Visualizing the Invisible*. Wood is also a member of the photography research collectives The Toronto Photography Seminar and The Family Camera Network.

ANDRÉS MARIO ZERVIGÓN is Associate Professor of the History of Photography at Rutgers, The State University of New Jersey. He is author of *John Heartfield and the Agitated Image: Photography, Persuasion, and the Rise of Avant-Garde Photomontage* (2012) and *Photography and Germany*, for the Reaktion Books *Exposures* series (2017). With Tanya Sheehan he coedited *Photography and Its Origins* (2014) and with Sabine Kriebel he coedited *Photography and Doubt* (2016). His current book project is *Die Arbeiter-Illustrierte Zeitung—The Worker's Illustrated Magazine, 1921–1938: A History of Germany's Other Avant-Garde*, for which he received a CASVA Senior Fellowship (2013–14).

INDEX

Note: Page numbers followed by *f* indicate a figure.

www.ingramcontent.com/pod-product-compliance
Lightning Source LLC
Chambersburg PA
CBHW072129170526
45158CB00004BA/1303